D0152100

Sixth Edition

IDEOLOGY AND THE DEVELOPMENT OF SOCIOLOGICAL THEORY

IRVING M. ZEITLIN

University of Toronto

Prentice Hall, Upper Saddle River, New Jersey 07458

Library of Congress Cataloging-in-Publication Data

Zeitlin, Irving M.
Ideology and the development of sociological theory / IRVING M. ZEITLIN.—6th ed.
p. cm.
Includes bibliographical references and index.
ISBN 0-13-255308-2
1. Sociology—History. I. Title.
HM19.Z4 1997
301′.09—dc20 95-48110

For Esther, Ruthie, Michael,
Bethie, and Jeremy

Editor in Chief: *Nancy Roberts*
Acquisitions Editor: *Fred Whittingham*
Associate editor: *Sharon Chambliss*
Editorial/production supervision: *Joanne Riker*
Buyer: *Mary Ann Gloriande*

This book was set in 10/12 Palatino by East End Publishing Services and was printed and bound by Courier Companies, Inc. The cover was printed by Courier Companies, Inc.

Printed in the United States of America

10 9 8 7 6 5 4 3 2 1

ISBN 0-13-255308-2

PRENTICE-HALL INTERNATIONAL (UK) LIMITED, *London*
PRENTICE-HALL OF AUSTRALIA PTY. LIMITED, *Sydney*
PRENTICE-HALL CANADA INC., *Toronto*
PRENTICE-HALL HISPANOAMERICANA, S.A., *Mexico*
PRENTICE-HALL OF INDIA PRIVATE LIMITED, *New Delhi*
PRENTICE-HALL OF JAPAN, INC., *Tokyo*
SIMON & SCHUSTER ASIA PTE. LTD., *Singapore*
EDITORA PRENTICE-HALL DO BRASIL, LTDA., *Rio de Janeiro*

Contents

Preface

First published in 1968, this book has now gone through six editions, each of which has introduced new thinkers and materials with the aim of enriching the book's contents. It should come as no surprise that most of the thinkers discussed in any book on the history of social thought are men. By now all thoughtful persons are aware that the conspicuous absence of women from certain intellectual and cultural fields cannot be explained by any natural incapacity on their part for careful and profound reflections on the nature of society. It is a fact too well known to require substantiation here that the general subordination of women has meant, among other things, that certain professional and academic areas, such as philosophy, science, and the arts, were closed to them. Historically, the obstacles to women entering those fields were legal and ideological; the very education of women from early childhood was a most formidable obstacle, for women were thoroughly indoctrinated with the view that their chief role in life was to serve as helpmates to men. A woman's primary responsibility was to marry and care for her husband and children. And yet, against all odds, women succeeded in achieving excellence whenever they were able to engage in their creative activities without the need to break into a closed male institution. Literature is an outstanding example of a culturally creative area in which women early demonstrated superior gifts. Some of the greatest writers of all time, in poetry and prose, have been women.

However, since universities prior to the twentieth century were virtually closed to women in the fields of social and political theory, only a few self-educated women could make their mark there. It is urgent that those women receive the recognition they deserve for their contributions to our understanding of the human condition.

In the fourth edition of this book, I introduced the work of Mary Wollstonecraft, a pioneer feminist who challenged some of Rousseau's views on women. In the present edition I have added Harriet Martineau, the first female journalist writing for her living under her own name, and Harriet Taylor, who profoundly influenced John Stuart Mill, and who, as he acknowledged, deserves equal credit for the ideas in several of his major works.

The central thesis of this edition remains the same as it has been in all previous editions, namely, that much of classical sociology emerged in the context of a debate, first with the eighteenth-century Enlightenment and later with the Marxian legacy. By employing the organizing principle of a debate or dialogue, we gain a definite intellectual advantage, for we learn from both sides by discerning their strengths and weaknesses.

The thinkers considered in this book lived in an era when it was quite customary to use "man" and "men" to refer to human beings in general. Such usages were so integral to their language that when we try to replace "man" with "human being," "person," or other terms, the result is stylistically awkward. I have therefore thought it best to retain their way of expressing themselves. But the reader may rest assured that no sexism is intended either in that practice or in the use of masculine pronouns.

Irving M. Zeitlin

1

The Enlightenment
Philosophical Foundations

The term "Enlightenment" refers to the intellectual movement that developed within the hundred-year span beginning with the English Revolution and culminating in the French Revolution.[1] Montesquieu was born in 1689 and Holbach died in 1789. The movement's leading representatives were religious skeptics, political reformers, cultural critics, historians, and social theorists who exercised considerable influence from Edinburgh to Naples, Paris to Berlin, Boston to Philadelphia. Although all these men were committed to the rational pursuit of truth, they also had their philosophical and political differences. In spite of the merciless criticism leveled against Christian dogma and myth, a few of these thinkers held tenaciously to the vestiges of their former religious beliefs. Others embraced materialism and atheism. Some, a distinct minority, remained loyal to dynastic authority, while radicals developed democratic ideas. The British thinkers were relatively content with their social and political institutions. The Germans were almost entirely unpolitical. In sharp contrast to both the British and the Germans, however, it was the French *Philosophes* who most vehemently criticized both church and state, campaigning unrelentingly for the basic freedoms—freedom from arbitrary power, freedom of speech, freedom of trade, freedom to realize one's talents. It was in eighteenth-century France that the conflict of the Enlightenment with the Establishment became the most intense and dramatic. Typically, the French *Philosophe* was most uncompromising in his opposition to the old regime. He tore it down intellectually, thus paving the way for its actual destruction by the revolution of 1789.

The Enlightenment, of course, had its prehistory, its roots in the past. Several centuries earlier a secular mode of thought had been slowly developing. In the four hundred years between 1300 and 1700 social forces first weakened and then shattered whatever unity western Christendom had possessed. Those social forces may be summarized with the catch phrase, "Protestantism, science, and capitalism." We must remember, however, that medieval science was teleological: Its purpose was to attain knowledge for the sake of God. The purpose of science was to discover God's intentions for his creation. Even the most rational of medieval thinkers conceded that there were sacred areas into which they must not venture, spheres in which revelation, faith, tradition, and ecclesiastical authority offered the answers and gave the orders. Scientific curiosity as applied to those spheres was an unwelcome intrusion into holy ground. It was this inviolable domain of the *sacred* that distinguished the Middle Ages at its most scientific and skeptical from the later ages of criticism. The medieval mind was dominated by the Church, literally, emotionally and intellectually. "A Revolution was necessary," wrote Rousseau, "to bring men back to common sense."[2]

In contrast to the medieval era, the men of the Enlightenment regarded all aspects of human life and works as subject to critical examination—the various sciences, religious beliefs, metaphysics, aesthetics, education, and so on. Self-examination, a scrutiny of their own actions and their own society, was an essential function of thought. By gaining an understanding of the main forces and tendencies of their epoch, human beings could determine their direction and control their consequences. Through reason and science, humanity could attain ever greater degrees of freedom and, hence, ever greater degrees of perfection. Intellectual progress, an idea permeating the thinking of that era, would serve to further humanity's general progress.

The *Philosophes* waged an unceasing war against superstition, bigotry, and intolerance; they fought against censorship and demanded freedom of thought. They attacked the privileges of the feudal classes and their restraints upon the commercial and industrial classes. It was the Enlightenment faith in science and education that provided so powerful an impetus to their work, making them humanitarian, optimistic, and confident. Philosophy was no longer merely a matter of abstract thinking. It acquired the practical function of asking critical questions about existing institutions and demanding that the unreasonable ones, those contrary to human nature, be changed. All social obstacles to human perfectibility were to be progressively eliminated. Enlightenment thinking, then, had a *negative-critical* as well as a positive side.

Unlike the rationalists of the seventeenth century for whom explanation was a matter of strict deduction, the *Philosophes* constructed their ideal of explanation on the model of the contemporary natural sciences. They turned not to Descartes but primarily to Newton whose investigations rested on the data of experience and observation. Newton's empirical method was based on the assumption of universal order and law in the material world. Facts appear to fall into patterns, exhibiting definite regularities and relationships. Order is immanent in the universe, Newton believed, and is discovered not by abstract reasoning alone, but by observation. That became the methodological premise of eighteenth-century thought, and it is this premise that distinguishes it from that of the seventeenth-century continental philosophers (e.g., Descartes, Leibniz, and Spinoza). Condillac, for example, in his *Treatise on Systems*, explicitly defends the empirical method and criticizes the great rationalists of the seventeenth century for having failed to adhere to it. The phenomena of the real world were, for all practical purposes, ignored by the seventeenth-century system builders. Ideas and concepts were elevated to the status of dogma. Thus Condillac argues the necessity of a new method that unites the empirical with the rational. One must study the phenomena themselves if their forms and connections are to be known. Condillac, d'Alembert, and others now call for this new method as a prerequisite to intellectual progress. The logic of this method was indeed new, for it was neither the logic of the medieval scholastic nor even of the purely mathematical concept; it was rather the "logic" of the facts.

Employing Galileo's discovery that falling bodies accelerate at a constant rate, and Kepler's observation that there exists a fixed relationship between the distance of a planet from the sun and the speed of its revolution, Newton arrived at the law that the sun attracted planets to itself at a rate directly proportional to their mass and inversely proportional to the square of the distance between them. Eventually, he was able to demonstrate that all bodies of the universe took their positions and movement through the force of gravitation. Moreover, the force that held the planets in orbit also made objects fall to the ground. The law was operative throughout the universe. The finite universe had become an infinite machine eternally moving by its own power and mechanisms. External causation accounted for its operation, which was apparently devoid of purpose or meaning. Space, time, mass, motion, and force were the essential elements of this mechanical universe that could be comprehended in its entirety by applying the laws of science and mathematics. This conception had an incalculable impact on the intellectuals of the Enlightenment. Here was a magnificent triumph of reason *and* observation, the new method that takes observed facts and advances an interpretation that accounts for what is observed, so that if the interpretation is correct, it can guide observers in their quest for new facts.

What is new and original about Enlightenment thought, therefore, is the whole-hearted adoption of the methodological pattern of Newton's physics, and immediately with its adoption it was generalized and employed in realms other than the mathematical and physical. It became an indispensable tool in the study of all phenomena. "However much individual thinkers and schools differ in their results," writes Cassirer, "they agree in this epistemological premise. Voltaire's *Treatise on Metaphysics*, d'Alembert's *Preliminary Discourse*, and Kant's *Inquiry Concerning the Principles of Natural Theology and Morality* all concur on this point."[3] Here again this may be contrasted with the seventeenth-century rationalists' understanding of the term "reason." For Descartes, Spinoza, and Leibniz, to select the most typical thinkers of that period, reason was the realm of "eternal verities"—truth held in common by man and God. That is not the view of the eighteenth century, which, Cassirer maintains

> takes reason in a different and more modest sense. It is no longer the sum total of "innate ideas" given prior to all experience, which reveal the absolute essence of things. Reason is now looked upon rather as an acquisition than as a heritage. It is not the treasury of the mind in which the truth like a minted coin lies stored; it is rather the original intellectual force which guides the discovery and determination of truth. . . .The whole eighteenth century understands reason in this sense; not as a sound body of knowledge, principles, and truths, but as a kind of energy, a force which is fully comprehensible only in its agency and effects.[4]

Reason bows neither to the merely factual, the simple data of experience, nor to the "evidence" of revelation, tradition, or authority. Reason together with observation is a facility for the acquisition of truth. Even the authors of the *Encyclopedia* viewed its function from this standpoint, not merely to provide knowledge and information but also and primarily to change the traditional mode of thinking. The change did indeed become increasingly manifest, and analysis was now applied to psychological and even sociological phenomena. In these realms, too, it had become clear that reason is a powerful instrument when employed in that special method—analysis into separate elements as well as synthetic reconstruction.

The eighteenth-century thinkers were aware of the two philosophical and intellectual tendencies of the previous century that had remained relatively separate from each other and thus without any significant reciprocal influence: rational philosophy and empirical philosophy. Descartes had a fundamental influence in founding the first movement, while Galileo used experimentation and Bacon explained its particular virtues. One way, then, of viewing the special contribution of the Enlightenment is to see its sustained effort at bringing together these distinct philosophical approaches into one unified methodology. The *Philosophes* believed that they had synthesized the best elements of both philosophical movements. Empirical philosophy had a very profound impact upon the *Philosophes'* thinking and from that standpoint the influence of John Locke, the great exponent of empiricism, was almost as great as that of Newton.

In his famous *Essay Concerning Human Understanding*, Locke asserted in opposition to certain of his contemporaries, that ideas are not innate in the human mind. Quite the contrary, at birth the mind is a *tabula rasa*—that is in a blank and empty state; only through experience do ideas enter the mind. The function of the mind is to collect the impressions and materials provided by the senses. In this view, the role of the mind is essentially a passive one, with little or no creative or organizing function. Clearly, this lent great support to the empirical and experimental methods: Knowledge could be increased only by extending the experiences of the senses. Moreover, Locke further supported the scientists' method of focusing on measurable qualities, and ignoring the other aspects of the things they were investigating, by advancing a classification of the qualities of matter into primary and secondary: Extension, number, and motion could be directly and immediately experienced. On the other hand, color and sound had no existence outside of the observer's mind. Subsequently, Locke's epistemology led to idealism and skepticism among English philosophers and to materialism among the French.

In England, Bishop Berkeley, for example, argued that Locke's distinction between "primary" and "secondary" was a dubious and tenuous one; neither of these qualities had any existence apart from the perceiver's mind. This was tantamount to saying that matter does not exist—or at least that there was no way of proving the existence of matter. Indeed, Berkeley insisted that only spirit exists and that this spirit is God. Thus, spirit, the subject of religion, was defended by attacking matter, the subject of science. A further step was taken by David Hume: The mind could know nothing outside itself; all human knowledge of the external world is therefore impossible. Hume's work will be discussed in a later context since it was at this point that Immanuel Kant began his own philosophical system.

Among many French philosophers, in contrast, Locke's ideas were translated into scientific materialism—a development probably related to the rigid and capricious absolutism in France and its support of the Church. Materialism appeared as an effective ideological weapon against Church dogma. Condillac expounded and elaborated Locke's theory of the origin of knowledge. The most thoroughgoing in this respect was Holbach, who rejected all spiritual causes and reduced consciousness and thought to the movement of molecules within the material body. While Helvetius, Holbach, and La Mettrie became exponents of materialism, Condillac, though accepting Locke's theory in most of its essentials, introduced important modifications whose implications Kant was later to develop even further. If Locke's theory implied a passive role on the part of the observer—merely receiving sensory impressions, with the mind playing no active role in their organization—Condillac now argues that once the power of thought and reasoning is awakened in man, he is no longer passive, and no longer merely adapts himself to the existing order. Now thought is able to advance even against social reality. Condillac thus assigned a decisive role to judgment and reason even in the simplest act of perception; this was true whether one was perceiving the natural world or the social world. The senses in themselves could never produce the world as we know it in our consciousness; the cooperation of the mind is an absolute necessity.

It should be clear, then, why the Enlightenment is a most logical point of departure if one is interested in the origins of sociological theory. It is in that period that one may see more consistently than before the emergence of the scientific method. Reason in itself will not yield a knowledge of reality; neither will observation and experimentation alone yield such knowledge. Knowledge of reality, whether natural or social, depends on the unity of reason and observation in the scientific method. The Enlightenment thinkers were as interested in society and history as they were in nature, and these were treated as an indivisible unity. By studying nature—including the nature of man—one could learn not only what *is*, but also what is *possible*; likewise, by studying society and history, one could learn not only about the workings of the existing factual order, but about its inherent possibilities. These thinkers were "negative" in that they were critical of the existing order which, in their view, stifled the human potential and did not allow the possible to emerge from the "is." The existing factual order was studied scientifically to learn how to transcend it. These premises, as will be seen, were either accepted, modified, or rejected in the subsequent development of *sociological* thought. In these terms, early sociology developed as a reaction to the Enlightenment. But before examining that reaction, it would be well to consider two *Philosophes*, Montesquieu and Rousseau, who may be regarded as forerunners of sociological theory.

NOTES

1. My interpretation of this intellectual movement has been heavily influenced by two studies in particular: Ernst Cassirer, *The Philosophy of the Enlightenment*, trans. Fritz C. A. Koelln and James P. Pettegrove (Princeton, N.J.: Princeton University Press, 1951), and Peter Gay, *The Enlightenment: An Interpretation* (New York: Alfred A. Knopf, 1976).
2. *Discours sur les sciences et les arts*, in *Oeuvres*, Vol. III, p. 6, cited in Gay, *The Enlightenment*, p. 208.
3. See Cassirer, *The Philosophy of the Enlightenment*, p. 12.
4. Ibid, p. 13.

2

Montesquieu (1689–1755)

With the exception of Giovanni Vico, who exerted no influence on the Enlightenment (and who remained relatively unknown outside Italy until his name was discovered by Jules Michelet in 1824), it was Montesquieu who made the first attempt in modern times at constructing a philosophy of society and history. Vico had read Francis Bacon, simultaneously with the *Philosophes* and apparently independently of them, and had decided it ought to be possible to apply to the study of human society the method advocated by Bacon for the study of the natural world. In 1725, Vico wrote and published a work informed by that point of view: *Principles of a New Science Dealing with the Nature of Nations, Through Which Are Shown Also New Principles of the Natural Law of Peoples.* "The nature of things," wrote Vico, "is nothing other than that they come into being at certain times and in certain ways. Wherever the same circumstances are present, the same phenomena arise and no others."[1] Thus, Vico perceived order, regularity, and perhaps even causation in the natural world; and this, he believed, was equally true of the social realm: "the social world is certainly the work of men; and it follows that one can and should find its principles in the modifications of the human intelligence itself. Governments must be conformable to the nature of the governed; governments are even a result of that nature."[2] Nonetheless, human progress and the perfectibility of man in the secular realm, the central ideas of the Enlightenment, are nowhere expressed in Vico's writings. He remained essentially medieval and theological in his outlook and viewed improvement and salvation as dependent on the grace of God. Though Vico saw successive phases of development, they were cyclical and repetitive rather than progressive in the Enlightenment sense.

Montesquieu, on the other hand, was a true son of his age, for he had thoroughly emancipated himself from the medieval heritage.[3] His concern with regularities was more in keeping with the modern conception; he sought the *laws* of social and historical development, his main purpose in studying the social facts. Facts are studied not for their own sake but for the laws that become manifest through them. In the preface to his *Spirit of the Laws*, Montesquieu wrote: "I began to examine men and I believed that in the infinite variety of their laws and customs they were not guided solely by their whims. I formulated principles, and then I saw individual cases fitting these principles as if of themselves, the history of all nations being only the consequence of these principles and every special law bound to another law, or depending on another more general law." Particular facts become the medium through which he hopes to gain an understanding of general forms and tendencies. His major work, *Spirit of the Laws*, and all his other writings to a somewhat lesser extent, is an analysis based on political and sociological types. The "ideal-type" was an indispensable intellectual tool by means of which one could make sense out of an otherwise incomprehensible welter of facts.

There are forms of government called republic, aristocracy, monarchy, and despotism; these forms are not aggregates of accidentally acquired properties. Rather, they express certain underlying social structures. Such structures remain hidden so long as we merely observe political and social phenomena, so long as we merely observe the facts. They seem so complex and varied that they appear to defy understanding. Yet, understanding becomes possible, writes Cassirer describing Montesquieu's conception, "as soon as we learn to go back from appearances to principle, from the diversity of empirical shapes to the forming forces. Now we recognize among many instances of republics the *type* of republic, and among the countless monarchies of history we find the type of the monarchy."[4] What are the principles underlying the types? The republic rests on civic virtue; monarchy depends on honor, and despotism on fear. Again this is proposed in an ideal-typical sense. No actual political form will conform precisely to its ideal qualities; but those qualities enable us to study the actual forms.

Montesquieu views all the institutions making up a society as having an interdependent and correlative relationship to one another and as depending on the form of the whole. Education and justice, forms of marriage and the family, and political institutions have not only a reciprocal influence but also depend on the basic form of the state, and the character of the state in turn rests upon these aspects of society. While Montesquieu's ideal-types are static forms employed in the study of social structures, he has no doubt of their usefulness for the study of process. If the study of a society discloses a certain interdependence among its elements, and if a number of societies have so much in common that they may be classed under the same type, then the functioning processes of such societies may also reveal certain similar, characteristic tendencies. Social processes and the fate of peoples are not determined by accidents. In Montesquieu's study of Roman civilization, for example, he proposed to show that there are cultural as well as physical causes that bring about the rise, maintenance, and fall of systems of power and even civilizations. Although much has been made of Montesquieu's attention to physical conditions like climate, soil, and so on, he sees them as primarily limiting factors and assigns to them much less importance than to sociocultural variables in determining the forms of government, laws, and other institutions.

Montesquieu was perhaps the most objective of all the *Philosophes.* He was so interested in the "facts" that Condorcet once remarked that Montesquieu would have done better if he had not been "more occupied with finding the reasons for that which is than with seeking that which ought to be."[5] Montesquieu did not hesitate to point out virtues as well as faults in all forms of government. His conspicuous moderation and objectivity provided all parties on the political spectrum with arguments supporting their respective positions.

Though he may have been somewhat less critical than his contemporaries, Montesquieu nonetheless shared their ideal of human freedom. One of his major concerns was power and its relation to freedom. Power should be distributed among the individuals and groups of a society so as to ensure maximal freedom. Individuals are not free because they have natural rights, or because they revolt if oppression becomes unbearable; they are free to the extent that power is distributed and organized so as to prevent, or at least minimize, its abuse. Liberty is best preserved where interest groups or organized publics check one another as well as the government, and where laws provide for such checks.

Throughout his life, Montesquieu retained an insatiable curiosity about other countries and cultures; his comparative approach to society and culture was in a large part based upon his own travels as well as those recounted by others.[6] When he was not actually traveling, he fancied himself to be. For example, when he wrote and published his *Persian Letters* in 1721, it was for comparative methodological reasons. Two traveling Persians were writing to their friends at home and giving their impressions of France as a foreign culture. In that way, Montesquieu could adopt another perspective and view French institutions through foreigner's eyes. That was a way of illustrating the variety and relativity of man's institutions. Though he had never actually traveled outside of Europe, in 1728–1729, he did visit Germany, Austria, Italy, Holland, and, finally, England, where he stayed about two years. His English experience was to influence Montesquieu profoundly, for he remained throughout his life quite impressed with the English political system, particularly with the constitutional separation of powers. When he returned to France, he prepared his chief work, *The Spirit of the Laws,* and then a second one, *Considerations on the Greatness and Decadence of the Romans,* published in 1734. When his *Spirit of the Laws* finally appeared in 1748, it met with immediate and almost universal enthusiasm in European intellectual circles. The new questions Montesquieu asked and the new assumptions he employed, together with his obvious attempt at maintaining objectivity, earned him a reputation for originality. The latter quality had already become evident in his first work, the *Persian Letters,* where for the first time, perhaps, many institutions of a European society were examined from the standpoint of an outsider.

His book on the Romans was also quite innovative, in that he studied Roman society and institutions not merely to describe them but also in order to put forward a theory that might account for the rise, development, and decay of Roman civilization. Roman institutions are treated as functionally interdependent and interrelated elements of a complex system. Rome's victories and conquests are explained as the effects of specific social and political conditions. Her success, which required changes in the political structure, led inevitably to decline and, finally, to collapse. The final collapse is viewed as a consequence of the initial success which so transformed the whole structure of society as to destroy the very conditions that made for success.

Montesquieu viewed the social institutions of a society as intimately connected; even forms of thought were considered in their relation to institutions. As he was among the first to take this approach, he may be regarded as a founder of the subdiscipline called the sociology of knowledge.[7] He looked at a people not as a multitude of individuals but as a society that could be distinguished from others by its customs and institutions, variables so intricately connected that a significant change in one is bound to affect the others. Political, economic, and other institutions are viewed as aspects of a people's life related to still other aspects. And the focus is most often on the social rather than on the nonsocial. Traditional interpretations notwithstanding, Montesquieu was not a climatic or geographical determinist. Climate and geography, which he did indeed take into account, are treated as extrasocial conditions that impose certain limits, at least temporarily, on a given society. The limiting effect of those conditions is regarded as temporary and variable because the further a particular people is from nature—that is, the more developed its institutions and technology—the less is the influence of these nonsocial conditions. "Spirit" for Montesquieu refers to the distinctive character of a system of laws. The way they are related to one another and to other aspects of a people's life distinguishes one society from another.

Montesquieu's sociology of knowledge, however rudimentary, anticipates many, if not all, of the major postulates about a society and its consciousness. How one views the customs and ideas of society depends on the social position one occupies and hence on the cultural perspective one adopts. That Montesquieu understands this is clear from the reactions of his Persian travelers. They begin to doubt their own customs and ideology as soon as they leave their own society; the longer they are in Europe, the less strange do the new customs appear. He posited the social genesis of ideas, and the functional interdependence of social action and ideas; and while, at times, he invokes physical causes, too, they are generally subordinate to sociocultural conditions. He was more aware than most of his contemporaries of the human "cultural variety."

He posited a constant, ubiquitous nature in man that is modified by the specific culture; within a given society and culture, the position one occupies in the division of labor—occupations and professions—tends to influence one's character as well as one's outlook on life. Montesquieu also speaks of laws of nature that he regards as eternal and universal. Men must try to discover those laws and truths and bring their society into harmony with them. That is an ideal that can be approached but never attained. For man, even with the sharpest of reasoning powers, cannot know those truths because of error and ignorance. Man's limited perspectives—the particular position from which he views the world—and his special interests make error and ignorance unavoidable.

It is with good reason, then, that Montesquieu is regarded as a forerunner of sociological theory and method. His consistent concern with laws of development and his utilization of the ideal-type construct were something of an innovation in his time. He delineated the subject matter of sociology and pioneered in sketching out a method. That is why Emile Durkheim referred to Montesquieu as a *précurseur.*[8] A closer look at Montesquieu's work is necessary in order to see that the attention given him is altogether warranted.

The study of "reality," Montesquieu understood, is an enormously complicated enterprise involving many difficult problems. One of the tasks of science is to describe the realities with which it deals, but if those realities differ among themselves to such a degree that they cannot be classified or subsumed under types, then they truly defy rational comprehension. If there were nothing generally discernible about such realities, they would have to be considered one by one and independently of one another; but because each individual phenomenon involves an infinite number of properties, that would be a hopeless and impossible task. In short, without classification and without typologies, science is impossible and, of course, so is a science of human phenomena.

Was that not understood before Montesquieu? Yes it was, but to a very limited extent. Aristotle, for example, did indeed employ the concept of type but confined it to political states. Moreover, even if two societies differed greatly but both were ruled by kings, Aristotle was satisfied to classify them as monarchies. His types therefore tell us little about the nature of a specific *society* and its system of government. Aristotle established a tradition in that respect and was followed by a great number of philosophers who adopted his classification and made no attempt to modify it or provide another. As Durkheim observed, those philosophers "thought it impossible to compare human societies in any respect other than the form of the state. The other factors, morality, religion, economic life, the family, etc.,. . . seemed so fortuitous and variable that no one thought of reducing them to types. Yet these factors have a strong bearing upon the nature of societies; they are the actual stuff of life and consequently the subject matter of social science."[9] Precisely because Montesquieu did give attention to the "actual stuff of life," and employ the ideal-type method to comprehend it, his work may be regarded as innovative.

MONTESQUIEU'S CLASSIFICATION OF SOCIETIES

When Montesquieu speaks of a republic (including aristocracy and democracy), a monarchy, or a despotism, those terms refer to whole societies, not just to political systems as is the case with Aristotle. The types are not derived from an a priori principle but are founded on observation. His study of history and travelers' accounts and his own travels all serve as comparative empirical material for his classification. When he talks, for instance, about "republic," he has in mind the Greek and Italian city-states—Athens, Sparta, and Rome. He argues that there is a definite relationship between political systems and other social and nonsocial conditions. Monarchy is suited to the conditions of the large nations of modern Europe. The peoples of antiquity also had "kings": the Greeks, the Germans, and the Latins, for example. But they impressed him as quite different from the absolute monarchies of modern Europe upon which he based his ideal-type. Forms of despotism have also been known to exist in various places and periods, often resulting from corruption of other political forms. Nonetheless, despotism had its "natural" or "perfect" existence only in the Orient. Thus, when Montesquieu puts forward his types, he is intent upon showing that they are to be distinguished from one another not only as different systems of government, but also as systems functionally interrelated with other conditions. Among the latter, he includes, for example, the population size of a society.

The republican form, he argues, has been found in towns and cities and is best suited to a small population. When numbers grow beyond a certain point, the republican form may break down. So Montesquieu proposed that several or even many small republics may be joined together to form one large *federal* republic. This idea was applied in practice by the framers of the American Constitution. The despotic state, on the other hand, is found in large societies and is spread over vast areas, especially in Asia. The monarchical state stands in between; it is of medium size and has a population larger than that of the republic but smaller than that of the despotic state. More important, however, social forms are distinguished with regard to their respective social structures. All citizens are equal, and even alike, in a republic; this is particularly true of a democracy. A kind of social homogeneity, and hence order, are evident. There are definite restrictions on excessive accumulation of wealth and power which, it is suspected, might undermine the solidarity and the very existence of the republic. Thus democracy can become debased by transforming itself into an aristocracy, and the more democratic the republic, the more "perfect" it is. In a democracy, the common welfare of all is emphasized. A democratic republic, then, is relatively small, equalitarian, and homogeneous, and is characterized by solidarity.

In a monarchy social classes have emerged. Farming, trade, and industry, and an increasingly complex division of labor make for a system of stratification that was absent from the republic but now reaches its maximal development in the monarchy. Yet, it is here that Montesquieu envisions maximal political freedom. Classes check and limit not only the power of the monarch but one another as well. Each prevents the other from becoming too powerful and is thus free to pursue its special interests, but in moderation. As the monarchy is structurally complex—composed of classes and groups with varying degrees of wealth, power, and prestige—personal interest, envy, rivalry, and class interest emerge as strong forces. Individuals and groups now tend to disregard the general welfare of society in favor of personal and class interests. In that way Montesquieu anticipates the utilitarian doctrine, for he argues that class and personal rivalry lead the members of society to perform their respective functions as well as possible and that this conduces ultimately to the common good. Honor, too, becomes a major incentive in the public life of a monarchy as men seek to raise their status as high as possible.

Finally there is the third type, despotism, a system in which all orders of the society have become so weakened that they can offer no organized resistance to the despot. This is a regime in which all but the ruler are equal in their condition of servitude. If *virtue* is the basis for participation in the republic, and *honor* is such a basis in a monarchy, then *fear* is the basis for submission to a despot.

The reasoning underlying Montesquieu's classification is still cogent today. He understood that the growth in complexity of economic and social structures, the growth of differentials in wealth, the emergence of strata, and so on, force changes in the political structure. He grasped the fact that a small republic, in which private property was little developed, would logically exhibit a high degree of social solidarity, and that a modern society, characterized by a complex division of labor, classes, and special interest groups, would exhibit a lower degree. Social solidarity, to the extent that it exists in modern society, springs from a different source. It no longer depends on equality and sameness, but precisely upon the division of labor that makes individuals and groups mutually interdependent. Later, Durkheim borrows this idea from Montesquieu and develops his own classification of types of society and their corresponding types of solidarity.

Before concluding the discussion of Montesquieu's classification of societies, attention should be drawn to a fourth type he presented. There are societies that live by hunting or cattle raising. Typically, they have small populations and hold the land in common. Conduct is regulated by custom, not laws. This type is further divided by Montesquieu into two subtypes: savages and barbarians. Savages are generally hunters living in small, relatively nonsedentary societies, while barbarians raise cattle, live in larger societies, and are relatively sedentary. Those distinctions are still tenable and useful today in studying nonliterate and traditional societies. The fourth type, in particular, shows clearly that Montesquieu did not merely take over Aristotle's classification but produced an original system.

MONTESQUIEU'S CONCEPTION OF LAWS

As was stated at the outset, Montesquieu's originality with respect to sociology lies basically in two areas: his classification of societies into types, which enabled him to compare all their important aspects, and his concern with "laws"—that is, *the necessary relations arising from the nature of things*. Laws apply not only to nature but also to human societies. In the social realm, laws depend on the form of a society; thus the laws of a republic differ from those of a monarchy. Forms of society in turn depend on certain conditions—a major one being the "volume of society." The republic, as we have seen, has a small population and is confined to relatively narrow limits. The affairs of the community are known to every citizen. As differentials in wealth are small, conditions are approximately the same for all citizens. Even the leaders of the community have limited authority and are viewed as first among equals. But if the volume of the society increases—population grows and the geographical limits are widened—all aspects of the society will change accordingly. The individual can no longer perceive the whole society; he tends to see only the interests of his special interest group or class. Increasing stratification gives rise to divergent viewpoints and objectives; great differentials in private property give rise to great inequality in political power. The leader is now a sovereign who stands far above everyone else. As such changes occur, the society inevitably evolves from a republican to a monarchical form of government. If those developments continue in the same direction, monarchy will yield to despotism, which is now necessary to control the masses.

A "sociological" approach is taken toward all the institutions of a society and is applied to an analysis of custom and law. Custom has definite social correlates that are different from those of law. Customs emerge spontaneously from social existence; laws, on the other hand, are established by a lawgiver in a formal and explicit fashion. In the latter case, the "law" emerges spontaneously, too. The more complex social structure seems to require certain definite laws most appropriate to that structure. But they would remain hidden and implicit, Montesquieu believed, if some lawgiver had not discerned them and formulated them explicitly. Laws may nevertheless be at variance with the requirements of a certain society because what the nature of a society requires is a matter of judgment. Men have the ability to deviate from that nature because their judgments are subject to ignorance and error. An element of contingency is thus introduced. A society would be what its nature prescribes were it not for the ignorance and errors of those interpreting what the prescriptions are.

Montesquieu's conception of law as expressing *the necessary relation among things* retains ambiguous elements. He seems to believe that by studying a society one can discover its laws (what its nature requires) and therefore create legal forms and other institutions that best suit that nature. The creation of those institutions involves interpretation of what a society's true nature is, and, therefore, is subject to error. In the absence of the element of contingency—ignorance and/or error—human beings would devise laws in perfect accord with society's nature. The elements of contingency which Montesquieu introduces seem to imply that human beings can never achieve such perfect accord. Moreover, those elements lead to no small deviations from the natural laws. For example, though the institution of slavery was present in all the ancient Greek and Italian republics, Montesquieu insists that that institution is repugnant to the nature of republics. If men had not made mistakes in interpreting the nature of republics, slavery would not have emerged. In a republic, slavery is not natural and is, therefore, unnecessary. Slavery may be the necessary result of certain social conditions, but one of those conditions is the misinterpretation by man of the true nature and requirements of a republic. The true nature, which expresses not what is but what ought to be, has remained hidden from the view of society's members. Montesquieu's social laws, then, sometimes are, and sometimes are not, like other laws of nature, inherent in phenomena. Laws in the social realm are sometimes *above* the phenomena, where they remain unrecognized and therefore inoperative.

The ambiguity in Montesquieu's conception of "laws" flows from his recognition of certain degrees of freedom in man. Human beings are not mindless creatures adapting themselves passively and automatically to existing conditions. Montesquieu understood that humans also act upon the conditions of their environment and change them. Such action involves an interpretation of what those conditions are. Being subject to ignorance and error, men very often bring about conditions that are contrary to their nature. However, the degrees of freedom that enabled men to institute slavery—which is contrary to the true nature of a republic—also enable them, once having recognized their mistake, to eliminate it.

Montesquieu thus appears to have seen two kinds of laws—both "natural"—one of the physical world and the other of human life. The first works itself out automatically, "naturally." The second refers to the "laws of nature of human life," which ought to regulate the affairs of men. But acting in accordance with those laws is difficult due to the unavoidably limited perspectives of men in their respective social positions.[10]

We see, then, that Montesquieu innovated in his employment of the concepts of ideal-type and laws. He understood the need for comparative studies, and he advanced the assumption that the elements of a society are functionally interdependent. For all these reasons Montesquieu may be regarded as an important forerunner of sociological thinking.

NOTES

1. Edmund Wilson, *To the Finland Station* (Garden City, N.Y.: Doubleday, 1940), p. 3.
2. Ibid., p. 3.
3. In the present discussion I rely, in addition to primary sources, on Cassirer's work earlier cited and the following: John Plamenatz, *Man and Society* (London: Longmans, Green, 1963); Emile Durkheim, *Montesquieu and Rousseau* (Ann Arbor: University of Michigan Press, 1960); Werner Stark, *Montesquieu: Pioneer of the Sociology of Knowledge* (London: Routledge and Kegan Paul, 1960).
4. Ernst Cassirer, *The Philosophy of the Enlightenment* (Princeton, N.J.: Princeton University Press, 1951), pp. 210–11.
5. Carl Becker, *The Heavenly City of the Eighteenth-Century Philosophers* (New Haven, Conn.: Yale University Press, 1932), p. 101.
6. For these and other biographical details, see Plamenatz, *Man and Society,* pp. 253–98.
7. See Stark, *Montesquieu: Pioneer.*
8. Durkheim, *Montesquieu and Rousseau.*
9. Ibid., p. 9.
10. See Stark, *Montesquieu: Pioneer,* p. 210.

3

Rousseau
(1712–1778)

Rousseau is perhaps best known for his conception of the "state of nature" and for his *social contract.* It would be wrong to interpret Rousseau's concern with the "state of nature" as evidence of a yearning for that lost condition to which men must return in order to regain their freedom and happiness. For Rousseau, man's freedom remained a fundamental ideal but one that was not to be attained by shaking off all society and civilization or by reverting to a so-called natural state. The perfectibility of man, his freedom and his happiness, and the increasing mastery of his own fate all depended on a clear understanding of the laws of nature. In common with the other *Philosophes,* Rousseau believed that nature and society worked according to such laws; like Montesquieu, he believed that society could depart from the requirements of its natural laws. Men act of themselves; it is they who must interpret those laws. Because of limited perspectives and insufficient knowledge, they err—that is, they act contrary to their nature by establishing a social order that violates their basic nature. Rousseau's chief objective, therefore, was to find a social order whose laws were in greatest harmony with the fundamental laws of nature. He sought an alternative to the prevailing order which, to his mind, precluded man's perfectibility and even deformed and violated his nature.

For Rousseau, then, there were two conditions, the natural and the social; though the chasm between them was already very great, they could in large measure be reconciled. To accomplish that, one must always keep in mind the dual aspects of man. To assert that the social order is at variance with man's nature, one must know something about that nature. How can one speak of social man doing violence to natural man unless one really knows something about natural man? And, how can one know "natural man" when men nowhere live outside of society? It was precisely with the purpose of addressing himself to such questions that Rousseau postulated man in a "state of nature," a hypothetical construct by which man is theoretically divested of his social and cultural aspects. If one could determine how men departed from their natural condition and how they imposed upon themselves a social order at variance with that condition, then, perhaps, one could know better how to change that order and replace it with a better one.

THE STATE OF NATURE

In the development of this concept, Rousseau is engaged in an imaginative thought experiment, but the concept also rests, as will be seen, on an experiential basis. He knew that there was no such state in which man lived before and outside society; in their "presocial" state men were not men. He says clearly that it is a state "which no longer exists, which perhaps never did exist, and probably never will exist; and of which it is, nevertheless necessary to have true ideas in order to form a proper judgment of our present state."[1] "Natural man" is simply man divested of what he has acquired in society. Think away all his social qualities and the residue is biopsychological man, or man reduced to what he might have been if he had actually lived in isolation. That this idea is being used in a strictly heuristic sense becomes clear when Rousseau insists that his description of natural man should not be taken as historical truth but as a hypothetical condition. Speculation about the primitive state may throw some light on the basic nature of man.

Even savages yield a very inaccurate picture of the state of nature, for despite their primitive condition they are quite remote from that state. Therefore, Rousseau argues, those who have imputed to natural man cruel and warlike tendencies are wrong; they have attributed to natural man characteristics acquired in society. How then does one acquire an adequate conception of the hypothetical state? Fully realizing how complex a problem that was, Rousseau asked: *"What experiments would have to be made to discover the natural man? And how are those experiments to be made in a state of society?"*[2]

Such experiments would be extremely difficult if not impossible. Therefore Rousseau suggests some alternative techniques with which to approach the problem. One can observe animals in their natural habitat to gain insight into natural behavior uninfluenced by society. Second, one can study primitive peoples—savages—keeping in mind that they have acquired definite sociocultural attributes. Finally, one could deduce all the factors implied by man's subsequent social development, such as language, and think them away. Rousseau thus sought an objective, nonideological yardstick by which to evaluate society.

If we know something about man's real nature, he reasoned, we can ask whether or not certain historical societies have been suited to that nature. If it is concluded that a particular social order is unsuited, and we therefore decide to change or replace it, an analysis of natural man must provide the principles by which to guide the process of change. In order that such principles be as free from ideology as possible, we must arrive at "natural man" by putting aside all those elements that have been implanted in man as a result of his social existence. Otherwise, our judgments would be purely ideological—that is, we would simply be justifying what we desire and condemning what we do not, and in both cases the judgment would be based on the special position and interests we have in the society. In such a case, one would be demonstrating one prejudice by another—an error Rousseau observed in others and wanted to avoid. Hobbes, for example, had, in Rousseau's view, invested his "natural men" with very social qualities indeed.

Rousseau's method therefore required that one subtract all the qualities of sociocultural origin until only the "natural foundation" remained. In his "state of nature," then, Rousseau was not describing a lost golden age; rather, he was proposing a methodological device by which one might lay bare the components of man's basic psychological makeup. In more recent times, too, similar approaches have been taken: Freud, for example, having employed some premises about man's basic nature, concluded that there is an irremediable antagonism between natural man and civilized man. Marx, as we shall see, also based his theory on a conception of natural man. "Species-being," an idea derived from Feuerbach, resembles in some ways Rousseau's notion that there is a natural man and that the best social system is that which enables him to realize his potentialities to the fullest. Man is perfectible and social systems should be judged by the degree to which they facilitate his perfection. Clearly, if such evaluative judgments are to be made about particular societies most objectively and least ideologically, then a reliable conception of natural man is required. That is the task that Rousseau set himself when he advanced his ideal construct, the "state of nature."

How does Rousseau conceive of the ideal state that is to provide insight into man's basic psychological nature? It is a perfect balance between man's needs and the resources at his disposal. He desires and needs only what is to be found in the immediate physical environment. Like other animals, he has only sensations, but no knowledge and no language. Accepting Condillac's theory that general, abstract knowledge is impossible without language, Rousseau postulates that since language is the product of society, one can safely conclude that man in nature has neither language nor knowledge. His needs are extremely simple and purely physical—food, a mate, and rest; he cannot conceive of the future and is oriented exclusively to the present. Harmony is achieved between internal nature and external nature through satisfaction of all needs; conditions for discord are wholly lacking. Then what, if any, is the relation among humans? Certainly not a state of war. Rousseau rejects the Hobbesian notion of the natural state as a "war of each against all."

To understand Rousseau's state of nature we must see how sharply it contrasts with that of Thomas Hobbes (1588–1679). In the tumultuous days of the English Civil War, Hobbes produced his *Leviathan* (1651), a classic study of power as a precondition of social order and peace. Hobbes defines power as a man's "present means to obtain some future apparent Good."[3] For Hobbes, there exists in all men a *natural* and restless desire for power. The desire ceases only in death. Indeed, men pursue more and more power. The reason for that is not that a man hopes for a greater delight that increments of power will bring him; nor is the reason that he cannot rest content with moderate power. Rather, the reason is that he cannot secure the present power he has to live well without acquiring more.

Hobbes makes another assumption about man's nature: The natural condition of humanity is one of *equality*. In the presocial state of nature that he postulates, men are equal in the faculties of both body and mind. True, one man may be physically stronger or mentally quicker than another, "yet when all is reckoned together, the difference between man, and man, is not so considerable, as that one man can thereupon claim to himself any benefit, to which another may not pretend, as well as he. For as to strength of body, the weakest has strength enough to kill the strongest, either by secret machination, or by confederacy with others, that are in the same danger with himselfe." And in faculties of mind, Hobbes saw even greater equality among humans. "For Prudence, is but Experience; which equall time, equally bestowes on all men, in those things they equally apply themselves unto. That which may perhaps make such equality incredible, is but a vain conceit of one's owne wisdome, which almost all men think they have in a greater degree, than the Vulgar . . . " (pp. 183–84).

The condition of fundamental equality among men gives rise to equality of hope in the attainment of their ends. Therefore, "if any two men desire the same thing, which neverthelesse they cannot both enjoy, they become enemies; and in the way to their End, . . . endeavour to destroy or subdue one another." The result is that men quarrel and fight for gain, for safety, and for reputation. Hence, the *natural* state is one in which men are engaged in *war*—a war of every man against every man. War, for Hobbes, refers not only to the act of fighting itself, but also to the will to contend. The consequences of such a war are that men live without culture and without society. Worst of all, they live in continual fear and danger of violent death; the life of man is "solitary, poore, nasty, brutish, and short" (p. 186).

In Hobbes's view, then, the state of nature is one in which force and fraud prevail. In that state, there is no right or wrong, no just or unjust, for those are social, not natural, qualities that men acquire only in Society. The single, most important condition that makes Society possible is a "common Power to feare." Wherever and whenever no such common power exists, men revert to a state of nature and war. The fear of falling back into that state, and their will to survive, evoke in men a modicum of reason, which leads them to the formation of a *social contract.* Under its terms, men agree to give up their natural liberty and to subordinate themselves to a sovereign authority who, in turn, guarantees them security and protection from force and fraud. It is only the common terror of the sovereign that holds the war of all against all in check. The contract with the sovereign is guaranteed by the sword, for contracts "without the Sword, are but Words, and of no strength to secure a man at all" (p. 223). In thus conferring all their strength on one sovereign, men form Society, or what Hobbes calls a Commonwealth. It is "that great Leviathan, or rather (to speake more reverently) . . . that *Mortall God,* to which we owe under the *Immortall God,* our peace and defence" (p. 227). Thus Hobbes sees men as warlike in nature; it is only in Society that their fighting and disposition to fight are restrained. War is natural and peace is social.

In part one of his *Discourse on the Origin of Inequality,*[4] Rousseau presents his own view in opposition to Hobbes. In the primitive, natural state, men are isolated from, and indifferent to, one another. The incentive to war, arising from unmet needs, is lacking. If he has what he needs, why should man attack others? Men have no moral or sentimental bonds, no sense of duty or feeling of sympathy; each man lives for himself and strives for self-preservation. Rousseau agrees with Hobbes that natural man is egoistic, solitary, and perhaps even brutish, but he disagrees that that results in war. Hobbes had not succeeded in divesting natural man of all the elements he acquired in society. War is a social institution and men learn to make war, Rousseau argued, only in society. Robbery, domination, and violence are unknown to natural man; not violent subjection of others, but indifference to them, is the rule. Man is withdrawn and tends to live separately. He is, however, capable of sympathy, which is not rooted in his instincts but is rather a product of his imagination. Even without knowledge and without language, man has the ability to place himself in the position of another and to sense his feelings; he can empathize with others and to a certain degree feel their sorrows. Not being belligerent toward his fellows, however, does not mean that he is inclined to join with them to form a society. He has neither the means nor the need to do so. In the state of nature, then, men are in many respects like other animals: They are neither good nor evil, neither quarrelsome nor domineering. In that state, there is no education, no progress, and no speech; generations follow one another, but sons are no different from their fathers. In short, men do not live in society and have no culture.

In this state a perfect balance exists between man and his physical environment. But changes occur and the balance is upset. That is not bad in Rousseau's view, for it reveals certain previously hidden potentialities in man. It is not society in general that stands opposed to man's nature but a certain kind of society that divides man against himself.

THE ORIGIN OF SOCIETY

The harmonious balance would have prevailed if something in the physical environment had not upset it. Man would never have voluntarily surrendered a perpetual springtime on earth, a paradise of plenty and sunshine. Probably, two developments eventually forced men to come together in society: "In proportion as the human race grew more numerous, men's cares increased. . . . " And "Barren years, long and sharp winters, scorching summers which parched the fruits of the earth, must have demanded a new industry."[5]

Now men had to unite and coordinate their efforts and they could do so because they had the potential for society. They were intelligent and resourceful enough to respond to the challenge; they discovered that they could not only adapt to the changed natural conditions but could also, to an increasing degree, bend those conditions to their own collective will. First, families formed, and then they banded together to form societies; as they learned to act together they learned to speak, and with speech they acquired the ability to accumulate knowledge and pass it on to their children. Man had invented culture. At that stage there was as yet no social inequality. Such inequalities as did exist were within families and not among them; children were dependent for survival upon parents. That was not a harmful dependence because it was natural and temporary. This was the happiest period for man, for though now capable of vanity and envy, he was also capable of love, loyalty, and the desire to please. For that reason Rousseau prefers this period to the natural state in which lonely and natural man never experienced such feelings; he prefers it also because men have not yet become masters and slaves.

The cultivation of plants, the domestication of animals, and the division of labor generally opened the way to all kinds of social inequalities which appeared for the first time. Some men begin to prosper more than others, accumulate wealth, and pass it on to their children. Once inequalities come into being, they create greater opportunities for the rich than the poor; the rich increasingly dominate the poor who become correspondingly resentful and envious. Strata and classes emerge; society is now for the first time divided against itself. Some of the poor acquiesce in their condition of servitude while others prefer to live by plundering the rich. Insecurity and violence—

from which everyone stands to lose, but the rich more than the poor—are now felt and feared. Under such circumstances, the rich think of a device from which all can benefit, but the rich more than the poor. Laws are instituted and political society comes into being.

Like Locke, then, Rousseau believed that government originated to protect property—ultimately to protect the rich. Rights, obligations, and rules of property are therefore products of society, because for the first time man learns to act against another, to attack him. War, therefore, is not a conflict of individual men in a state of nature; it is a social phenomenon. Hobbes is wrong, Rousseau argues, to assume that men made society and submitted to a strong central power to escape the war in nature. On the contrary, man makes war as a member of an organized community—his own community against another. He becomes a warrior only after he has become a citizen.

However, aggression and war also emerge within society and that—what later thinkers called class and civil conflict—is the result of social inequalities. Social relations among men, in which some are rich and some poor, in which some dominate and some serve, also give rise to hostility and conflicts among them. It is for the purpose of controlling that war that the civil state is established. That is quite the reverse of Hobbes's view, in which war in the natural state led men to establish a civil state for their mutual security and protection. For Rousseau, in contrast, tranquillity and peace reigned in the natural state, where plenty, not scarcity, was the rule and thus allowed for a perfect equilibrium between man and his environment. It was only after that equilibrium was disturbed and finally upset that men created society. The social condition led to inequality, inequality to war, and war to the civil state.

For Rousseau, man is perfectible, and that distinguishes him from other animals. Perfectibility is possible only through society, but man has that potential already in a state of nature. With society, inequalities come about and the civil state arises. Rousseau conceives of society at this stage as a new kind of entity. It is a single, definite body distinct from the individuals who compose it, but since only the individual is real and natural, the society is not; it is a product of interaction and interdependence. Since individuals compose it, are its matter and substance so to speak, society can never attain the unity of a natural organism. "It is impossible," says Rousseau, "to prevent each one from having an individual and separate existence and attending to his own needs."[6] Whatever unity society has is a function of mutual need, coercion, and—least often—reason. In the society of unequals that has now arisen, "mutual need" is highly asymmetrical, even spurious. Rousseau writes: "You need me, for I am rich and you are poor. Let us therefore make a contract with one another. I will do you the honor to permit you to serve me under the condition that you give me what little you still have left for the trouble I shall take in commanding you."[7]

Since such a relationship involves elements of coercion, Rousseau replies to Hobbes that this "contract" is absurd and unreasonable. Instead of inwardly uniting their individual wills, members are compelled to unite in a society which is inherently unstable and devoid of an ethical foundation. For authority to have moral value, the individual will must freely submit to the general will. Social unity must be founded on liberty; liberty includes the active submission of the individual to the *general* will—not to another individual or group. But that is far from being the case, Rousseau argues, in society as it is today. Men are not united by reason in liberty; they are divided by artificial inequalities and are held together by force. Such a society is contrary to man's nature and hence unreasonable. The prevailing social inequalities have no direct relationship to natural differences—differences of age, health, physical strength, and mental abilities. In society some men enjoy privileges to the detriment of others, some are richer, more respected, and more powerful than others; such differences are not natural. Social institutions and conventions invest certain individuals and groups with a "superiority"; those same individuals and groups, in a state of nature, would not be superior and might even have been inferior. In Rousseau's words, "it is plainly contrary to the law of nature, however defined, that children should command old men, fools, wise men, and that the privileged few should gorge themselves with superfluities, while the starving multitude are in want of the bare necessities of life."[8] The unnatural inequalities, perpetuated by the social institution known as inheritance, soon acquire stability and legitimacy. So man, who began independent and free, now becomes the tool and victim of another. "Man is born free; and everywhere he is in chains."[9]

But if society as it is now constituted violates man's nature, will that be true of every society regardless of its form? Is there some irremediable antagonism between man's nature and life in society, or can they be reconciled? For Rousseau, the suffering caused by civilization seemed far to outweigh its "grandeur." Since, however, man is reasonable, perhaps the present evils could be eliminated, thus leading to a new level of perfection superior even to his original state. The prevailing condition was neither inevitable nor necessary. Rousseau proposed, therefore, to emancipate the individual not by releasing him from society altogether, which he recognized as quite impossible, but by releasing him from a particular form of society. The problem was to find a form of society in which every member would be protected by the united power of the entire political organization and in which each individual, though uniting with others, remains free and equal, obeying nobody but himself. In short, "each man, in giving himself to all, gives himself to nobody; and as there is no associate over which he does not acquire the same right as he yields others over himself, he gains an equivalent for everything he loses, and an increase of force for the preservation of what he has."[10] That is the ideal solution Rousseau proposes in his *Social Contract.*

THE SOCIAL CONTRACT

All other contract theorists, such as Hobbes, Locke, and Grotius, viewed society as a contract which establishes the State by the *subjection* of its members. Rousseau, in contrast, posits freedom and equality: The social contract was to be formed by free and equal individuals. That was the fundamental premise of his *Volonté Genérale,* or General Will. Previous theorists had allowed for a change of the contract only when the monarch or State abused its power. Rousseau went farther and posited *popular sovereignty.*

Some commentators have misunderstood Rousseau's *Social Contract,* attributing to him a glorification of an allegedly unbounded absolutism of the State. They have erroneously interpreted him as having advocated the subordination of every particular Will to the General Will. Yet Rousseau emphasized time and again that the individual does not simply subordinate himself, but rather assents only to such obligations that he himself recognizes as valid and necessary.

Rousseau did, however, allow for certain inequalities in the new society. "Physical inequality," under which he included *inequality of property,* is unavoidable and ought not be deplored. Rousseau therefore had no truly communitarian ideas concerning property. The State was entitled to interfere only when inequality endangered the moral equality of the citizens. An example would be specific classes of citizens who are subject to an economic dependence that threatens to make them mere instruments in the hands of the wealthy and powerful. The remedy, for Rousseau, was to place limits on the inheritance of wealth. He attacked not poverty as such, but the political and social disfranchisement resulting from it.

The new society, or social contract, enables the individual to be absorbed into the common, general will without losing his own will, because in giving himself to the common will he gives himself to an impersonal force. When a man submits to it, no immoral dependency results. He loses little or nothing and gains in return the assurance that he will be protected by the full force of society against the encroachment of individuals and groups. He is now a member of a society of equals and has regained an equality not unlike the one he enjoyed in nature—but in a new form and on a higher level. Freedom and equality are now not only preserved but are more perfect than in the state of nature. There is a vast moral difference, Rousseau believed, between subjection to an individual and subjection to the whole community. The general interest is expressed in the fact that all desire the happiness of each. Yet, when Rousseau set about examining the prerequisites of such a society, he made many compromises.

In the new society, Rousseau had argued, sovereignty is inalienable and indivisible. In practice, however, he recognized that it was impossible outside a very small community to have democracy without representatives and without the delegation of powers. He understood that the force of government, though it called itself a public force and though it professed to represent the general will, could usurp power and act against the common good. Government is a constant threat to man's freedom and yet it is indispensable; government is the corrupting element in society and threatens continually to undermine the sovereignty of the people. Thus Rousseau's judgments about realizing his good society were not altogether confident and optimistic. If democracy is open to constant threat from the very government it requires, then "aristocracy" may be the best form of government. That seemed to be the best compromise between democracy and monarchy. Aristocracy was to be a government composed of a minority chosen on the basis of age and experience. But even then, those who govern will have to be guided by divine wisdom and patience.

Even the wisest, most patient, and best of legislators, however, are doomed to failure in the absence of certain preconditions. If legislation is to facilitate the desired profound transformation, then the people for whom it is intended must be neither too young nor too old. In the latter case, they are set in their ways and immune to change; and if they are too young, they are not ready for the efforts and discipline required. Then, too, the nation must not be so large that it will lack homogeneity, for where that is lacking, a general will is impossible. Neither must it be so small that it cannot maintain itself. The critical moment must be seized before it passes. "The whole *Social Contract* favors the establishment of a small society on the model of the ancient city-state or the Geneva Republic."[11] Finally, peace and plenty must prevail. Although the role of the legislator is a very important one, his success depends on certain conditions that are at best problematical. Rousseau appears to have believed that the new society will have to wait for some charismatic figure who would emerge in an unpredictable way, quite by accident. If and when that occurred, and if the other objectively necessary conditions were present, success might be possible. On balance, however, he was somewhat pessimistic.

Late in life, when he was asked for some practical advice by the government of Poland and thus had to address himself quite concretely to the question of transforming a society, Rousseau advocated slow change and suggested the institution of several formal democratic mechanisms. Emancipate the serfs, he counsels, only when they prove their fitness for liberty, because men who have been servile cannot become citizens overnight. Do not get rid of the "old" hastily, but change it slowly. The national assembly is to be elected by provincial assemblies; the executive is to be appointed by the legislative, and the king is to have great honor but little power. Finally, those elected are to be closely bound by instructions. In sum, Rousseau sees social change as a deliberate and slow process.[12]

Later, when the French revolutionaries were to turn their attention to Rousseau, they ignored that part of his teachings; it was only after the

Revolution that his emphasis on "organic" change was discovered and elaborated by the Romantic-Conservative Reaction to the Enlightenment and the Revolution.

There are, then, several reasons why Rousseau may be regarded as a forerunner of sociology. As a result of his attention to "natural man" and the methodological device he employed to deduce him, he had an accurate conception of culture—or what man acquires in, through, and from society. He was among the first to address himself in a relatively systematic manner to the origins, forms, and consequences of inequality in society. He saw clearly that the existence of classes affected all aspects of men's lives. Inequality had definite consequences leading to strife and war within and among societies. Finally, he saw the possibilities of change. There should be a way, he believed, to change or remake the society that man's own action has produced but in which he is not his own master.

NOTES

1. Jean Jacques Rousseau, *The Social Contract and Discourses,* trans., with an introduction, by G. D. H. Cole (New York: E. P. Dutton, 1950), p. 191.
2. Ibid.
3. Thomas Hobbes, *Leviathan* (New York: Penguin Books, 1968), p. 150. (Originally published in 1651.) (Hereafter all page references to this work will be indicated in parentheses immediately following the quoted passage.)
4. Ibid., pp. 222–26.
5. Ibid., p. 236.
6. Quoted in Emile Durkheim, *Montesquieu and Rousseau* (Ann Arbor: University of Michigan Press, 1960), p. 84.
7. From Jean Jacques Rousseau's article, "Economie Politique," Encyclopédie (Paris, 1755, v. 347). Quoted in Cassirer, *The Philosophy of the Enlightenment* (Princeton, N.J.: Princeton University Press, 1951), p. 260.
8. Rousseau, *Social Contract,* p. 272.
9. Ibid., p. 3.
10. Ibid., p. 14.
11. Durkheim, *Montesquieu and Rousseau,* p. 120.
12. See John Plamenatz, *Man and Society* (London: Longmans, Green, 1963), pp. 387–88.

4

Perfectibility Through Education

Rousseau's Émile—and Sophy

Rousseau is justly famous not only for his political theory, but also for his ideas on education. Indeed, soon after the publication of *Émile,* with its advocacy of maternal breast-feeding and its opposition to the swaddling of infants, Rousseau's ideas acquired considerable influence. More and more mothers took to nursing their own babies, and it became fashionable among "enlightened" parents to bring up their children *à la Jean-Jacques* ("in the Rousseau manner").

Émile is a classic which deserves to be read and studied, not only as a historical document but also for what it has to say to us today. That is especially true regarding Book V, where Émile, having reached manhood, is ready for his promised helpmeet whom Rousseau calls Sophy. It is in this final part of Rousseau's work that he sets forth his principles for the education of woman. There, as we shall see, Rousseau maintains that the natural differences between the sexes requires that they be educated differently. The knowledge to be imparted to the sexes and the shaping of their personalities must correspond to their respective natures. This conception of things soon met with vehement opposition in the work of Mary Wollstonecraft, a pioneer feminist whose *Vindication of the Rights of Woman* (1792) may be regarded as the first feminine declaration of independence. So let us first listen to Rousseau on the education of man and woman and then hear what Wollstonecraft had to say by way of criticism.

Rousseau referred to *Émile* as *"mon traité d'education,"* and it is true that *Émile* is a treatise on education insofar as its content is concerned. As many commentators have observed, however, the most striking feature of this work is its form, half essay and half novel, which becomes in Book V, with the love story of Émile and Sophy, more novel than treatise. But *Émile* is also and perhaps primarily an essay on moral philosophy founded on Rousseau's belief that the human being is naturally good. The essay is directed to the good mother who thinks for herself and wishes to shield her child from the crippling effects of social conventions which are unreasonable and contrary to human nature.

The mother's role in child rearing is fundamental, since a child's earliest education is most important and is, undoubtedly, woman's work. "If the author of nature," wrote Rousseau, "had meant to assign it to men he would have given them milk to feed the child."[1] Education is not just a matter of preserving the child's life; that is not enough, for he must be taught how to preserve his own life when he becomes a man, how to bear the ups and downs of fortune, how to live, if need be, in the snows of an icy, wind-swept terrain or on the edge of a scorching desert. But, alas, the human being, instead of developing his natural gifts and powers, is everywhere subject to control, constraint, and compulsion. He is imprisoned by his institutions and, indeed, prepared for such imprisonment in infancy by being bound up in swaddling clothes. The infant's vital impulses thus meet an insurmountable obstacle. He is now less free and more constrained than he was in the womb. Where this absurd convention prevails, men are lame, rickety, and deformed, not tall, strong, and well made.

"What is the origin of this shameless and unnatural custom?" asks Rousseau. It emerged, he suggests, with the refusal of mothers to fulfill their first duty and to nurse their own children, entrusting them instead to hired strangers who swaddle their employer's children to save themselves trouble. An unswaddled child would need constant watching; a well-swaddled one may be cast into a corner where its cries go unheeded. So while the gentle mother, having got rid of her baby, devotes herself gaily to the pleasures of the city, her child, if the nurse is at all busy, ". . . is hung up on a nail like a bundle of clothes and is left crucified while the nurse goes leisurely about her business" (p. 2). The upper-class woman, in particular, has not only ceased to suckle her own child, but she also shirks the main duty of motherhood; there is no substitute for a mother's love, which the child needs even more than her milk.

The real nurse is and should be the mother and the real teacher, as the child grows and develops, is the father. Let the mother and the father agree on the ordering of their duties and method, and the child will learn effectively from both. He will be better educated by a sensible though ignorant father than by the cleverest stranger. Believing this, and feeling deeply the importance of a tutor's duties, Rousseau declares himself unfit to accept such a task. He therefore takes up not the task but the pen in order to describe how he would educate an orphan—an imaginary pupil of good health and ability—and guide him from birth to manhood.

Émile, the new-born child, will first of all require a nurse, healthy in mind and body, who has recently become a mother. He will be accustomed to a daily bath, to plenty of fresh air, and to the extremes of heat and cold. Far from being confined in tight wrappings, he shall be clothed in loose and flowing flannels, light enough to leave his limbs free and to allow the air to flow through. Freedom of movement is essential, for that is how the child learns the difference between self and not-self. His mind soon distinguishes between the pain caused by things and the pain caused by other individuals, the latter experience helping him to develop his innate sense of the difference between justice and injustice. When he perceives the pain inflicted upon him as unjust, this gives rise to anger and resentment.

Émile now enters the second phase of life. He no longer cries in pain, for he can now say, "It hurts me!" The long process of acquiring wisdom through experience and striving for liberty has begun. For Rousseau, it was self-evident that when our natural tendencies are unhampered by human prejudices and institutions, children and adults alike fully enjoy their liberty. So Émile is ready to begin to learn the difference between two kinds of dependence: "dependence on things, which is the work of nature; and dependence on men, which is the work of society. Dependence on things, being non-moral, does no injury to liberty and begets no vices; dependence on men . . . gives rise to every kind of vice, and through this master and slave become mutually depraved" (p. 49). The words *command* and *obey* will be excluded from Émile's vocabulary, and he will learn primarily through experience, not by means of verbal lessons. His earliest notion of justice will come from reflection on what is due to him and not on what he owes to others. He must also possess something of his own so that he may grasp the idea of property. And he must now learn the only moral lesson suited for a child and yet the most important moral lesson for every time of life: "Never hurt anybody." Such negative virtues are also the noblest, "for they make little show, and do not even make room for that pleasure so dear to the heart of man, the thought that someone is pleased with us. . . . It is not in talking about this maxim, but in trying to practice it, that we discover both its greatness and its difficulty" (p. 69).

At the same time Émile's body is to be strengthened through daily rigorous exercise. Just as the practice of an art or craft requires tools sufficiently strong to stand use, the senses, limbs, and bodily organs must be strong and healthy, for they are the tools of the intellect. Émile should go about bareheaded the year round, and when thirsty, he should drink fresh, cold water, even in the depths of winter. If he has a fear of darkness, "take him often into dark places and be assured this practice will be of more avail than all the arguments of philosophy. The tiler on the roof does not know what it is to be dizzy, and those who are used to the dark will not be afraid" (p. 100). Let Émile also go barefoot the year round; let him do anything that leads to the agility of his body; let him run, jump, leap, and climb. And let him engage in any activity that expands his mental prowess and develops his gifts: geometry, music, the art of drawing, and so on.

Émile's diet will require special attention. Children, says Rousseau, are indifferent toward meat, which proves ". . . that the taste for meat is unnatural; their preference is for natural foods, such as milk, fruit, and vegetables. Beware of changing this natural taste and making children flesh-eaters, if not for their health's sake, then for the sake of their character. . . . Homer makes his flesh-eating Cyclops a terrible man, while his Lotus-eaters are so delightful that those who went to trade with them forgot even their own country to dwell among them" (p. 118). Rousseau then cites Plutarch on the same subject:

> You ask me why Pythagoras abstained from eating the flesh of beasts, but I ask you, what courage must have been needed by the first man who raised to his lips the flesh of the slain, who broke with his teeth the bones of a dying beast, who had dead bodies, corpses, placed before him and swallowed down limbs which a few moments ago were bleating, bellowing, walking, and seeing? How could his hand plunge the knife into the heart of a sentient creature, how could his eyes look on murder, how could he behold a poor helpless animal bled to death, scorched and dismembered? How can he bear the sight of this quivering flesh? Does not the very smell of it turn his stomach? Is he not repelled, disgusted, horror-struck, when he has to handle the blood from these wounds, and to cleanse his fingers from the dark and viscous bloodstains?. . . But you, oh, cruel man! Who forces you to shed blood? Behold the wealth of good things about you, the fruit yielded by the earth, the wealth of field and vineyard; the animals give their milk for your drink and their fleece for your clothing. What more do you ask? (pp. 118–19)

"Ruthless men," Plutarch continues,

> you not only slay the animal, you turn against the dead flesh, it revolts you, it must be transformed by fire, broiled and roasted, seasoned and disguised with drugs; you must have butchers, cooks, turnspits, men who will rid the murder of its horrors, who will dress the dead bodies so that the taste deceived by these disguises will not reject what is strange to it, and will feast on corpses, the very sight of which would sicken you. (p. 120)

Émile has now reached puberty; he is about twelve, thirteen years of age. He is ready to transform sensations into ideas. But Rousseau, as imaginary tutor, would not jump too quickly from objects of sense to objects of thought. His general rule is to stay within the realm of Émile's environmental experiences. Avoid substituting a symbol for the thing signified, unless it is impossible to show the thing in itself. Émile's lessons in geography, for example, will begin with the village in which he lives and the places which he visits; he will make his own map. He will also begin to learn about the world of work. He comes to recognize with the aid of his tutor, that every form of work must be judged in terms of its usefulness, safety, or comfort for human beings. He learns to have more respect for the shoemaker or mason than for the jeweler. He sees agriculture as the most honorable of arts, but metalwork and carpentry as honorable too. He learns about the interdependence of human beings and that the exchange of goods and services is essential in any society. He learns that the human being is bound to work and that every idler is a thief. Émile will learn a trade, an honest trade. It is here, in his choice of a trade for Émile, that Rousseau anticipates an argument he will make later in his discussion of Sophy—Émile must learn a trade befitting his age and *sex*:

> Sedentary indoor employments, which make the body tender and effeminate, are neither pleasing nor suitable. No lad ever wanted to be a tailor. It takes some art to attract a man to this woman's work. The same hand cannot hold the needle and the sword. If I were king I would only allow needlework and dressmaking to be done by women and cripples who are obliged to work at such trades. (p. 162)

Rousseau also forbids for Émile

> those stupid trades in which the workmen mechanically perform the same action without pause and almost without effort. Weaving, stocking-knitting, stone-cutting; why employ intelligent men on such work? It is merely one machine employed on another. (p. 163)

After these considerations Rousseau decides that Émile will learn carpentry, a clean and useful trade that strengthens the muscles and calls for skill, industry, creativity, and taste.

Émile in his growing adolescence has become more and more aware of his moral nature, of his relation to his fellow men—and women. He feels the impulses of nature and, hence, the need for a companion. Being a well-educated youth, however, his first sentiment is not love but friendship. The first work of his rising imagination is the appreciation of his fellows. It is at this stage of dawning sensibility that the first seeds of humanity may be effectively sown in the heart of the young adolescent. Otherwise, Rousseau feared, Émile might become like those young men who were early addicted to women and debauchery. Their passionate temperament and frustrations made them impatient, vindictive, angry, cruel, and inhuman, but Émile at sixteen knows what it is to suffer, for he himself has experienced suffering. Under the guidance of his tutor and with the expansion of his sympathetic imagination, Émile begins to see himself in his fellow creatures, to be touched by their signs of pain. Émile is now beginning to put himself in the place of those who can claim his pity. It dawns on him that the fate of miserable and wretched individuals may one day be his own, ". . . that his feet are standing on the edge of the abyss, into which he may be plunged at any moment by a thousand unexpected, irresistible misfortunes" (p. 185). Émile must learn to put no trust in his good health and fortune, since it may be entirely temporary. When he looks at the rich and compares them with the poor, he sees an essential difference: The rich man's ills are largely of his own making, but the poor man's come from the external hardships fate has imposed on him—hunger, fatigue, exhaustion. Not only that, Émile now recognizes that it is in fact fate that has placed these human beings in such circumstances and that they are, on the whole, no less wise than he. When he carefully observes persons in this class, he sees that although they have a different way of speaking, they have as much intelligence and more common sense than he has. Émile is gaining a sensitive human conscience and is trying to live in accordance with the golden rule. He has also begun to think for himself, and once he has begun, he will never leave off. And yet until now, his tutor has not spoken to him of religion as such. Why not? Because, "The chief harm which results from the monstrous ideas of God which are instilled into the minds of children is that they last all their life long, and as men they understand no more of God than they did as children" (p. 222). But now that Émile is becoming a young man and learning to think for himself, he is ready to learn what it really means to be a truly religious human being.

THE CREED OF A SAVOYARD PRIEST

It is highly probable, Rousseau scholars believe, that the aspect of the book *Émile* that had the greatest impact on Rousseau's contemporaries was the discussion of religion in the *Profession de foi du Vicaire savoyard*. Although this section of the book is supposed to be an important element in Émile's education, it is clear from the text alone that the "profession of faith" is more than just that. As P. D. Jimack has observed, it is more, too, than the advice given to Rousseau some thirty years earlier, as he claims in the introductory remarks to this section of the book. Rousseau himself acknowledged in a letter to a friend and in his *Reveries du Promeneur solitaire* that the "profession of faith" was his own, and that it was his aim to set down the basic religious-moral principles with which he would guide his conduct for the rest of his life. In these terms, although "The Creed of a Savoyard Priest" is an integral part of *Émile,* it can be read as an independent essay. And if we place this essay in its historical context, we can more fully appreciate its meaning and the nature of Rousseau's achievement. France at the time was split between two bitterly opposed, religious camps: the intolerant and authoritarian Catholic church, on the one hand, and the severe critics of religion, on the other. Most of Rousseau's friends among the *Philosophes* were deists, materialists, and even atheists, "and it was to a large extent the disquieting ethical implications of the more extreme materialist views which prompted him to seek to clarify and formulate his own religious position."[2]

Rousseau begins by rejecting both the stance of the church, which permitted no doubt, and the attitude of the *Philosophes*, who were no less dogmatic in their assertions of materialism. Matter, says Rousseau, receives and transmits motion, but cannot produce it. The more he reflected on the action and reaction of natural forces, the more he was inclined to arrive at a first cause in some will. And if matter in motion points to a will, then matter in motion according to fixed laws points to an intelligence. "Unless the eyes are blinded by prejudices, can they fail to see that the visible order of the universe proclaims a supreme intelligence?" (p. 237). That the world is governed by a wise and powerful will was therefore fundamental to Rousseau's creed. As for the human being, the motive power of all his action lies in the will of a free creature. The human being is active and free and thus acts of his own accord. God is no puppeteer who pulls strings and thus determines the conduct of his creatures. No, providence has made the human free so that he may choose good and reject evil. If God is good and all powerful, what is the source of evil? This is the question with which theodicy concerns itself. God's omnipotence precludes the existence of a second domain as the source of evil. Rousseau rejects all notions of the so-called devil as pure silliness. Then what is the source of evil? For Rousseau the answer is clear: Evil is the result of the human being's failure to live according to God's ethical and moral teaching, the failure to construct a society that will preserve humanity's original goodness. In these terms, then, Rousseau also rejects the doctrine of "original sin." "O man!" he declares, "seek no further for the author of evil; thou art he. There is no evil but the evil you do or the evil you suffer and both come from yourself" (p. 224).

It is no less certain, for Rousseau, that the human individual is a thinking, willing, moral being: "I am aware of my soul; it is known to me in feeling and in thought; I know what it is without knowing its essence; I cannot reason about ideas which are unknown to me" (p. 246). But

> Do not ask me whether the torments of the wicked will endure for ever . . . . How does the fate of the wicked concern me? I take little interest in it. All the same, I find it hard to believe that they will be condemned to everlasting torments. If the supreme justice calls for vengeance, it claims it in this life. . . . Justice uses self-inflicted ills to punish the crimes which have deserved them. It is in your own insatiable souls, devoured by envy, greed and ambition, it is in the midst of your false prosperity, that the avenging passions find the due reward of your crimes. What need to seek a hell in the future life? It is here in the breast of the wicked. (p. 247)

Are the ideas of what is right, good, and just the monopoly of any one religion? Rousseau answers this question with a resounding "no"! In spite of the amazing variety of manners and customs, one finds everywhere the same ideas of right and justice. Every human being has an intuitive knowledge of moral truth. There is at the bottom of every human heart an innate principle of justice and virtue. The motive power of conscience lies in both feeling and reason. Rousseau's "natural religion" stresses the moral and regards it as a "strange sort of conceit which fancies that God takes . . . an interest in the shape of the priest's vestments, the form of words he utters, the gestures he makes before the altar and all his genuflections" (p. 259). The real duties of religion are independent of human institutions. A righteous heart is the true temple of the Godhead. The essence of religion is therefore this: "to love God above all things and to love our neighbor as ourself . . . ; remember, there is no religion which absolves us from our moral duties . . . " (p. 276).

> Émile is now a man. He is twenty years of age and requires a companion, and with the aid of his tutor he will go in search of a fitting one.

SOPHY, OR WOMAN

For Rousseau, it is the divergent *nature* of the sexes that should determine the form and content of education. "The man," he declares,

> should be strong and active; the woman should be weak and passive; the one must have the power and the will; it is enough that the other should offer little resistance. When this principle is admitted, it follows that woman is specially made for man's delight. If man in his turn ought to be pleasing in her eyes, the necessity is less urgent, his virtue is his strength, he pleases because he is strong. I grant you this is not the law of love, but it is the law of nature, which is older than love itself. (p. 322)

But Rousseau also acknowledges the distinctive power of woman. The different constitutions of the sexes make it plain that the man seems to be master but is, as a matter of fact, dependent on the woman, and that is an inexorable law of nature.

> For nature has endowed woman with a power of stimulating man's passions in excess of man's power of satisfying those passions, and has thus made him dependent on her good will, and compelled him in his turn to endeavour to please her, so that she may be willing to yield to his superior strength. Is it weakness which yields to force, or is it voluntary self surrender? This uncertainty constitutes the chief charm of the man's victory, and the woman is usually cunning enough to leave him in doubt. (p. 323)

Rousseau goes on to argue that the woman's biological makeup, at least in her youth, always reminds her of her sex and her special functions. She needs care during pregnancy and when she gives birth and nurses her children. "Women do wrong to complain of the inequality of man-made laws," Rousseau insists. "This inequality is not of man's making, or at any rate it is not the result of mere prejudice, but of reason" (p. 324). And if someone reminds Rousseau that women are not always bearing children, he responds,

> Granted; yet that is their proper business.
> . . . can a woman suddenly change her way of life without danger? Can she be a nursing mother today and a soldier tomorrow? (p. 325)

It followed, for Rousseau, that if men and women are unlike in constitution and temperament, their education must be different:

> To cultivate the masculine virtues in women and to neglect their own is evidently to do them injury. . . . Do not try to make your daughter a good man in defiance of nature. (p. 327)

Rousseau does not intend by this that woman should be brought up in ignorance and kept to housework only. She is to be man's helpmeet, not handmaid! Women should learn to think, to will, to love, to cultivate their minds as well as their persons. Woman should learn many things, "but only such things as are suitable" (p. 327). And what are those suitable things?

> A woman's education must therefore be planned in relation to man. To be pleasing in his sight, to win his respect and love, to train him in childhood, to tend him in manhood, to counsel and console, to make his life pleasant and happy, these are the duties of woman for all time, and this is what she should be taught while she is young. (p. 328)

Rousseau acknowledges that for both sexes the training of the body is desirable and that it must precede and accompany the cultivation of the mind. But

> the aim of physical training for boys and girls is not the same; in the one case it is the development of strength, in the other, of grace; not that these qualities should be peculiar to either sex, but that their relative values should be different. (p. 329)

However, Rousseau then goes on to make other assertions that exaggerate the role of nature and underestimate the role of nurture in the formation of the personalities of boys and girls. "The doll," he declares,

> is the girl's special plaything; this shows her instinctive bent towards her life's work. (p. 331)
> . . . Little girls always dislike learning to read and write, but they are always ready to learn to sew. (p. 331)

Girls, Rousseau continues, should not only be kept busy at sexually appropriate tasks, they should be accustomed to restraint.

> All their life long, they will have to submit to the strictest and most enduring restraints, those of propriety. This habitual restraint produces a docility which woman requires all her life long, for she will always be in subjection to a man, or to man's restraints, and she will never be free to set her own opinion above his. (pp. 332–33)

Furthermore, Rousseau perceives significant differences in the mental capacities of the sexes:

> The search for abstract and speculative truths, for principles and axioms in science, for all that tends to wide generalization, is beyond a woman's grasp; their studies should be thoroughly practical . . . ; for the works of genius are beyond her reach, and she has neither the accuracy nor the attention for success in the exact sciences. (p. 349)

On the other hand, women are the best and most natural judges of a man's worth:

> Alas for the age whose women lose their ascendancy, and fail to make men respect their judgment! This is the last stage of degradation. Every virtuous nation has shown respect to women. . . . Every great revolution began with the women. (pp. 353–54)

It is in the spirit of such maxims that Sophy has been educated. Although she is not beautiful, the more one sees her, the prettier she becomes. She dresses simply but elegantly; far from displaying her charms, she conceals them, but in such a manner as to enhance them. She is above all, modest. "Needlework is what Sophy likes best; and the feminine arts have been taught her most carefully . . . " (p. 357). Sophy wanted a lover, but the lover must be her husband. She was in love with the mythical Telemachus, and she sought someone like him. From the moment she and Émile were introduced, they knew they were made for each other.

Rousseau thus proposed to educate woman in accordance with her presumed nature. One can readily see why some of his views would have generated an impassioned rebuttal on the part of a thinking person. Indeed, there is at least one passage in Rousseau's discussion of women in which he comes close to contradicting and even repudiating much of his central argument. "In both sexes alike", he writes,

> I am only aware of two really distinct classes, those who think and those who do not; *and this difference is almost entirely one of education.* (p. 371, italics added)

Not surprisingly, this passage did not slip by unnoticed in Mary Wollstonecraft's rejoinder.

NOTES

1. Jean-Jacques Rousseau, *Émile*, trans. by Barbara Foxley, with an introduction by P. D. Jimack, (London: Dent, Everyman's Library, 1986), first published in 1911. (Hereafter all page references to this work will be indicated in parentheses immediately following the quoted passage.)
2. See Jimack's introduction in ibid., p. xx.

5

Mary Wollstonecraft
(1759–1797)

A true child of the Enlightenment, Mary Wollstonecraft was profoundly influenced by the outstanding thinkers of that movement, notably by Rousseau whose writings she much admired and yet criticized for his attitude toward the education of women. In his *Émile,* as we have seen, Rousseau proposed an educational program for women which, in Wollstonecraft's judgment, was founded not on reason but on age-old prejudices. It was in response to the views of Rousseau and to those of several British writers that Wollstonecraft composed her major work, *Vindication of the Rights of Woman* (1792).

In an earlier work she had defended the first phase of the French Revolution as the practical application of Enlightenment principles.[1] Edmund Burke, in his *Reflections* on the Revolution, had condemned the events in France as threatening to break up the established social order throughout Europe, an order embodying, in his view, the sum of political wisdom. Wollstonecraft replied to Burke in her *Vindication of the Rights of Men.*

Burke, as his political record demonstrated, was no out-and-out reactionary. He supported the American claim to independence, abhorred slavery, condemned the harshness of the penal system, and threw his weight behind the reforms of the British colonial administration of India. In his *Reflections on the Revolution in France,* however, Burke maintained that the laws of inheritance and inequalities of rank were the chief elements of a civilized society. This, together with his attitude toward the poor, aroused Wollstonecraft's greatest indignation. Burke, advocating what he called "the principles of natural subordination," wrote:

> They [the poor] must respect that property of which they cannot partake. They must labour to obtain what by labour can be obtained; and when they find, as they commonly do, the success disproportioned to the endeavour, they must be taught their final consolation in the final proportions of eternal justice.[2]

In Wollstonecraft's view, such an attitude was an affront to both humanity and God:

> This is contemptible, hard-hearted sophistry, in the specious form of humility, and submission to the will of heaven. It is, Sir, possible to render the poor happier in this world, without depriving them of the consolation which you gratuitously grant them in the next. They have a right to more comfort than they, at present, enjoy; and more comfort might be afforded them, without encroaching on the pleasures of the rich; not now waiting to enquire whether the rich have any right to exclusive pleasures.[3]

But it was Burke's views of women that Mary Wollstonecraft found to be especially repugnant. In his *A Philosophical Enquiry into the Sublime and Beautiful* (1757), Burke ascribed women's beauty to their "littleness and weakness," which "clearly proved that one half of the human species, at least, have not souls."[4] For Mary Wollstonecraft this concept of beauty was far from sublime, implying, as it did, that women should not cultivate such "manly" virtues as might interfere with the pleasurable sensations women were presumably created to inspire. In his attitude toward women, Burke had separated love from respect, making them antagonistic principles. It is this attitude that Wollstonecraft assailed in her major work on the rights of woman. There she applied to the status of women the same Enlightenment principles she had earlier affirmed as self-evident in her *Vindication of the Rights of Men:*

> that there are rights which men inherit at their birth, as rational creatures, who were raised above the brute creation by their improvable faculties; and that, in receiving these, not from their forefathers but, from God, prescription can never undermine natural rights.[5]

From the general injustices of the old regime, she turned her attention to the specific wrongs perpetrated against the female half of the species.

Doubtless, Mary Wollstonecraft's own childhood experiences contributed to her acute awareness of the plight of women. As the eldest daughter of a drunken, brutish father and a weak but harsh mother, she was made painfully aware in her early years of the "wrongs of women."[6] And it appears that her experiences were not untypical of the condition of women in the eighteenth century. As Margaret Tims has remarked, "The uncouth, overbearing father was evidently a commonplace character and he crops up in much of the literature of the day. . . ."[7]

The outstanding advances in eighteenth-century philosophy and science had left the status of women untouched, and Wollstonecraft recognized that this was partly due to the general submission of women to the prevalent view of them propounded by men. Indeed, these deeply rooted, antiwoman prejudices could be traced back to the Bible and to classical Greece. Erroneous and debilitating conceptions of women could be eliminated, Wollstonecraft believed, by the right kind of education. Education was the foundation on which women's rights could be established. This was not an entirely new idea, since several Enlightenment thinkers had already made similar proposals.

Baron d'Holbach defended women's rights in his *Système Sociale* (1773), and Condorcet provided for the education of girls as well as boys in his first "memoir on public instruction" in 1790. By and large, however, the men of the French Revolution ignored the rights of women. In England it was Catherine Macauley, the author of several significant works including a *History of England,* who anticipated and most directly influenced Wollstonecraft's *Rights of Woman.* She had written a lengthy review of Macauley's *Letters on Education* (1790) in the *Analytical Review,* and most of the principles expounded in the *Rights of Woman* are to be found in Macauley's work.

VINDICATION OF THE RIGHTS OF WOMAN

Mary Wollstonecraft's main argument in her rebuttal of Rousseau is that women deserve social equality with men and should be given the education necessary to achieve it. The woman who strengthens her body and develops her mind will become the friend, and not the humble dependent, of her husband. If women appear to be inferior, that is only because they are indoctrinated from infancy with so-called feminine virtues: gentleness, passivity, submission, a spaniel-like affection for fathers, brothers, and husbands. But just give women the opportunity to unfold and sharpen their physical and mental faculties, and then we shall see where they stand in the scale of excellence. That woman is essentially inferior to man cannot be demonstrated so long as she is held in a state of subjugation. "I will allow," wrote Wollstonecraft,

> that bodily strength seems to give man a natural superiority over woman; and this is the only solid basis on which the superiority of the sex can be built. But I still insist that not only the virtue but the *knowledge* of the two sexes should be the same in nature, if not in degree, and that women, considered not only as moral but rational creatures, ought to endeavour to acquire human virtues (or

> perfections) by the *same* means as men, instead of being educated like a fanciful kind of *half* being—one of Rousseau's wild chimeras.[8]

When Rousseau denies to woman the same rigorous physical and intellectual education he proposes for man, the effect is to perpetuate not a natural but an artificial inferiority. If, therefore, mothers wish to give their daughters a true dignity of character, they should proceed on a plan diametrically opposed to that of Rousseau. Mothers should recognize that their daughters are made even weaker than nature intended when their ". . . limbs and faculties are cramped with worse than Chinese bands" and when they are condemned to lead a sedentary life while boys run, jump, climb, and frolic in the open air. "As for Rousseau's remarks, which have since been echoed by several writers, that they [girls] have naturally, that is, from their birth, independent of education, a fondness for dolls, dressing and talking, they are so puerile as not to merit a serious refutation" (p. 128).

We need to remind ourselves that in Wollstonecraft's time the "civil death" of women was written into law. The common law of England ruled that whatever property a woman owned before marriage or might receive thereafter became automatically her husband's. This is how William Blackstone, the distinguished professor of law at Oxford, interpreted the legal status of married women:

> By marriage the husband and wife are one person in law; that is, the very being or legal existence of the woman is suspended during the marriage or at least is incorporated and consolidated into that of her husband; under whose wing, protection and cover, she performs everything.[9]

The wealthy woman, then, was no less subordinate than the poor.

Mary Wollstonecraft had a vision of a reformed society in which the subjection of women would disappear together with other basic social inequalities:

> . . . we shall not see women affectionate till more equality be established in society, till ranks are confounded and women freed . . . (p. 315)

And yet, as we shall see, her proposals for the emancipation of women presuppose the perpetuation of certain social inequalities. A careful reading of the *Vindication* reveals that Wollstonecraft directs her argument to the middle-class woman, effectively excluding both the aristocratic and the poor woman from her audience. Aristocratic women are incapable of improvement by means of education. They are ". . . weak, artificial beings" who "undermine the very foundation of virtue, and spread corruption through the whole mass of society! As a class of mankind they have the strongest claim to pity; the education of the rich tends to render them vain and helpless. . . . They only live to amuse themselves, and by the same law which in nature invariably produces certain effects, they soon only afford barren amusement" (p. 81).

And although Wollstonecraft exhibits a sincere and profound compassion for the poor, she seems to believe that the oppressive routine of domestic drudgery makes it virtually impossible for the impoverished woman to emancipate herself through education. Moreover, it is worth noting that Wollstonecraft does not envision the elimination of a servant class in her more egalitarian society. Indeed, for Wollstonecraft, the middle-class woman's education and emancipation is unattainable without the existence of servants:

> To render the poor virtuous they must be employed, and women in the middle ranks [i.e., class] of life, did they not ape the fashions of the nobility, without catching their ease, might employ them, whilst they themselves managed their families, instructed their children, and exercised their own minds. (p. 170)

Wollstonecraft contemplates with pleasure the emancipated woman,

> . . . nursing her children, and discharging the duties of her station *with perhaps merely a servant-maid to take off her hands the servile part of the household business.* (pp. 254–55, italics added)

For Wollstonecraft a woman was to be educated not only in her own interest, but especially in the interest of creating more enlightened mothers and wives. Speaking of women in general, she affirms again and again, that women's

> . . . first duty is to themselves as rational creatures, and the next, in point of importance, as citizens, is that, which includes so many, of a mother. The rank in life which dispenses with their fulfilling their duty, necessarily degrades them by making them mere dolls. (pp. 257–58)

And in the same vein,

> As the care of children in their infancy is one of the grand duties annexed to the female character by nature, this duty would afford many forcible arguments for strengthening the female understanding, if it were properly considered. (p. 265)
>
> To be a good mother, a woman must have sense, and that independence of mind which few women possess who are taught to depend entirely on their husbands. Meek wives are, in general, foolish mothers . . . (p. 266)

And in this important respect she agreed with Rousseau. A woman's

> parental affection, indeed, scarcely deserves the name, when it does not lead her to suckle her children, because the discharge of this duty is equally calculated to inspire maternal and filial affection . . . ; and what sympathy does a mother exercise who sends her babe to a nurse, and only takes it from a nurse to send it to school? (p. 266)

Mary Wollstonecraft was also a pioneer in calling for universal suffrage:

> . . . I really think that women ought to have representatives instead of being arbitrarily governed without having any direct share allowed them in the deliberations of government. (p. 260)

In her discussion of national education, she was also among the first to call for public schools in which boys and girls would be educated together. The schools for the younger children, ages five to nine, would be absolutely free and open to all social classes. But just as Wollstonecraft's proposal for the emancipation of woman retains a servant class, her proposals for national education tend to perpetuate and reinforce social-class distinctions. "After the age of nine," she wrote,

> girls and boys, intended for domestic employments, or mechanical trades, ought to be removed to other schools, and receive instruction in some measure appropriate to the destination of each individual. . . .
>
> The young people of superior abilities, *or fortune,* might now be taught, in another school, the dead and living languages, the elements of science, and continue the study of history and politics, on a more extensive scale . . . (p. 287, italics added)

As Miriam Brody has observed, "not all these visions of a reformed society are reconcilable with Wollstonecraft's egalitarian principles. And she has not attempted to make them so."[10]

As we reflect on the *Vindication* taken in its entirety, we can see that Wollstonecraft's response to Rousseau was effective in at least one crucial respect. For she certainly succeeded in challenging his central thesis that woman's nature made her unfit for intellectual pursuits. Indeed, it is surprising that Rousseau, who so clearly recognized the role of indoctrination in making men into warriors ("man becomes a citizen before he becomes a soldier"), failed, somehow, to recognize the role of education and upbringing in the shaping of a woman's mind and conception of self.

Wollstonecraft believed that women are capable of achieving intellectual equality with men and that once they have done so, they should acquire political equality as well. She demanded honorable vocations for women, but she also always insisted that women should direct most of their energy to their tasks as wives and mothers. In her words, ". . . whatever tends to incapacitate the maternal character takes woman out of her sphere" (p. 298).

Critics have noted numerous faults of style and organization in the *Vindication,*[11] and we have noted Wollstonecraft's failure to reconcile her egalitarian vision of a future society with the class distinctions she left intact in her proposals for woman's emancipation. In spite of these shortcomings, however, the *Vindication* has to be considered a major pioneering achievement, alerting men and women alike to the plight of oppressed womankind.[12]

NOTES

1. As the Revolution ran its course, however, she was shocked and horrified that so many men and women had been guillotined merely because they were members of the nobility. She now developed serious doubts that human perfectibility could prevail against human viciousness.
2. Quoted in Margaret Tims, *Mary Wollstonecraft: A Social Pioneer* (London: Millington Books, 1976), p. 117.
3. Ibid., p. 117.
4. Janet M. Todd, *A Wollstonecraft Anthology* (Bloomington: Indiana University Press, 1977), p. 64.
5. Ibid., p. 117.
6. This is the title of a largely autobiographical novel, exploring the parallels between domestic and political life. See Mary Wollstonecraft, *Mary* and *The Wrongs of Woman,* edited with an introduction by Gary Kelly (Oxford: Oxford University Press, 1976).
7. Tims, *Mary Wollstonecraft,* p. 122.
8. Mary Wollstonecraft, *Vindication of the Rights of Woman,* edited with an introduction by Miriam Brody (Middlesex, England: Penguin Books, 1986), p. 124, italics in original. (Hereafter all page references to this work are indicated in parentheses immediately following the quoted passage.)
9. *Commentaries on the Laws of England* (New York, 1847), vol. I, p. 441.
10. See Miriam Brody's exceptionally thoughtful introduction to Wollstonecraft's *Vindication of the Rights of Woman,* p. 44.
11. Miriam Brody's criticism is fairly typical: Wollstonecraft's "prose is an imitation, and not a particularly felicitous one, of the rounded sentences of eighteenth-century prose; one comes all too often, panting to the end of hopelessly long sentences, a little unsure of what the subject was. . . . There are many digressions in the text, with the argument turning suddenly from one subject to another." See ibid., p. 41.
12. In addition to the secondary sources already cited, the reader might wish to consult Ralph M. Wardle, *Mary Wollstonecraft: A Critical Biography* (Lawrence: University of Kansas Press, 1951), and Claire Tomalin, *The Life and Death of Mary Wollstonecraft (London: Weidenfeld and Nicolson, 1974).*

6

The Romantic-Conservative Reaction

The philosophy of the Enlightenment, as we have seen, was rooted in the thought of the seventeenth century. The two main philosophical currents of that century—rationalism and empiricism—were synthesized rather successfully by the *Philosophes*, who expressed great confidence in reason and observation as means of solving human problems. The universe was governed by immutable laws, and man and society could be made better by ordering the social and political environment according to those discoverable laws. These ideas became the foundation of the intellectual movements of the nineteenth century as well, but they were modified considerably by Romantic and Conservative thinkers. They turned away from what they considered to be the naive optimism and rationalism of the eighteenth century; they did so not only by recognizing the irrational factors in human conduct but also by assigning them positive value. Tradition, imagination, feeling, and religion were now regarded as natural and positive. Generally deploring the disorganizing consequences of the French Revolution for Europe, the Romantic and Conservative thinkers attributed those consequences to the folly of the revolutionaries, who had uncritically accepted Enlightenment assumptions and had attempted to reorder society according to rational principles alone. In reaction to the eighteenth-century exaltation of reason, then, the nineteenth century extolled instead emotion and imagination, leading to a great revival of religion, poetry, and art. In addition, *the group, the community,* and *the nation* now became important concepts. Historic memories and loyalties were viewed as binding the individual to a *nation,* a category now elevated to a position of supreme importance. Gone was the cosmopolitanism of the Enlightenment. Increasingly, the nineteenth century turned to the investigation of the origins of existing institutions rather than to their transformation according to rational principles. An historical attitude emerged in which more than ever before institutions were regarded as the product of slow organic development and not of deliberate rational, calculated action.

Although the Romantic movement was in evidence throughout Europe, its form varied from one country to another. In England, and especially in Germany, the movement reflected a strong national reaction to the radicalism of the Enlightenment as expressed in the Revolution and against Napoleonic expansionism. In general, the Enlightenment conception of a rational, mechanistic universe was now rejected. In every field—literature, art, music, philosophy, and religion—an effort was made to free the emotions and the imagination from the austere rules and conventions imposed during the eighteenth century. In religion, the importance of inner experience was restored; in philosophy, the individual mind was assigned a creative role in shaping the world. It is the philosophical movement, in particular, that is most directly pertinent to our discussion of social theory.

This movement, which began with the work of Rousseau and Hume and was further developed in the philosophy of Immanuel Kant, expressed a shift in emphasis from the mechanistic universe of Newton to the creative character of the personality, having as its intention the liberation of the mind from purely rationalistic and empirical thinking. Rousseau, as we have seen, though an Enlightenment thinker, departed somewhat from the "typical" standpoint; he was less inclined than his contemporaries to counsel the reconstruction of society according to abstract rational principles alone. Inner moral will, conscience, and convictions are also important if man is to free himself.

The most dramatic break with the Enlightenment, however, was expressed in the work of David Hume.[1] His critical examination of its leading assumptions served to undermine the prevailing faith in the universe as a network of cause-effect relationships. These are far from being immanent in the universe; instead, he argued, "causality" is simply an idea, a customary way of thinking. Because phenomenon B follows phenomenon A, one assumes that B is the effect of A. Hume thus assigned a creative role to the mind by insisting that the mechanistic conception is merely a way of thinking whose relationship to the real world is an open question. In that way, Hume along with other thinkers, notably Leibniz—who accepted the Newtonian conception but saw in it personal, idealistic, and teleological elements—laid the groundwork for Kant's epoch-making philosophy.

To appreciate the importance of Kant's new epistemology, we need to understand that he was arguing against the theory of knowledge advocated by John Locke and his followers. Locke likened the human mind to a dark room wholly shut off from light except through a single opening.[2] He called that hypothetical construct a *tabula rasa*, a blank or empty state. At birth the mind contains nothing. Then as the infant begins to experience sensations of the outside world, the mind begins to acquire knowledge. The *tabula rasa* is illuminated by means of sensory experience, which conveys a faithful and complete representation of things as they actually exist outside the mind. It is as if the mind were a camera producing photographs of the outside world. For that reason, Locke's theory has been called "empiricism"—that is, a theory that all knowledge originates in sensory experience. It has also been called a photographic or copy theory of knowledge.

For Locke, the mind is wholly *passive* in receiving sensory impressions; it is like a receptacle or mirror. Locke allows the mind no creative role in selecting, modifying, or organizing the materials it receives. His conception of what the mind is capable of is quite mechanical:

1. It combines simple ideas into complex ones.
2. It sets ideas side by side without, however, uniting them.
3. It separates an idea from all the others accompanying it in reality.

The third process is called *abstraction,* which is how all general ideas are made. The three processes are analogous to human powers in the material world, where men combine things, set them side by side, and separate them. The mind, thus working like a mechanical instrument, arrives at the concepts of "infinity" by adding space to space, and "eternity," by adding stretches of time.

In contrast to Locke, Kant maintained that the mind is an active and creative entity that always plays a role in sensory experience.[3] Kant argued that there exist certain universal and necessary elements in all knowledge, the origin of which is to be found in the nature of human thinking and *not* in the objects of experience themselves. He called those elements "a prioris" because they are inherent in the mind; he called his theory of knowledge "transcendental logic" because those elements are a necessary factor in all experience.

Hume was right, Kant believed, to say that cause, effect, and so on are somehow added, and are not immediately given by sensory experience; but Hume had not seen the a priori origin of the added ideas. For Kant, the very possibility of experience presupposes that it will occur in relation to other experiences—before, after, together, and so forth. Sequence, coexistence, and other such processes are what the mind, by its very nature, demands. To support his argument, Kant asked this key question: What elements are *not* objects of perception but are nevertheless necessary for perception? His answer was *space* and *time*. All objects of experience appear in space and time; they are "aprioris," or organizing principles of the mind that are inherent in it. It followed that there is an unavoidably *subjective* element in all experience, and that knowledge of the world as it exists independently of a knowing subject is impossible. The mind, far from "photographing," *interprets* according to its own nature and laws.

In that way Kant tried to free the mind from its dependence on solely external sources for knowledge and to give a renewed validity to truth derived from the spiritual realm—religion, morality, and art. The *Philosophes* had regarded "knowledge" derived from those realms as inferior to that provided by science; only science could provide a true conception of nature and society—that is, a conception of the world as it actually is. For Kant, the knowledge derived from both realms, the spiritual as well as the scientific, had the same validity. If the concepts "causality" and "necessity" are also the product of the creative activity of the mind, why should scientific knowledge have greater validity than nonscientific knowledge? By demonstrating the limitations of scientific knowledge, Kant intended to restore the validity of faith and intuition. And, indeed, in sharp contrast to the Enlightenment, the Romantic thinkers regarded faith and intuition as essential for an understanding of nature and society.

If it was Kant who challenged the general methodological assumptions of the *Philosophes*, it was Edmund Burke who criticized their sociological assumptions. Burke expressed the growing national and conservative reaction to both the principles of the Enlightenment and the French Revolution. Burke's views, as well as those of Hegel, provide an important background for an understanding of the intellectual and historical context in which the founders of sociology, Saint-Simon and Comte, developed their own ideas. Burke's critical reflections contributed greatly, not only in England but also on the continent, to the formation of a conservative political and social philosophy. Although he criticized and condemned the French revolutionary leaders, he had a different view of the American Revolution. The American colonists were attempting to preserve the organic character of society by struggling to retain their ancient rights and privileges; in effect, it was George III who was undermining that organic character by attempting to deprive them of their privileges. Society is an "organism," but its separate organs are not necessarily perfectly coordinated as they are in a natural organism. In the social organism some parts may change more rapidly than others. When that occurs, reforms are necessary to bring the parts into harmony again. Reforms, not revolution. That Burke favored reforms is clear from his stand with respect to British rule in India and Ireland. Reforms were necessary to bring the state into harmony with the other social conditions. But there should be no sudden breaks with the past as had been the case in France.

In advancing his *organic* conception of society, Burke was explicitly repudiating the abstract rational conception of the *Philosophes*—namely, that there were general natural laws and natural rights that could be discovered by the mind, and that the laws men make should conform with the ideal principles as nearly as possible. In their application of that doctrine, Burke argued, the revolutionaries had treated society as a machine, thinking they could simply pluck out the obsolete parts and replace them with new ones. They therefore discarded old and established institutions, which had developed through time and which were integral parts of the social order and tried to replace those institutions on the basis of some abstract formula. The individual was proclaimed more important than the nation or state, the element more important than the whole; the state, far from being conceived as organically related to the rest of the social order, was treated as a mere contractual relationship. The implications were clear: If the state is a mere contract, then it can, and indeed should, be dissolved as soon as the contracting parties decide that it no longer satisfies their interests.

In his *Reflections on the Revolution in France*, Burke presents a point-for-point rebuttal of the rationalistic position.[4] The individual has no abstract rights. On the contrary, he has only those rights and privileges that prevail in a given community and which he acquires by virtue of having been born there. Rights and privileges develop slowly and organically; they are historical in character, not abstract. A community does not exist merely in the present; it is an endless chain of generations, each one inheriting from its predecessors and each individual being but one link. The generation of the Revolution therefore had no right to destroy customs and institutions that belonged not solely to them but to past generations and even future generations. Twenty-six million Frenchmen had no right to regard themselves as having sovereign authority over what belonged equally to the past and the future. Each generation should merely add to what the dead have achieved and left behind and pass on the total to its heirs.

As for the State, it is no mere contract made by individuals for the attainment of limited ends and therefore to be dissolved when the ends are attained or the agreement breached. Quite the contrary, the State is a higher organic unity, an integral part of the national community. The State, Burke wrote, "is a partnership in all science; a partnership in all art; a partnership in every virtue, and in all perfection. As the ends of such a partnership cannot be obtained in many generations, it becomes a partnership not only between those who are living, but between those who are dead and those who are to be born."[5] The State and the Nation are organisms and hence the product of a long process of growth; they are not deliberate calculated inventions out of whole cloth. Moreover, it is not calculated interest nor rational convictions that hold nations and societies together, but certain nonrational factors. Not only material interests but spiritual ties and sentiments bind the members of a community together. Such ties may be as "light as air" but they are "as strong as links of iron."[6] Burke had thus formulated his conservative reflections on the Revolution.

Burke's philosophy embodied within it a new conception of society, which now alerted social thinkers to a variety of factors the Enlightenment had ignored. Burke had advanced an historical, developmental, organic view of society and, together with his emphasis on the nonrational elements in human conduct, presented an important perspective from which to view the structure of a society and the process by which it changed. Burke's historical and conservative conception of the state and nation was given a more explicitly philosophical foundation by the German philosopher, Georg Wilhelm Friedrich Hegel.

HEGEL'S HISTORICAL SYNTHESIS

For Hegel, the Romantic-Conservative conception of "historical development" and the Enlightenment emphasis on reason were each in their own way very important ideas. He therefore attempted to bring them together in one philosophical synthesis. Reason, he argued, is not merely a faculty existing in the individual by which he might measure customs and institutions; reason is inherent in the process of development itself. That is the meaning of his celebrated notion that "what is rational is real" and "what is real is rational." Reason is not, as the *Philosophes* had regarded it, a mere abstraction from the real; it is an immanent force which determines the structure and development of the universe. In that way Hegel transforms reason into a great cosmic force that he variously calls the Idea, the Spirit, the Absolute, or, finally, God. The Idea is not an unchanging essence but is continually developing and becoming. Moreover, it is an impersonal, logical, and cosmic process which unites the social as well as the natural realm; all customs, habits, institutions, and conceptions are united into one dynamic and organic whole.

The historical process is the manifestation of the progressive unfolding of Reason in the various social and cultural institutions; that development follows a form not dissimilar to the way human thought develops. The cosmic reason objectifies itself in institutions by the process of fusion of contradictions; fusion produces new contradictions, which in turn are brought together in a new synthesis, and so on, to infinity. In other words, each thesis engenders its own antithesis; both are then resolved in a synthesis, which in turn becomes a new thesis. If the cosmic reason is to be distinguished in any way from individual reason, it is by the greater or more complete unfolding of the former's inherent potentialities. The individual mind can comprehend only aspects of reality; the acorn, however, becomes what it can become; it unfolds into an oak tree.

In the human realm, the nation stands higher than all other institutions, for it is the vehicle through which the cosmic reason realizes its destiny. That becomes clear from Hegel's philosophy of history in which he divides history into a series of succeeding epochs, each of which expresses a particular phase in the development of the World Spirit. When a nation is still in its ascending phase, it embodies not the whole of cosmic reason, but only a particular phase of its ultimate fulfillment. A nation is an individualized expression of the World Spirit and is therefore the medium through which the spirit achieves self-consciousness. In his *Philosophy of History*, one learns, much to one's astonishment, that Hegel concludes the process with the Spirit ultimately having reified itself in the Prussian state, the highest expression of the Cosmic Reason on earth. A surprising conclusion indeed! One can see, then, two distinct and opposing tendencies in Hegel's thought. On the one hand, it led explicitly to the ideological defense of the Prussian state and of German society at the time; many concluded that what is, is rational and therefore necessary and unavoidable. In those terms Hegel's philosophy became definitely conservative in its influence. But on the other hand, there was the emphasis on constant change, a dynamic and dialectical development that would continue ceaselessly and inexorably.

To perceive more clearly the two tendencies in Hegel's thought, it will be instructive to examine more closely his conception of dialectical development.[7] On the one side, one can see the emphasis on slow, organic growth determined by immanent rational laws. Between phases, however, as in the transition from the acorn to the oak tree, there is a kind of "dialectical leap" from one quality (acorn) to another (oak tree). That takes place when the quantitative accumulation of slow organic change reaches a nodal point at which an increment produces a *qualitative* change. This process may also be described as the "negation of the negation." The acorn in this example was itself a negation of the previous form (the seed), in which the acorn was inherent. With the continuation of the quantitative changes it, too, is negated by the new and potential form within it—the oak tree. Contained already within the seed is the chain of opposing forces which, if the seed is to develop, must continue to negate one another until its full potential is actualized. Each thing or form contains its own negation, and each is a unity of opposites. When a particular thing is "negated," it is superseded by a new force, which continues to develop until it, too, engenders its own negation. That is precisely what "development" means—changing according to the immanent pattern of a given thing. Negation, then, is not synonymous with outright destruction. The seed, or acorn, or even the tree, is not *negated* when it is destroyed—for example, by crushing the seed. Negation occurs only when the initial form is transcended by new qualities inherent in the first, and when the new qualities in their subsequent development actualize the full potential of the initial form.

Things strive to attain *actually* what they always were *potentially*, Hegel is saying, in his own formulation of an essentially Aristotelian notion. In natural organisms, this takes place in a "direct, unopposed, unhindered manner." Why? Because between "the Idea and its realization—the essential constitution of the original germ and the conformity to it of the existence derived from it—no disturbing influence can intrude."[8] In nature, typically, essence is actualized in existence as an undisturbed process, harmoniously. The opposite, however, is true in relation to Spirit, or the human, sociocultural realm: " . . . the realization of *its* Ideal is mediated by consciousness and will. . . . Thus Spirit is at war with itself; it has to overcome itself as its most formidable obstacle. That development which in the sphere of Nature is a peaceful growth, is in that of Spirit, a severe, a mighty conflict with itself. What Spirit really strives for is the realization of its Ideal being; but in doing so, it hides that goal from its own vision, and is proud and well satisfied in this alienation from it." The development of the sociocultural sphere, therefore, ". . . does not present the harmless tranquillity of mere growth, as does that of organic life, but a stern reluctant working against itself."[9]

In metaphysical terms, Hegel is saying that the dialectical development in the social realm is a process characterized by conflict; if development means that each succeeding phase is a step forward or "higher" than the preceding phase, then progressive development is conflictive. It is easy to see some of the radical implications of this philosophy, particularly those which Marx later found so appealing. For in the cultural realm, Hegel had emphasized that development toward freedom, far from being a natural and mindless process, was contingent upon consciousness and will. "Universal history . . . shows the development of the consciousness of Freedom on the part of the Spirit, and the consequent realization of that Freedom. This development implies a gradation—a series of increasingly adequate expressions or manifestations of Freedom, which result from its Idea."[10]

Yet, this philosophy, as we have seen, had its conspicuously conservative side. Much like Burke, Hegel argued that it is not the individual, nor even the family, but the State that is the embodiment of Law. The State is the highest order to which all others must subordinate themselves. Real World History, for Hegel, begins with the State; its Right and Law supersede all prehistorical forms—family, community, and so on—with their right and law. But in the final analysis, it is not just any state or nation, but the German state which embodies the true, the eternal wisdom of the Spirit—of God. Thus Hegel concludes: "We have now arrived at the third period of the German World, and thus enter upon the period of Spirit conscious that it is free, inasmuch as it wills the True, the Eternal—that which is in and for itself Universal."[11]

As will be seen later in a discussion of Marx's intellectual origins, he adopted some of the negative-critical or radical aspects of Hegel's thought but rejected the others. Marx's theory is of a completely different order and cannot be adequately comprehended as an extension of any of Hegel's themes. But before that can be taken up, other aspects of the Conservative Reaction to the Enlightenment and the Revolution must be explored.

NOTES

1. See V. C. Chapell, ed., *The Philosophy of David Hume* (New York: Modern Library, 1963).
2. John Locke, "An Essay Concerning Human Understanding," in *The English Philosophers from Bacon to Mill,* ed. Edwin A. Burtt (New York: Modern Library, 1939 and 1967).
3. Carl J. Friedrich, ed., *The Philosophy of Kant: Immanuel Kant's Moral and Political Writings* (New York: Modern Library, 1949 and 1977).
4. Edmund Burke, *Reflections on the Revolution in France* (New York: E. P. Dutton, 1960).
5. Ibid., p. 117.
6. Ibid., p. 219.
7. See G. W. F. Hegel, *Science of Logic,* trans. W. H. Johnston and L. G. Struthers (New York: Macmillan, 1951), Vol. I, pp. 147–70.
8. G. W. F. Hegel, *The Philosophy of History* (New York: Dover Publications, 1956), p. 55.
9. Ibid., p. 55.
10. Ibid., p. 63.
11. Ibid., p. 412.

7

Bonald and Maistre

The Conservative Reaction to the Enlightenment, and particularly to the Revolution, was felt throughout Europe. While outside France, especially among German thinkers, the movement took on a strong nationalistic character as a reaction against Napoleonic imperialism, among French thinkers, the movement assumed both a religious and reactionary character. The French conservatives who reflected on the Revolution and its aftermath regarded the period after 1789 as a terrible ordeal and generally abhorred its events and consequences. Two thinkers in particular, Bonald and Maistre, developed the Catholic counterrevolutionary philosophy, which not only provided an ideological defense of the post-Revolutionary order—the Restoration—but also called for additional regression to the order of the old regime. These men were traditionalists who idealized the lost medieval order and yearned for its providentially arranged harmony. Contradicting the ideas of the Enlightenment, they posited the inferiority of individual reason as compared with revealed and traditional truth. They put forward a religious and philosophical doctrine in which the human being acquired knowledge not by means of his individual reason, but rather as a social being through tradition—that is, by growing up in a cultural community. However, unlike the secularists whose conceptions of that process emerged only later, Bonald and Maistre viewed tradition as beginning with an original revelation, afterward transmitted and supported by the Church and other fundamental institutions. That was a reaction against the optimistic faith of the eighteenth century in the power of individual reason to fashion and refashion social systems. The traditionalists rejected the major premise of the Enlightenment thinkers and revived all the elements of a transcendental philosophy of history—Divine Providence, original sin, final causes, and an infallible Church. Thus Bonald and Maistre rejected the *immediate* past by defending Providence against the naturalism of the *Philosophes*. Resisting the secularization of thought and society by insisting that Providence worked through historical and social laws, Bonald and Maistre furthered the tendency toward historicism begun by the Romantics. Ironically, however, they thus unknowingly provided the major concepts that ultimately became the elements of secular social science. The philosophy of Bonald and Maistre merits consideration, then, in the light of the proposition that philosophical conservatism is the source, historically, of major sociological concepts and ideas.

LOUIS DE BONALD (1754–1850)[1]

Bonald's first and best known work, *Théorie du Pouvoir,* was a polemic against Rousseau's *Social Contract* and Montesquieu's *Spirit of the Laws*. In his *Théorie,* Bonald treats all forms of "knowledge," such as art and literature, as products and expressions of the society that produces them. Literature, for example, is a manifestation of the moral aspect of society, of its constitution, which is the soul, the spirit, and the character of a society. Bonald thus denies the efficacy of individual action or creativity by treating literature and other arts as social products. Every art is a collective effort and therefore the individual is simply the tool rather than the creator of an art work. Not only are the positive achievements of an artist viewed as the achievements of society, but his errors as well are viewed as the fault of an age, not of the person. Here, as in all his subsequent work, Bonald is intent upon proving the errors of individualism and the validity of traditional ideas. His "sociology" is thus developed in the course of a sustained polemic against the Enlightenment; liberty, equality, and other such ideas, are not general abstractions, nor are they the results of natural law as the *Philosophes* understood it. Quite the contrary, rights exist only in definite and concrete social relationships.

The term *natural* as it was used by Rousseau and his contemporaries implied to Bonald simply the existence of natural man anterior to society. Men's rights, thus understood, were natural and did not result from social organization. That conception of natural man was a meaningless abstraction for Bonald. There is no natural man, he argues, only social man; there are no natural rights, only social rights, and they are relative to a particular social order. The men of the Enlightenment had wrenched words out of their social context and had transformed them into weapons for criticism and revolution.

Bonald also attacked Condillac's view of ideas and language—namely, that ideas were the result of sensory experience and that men invented language by transforming their gestures and natural signs into spoken words. Bonald rejected that theory because of its secular and revolutionary implications. If men could invent language and language in turn was necessary for social existence, then men could create and re-create society according to their desires. It reinforced the view that man had not always been a social being but evolved into a social state from a natural one. Condillac's view was offensive, because it denied revelation and affirmed that man *not* God made society, that man could make, change, and destroy its forms. In opposition to that view, Bonald wanted to demonstrate logically the divine origin of society, the organic links between the present and the past, the unbroken chain of tradition, the divine basis of authority, the superiority of society over the individual, the general over the particular, and duties over rights. In short, his work was an attempt to undermine every major assumption of the Enlightenment.

Ideas, for Bonald, were innate, but not, in the Cartesian sense, in the individual man. Knowledge of moral truth is innate in society and is transmitted to the individual through speech. Thus "the word" is the principal instrument of Truth. Man did not invent language—it had a divine origin as the Old Testament had shown. Language did not arise out of social interaction; the opposite is true: Knowledge and language preceded society. In the beginning, there was the word. The word was given by revelation that imparted general truth, and society became the context for language and truth. The family, the Church, and the State derived their respective aspects of the truth from the general Truth. Man is born into society and becomes a part of it by acquiring language and the social truth. He learns aspects of the truth within the respective social institutions. In that way, Bonald sought to restore revelation, tradition, and authority as the bases of Truth. Man receives the word from God and tradition is preserved in the continuity of the family, the Church, and the state authority, the last of these being the main defender of tradition. The individual should therefore obey God's will by subordinating himself to the domestic, religious, and political traditions and institutions of society.

Clearly, Bonald was developing a point-for-point rebuttal of the Enlightenment ideas whose consequences he decried and whose implications he still feared. The assumption that language was a human product he found particularly abhorrent. If men invented language, then the meaning of words was arbitrary and conventional; meanings could be changed. "The Church," contrary to the meaning it had in its original context, could be construed as the guardian of superstition, and "the State" could be conceived as a despotism and therefore criticized and undermined with all the fearful results of the French Revolution. On the other hand, if language were a divine gift, a tool of Providence, and the word acquired its meaning from the traditional social complex, then the individual by his own reason could not know meanings and could learn them only in particular social relationships. In that way, Bonald reasoned, God's order could be protected from individual reason and criticism. God imposed language, society, and authority, and individual men had no right to tamper with them. Apparently, Bonald did not see how quite opposite conclusions could be drawn from his theory, as in fact they later were. If meaning is dependent on definite social relationships, then by rejecting his first premise of divine revelation, one could argue that knowledge is a function of social conditions. In those terms one may propose, as indeed a sociologist might, that both the ideas of the Enlightenment and of Bonald—indeed all ideas—are a function of the sociohistorical conditions in which they are conceived and formulated. And that, of course, eventually became a major postulate of Marx's theory of ideology and later of the sociology of knowledge—both eminently *secular* theories.

For Bonald, authority, like language, was divinely established and fit into the providential scheme. His fondness for the number "three," no doubt inspired by the Catholic conception of the Trinity, led him to posit three functions that expressed the divine: "A general will, a general love, (and) a general force achieve the aim which is the conservation of social beings."[2] Authority is a unity that must be both general and perpetual in order to avoid social divisiveness and strife. The father guarantees the perpetuity of domestic authority and the Church, as the expression of Christ, guarantees religious authority. If, however, unity and perpetuity in those realms are not guaranteed in the political realm, the society will be wracked by conflict and revolution. The continual authority of the State must therefore be assured, and that is best accomplished by a hereditary monarchy.

The family, the Church, and the State must assure general social stability and cohesion. Those institutions are based on fundamental laws, for the structure of society has been decreed by God, nature, and history as a unity. Society's structure is an ensemble of laws or necessary relationships that exist between the beings who compose them. Laws and relationships are based on the nature of man—a God-given nature. Social laws express the will of God, the ultimate author of the underlying social relationships. The purpose of society is the conservation of being that is desired by the *general will*. That will, unlike Rousseau's, is not the sum of particular wills, but an expression of the divine, natural order, the will of God.

Bonald also rejected, as did Burke, the Enlightenment idea of the *Social Contract*. There was no evidence of such a contract in any social relationship—between God and man, father and son, monarch and subject. Society was not, as implied in the contract notion, dependent on the will of man. There was no contract, but natural (divine) and necessary relationships. Society must have three elements. They are monarchy, nobility, and subjects, the best and most natural elements. A single hereditary monarch must reign supreme in a given society, best administered by a hereditary nobility serving both monarch and subjects and acting as a buffer between them. In order to do so, the nobility must remain an independent class—that is propertied and thus financially independent. The best form of society is one guided by a paternalistic monarchy and nobility; all other forms, including, of course, democracy and aristocracy, are inherently unstable because they lack a definite center of authority and are therefore destined to suffer from chronic conflict and disorder. Against the Enlightenment, Bonald thus argued that anything that undermined the patriarchal, monogamous family, the Catholic church, and the monarchical state would result in anarchy. For that reason he inveighs against divorce, which had been legalized in 1792.

It is clear, then, that Bonald's theory was an idealization of the *status quo ante*, the medieval order, which for him symbolized perfection. That was his model for the reconstruction of post-Revolutionary society; in fact, he supported the Restoration as an attempt to reestablish such a society. Subjects must obey authority which represents the general will of society and which in turn is a manifestation of the will of God. Anything that contradicts that order—popular sovereignty, representative government, separation of powers—he abhors. Naturally, most of all he detests the two historical events that contributed most to the downfall of the old order—the Reformation and the French Revolution. The first had destroyed the unity of the Church and the second, the feudal social system.

If Bonald admired the feudal order, it followed that he would despise what the bourgeoisie stood for—commerce and industry. It was the very same principles of the *Philosophes,* he noted with irony, that held up natural man as a standard for measuring existing societies and for condemning their crippling and deforming tendencies, that led to the Industrial Revolution—a far cry from the original image and ideal. Bonald's work thus became in part a severe critique of bourgeois society, a critique that anticipated in many respects later socialist thinking, but from a different standpoint.

Bonald longed for the "good old days" of the prebourgeois era, while the socialists looked forward to a future condition that would transcend and supersede bourgeois civilization. Bonald scoffed at those who now saw industry as providing for man's needs and pleasures, at those who wished " . . . to see us all in palaces, spinning cloth of gold and silk. . . . Everything is resolved for man in society to produce in order to consume and to consume in order to produce; and to their eyes all of society is divided into two classes, producers and consumers. . . . "[3] Bonald derided them for seeing industry as an independent force that guarantees peace and liberty, while, in fact, it was agricultural society that was in all respects superior to industrial society. The agricultural family can feed and nourish itself; it is not dependent on other men and other social events to assure its continued existence. The industrial family, on the other hand, produces children whom it cannot be sure of supporting, dependent as it is on the vicissitudes of the market. In the agricultural family, moreover, the natural and divine order is respected because the father is the authority, which is not at all the case in the industrial system where the father, mother, and children are isolated, and family unity is disturbed. The industrial system thus undermines the most natural and sacred of social units. It imposes harsh labor on children, thereby preventing their education and destroying their health in an artificial and foul environment. And while it cripples the young, it also discards the old and weak who cannot work.[4] Agriculture, therefore, unifies society while industry tends to divide it into hostile classes and factions. Bonald's critique of bourgeois-industrial society, though made from a conservative standpoint, did anticipate some of the criticisms of later socialists. For example, Saint-Simon, as we shall see, acknowledged Bonald's influence and expressed admiration for his ideas.

Ultimately, Bonald justified his conception of things by arguing that society must express the fundamental laws of God or suffer from crisis and anarchy. God's laws gave order to society and guaranteed the conservation of being. The individual learns those laws only through his social existence—that is, within social institutions that are the depositories of tradition and thus impart truth to man. Knowledge (culture) is transmitted by tradition, historical development, and revelation. The individual, an integral part of society, may in no instance place his individual will above the general will. Man must not arrogate to himself the right of judging, changing, or rebelling against general society, for then he is dethroning the general, providential reason and wisdom, historically arrived at, and putting in its place individual reason.

In Bonald's scheme, then, the words "nature" and "natural laws" have a meaning quite different from that of the *Philosophes*. For Bonald, God was beyond nature, not in it nor of it. He was the great conserver of being who employed toward that end nature, history, and men. Yet, in one ambiguous formulation, he comes close to compromising that view and thus opens the way for the secularization of his theory; indeed, later thinkers were to note that, divested of its metaphysical assumptions, Bonald's theory could be transformed into a secular, sociological one. "The general will of society," Bonald writes, "of the social body, of social man, the nature of social beings or of society, the social will, the will of God are synonymous expressions in this work."[5]

One sees how easily that could lead to a proposition quite the reverse of Bonald's: that "God" is an expression of society—as Durkheim later formulated it. Stripped, then, of its theological assumptions, Bonald's work becomes the source of major sociological concepts and ideas. Society is a historically evolved, organic unity of institutions. Common values and traditions constitute its major binding force. Language and culture, though not viewed as products of social interaction by Bonald, are nonetheless seen as embedded in the social context and inseparable from that context. It is the "individual," not society, that is an abstraction; for outside society, an individual is nonexistent—an impossibility. Furthermore, Bonald saw clearly the historical forces and trends that had led to the dissolution of the medieval unity; he saw and feared the growing secularization that had accompanied the Reformation, the Enlightenment, and the Revolution and thus anticipated the various theorists who later centered attention on the historical shift in Europe from the *Gemeinschaft* of the Middle Ages to the increasingly *gesellschaftliche* character of the modern era. Finally, he saw clearly some of the repressive and alienating consequences of industrial civilization.

Bonald had written his *Théorie du Pouvoir* as an emigré in Heidelberg. Although the police of the Directory had destroyed almost the entire edition of the book, a copy sent to Napoleon impressed him so favorably that he had the author's name removed from the list of the exiled. Little wonder that Bonaparte was so impressed. In Bonald's view, history expressed the tension between the divine will to order society according to a larger providential design and man's ability either to sabotage that design or to cooperate in bringing it about. Being a free agent but tainted with original sin, man does, in fact, at least periodically, obstruct and even destroy that design. Whenever that happens, there is little doubt that Providence will sooner or later prevail. The obstruction of the design and the consequent social chaos is always temporary, because it cannot long oppose the nature of being. In those terms, even that most violent of upheavals, the French Revolution, was a "salutary crisis." The revolutionaries were instruments of Providence, and the obstructions they had erected before the providential design were eventually turned against the revolutionaries themselves.

The Revolution, therefore, even for Bonald, was not purely negative and destructive. It was a kind of chastisement of man by Providence which, despite its temporary catastrophic results, was bound, like all other crises, ultimately to have salutary effects, because it cleared the way for the reestablishment of order. Napoleon could not fail to be impressed, then, when Bonald taught that revolutions begin with the subjects but end with the ruler; that they break out because the authorities have become weak and have yielded, but subside when authority has been restored and strengthened. Every disturbance will ultimately serve only to strengthen authority. Bonald had prophesied that the revolution that had begun with the declaration of the rights of man would culminate in the declaration of the rights of God; since those were the very rights Bonaparte was now proclaiming, Bonald's position was very secure indeed.[6]

Before turning to a more detailed examination of Bonald's sociological concepts, it will be instructive, first, to consider briefly the ideas of another conservative thinker, Bonald's contemporary and "partner in arms," Joseph de Maistre.

JOSEPH DE MAISTRE (1754–1821)

Joseph de Maistre was born in the same year as was Bonald; although the two men had never met personally, they agreed on all the fundamentals of their respective theories and expressed great admiration for each other. Bonald telis of a letter he received from Maistre not long before he died: "Je n'ai rien pensé que vous ne l'ayez écrit; je n'ai rien écrit que vous ne l'ayez pensé."[7]

Maistre's work, like that of Bonald, may be read as a sustained polemic against the philosophy of the Enlightenment. He also devoted his life to discrediting those principles that had led to the Revolution and to defending those of the counterrevolution.

Maistre found particularly offensive the Enlightenment conception of the origin of society. He had read Rousseau's discourses less as an attempt to fashion a device by which natural man could be "separated out" by stripping him of his sociocultural attributes, than as an assertion that there was in fact a presocial state of man. Thus understood, Rousseau's conception offended Maistre because it implied that human society had a beginning without the intervention of the Divine and that there had existed somewhere in the remote past a pre- or nonsocial condition of man. That assumption Maistre rejected altogether. Man is unthinkable, an impossibility, before, or outside, society; if such creatures did exist, whatever they were, they were not men. He insists that the opposite possibility be entertained—that society had no beginning in a temporal or historical sense, and, therefore, that it may very well be an aspect of human nature by definition.[8]

That approach is on firmer ground than the other, Maistre argues, because it coincides with our experience and our historical knowledge. He misreads Rousseau as having posited an antithesis between nature and society, between natural and social man, and ignores the fact that Rousseau posited such an antithesis only between "natural man" and *certain definite forms* of society—not society in general. Rousseau was not, as Maistre assumed he was, positing the superiority of the state of nature ("man is born free") to all society ("and everywhere he is in chains"). But having understood it in that way, Maistre resented the implication that society was inferior to the state of nature. Apparently, he conveniently ignored the proposition that Rousseau insisted upon—namely, that certain social states were unquestionably superior to the so-called natural state (which he admitted probably never existed), because they allowed for man's perfectibility, a goal he cherished and considered impossible outside of society.

Maistre really understood that Rousseau was exercising his imagination when talking about the "state of nature," and that he had advanced that concept for heuristic purposes. Even so, Maistre found himself indignant at the way in which Rousseau had raised and resolved the issue in question: Is man essentially a natural being or a social being? Rousseau had suggested that man in the "natural state," though he had the potential for society and thus for perfection, lived out his life as a nonsocial being. And what bothered Maistre most about that image was both the amoral character of man's natural life as Rousseau had depicted it, and the fact that when he spoke of man's acquiring "conventions" he treated them negatively and thus tended to stigmatize basic moral conceptions of Western and Christian civilization.

When Rousseau had said that in the state of nature, man gets together with woman for physical love only, and that immediately with the mutual satisfaction of their needs they parted and became independent again; when he said that children remained with parents only so long as it was necessary for their survival and then cut off the natural relation, after which neither parents nor children had any mutual obligations; when he argued, in short, that the family as a moral unit did not exist in the natural state, that offended Maistre's religious sensibilities. For in that description, Rousseau was not only being cavalier about historical and anthropological fact, he was questioning the sacred character of one of the most fundamental institutions of Western Christendom: the monogamous family.

First, on the anthropological level, Maistre criticizes Rousseau for his inconsistencies. He observes that Rousseau himself had noted the brutality of savages and had tried to save himself from a contradiction by asserting that even the most primitive savage was far removed from the state of nature. Maistre attacks Rousseau for his ambiguity and, for all practical purposes, dismisses his views as nonsense. The brutality of the savage does pose a problem, Maistre admits: That is not a *later* stage than the tranquil *first* state, as Rousseau had suggested, but a degraded state, an objectification of original sin. The savage state follows the civilized state, and, wherever it is in evidence, it represents the degeneration of a civilized people. Maistre thus reversed Rousseau's picture in keeping with Christian mythology. Savagery is not an original condition of mankind but a terminal state in which man has completely lost his original and natural perfection.

Maistre insists that history is the full account of man's stay and development on Earth, and that if we address ourselves to history, we shall see the incontrovertible fact that man is and always has been a *social* being.[9] And if anyone believes differently, the onus is upon him to prove it. But since in fact such proof is impossible, Maistre believes that history and anthropology have demonstrated beyond any doubt that man has always dwelt in society and that he is social by nature. Was there, however, an historical origin to society? Treating the Old Testament as an historical document, Maistre builds upon the story in Genesis.

The family is prototypical of society. Sexual differentiation was constituted with the divine purpose of peopling the Earth. It was a kind of secondary causal force by which Providence intended to carry out its purpose. The end, the total human society, or series of societies, was posited in the first sexual pair and their offspring. The first pair was physically mature. When blood line no longer suffices to unite a group, when the genitor can no longer be the sole source of authority due to multiplication, death, and so on, then a "lawgiver" like Moses must arise to substitute a moral for a physical bond of unity. The "nation" emerges. Here Maistre views all aspects of culture—morals, religion, government, art—as fulfilling essential social functions: the conservation of being through society.

A nation has a common consciousness, a common soul, a common language; it is a cultural unity. A society's continuity requires as much moral unity, even unanimity, as possible. For Maistre, as for Bonald, the ideal form of this unity was approximated in the Middle Ages. Unlike Burke, however, who saw the necessity and desirability of reforms, Maistre regarded reforms as dangerous. Reforms will inevitably lead to unforeseen consequences, worse than the original, alleged wrongs that one wants to correct. Reforms are dangerous because man has incomplete knowledge. In order to reform, man would have to possess a thorough knowledge of the course and trend of the historical process, a complete survey of its elements. That is impossible. Therefore, it is in the best interest of man to leave the entire matter in the hands of Providence, the sole force capable of perfecting social forms.

Both Maistre and Bonald, then, maintained that man by his very nature is a social, moral, and cultural being. Man had never had an existence before or outside society, and to the extent that Rousseau or his followers believed otherwise, their speculations were immoral as well as absurd. If Rousseau had wanted to use the concept of "natural man" as a criterion for evaluating specific social systems, and thus for providing man with some guidance in changing society to facilitate his perfection, Bonald and Maistre now insisted that man is and always has been social and that the historical development of society is guided by an omniscient Providence. Man, being less than omniscient, must not tamper with society nor attempt to reform it, because the cure will always be worse than the alleged disease. In developing their ideological standpoint, however, Bonald, Maistre, and other representatives of the Conservative Reaction advanced a number of ideas that have since been incorporated into sociology as important working concepts and assumptions.

CONSERVATIVE PHILOSOPHY AND SOCIOLOGY: A SUMMARY

We have seen how the principles of the Enlightenment, as they became manifest in the Revolution, engendered a conservative philosophical reaction. That reaction, in turn, engendered a new interest in *social order* and various related problems and concepts.

Conservatives, like Burke, Hegel, Bonald, and Maistre, are so called because they desired quite literally to conserve and maintain the prevailing order. Moreover, some of them, as we have seen, sought not so much to conserve the existing order as to regress to a *status quo ante*. The disorder, anarchy, and radical changes those thinkers observed after the Revolution led them to generate concepts that relate to aspects of order and stability: tradition, authority, status, cohesion, adjustment, function, norm, symbol, ritual. As compared with the eighteenth century, the conservative concepts constituted a definite shift of interest from the individual to the group, from criticism of the existing order to its defense, and from social change to social stability.[10]

From the conservative standpoint, the social changes following in the wake of the Revolution had undermined and destroyed fundamental social institutions and had resulted in the loss of political stability. The conservatives traced those results to certain preceding events and processes in European history that had led, they believed, to the progressive weakening of the medieval order and hence to the upheaval of the Revolution. Quite precisely, they singled out Protestantism, capitalism, and science as the major forces. Those processes, furthermore, which were hailed as progressive by their liberal and radical contemporaries, were leading even now to an increasing atomization of peoples. Large "masses" now appeared, presumably unanchored in any stable social groups; widespread insecurity, frustration, and alienation became evident; and, finally, a monolithic secular power had emerged that was dependent for its existence on the mass of rootless individuals.

The conservatives had idealized the medieval order, and from that standpoint the modern era was very wanting indeed. As an antidote to the principles of the *Philosophes*, and as a critique of the post-Revolutionary *"disorder,"* the conservatives advanced a number of propositions about society:

1. It is an organic unity with internal laws and development and deep roots in the past, not simply a mechanical aggregate of individual elements. The conservatives were "social realists" in the sense that they firmly believed in society as a reality greater than the individuals who comprise it. That was in direct opposition to the social nominalism of the Enlightenment, the view that only individuals exist and that society is simply the name one gives to those individuals in their interrelationships.

2. Society antedates the individual and is ethically superior to him. Man has no existence outside of a social group or context, and he becomes human only by participating in society. Far from individuals constituting society, it is society that creates the individual by means of moral education, to employ Durkheim's term.

3. The individual is an abstraction and not the basic element of a society. Society is composed of relationships and institutions; individuals are simply members of society who fulfill certain statuses and roles—father, son, priest, and so on.

4. The parts of a society are interdependent and interrelated. Customs, beliefs, and institutions are organically intertwined so that changing or remaking one part will undermine the complex relationships maintaining the stability of society as a whole.

5. Man has constant and unalterable needs, which every society and each of its institutions serve to fulfill. Institutions are thus positive agencies by which basic human needs are met. If those agencies are disturbed or disrupted, suffering and disorder will result.

6. The various customs and institutions of a society are positively functional; they either fulfill human needs directly or indirectly by serving other indispensable institutions. Even prejudice is viewed in those terms; it tends to unify certain groups and also increases their sense of security.

7. The existence and maintenance of small groups is essential to society. The family, neighborhood, province, religious groups, occupational groups—those are the basic units of a society, the basic supports of people's lives.

8. The conservatives also conceived of "social organization." The Revolution, as they saw it, had led not to a higher form of organization, but to social and moral disintegration. They wanted to preserve the older religious forms, Catholicism not Protestantism, and sought to restore the religious unity of medieval Europe. Protestantism, in teaching the importance of individual faith, had undermined the spiritual unity of society. And, as we have seen in the case of Bonald, the disorganizing consequences of urbanism, industry, and commerce were recognized.

9. The conservatives insisted, in addition, on the essential importance and positive value of the nonrational aspects of human existence. Man needs ritual, ceremony, and worship. The *Philosophes,* in their merciless criticism of those activities as irrational vestiges of the past, had weakened the sacred supports of society.

10. Status and hierarchy were also treated as essential to society. The conservatives feared that equality would destroy the "natural" and time-honored agencies by which values were passed on from one generation to another. Hierarchy was necessary in the family, the Church, and the State, without which social stability was impossible.

Those are some of the major sociological tenets of the conservative legacy—a legacy that greatly influenced such thinkers as Saint-Simon, Comte, and, later, Durkheim. Those thinkers attempted to take conservative ideas and concepts out of their theological-reactionary context and to make them part and parcel of a scientific sociology. To see the beginnings of that attempt, the work of Saint-Simon and Comte, the founders of modern sociology, has to be considered.

NOTES

1. The following discussion is based on Bonald's *Oeuvres*, and particularly on his *Démonstration Philosophique du Principe Constitutif de la Société* (Paris: Libraire D'Adrien Le Clere et C, 1840). This work, Volume 12 of his *Oeuvres*, which he wrote in 1829, is a general summary of his social philosophy. In addition, I have consulted the following secondary sources: Émile Faguet, *Politiques et Moralistes du Dix-Neuvième Siècle* (Paris: Société Française D'Imprimerie et de Librairie, 1890), and George Brandes, *Main Currents in Nineteenth-Century Literature* (New York: Macmillan, 1906).
2. Bonald, *Oeuvres*, Vol. I, p. 146.
3. Ibid., Vol. II, p. 237.
4. Ibid., Vol. II, p. 239.
5. Bonald, *Théorie du Pouvoir, Oeuvres*, Vol. I, p. 133.
6. See Brandes, *Main Currents*, p. 113.
7. Bonald, *Oeuvres*, Vol. XII, pp. 198–99.
8. Joseph de Maistre, *Oeuvres Complètes* (Lyon: Vitte et Perrussel, 1884–86), Vol. I, p. 315. Translated selections may be found in Joseph de Maistre, *Works*, selected, translated, and introduced by Jack Lively (New York: Macmillan, 1965).
9. Ibid., Vol. VII, p. 541.
10. In the present discussion, I have drawn upon a number of points made by Robert A. Nisbet in his article entitled "Conservatism and Sociology," *American Journal of Sociology* (September 1952).

8

Saint-Simon (1760–1825)

The conservatism of Louis de Bonald and Joseph de Maistre, as we have seen, took the form of a reactionary response to the Revolution and to the principles of the Enlightenment. They called for a post-Revolutionary society similar to that of medieval times. In advancing their philosophy, they centered attention on a number of aspects of society which later became a major source of sociological concepts. In fact, both Saint-Simon and Comte, the official founders of sociology, were directly influenced by Bonald and accepted some of his basic assumptions even while reinterpreting them and placing them in a different theoretical context.

From an ideological standpoint, Comte was conservative in a different sense from that of Bonald and Maistre. Comte wanted to conserve not the *status quo ante* but the status quo—that is, middle-class society then in the process of emerging and consolidating itself. Comte's so-called *positive philosophy* was an explicit repudiation of the "negative" philosophy of the Enlightenment and the Revolution. Comte wanted to preserve the "is." Each stage in the evolutionary development of society as he saw it was necessary, and the improvement of social conditions could only come about slowly, stage by stage.

Saint-Simon has sometimes been regarded as a founder of socialism. Karl Marx, for example, dubbed him a "utopian socialist," meaning that

Saint-Simon lived and wrote before industrial development had reached the critical point at which the "contradictions" of capitalism had become clear—that is, before class conflict between the bourgeoisie and the proletariat had become a normal phenomenon. In Marx's view, then, Saint-Simon apparently could not, or did not, see the conflict of interests between the major classes of the industrial system and therefore not only treated them as one class with common interests, but left bourgeois property institutions intact in his blueprint for the future society. Other students of Saint-Simon's thought have argued that there is no appreciable difference from an ideological point of view between the ideas of Saint-Simon and Comte and that both thinkers advanced a sociological theory that is little more than a "scientific" rationale for a totalitarian type of society.[1]

In comparison with his students, particularly Thierry and Comte, and despite his aristocratic background, Saint-Simon's education was relatively unsystematic. For the most part he was self-educated except for the help of some private tutors, the best known being d'Alembert, the encyclopedist.[2] Because, in addition, Saint-Simon had once visited Rousseau, it is clear that he had some firsthand contact with the Enlightenment thinkers. The versatility of his interests and activities is demonstrated by the fact that, among other things, he had fought with distinction in the American Revolution and had been among the first to advance a scheme for a canal to join the Atlantic with the Pacific. As for the French Revolution, he was ambivalent toward that momentous event: "I did not wish to take part in it, because, on the one hand, I was convinced that the *Ancien Regime* could not be prolonged, and, on the other, I had an aversion to destruction."[3] Records from the revolutionary period reveal, however, that he had been much more enthusiastic a follower of the Revolution than he afterward admitted. He had, for instance, given up his artistocratic title, prepared the *cahier* of his local canton for the Estates-General, and presided at the first meeting of his commune. In addition, in 1793, he was awarded two certificates of *civisme* (good citizenship) and in the autumn of the same year was active in *Hébertist* and other radical circles in Paris. Saint-Simon's ideas retained to the end elements of Enlightenment and Revolutionary thought, but they, as we shall see, were fused with Romantic and conservative elements.

Scholars have now firmly established that Saint-Simon developed before 1814 all the major ideas which Thierry and Comte later claimed as their own. Those ideas—positivism, industrialism, internationalism, a "new religion"—and the originality with which he approached them make Saint-Simon one of the most important social thinkers of the nineteenth century.

Like Bonald before him, Saint-Simon attributed the great stability of medieval civilization to its universally accepted religion; like Marx after him, Saint-Simon viewed the historical transformation of European society as the result of forces that had been maturing in the womb of the old order. The growth of science, the emergence of an industrial and commercial bourgeoisie, the Protestant Revolution, and finally, the negative-critical philosophical movement of the Enlightenment, all served to undermine the Catholic church and hence the unity of medieval society. The *Philosophes*, Saint-Simon argued, with their insistence on the principles of equality and natural rights, had contributed to the disintegration of the old order. Their principles were destructive of the old society and led ultimately to that great revolutionary crisis of his time. Yet, those same principles gave little or no guidance for the successful reconstruction of society. Saint-Simon therefore saw it as his task and the task of his contemporaries to create a new and organic social order based upon the new principles and forces that had come into view. Thus he wrote, "The philosophy of the eighteenth century has been critical and revolutionary; that of the nineteenth century will be inventive and constructive."[4]

If Saint-Simon admired the social unity of the medieval order quite as much as Bonald, he also recognized that there was no going back to that order, thus parting ways with the theorists of the Catholic revival. The new social unity must rest on a new unity in the realm of thought, on new intellectual principles. Human knowledge has passed through three stages in its development: from the theological to the metaphysical and finally to the scientific. The study of human conduct, which Saint-Simon called "social physiology," must become a positive science in much the same way as the study of physical phenomena had become scientific. Scientific knowledge will thus take the place of religious dogma, and scientists and industrialists will emerge as the new "natural" élite to replace the leaders of medieval society, the clergy and nobility. Again, like Bonald, Saint-Simon admired the educated international élite of the old order and believed that such an élite would also be necessary in the new society. The older cultivated and educated élite of the Middle Ages would be replaced by a new international, scientific-industrial élite. Science in the new order must fulfill the function of religion in the old. How? By means of positivism, or the application of scientific principles to all natural and human phenomena.

Saint-Simon drew his inspiration from the scientific work of his predecessors and modeled his approach after theirs. He hoped that the human sciences would attain the unity and elegance of the natural sciences and was particularly impressed with Newton's law of gravitation. He realized that he himself was not a scientist and admitted that he lacked the training to carry out the program of making the social studies positive. Although he eventually abandoned the idea of unifying the sciences, he held on to his conception of science as a body of verified and established beliefs that could take the place of religion as the binding force of society. Religion, whose essential function was to provide a coherent view of the universe and of human existence, and thus to unite people on the basis of common truths, would now be replaced by science. For those who are unable to grasp scientific truth intellectually, knowledge will be imparted by means of rituals, cults, and mystical processes. The educated élite, on the other hand, will learn the ideas directly as scientific principles.

A spiritual as well as a temporal élite remain essential in Saint-Simon's picture of the future society; the former is made up of scientists and the latter of industrialists and other "productive" property owners. It is an authoritarian society in which a scientific-technological élite will rule together with the property owners. That vision of the structure of the new society holds throughout his work. For example, in his *Letters from an Inhabitant of Geneva*, one of Saint-Simon's earlier works, he views the old society as divided into three classes. The first is made up of the scientists, artists, and men of liberal ideas; the second, the property owners, resists change and wants to preserve the old order; the third class, "which rallies to the word `equality,' comprises the rest of humanity." The class structure, in short, consists of the intellectuals, the "haves," and the "have-nots." As the class conflict between the haves and have-nots increased in intensity, and as the insurrection of the latter began to succeed, the intellectuals joined their movement as its leaders. The Revolution occurred because the haves could no longer contain the movement, could no longer control the have-nots. The reason for that was the loss of cultural and intellectual superiority on the part of the old élite consisting of monarch, priests, and nobles.

For the post-Revolutionary society to regain its unity, a new scientific élite, a council of Newton, must replace the spiritual authority of the Church by providing a unified scientific doctrine centered on Newton's law of gravitation. Thus the structure of the new society remains essentially the same: Science replaces religion as the main force holding society together and each élite of the old system is superseded by a new one—priests by scientists and feudal lords by industrialists. The conflict between the new haves and have-nots will continue, but the former may now regain control over the latter. In effect, Saint-Simon is imploring the propertied classes to align themselves with the most enlightened group in society, the intellectuals. Such an alignment will bring about a stable social order in which control over the have-nots is regained and revolution is thereby forestalled. Speaking to his imaginary audience of property owners, he asks them to do with good grace "what the scientists, artists, and men of liberal ideas, allied with the have-nots, will sooner or later compel them to do."

It is easy to see, then, the extent to which Saint-Simon's view of society was inspired by his conception of the social order of the medieval period. For Saint-Simon, that order was not a totally dark age as it had been for the Enlightenment thinkers. After all, the modern era had had its beginnings in that period; science, too, stimulated by the Arabs in Europe, had emerged in the Middle Ages. He admired the alleged spiritual and social unity of medieval society and the alliance between the spiritual and temporal élites which had maintained that unity. He differed with Bonald and Maistre, however, about the possibility of restoring that unity on the basis of Catholic theology. Science has made that impossible once and for all. The dualism of mind and matter that emerged as an attempt at compromise between spiritual and temporal powers must be eliminated. Mind and matter must again be viewed as aspects of one and the same unity—*but* this is to be accomplished not by an outmoded theology but rather by means of scientific laws.

Changes in history are thus related to changes in religious ideas, and those in turn represent the state of beliefs and knowledge in a given period. History has passed through polytheism and theism, and now with physicism has left the conjectural stages to arrive at a positive stage in which all knowledge will be unified on a scientific positive basis. The conclusion is therefore inescapable that Saint-Simon conceived both the name and the essentials of positive philosophy. Émile Durkheim was among the first to realize that and he sought tirelessly to demonstrate the fact: " . . . the idea, the word, and even the outline of positivist philosophy are all found in Saint-Simon. He was the first to conceive that between the formal generalities of metaphysical philosophy and the narrow specialization of the particular sciences, there was a place for a new enterprise, whose pattern he supplied and himself attempted. Therefore, it is to him that one must, in full justice, award the honor currently given Comte."[5] Durkheim goes on to show that the credit for founding positive sociology also belongs to Saint-Simon and not to Comte. Contemporary students of the problem agree with Durkheim; the judgment of F.M.H. Markham is typical in this regard: "The `Law of the Three Stages,' pompously announced by Comte as an original discovery, is merely a precise formulation of Saint-Simon's argument, which goes back to the *Letters from an Inhabitant of Geneva.*"[6]

That the medieval order is always the model for Saint-Simon's conception of society is also borne out by his approach to the *Reorganization of European Society.* In that work the influence of the theorists of the Catholic revival is again evident; for Saint-Simon viewed medieval civilization as an international order, resting on an international organization—the Church. Since there is no going back, one must go forward and establish a new international organization on the basis of new international principles. Are there any principles more international than scientific ones? Science and positive philosophy must bind the nations of Europe into one international community, for without international order there can be no order or stability in the individual societies of Europe.

In his later as well as his earlier works, the structure of each national society is the same: There are "producers" and there are "idlers." In the "productive" class, Saint-Simon lumped together bankers, industrialists, scientists, managers, *and* manual workers, assuming that they all share common interests. That was later to strike Marx as a very naive view of the class structure of industrial society and perhaps the weakest part of Saint-Simon's system. Moreover, in his projection of the "new" society, Saint-Simon leaves the class structure and, hence, the institution of private property intact; the only change he advocates is the compensation of tenants for improving the land they worked. Equality, he believed, is a foreign idea having no place in European civilization.

In the earlier years of his intellectual labors (1815–1821), Saint-Simon's views of economics are clearly laissez-faire. But he differs with the Classical Economists in several important respects. He sees production not as an end in itself but as a means of improving the conditions of life; that becomes possible in his hierarchical and organic society only by means of rational planning of production. In his work, *Organisateur,* he outlines a plan for an industrial parliament, or planning body, composed of three chambers: invention, examination, and execution. The first consists of the scientists, artists, and engineers who are to plan the various public projects; the second, of the scientists who are to supervise the projects and control education, and the third, of industrialists, who are to carry out the plans and control the budget. He also disagrees with the assumption of the Classical Economists that the pursuit of individual well-being will lead automatically to the general good. The unbridled egoism of the rich as well as the uncurbed rebelliousness of the poor will have disorganizing consequences in the absence of a worldly ethic of some kind; the new society will therefore require a secular equivalent of religion. Saint-Simon had been influenced by Sismondi's *Nouveaux Principes d'Economie Politique* (1819) in which he had shown that the poor suffer most from economic crises and therefore that the utilitarians and Classical Economists were wrong. In his *Système Industriel,* Saint-Simon begins to emphasize the necessity of improving the condition of the poorest classes and of founding the industrial system on the principle of brotherly love. The artists must contribute to the moral unity of society by shaping beliefs, opinions, and sentiments.

Thus as Saint-Simon viewed the historical transformation of European society, the supersession of the feudal nobility by the industrial bourgeoisie was inevitable; but as F. M. H. Markham has observed, for Saint-Simon to go on to predict, as Marx later did, that the bourgeoisie would in turn be superseded by the proletariat was unthinkable. Always keeping in mind as an ideal the spiritual élite of the Middle Ages, Saint-Simon could not conceive of a society governed by anyone but an educated élite. The scientists and industrialists were therefore to his mind the "natural" leaders of the working class. He did foresee conflict between owners and nonowners, between capitalists and workers, and between rich and poor generally, but he believed that such conflict could and should be averted in a truly organic society. Further, he argues that the main purpose of politics is to preserve property and that "the only barrier which the property owners can put up against the proletariat is a system of ethics."[7] Comte, as we shall see, becomes quite fascinated with that idea and his ideological defense of the bourgeoisie becomes more blatant. Later, the unresolved problems raised by Saint-Simon and Comte were to intrigue Durkheim, much of whose work can be read as an attempt to reconcile the structured inequality of modern society with the requirements of social solidarity.

From the foregoing discussion, one can truly wonder why the term *socialist* was ever applied to Saint-Simon's doctrine, particularly if that term is taken to mean the abolition of private property and the maximal equalization of life chances. Saint-Simon's doctrine is quite remote from the Marxian conception of the future society, in which class conflict and the classes themselves would be abolished. What remains, then, as the sole "socialist" element in Saint-Simon's new society is centralized planning of the economic system. More than Saint-Simon himself, it was his followers—Bazard, Enfantin, and others—who somewhat radicalized his critique of the "idlers" in society and who attacked the institution of inheritance, combining that with the advocacy of a planned economy. But their "socialism," too, was short-lived.

To summarize—knowledge, for Saint-Simon, is the underlying and sustaining factor of society; a social system is the application of a system of ideas. The historical growth of knowledge, or science, was a major cause of the transformation of European society. Knowledge, therefore, is both the moving power of progress and the binding force of society, which is, in fact, a *community of ideas*. Given the importance of ideas, Saint-Simon saw it as his task to determine which ideas were best suited to the condition of European society at the beginning of the nineteenth century. What unites people is their common way of thinking and of picturing the world, but the way of thinking among the people as a whole lags behind the progress of scientific knowledge, behind positive fact. Therefore, by systematizing scientific knowledge, one could define what the consciousness of a people should be at a given time. Inasmuch as a social system is the application of ideas, it will be impossible to build the new society until positive philosophy, which is to be its basis, has developed. Even though there already exist many sciences, the most important one is missing: a science of humanity. That is the only science that can *reconcile the interests of classes* and thus serve as the foundation of a unified organic society. The human science should be modeled after the natural sciences because man is, after all, a part of nature.

Saint-Simon thus looked forward to a time when politics would be a science and political questions would be handled in much the same way as other phenomena are treated by science. The main task of science is to discover the laws of social development, evolution, and progress; those laws are inevitable and absolute. All that man can do is submit. Progress takes place in stages and each stage is necessary and contributes something to the further progress of humankind. (As we have seen, medieval civilization was not all dark, since the elements of modern civilization had their origin there.) Once the laws of social development have been discovered, they will indicate the direction progress must follow. Thus the future can be deduced from the past and the present. The scientific élite will discover the principles or laws most appropriate to the new society and will appeal to the haves to cooperate in bringing that society about. Failing such cooperation, the haves are warned, the have-nots may again, as in the case of the French Revolution, win over the disaffected intellectuals, who will become the leaders of a new insurrection. Individual freedom has no place in this scheme and appears not to have concerned Saint-Simon. All considerations are subordinated to the establishment and maintenance of a hierarchical but "organically unified" society.

SAINT-SIMON'S DEVELOPMENTAL VIEW OF HISTORY

Simultaneously with Hegel, but independently of him, Saint-Simon advanced a remarkably similar conception of historical development. Hegel viewed the historical development of society as the increasing realization of reason; Saint-Simon placed scientific knowledge in that role. Both thinkers conceived of historical development advancing in stages; for Saint-Simon as for Hegel, each stage embodied some degree of rationality, and therefore some necessity. Both thinkers regarded development and progress as the struggle of opposing forces. Keeping Hegel's conception in mind, we can sketch Saint-Simon's conception of European history, as found in his *Organisateur*, and note the similarities underlying the general outlook of both thinkers.

As a social system comes into being, it enters its ascending phase, which continues until it reaches maturity; with maturity the system begins to decline. The feudal system, for example, reached maturity according to Saint-Simon during the tenth century or thereabouts and from that time to the eve of the Revolution showed an uninterrupted decline. During the period of decline, the industrial and scientific forces, which had formed in the midst of the old system, manifested themselves not only by their tendency to undermine and ultimately to destroy the old order, but also by giving rise to the new one. The new forces, while detaching consciences and wills from the old centers, which until then had provided direction and unity to the system, gathered momentum and increasingly became themselves new foci of common action and centers of organization. A new social system was emerging in the bosom of the old, which was now powerless to arrest the process and was thus moving inevitably to its demise. Émile Durkheim described Saint-Simon's general conception of those processes in the following terms:

> In the measure that the ancient social system gave way, another was formed in the very bosom of the first. The old society contained within itself a new society, in process of formation and every day acquiring more strength and consistency. But these two organizations are necessarily antagonistic to each other. They result from opposing forces and aim at contradictory ends. One is essentially aggressive, warlike, the other essentially pacifist. The one sees in other

> peoples enemies to destroy; the other tends to view them as collaborators in a common undertaking. One has conquest for its aim, the other, production. Similarly in spiritual affairs the first calls on faith and imposes beliefs which it puts beyond discussion. The second calls on reason and even trust—it requires a type of intellectual subordination which is essential to rationality, a commitment to further exploration and testing. Thus these two societies could not coexist without contradicting each other.[8]

In that formulation, Saint-Simon's organic and conflictive view of historical development becomes quite evident.

In his *Système Industriel*, Saint-Simon illuminates the process that eventually led to the French Revolution:

> This tremendous crisis did not have its origin in this or that isolated fact. . . . It operated as an overturning of the political system for the simple reason that the state of society to which the ancient order corresponded had totally changed in nature. A civil and moral revolution which had gradually developed for more than six centuries engendered and necessitated a political revolution. . . . If one insists on attributing the French Revolution to one source, it must be dated from the day the liberation of the communes and the cultivation of exact sciences in western Europe began.[9]

For Saint-Simon, the Revolution was necessary and inevitable; nevertheless, he criticizes the revolutionaries: It was rash to overthrow the old institutions without determining what to put in their place. He objects not to the Revolution but to its not having become what it might have; the Revolution stopped midway in its course and did not culminate positively. The critical, destructive, and negative work of the metaphysicians and revolutionaries was necessary to clear the way for the new order, but they never went beyond their negative, rigid, abstract principles to form a positive philosophical basis for the new order. The new organic society must be built exclusively on positive principles. Had it not become clear that societies based on conflicting tendencies and principles are doomed to instability, crisis, and revolution?

Saint-Simon perhaps meant well when he advocated the rule of scientists and industrialists. He wanted not the strongest to rule but the most capable and knowledgeable in science and industry. The scientific-industrial élite was not to dictate orders but was only to declare what conforms to the nature of things. "In the old system" he wrote, "society is governed essentially by men; in the new it is governed only by principles."[10] In the new society there was to be scientific administration, but no politics properly speaking. Those who direct and administer would not be "above," they would merely fulfill a different function. How would that be reconciled with the preservation of private property? Would not the ownership of productive resources on the part of the industrialists lead to the concentration of power in their hands? Perhaps, but more important is that property should not run counter to the general need; it must not be separated from so-called intelligence and capacity.

The check on egoism in the new society is to be Christian brotherly love. "Love one another" is the motto Saint-Simon inscribed on the first page of his *Système Industriel*. The condition of the proletariat is to be improved as much as possible, not only for its own sake but for the sake of social order. There are two ways of keeping that class in check: Either use force to impose social order, or make them love it. The latter is by far the more rational for the propertied and scientific élite and will ensure the social peace more effectively than repressive measures.

INTERNATIONALISM AND RELIGION

The transition to the new society cannot take place in a single country, independently of the developments in others. The European societies are not isolated from one another; there are definite bonds that unite them. Therefore they must become a community of nations where despotism is eliminated from each and every one. "The great moral movement," Saint-Simon wrote, "which should make society pass from the modified despotic regime to one most advantageous to the majority of society, cannot be effected except by being common to the most enlightened peoples."[11] Why is there interdependence among the societies of Europe? They are neighbors who share a similar social, economic, and religious history. They were all, at one time, subjected to feudal regimes and shared a common religion and clergy, whose head, the pope, was independent of all individual governments. Any important change in one European nation is bound to have repercussions in another, as was proved by both the revolution and the counterrevolution. Europe must be unified in peace. For how can one nation disarm and become peaceful while the rest remain armed and warlike? Peace would, in fact, be impossible, Saint-Simon argues, were it not for the newly emergent industrial forces and spirit, which now render the military spirit quite obsolete. National rivalries and hatreds as expressed in international military conflicts can only hinder the development of the industrial civilization on which the future well-being of all Europe rests. The industrial spirit will bind peoples instead of dividing them; for all the countries of Europe will now have the same interests in furthering production , which will increasingly be the case. All the societies of Europe will be united by the common need for security in production and liberty in exchange. "The producers of all lands are therefore essentially friends." Thus it is not only nationally but internationally as well that all "producers" have common interests conducing to social solidarity.

In addressing himself to the possibility of a peaceful and united European community, Saint-Simon did not adequately take into account the survival of feudal elements in each society. Nor did he foresee the new nationalism in Europe, which became manifest later in the century as a distinctly economic rivalry among nations and which led to ever more bitter and extensive military conflicts. The so-called common industrial spirit did not prove itself to be the internationally unifying factor Saint-Simon had assumed it would be.

Saint-Simon also regarded science as an antidote to nationalism. An international community of scholars and scientists—a new international spiritual élite to replace the old—would emerge as a unifying force. Although national rivalries would remain for a time, they would merely be vestiges of a transitional phase. Saint-Simon saw some kind of professional and occupational solidarity emerging, capable presumably of corroding the irrational nationalistic sentiments. The universalistic interests of the industrial professions and occupations would undermine and supersede all the particularisms of the old order. Eventually the industrial system would embrace all of Europe and perhaps, even all of humanity. Nations would not disappear entirely; they would retain some degree of cultural distinctiveness and political autonomy, but not the moral importance they have had historically.

Nationalism is a form of egoism that must be drastically reduced, if not eliminated, in the new society. Patriotism, Saint-Simon writes, ". . . is nothing but national egoism; and this egoism causes the same injustices to be committed by nation to nation as personal egoism does among individuals."[12] Saint-Simon did not expect the international community to develop in an altogether spontaneous fashion. Common institutions and organizations will be necessary; otherwise, everyone will continue to resort to force. Supranational forms of organization based on the common industrial spirit will bring about a revolution in international relations. However, those conditions, conducing to an international, temporal bond, are insufficient for real international peace and unity. In addition, a spiritual bond will be necessary—a common body of doctrines and beliefs affording moral unity to all European societies. And again, as in the Middle Ages, that will take the form of a common religion, for it is conflicting beliefs that lead inevitably to war. The spiritual and moral unity of men and nations would be based on the New Christianity.

Although *Le Nouveau Christianisme* did not constitute an about-face, it did represent a discernible change in his outlook. In his earliest writings, the emphasis is on the purely scientific. But in his *Système Industriel* and especially in his final work, the idea of God comes to the fore. Increasingly, Saint-Simon was led to the conclusion that interests and organizations were not sufficient to guarantee peace and unity, either within societies or among them. *Moral sentiments* were now assigned an important role. Thus he differs from the utilitarians who relied on self-interest to ensure the well-being of society. Saint-Simon, more emphatically and systematically than they, begins in his later works to stress the need for moral unity as an additional and equally essential basis of social order and unity. Charity, mutual obligation, and philanthropy are essential; although the new religion will have its creed and dogma, morality will be its central core. (Later, it will be seen how

Durkheim employs Saint-Simonian ideas in his attempts to reconcile the disorganizing effects of industrial development with the requirements of social order and unity.)

Saint-Simon's God is impersonal and immanent in all nature. His final doctrine is a form of pantheism in which spirit and matter are once again unified. For Saint-Simon, morality is basically secular, having no end beyond the temporal. It is only by procuring for humanity "the greatest degree of happiness it can achieve during its worldly life that you will succeed in establishing Christianity."[13] His final word on the subject, then, is that the new world will require religion as well as science. Positive philosophy and science, which were to supersede once and for all the theological and metaphysical stages, become a somewhat secularized religion. Eventually, as we shall see, things go so far in that direction that Comte, in his later work, *Politique Positive*, proclaims himself the pope of the new positive religion.

Looking back over Saint-Simon's doctrine as a whole, one sees clearly the two main intellectual currents that shaped it. He lived and wrote at the turn of the century, when the Romantic, conservative, and Catholic movements were challenging every single premise bequeathed by the Enlightenment. Like the *Philosophes*, Saint-Simon had great faith in the power of reason to change the world; he was optimistic and cosmopolitan in his outlook. As for the Revolution, he did not condemn it. It had simply not gone far enough, and that was mainly due to the negative-critical principles of the *Philosophes*. Where he parts company with the Enlightenment thinkers is in their evaluation of the Middle Ages. He rejects their total repudiation of that period as an age of superstition and ignorance. Here the influence of the reaction is clear. For like the conservatives and the theorists of the Catholic revival, he admired the "medieval unity" so much that he adopted it as the model for his new world. The medieval world, he believed, was for a time an intellectual and social unity; it was international, organic, hierarchical, and stable, and it was ruled by both a spiritual and temporal élite. But such social orders do not flower twice in history. Science and industry, from the moment they appeared in the bosom of the old order, sounded its death knell. And that is where Saint-Simon departs from Bonald and Maistre. Science and industry have not only led once and for all to the demise of the old order, they have also become the essential positive principles of the new one. The emergence of conflicting principles and forces within the old system inevitably led to the Revolution and to the destruction of the medieval order. The new society, therefore, must not be based on conflicting principles if it is to escape the fate of its predecessor. It, too, must be international, organic, hierarchical, and stable, ruled by a spiritual and a temporal élite, and, finally, unified by an international religion. In that way, Saint-Simon absorbs and reflects the influence of both the Enlightenment and the counterrevolution. On balance, however, his synthesis represents, ideologically, the bourgeoisie and the related professional and scientific élites who were struggling to consolidate and advance the position of power they had gained during the Revolution and the Empire. When the bourgeoisie finally repudiated him, it was not for his "socialism" but for his theological tendencies.

Saint-Simon viewed the new elements of his age not as conflicting forces but potentially as parts of an organic whole. In a large context, his thought patterns reflect the conditions of *early* nineteenth-century Europe: Nationalism was offset by a semblance of European unity; Catholicism seemed to be making its peace with liberal democracy, and large-scale industry with its accompanying proletariat had not yet appeared on the continent. Therefore, the intense class struggles of the latter part of the century were still unknown phenomena in Saint-Simon's time. The peoples of the nineteenth century failed to achieve an integrated industrial civilization, and those of the twentieth experienced a type of "technocratic utopia" not unlike the one Saint-Simon had advocated. He had ignored the problem of freedom and had looked forward to an essentially rigid, caste society.

Auguste Comte, though he denied it, appropriated virtually all of Saint-Simon's ideas, as we shall presently see.

NOTES

1. This view may be found in Albert Salomon, *The Tyranny of Progress* (New York: Noonday Press, 1955).
2. These and other biographical details may be found in F.M.H. Markham's excellent introduction to the selected writings of *Henri Comte de Saint-Simon* (Oxford: Basil Blackwell, 1952). See also Frank E. Manuel's *The New World of Henri Saint-Simon* (Cambridge, Mass.: Harvard University Press, 1956). Another important source, of course, is Émile Durkheim's *Socialism and Saint-Simon* (London: Routledge and Kegan Paul, 1958).
3. Claude Henri Saint-Simon, *Oeuvres Complètes de Saint-Simon et Enfantin*, 1865–76 (Paris, 1865–76), Vol. XV, p. 66.
4. Ibid., p. 92.
5. Durkheim, *Socialism and Saint-Simon*, p. 104.
6. F.M.H. Markham, *Henri Comte de Saint-Simon*, p. xxv n.
7. Saint-Simon, *Oeuvres Complètes*, Vol. XVIII, p. 221.
8. Durkheim, *Socialism and Saint-Simon*, pp. 118–19.
9. Quoted in Durkheim, *Socialism and Saint-Simon*, p. 120.
10. Saint-Simon, *Oeuvres Complètes*, Vol. IV, p. 197.
11. Quoted in Durkheim, *Socialism and Saint-Simon*, p. 170.
12. Ibid., p. 175.
13. Saint-Simon, *Oeuvres Complètes*, Vol. VII, p. 154.

9

Auguste Comte
(1798–1857)

The term "positive," as Comte employed it in his positive philosophy, was explicitly polemical, intended as an ideological weapon with which to combat the philosophical legacy of the Enlightenment and the Revolution. The critical and destructive principles of *negative* philosophy were to be discredited and repudiated so that they could be replaced by the affirmative and constructive principles of *positive* philosophy. Actually, this counterattack also took place in Germany, where positivists attempted to challenge the radical tendency in Hegel's thought. Their most fundamental objection to Hegel's negative philosophy was that it

> . . . "negates" things as they are. The matters of fact that make up the given state of affairs, when viewed in the light of reason, become negative, limited, transitory—they become perishing forms within a comprehensive process that leads beyond them. The Hegelian dialectic was seen as the prototype of all destructive negations of the given, for in it every immediately given form passes into its opposite and attains its true content only by so doing. This kind of philosophy, the critics said, denies to the given the dignity of the real; it contains the principle of revolution.[1]

In the present discussion, attention will be confined to France where Comte fought against the heritage of the *Philosophes* and in the process formed his own philosophy.

Comte saw a "deplorable state of anarchy" in his time, and he believed that his "social physics," bearing directly upon the "principal needs and grievances of society," would help bring order out of chaos.[2] He hoped to call this "science" to the attention of statesmen who "profess to devote themselves to the task of resolving the alarming revolutionary constitution of modern societies." Social and moral anarchy are the result of intellectual anarchy, itself a consequence of the fact that, on the one hand, theologico-metaphysical philosophy has declined and, on the other, positive philosophy has not yet reached the point where it can provide an intellectual basis for a new organization and thus deliver society from the peril of dissolution.

Order and progress, which the ancients thought irreconcilable, must be united once and for all. Comte considered it the great misfortune of his time that the two principles were regarded as contradictory and were represented by opposing political parties. What he called the retrograde party was for order, whereas the anarchical party was for progress. The principle of order was derived from the Catholic-feudal, or theological, state of social philosophy, whose exponents were Bonald, Maistre, and others. The principle of progress, on the other hand, was derived from the critical tendencies of the Reformation and the Enlightenment. Existing social classes, much to Comte's chagrin, tended to polarize and to support either one or the other—hence, conflict, disorder, and anarchy. In every crisis, the retrograde party argued that the problem was due to the destruction of the older order and therefore demanded its complete restoration; the anarchical party, in contrast, argued that the trouble stemmed from the fact that the destruction of the old order was incomplete, and, therefore, that the revolution must continue.

Comte, like Saint-Simon, appreciated certain aspects of the feudal-theological order and did not reject it altogether. True, it had become "pernicious" by outliving its usefulness, but it had facilitated the development of modern society. Because, however, it can no longer hold its own before the natural progress of scientific intelligence and other social changes, the theological polity can never again become the basis of social order. Thus, Comte, unlike Bonald, believed it was impossible to restore the old order. The decline of the old is not temporary; neither is it the work of Providence. Somehow, Comte argues, a synthesis of the opposing ideas, order and progress, must be achieved, because only through intellectual unity and harmony can social unity be restored.

Science and industry were the main causes of the decline of the feudal-theological order, and the rise of the scientific spirit now precludes the restoration of that order; likewise with the industrial spirit, which now prevents the recurrence of the feudal-military spirit. Moreover, the new spirit is so strong that the spokesmen for the theological school are themselves infected with it. De Maistre, for example, tried to justify the restoration on the grounds of *reason* rather than divine right, thereby showing he was a child of his times. Also, the spokesmen for this school are not unified; torn as they are by sects, they have even accepted many basic principles that are antagonistic to their theological spirit—for example, subordinating the spiritual to the temporal authority. If, finally, they could succeed even temporarily in restoring the old order, the crisis would break out all over again—but even more violently than before because the same disintegrating forces would constantly be at work within it. So much for the theological stage and any hopes for restoring it. What about the metaphysical?

The principles of the "metaphysicians," Comte's term for the Enlightenment thinkers, were essentially critical and revolutionary. They contributed to progress but only in a negative sense. The metaphysical stage was necessary because it broke up the old system and paved the way for the next stage—the positive one that would put an end to the revolutionary period by the formation of a social order uniting the principles of order *and* progress. The metaphysical stage, necessary but provisional, "must be dangerously active till the new political organization which is to succeed it is ready to put an end to its agitation" (p. 9). The metaphysical spirit was necessary to direct the struggle and organize the maximum energy for the overthrow of the great ancient system. But, it, too, has outlived its usefulness and has become obstructive. Comte is especially indignant at the metaphysical view that represents "all government as being the enemy of society, and the duty of society to keep up a perpetual suspicion and vigilance, restricting the activity of government more and more, in order to guard against its encroachments . . ." (p. 11). Liberty of conscience is a dogma which *had* value as a weapon against theological dogmatism but is no longer useful because it can never be a positive organic principle—that is, the basis for the reorganization of society. The various demands for liberty are strictly "negative" principles. Just as astronomers, physicists, and chemists would not allow laymen to question or interfere with their operations, so in social physics (the term "sociology" does not yet appear at this stage of his discussion), the scientific experts should not yield to the incompetent. Social reorganization requires intellectual reorganization, and that is impossible so long as individuals have the right of inquiry on subjects above their qualifications. Comte insists that unity and unanimity will be essential in the new organic society. Social order, he writes, " . . . must ever be incompatible with a perpetual discussion of the foundations of society" (p. 13).

Equality is another dogma: It has limited historical value as a weapon, but must not be turned into an absolute. It is an anarchic principle and hostile to order, as is the dogma of the "sovereignty of the people," which condemns the superior to dependence on the masses and opposes reorganization on different principles.

Comte also finds particularly objectionable Rousseau's "metaphysical notion of a supposed state of nature" and his representation of "civilization as an ever growing degeneracy from the primitive ideal type." Rousseau's presupposition that one can ask questions about the suitability of social systems for the nature of individuals was for Comte presumptuous and dangerous. He therefore dismisses Rousseau's conception as nothing more than the "metaphysical form of the theological dogma of the degradation of the human race by original sin" (p. 16). The disciples of the metaphysical school are also inconsistent if not hypocritical; for once in power they change their conduct and adopt many retrograde principles: war, centralization, natural religion, and so on.

Social crisis will continue so long as the two conflicting doctrines, the theological and the metaphysical, prevail. No order is possible until both are superseded by the positive state, which will be more *organic* than the theological and more *progressive* than the metaphysical. But one must not rush to bring about the new order. Rather, the people must wait patiently for the new system to emerge, and when the right conditions arise, society will submit to the rules that will assure its preservation. The new society will not arise so long as the theological and metaphysical spirits prevail, for they are mutually contradictory and cannot survive together indefinitely in one system. All contradictions must be banished from the new order. England's constitutional monarchy is based on contradictory principles and, therefore, predicts Comte, its "inevitable end cannot be very far off" (p. 22).

Comte despised intellectual anarchy and regarded it as the main cause of moral disunity. He had disdain for those laymen who expressed themselves about complex social and political issues as if such issues were not dependent on education and training. True moral order, Comte believed, "is incompatible with the existing vagabond liberty of individual minds if such license were to last; for the great social rules which should become customary cannot be abandoned to the blind and arbitrary decision of an incompetent public without losing all their efficacy" (p. 25). Comte feared and disliked social criticism and its disorganizing results. Criticism of the traditional patriarchal family, for example, had led to the legalization of divorce, and hence to personal and domestic disorder. Questioning and criticizing time-honored institutions is destructive and threatens to undermine all social life. No important social duties should be questioned or discussed until such time as the discussion is directed by "true" positive principles. Such principles will provide a basis for intellectual unity; lacking such unity, society also lacks a moral authority and degenerates into a state of terror, anarchy, and corruption.

Comte also feared the contemporary emphasis on "material" considerations and regarded it as fatal to progress. That emphasis had revolutionary implications, dangerously annulling the resignation and submissiveness of the lower classes that he so strongly desired. The source of social evils is not to be sought in basic economic and political institutions but in ideas and manners. "When all political evils," he writes, "are imputed to institutions instead of to ideas and social manners, which are now the real seat of the mischief; the remedy is vainly sought in changes, each more serious than the last, in institutions and existing powers" (p. 31). Private property, to be sure, brings with it certain evils, but "it is equally evident that the remedy must arise from opinions, customs, and manners, and that political regulations can have no radical efficacy" (p. 32). The point, then, is not to tamper with, or change, existing institutions but rather to bring about a moral reorganization—a euphemism for the acquiescence of the lower classes to their social condition. There will be neither order nor progress so long as men fail to recognize that their suffering is not of a physical but "of a moral nature."

THE ADVENT OF POSITIVE PHILOSOPHY

Comte had great confidence in the ascendancy of the positive doctrine. Its "perfect logical coherence" and its social function assured success, because this doctrine "will impart a homogeneous and rational character to the desultory politics of our day, and it will . . . establish a general harmony in the entire system of social ideas . . ." (p. 35). Positive philosophy, he believed, is undoubtedly superior to its predecessors. For, while the metaphysical school condemned all periods prior to the Revolution, and the retrograde school disparaged the whole of the modern era, only the positive principle is able to recognize "the fundamental law of continuous human development, representing the existing evolution as the necessary result of the gradual series of former transformations, by simply extending to social phenomena the spirit which governs the treatment of all other natural phenomena" (p. 36). And toward what end is this positive science to be developed? "It is plain that true science has no other aim than the establishment of intellectual order, which is the basis of every other order" (p. 36).

We must let Comte speak for himself to demonstrate the degree to which he advanced his positive doctrine with one purpose in mind—to avert revolution and to achieve the resignation of the "multitude" to the conditions of the existing order. He explicitly pushes to the extreme some of the conclusions which were only implicit in Saint-Simon's work and purges from that work every last critical element that might have remained:

> It is only by the positive polity that the revolutionary spirit can be restrained, because by it alone can the influence of the critical doctrine be justly estimated and circumscribed. . . . Under the rule of the positive spirit, again, all the difficult and delicate questions which now keep up a perpetual irritation in the bosom of society, and which can never be settled while mere political solutions are proposed, will be scientifically estimated, to the great furtherance of social peace. . . . At the same time, it [the positive polity] will be teaching society that, in the present state of their ideas, no political change can be of supreme importance, while the perturbation attending change is supremely mischievous, in the way both of immediate hindrance, and of diverting attention from the true need and procedure. . . . Again, the positive spirit tends to consolidate order, by the rational development of a wise resignation to incurable political evils. . . . A true resignation—that is, a permanent disposition to endure, steadily, and without hope of compensation, all inevitable evils—can proceed only from a deep sense of the connection of all kinds of natural phenomena with invariable laws. If there are (as I doubt not there are) political evils which, like some personal sufferings, cannot be remedied by science, science at least proves to us that they are incurable, so as to calm our restlessness under pain by the conviction that it is by natural laws that they are rendered insurmountable. Human nature suffers in its relations with the astronomical world, and the physical, chemical, and

> biological, as well as the political. How is it that we turbulently resist in the last case, while, in the others, we are calm and resigned . . . ? Finally, the positive philosophy befriends public order by bringing back men's understanding to a normal state through the influence of its method alone, before it has had time to establish any social theory. It dissipates disorder at once by imposing a series of indisputable scientific conditions on the study of political questions. By including social science in the scientific hierarchy, the positive spirit admits to success in this study only well-prepared and disciplined minds, so trained in the preceding departments of knowledge as to be fit for the complex problems of the last. The long and difficult preliminary elaboration must disgust and deter vulgar and ill-prepared minds, and subdue the most rebellious. (pp. 37–38)

The positive conception of progress is superior to all others, and especially superior to the revolutionary view in which progress consists of the continuous extension of freedom, and the "gradual expansion of human powers. Now, even in the restricted and negative sense in which this is true—that of the perpetual diminution of obstacles—the positive philosophy is incontestably superior: for true liberty is nothing else than a rational submission to the preponderance of the laws of nature . . ." (p. 39). The scientific élite will be the final authority of what those laws are and will indicate the degree to which the lot of the lower classes may be slowly improved. In that way the positive doctrine will provide a so-called constructive alternative to the insurrectionary solution advocated by the revolutionary school. Basic economic and political institutions are not to be changed, for history has shown that such change avails nothing. The class structure should remain as it is; and class conflict presumably will be reduced, even eliminated, through the moral reconciliation of the classes. That will be facilitated by imposing a moral authority between the working classes and the leaders of society.

Those who identify with the theological-retrograde school probably will not support the positive doctrine because they are not interested in just any order but in their unique one. The "stationary school," the defenders of the status quo, on the other hand, may be won over when they recognize that it will further their interests. But Comte's real target is the revolutionary school whose "doctrines will be absorbed by the new philosophy, while all its anarchical tendencies will be extinguished." The present generation of scientists, however, is too much infected with revolutionary principles to adopt the positive view. Therefore the chance of winning over the scientists will depend on the younger generation who will be given a really thorough positive education. In all cases, "progress" will depend on "an intellectual, and then a moral reorganization [which] must precede and direct the political" (p. 42).

THE POSITIVE METHOD IN ITS APPLICATION TO SOCIAL PHENOMENA

For Comte, what distinguishes the scientific spirit is its steady subordination of imagination to observation, of reason to "facts." That is quite different from the eighteenth-century conception in which reasoning and observing are coordinate functions of the scientific method. In Comte's view, prediction, or "prevision" as he calls it, will facilitate social control, a primary and even exclusive aim of his positive doctrine. In those terms, "to predict in order to control," becomes a totalitarian slogan in his hands. That becomes even clearer in his "scientific" conception of society.

Order and progress are the static and dynamic aspects of a society. Order refers to the harmony that prevails among the various conditions of existence, whereas progress refers to the society's orderly development according to natural social laws. Thus the two principles, previously mutually antagonistic, are reconciled. It is natural and normal for the elements of the social system, the institutions of society, to be interdependent and interrelated. Therefore, even for analytical purposes, social elements should not be contemplated separately as if they had an independent existence. All the parts of the system make up a harmonious whole, which, by definition, is divested of all conflictive, contradictory, and antagonistic elements. He enunciates as a scientific principle "that there must always be a spontaneous harmony between the whole and the parts of the social system," and he insists that harmony will establish itself through radical consensus, the only condition proper to the social organism. Emphasis is always on adjustment to the "natural" social laws, quite deliberately opposed to Enlightenment principles where the emphasis is on changing the social system to allow for the infinite perfection of the human individual. Again and again Comte stresses that the scientific method requires that society be studied as a whole and not separated into its component parts. It is as if he fears that the logical analysis of a society's institutions will inevitably lead to its actual dissolution; an analytical view of society, in which relationships are critically scrutinized, will revive the very same critical, negative, and revolutionary philosophy that positivism was to replace once and for all.

Social dynamics refers to the study of the patterns of evolutionary progress in which the sequences of development are necessary and inevitable. Social dynamics, then, is really "dynamic order" proceeding according to natural, orderly, and necessary laws. For "unless the movement was determined by those laws, it would occasion the entire destruction of the social system" (p. 72). Amelioration accompanies development but it is not unlimited. "The chimerical notion of unlimited perfectibility is thus at once excluded" (p. 73). The tendency toward improvement is spontaneous, and therefore does not require any special political action directed toward change. The latter is in effect "superfluous," because each stage is as perfect as it can be. Not only political action but human action in general is very limited in its effects and subject to the constriction of natural laws. Can those laws nevertheless be modified in any way? The human race could perhaps accelerate or retard certain tendencies but never change the nature of those tendencies. It certainly cannot reverse certain orders of development nor can it skip stages. The importance of human action, in general, and political action, in particular, has been greatly exaggerated.

As for other aspects of Comte's method, he emphasized such techniques as observation, experiment, and comparison. And in spite of the transparent ideological elements of his methodology, he does manage to grasp some of the principles of scientific method—which always remains subordinated, however, to the construction of his hierarchical, organic, authoritarian society. Observation is impossible without theory, first to direct it and then to interpret what is observed. Facts cannot speak for themselves, for "though we are steeped to the lips in them, we can make no use of them, nor even be aware of them, for want of speculative guidance in examining them" (p. 81). Facts must be attached at least by a tentative hypothesis to the laws of social development. But for Comte, as we have seen, those laws as well as all his other assumptions and concepts about society were in the first instance inspired by their ideological function. The whole apparatus of his positive doctrine is ideological in the strictest sense of that term, and science never achieves very much autonomy in his doctrinaire and totalitarian system. He remained blind throughout his work to the ideal of freedom even as it related to science and apparently failed to see how many aspects of society he had dogmatically closed off from the view of science by means of his doctrinaire pronouncements.

As Comte proceeds in his exposition of social statics, he considers the individual, the family, and society, "the last comprehending in a scientific sense, the whole of the human species, and chiefly, the *whole of the white race*" (p. 105, italics added). Not the individual but the family is the true social unit, because the family is the school of social life. Man is a social being whose social nature is formed in the family context. But those assertions and the like are always made with a specific ideological intention in mind. The subordination of woman is natural and will continue in the "new" society: The female sex is in a state of perpetual infancy. "Sociology will prove that the equality of the sexes, of which so much is said, is incompatible with all social existence . . . " (p. 112). Thus Comte argues the organic inferiority of woman and attempts to provide a "scientific" rationale for the same state of affairs that the theological school regarded as determined by Providence.

Generally, "providential wisdom," though in a secularized form, dominates Comte's conception of society and its development. The changes brought about by the inherent wisdom of the spontaneous evolutionary process are always "superior to any that the most eminent reformers would have ventured to conceive of before hand" (p. 114). Nevertheless, there are developments which, though natural, can threaten the very existence of society. Comte views the division of labor, growing increasingly complex, in that light. It seems to be an inexorable process, the very principle of society's development; but at the same time, as the division of labor is extended, it seems to decompose and fragment society. Thus government is assigned the role "to guard against and restrain the fundamental dispersion of ideas, sentiments, and ideals, which is the inevitable result of the very principle of human development, and which, if left to itself, would put a stop to social progression in all important respects" (p. 119). Every element and institution of the society, including government, must serve to further stability, solidarity, and order. Society is everything in Comte's scheme—the individual, nothing. Each must subordinate himself, but that has its rewards because "there can be no one who, in his secret mind, has not often felt, more or less vividly, how sweet it is to obey when he can have the rare privilege of consigning the burdensome responsibility of his general self-conduct to wise and trustworthy guidance . . ." (p. 122).

This review of Comte's work should suffice to show how much of it was explicitly justificatory and apologetic for his "best of all possible worlds." Despite the lip service paid to "science," virtually every assertion he makes is based not on experience, observation, and reasoning, but on values and sentiments. He refused to see that the human being is not merely an object but an active subject; that he *determines* and is not merely determined; that he can change society according to goals, " . . . something which positivism must deny, for goals, in their very nature, are something that have not as yet been experienced."[3]

In his later work, *Politique Positive* (1851–54), the religious and sentimental factor finally prevailed and Comte unabashedly proclaimed himself pope of the new positive religion—an ironic turn of events for the ardent defender of positive science. Little wonder, then, that J. S. Mill described Comte's later views as "the most complete system of spiritual and temporal despotism that ever issued from the brain of any human being—except, perhaps, Ignatius Loyola."[4]

Despite Comte's philosophic efforts, the peoples of Europe failed to achieve an organic, integrated, conflict-free civilization. It was Karl Marx who was to draw the most radical conclusions from that failure.

NOTES

1. Herbert Marcuse, *Reason and Revolution* (Boston: Beacon Press, 1960), p. 325. For a full discussion of the positive reaction, see pp. 323–74.
2. The present discussion of Comte is based on the second volume of Harriet Martineau's translation and condensation of his *Cours de Philosophie Positive*. It appeared in English as *The Positive Philosophy*, 2 vols. (London: Routledge and Kegan Paul, 1893). Martineau's rendition so impressed Comte that he recommended it over the original and as a result her version was retranslated into French. (Hereafter all page references to this work will be indicated in parentheses immediately following the quoted passage.)
3. See Frank Hartung, "The Social Function of Positivism," *Philosophy of Science*, Vol. 12, no. 2 (April 1945), pp. 120–33.
4. Quoted in F.M.H. Markham, *Henri Comte de Saint-Simon* (Oxford: Basil Blackwell, 1952), p. xviii.

10

☙ *Alexis de Tocqueville*
(1805–1859)

DEMOCRACY IN AMERICA

Alexis de Tocqueville is regarded as one of the most important social and political theorists of the nineteenth century because he grappled in a most enlightening manner with the implications of the two revolutions of his time—the democratic and the industrial—which were markedly transforming the social order of Europe. Born to a French noble family, he retained throughout his life certain aristocratic values and thus confronted the intense social conflicts of post-aristocratic France with considerable ambivalence. For although he had early become convinced of the inevitable advance of democracy, believing efforts to block it futile, he feared that the victory of the *demos* would lead to the erosion, if not outright destruction, of aristocratic values and institutions. The history of his homeland had shown that the rise of the masses could pave the way to despotism—the revolution of 1789 had culminated in the Napoleonic dictatorship; and Napoleon's nephew, Louis Bonaparte, seized power by force after the revolutions of 1848. In the light of French experience, then, there was a strong tendency for democratic revolutions to alternate with despotism. Yet the American Revolution was free of any despotic tendency. Indeed, the American experience strongly suggested that democracy offered the fullest scope for the growth and safeguarding of liberty.

Tocqueville arrived in New York on May 12, 1831, just at the moment when the antithesis, aristocracy-democracy, appeared to be a very lively public issue. Of course, aristocracy in the American context referred not to a hereditary landed nobility, but simply to the large, rich property holders. The issue, as the Jacksonian democrats saw it, was "whether people or property, shall govern? Democracy implies a government by the people . . . . Aristocracy implies a government of the rich."[1] This political atmosphere and the egalitarian ideals Tocqueville encountered in the United States contrasted sharply with his own aristocratic tastes. It is therefore not surprising that the struggle between aristocracy and democracy, and the irresistible movement from one to the other, became the master theme of his first great book and most of his subsequent works as well.

In his first major work, *Democracy in America,* Tocqueville wrote of America with one eye on his own country. In America, he believed, the people ruled. Yet, much of what he so strongly desired for France he found in the United States: order, government based on the separation and balance of powers, true freedom. And the phenomena he feared and despised in France were nonexistent in American society. For Tocqueville, the striking thing about America was that she had had her democratic revolution but had avoided France's fate—anarchy alternating with despotism. Tocqueville therefore studied America in the hope that it would provide guidelines for France where the continuing ascendancy of the people appeared to be inevitable. In Tocqueville's eyes America was a post-revolutionary, middle-class society—a one-class or "classless" society in which greater and greater equality was becoming the rule.

Tocqueville was among the first to recognize the uniqueness of the American social structure. America, he observed, had never had an old regime: no absolute monarchy, no feudal nobility, no established church, no centralized state bureaucracy. Nor, on the other hand, did America possess any large metropolitan areas or great industrial centers. It was the absence of these conditions that made the American form of order and liberty possible. America was one great, relatively homogeneous, agrarian middle class; and although there were also extremes of wealth and poverty, such extremes were comparatively rare. In America the democratic revolution had thus produced a high degree of social equality. In Europe, too, a universal democratic revolution was gathering momentum every day. For Tocqueville, one meaning of "democracy" was the historical ascendancy of the middle and lower classes to prominence and power. In France this movement had led to the collapse of the old regime; but the foundations of the new order now seemed as shaky as those of the old. Although capitalists were gaining in power, they appeared to be no more secure before the laboring classes than were the feudal lords in the face of the rising bourgeoisie. To Tocqueville, then, "democracy" referred to the permanent and seemingly inexorable revolt of the lower classes. "Can it be believed," he asked, "that the democracy which has overthrown the feudal system and vanquished kings will retreat before tradesmen and capitalists?"[2]

The irresistible character of the democratic revolution prompted Tocqueville to describe it as providential. This was also a useful metaphor with which to counter the ultraconservatives in France who regarded every departure from the old order as a violation of the divine will.

In Europe, the revolution had proceeded blindly, without the benefit of knowledgeable guidance: "A new science of politics is needed for a new world" (p. 7). The absence of such guidance accounts for the extremely violent character of social conflict in France, in contrast to the more peaceful nature of change in America. The French upper classes had failed historically to make the lower fit to govern, which would have required the sharing of power. Instead, the privileged and powerful were bent on excluding the people from government. For this reason—Tocqueville here directs his argument to the members of his own proprietary class—democracy has been perceived as evil, and the benefits it might confer ignored.

Democracy, Tocqueville argued, brings certain losses for a minority but definite gains for the majority. With democracy properly guided, comfort is more general and ignorance less common. The likelihood of violent conflict, disorder or despotism also diminishes. In France, however, the people's revolution has remained unguided, resulting in increased hostility between the classes even though the actual distance between rich and poor has diminished. In America, in contrast, the revolution has brought with it no such consequences. Americans reap the fruits of the revolution without paying the terrible price Tocqueville's countrymen have paid.

Like Montesquieu before him, Tocqueville admired English political institutions and recognized their influence in shaping American democracy. The English had brought to America that fruitful germ of free institutions, the township. From the beginning the predominantly middle-class origin of the pioneers militated against the formation of a landed aristocracy. Free farmers, each with his own private plot, worked a land that demanded the self-interested efforts of the owners themselves. Hence, there emerged in America not the aristocratic form of liberty of the mother country but rather that freedom of the middle and lower orders of which the history of the world had earlier furnished no example. In the North, and in New England in particular, the settlers shared class origin, religion, language and even political creed. America's democratic institutions were most "perfect" in New England, where the people directed their own public affairs. And although Tocqueville was not blind to the oppressive side of these communities, notably the "narrow sectarian spirit" of the Puritanical laws, he recognized the distinctive democratic virtues of these communities: personal liberty, trial by jury, and the accountability of the elected official.

Tocqueville continually highlights the contrasts between America and France. His praise for local autonomy and decentralized government in

America was intended as a critique of the highly centralized state bureaucracy in France—a phenomenon to which he devoted much attention in his final work, *The Old Regime and the French Revolution*, discussed later in this chapter. Already here in the *Democracy*, however, he saw the profound difference it made for political life when the community was rent into mutually hostile classes as in France, and when it was not, as in America. "In New England," he observed,

> no tradition exists of a distinction of rank; no portion of the community is tempted to oppress the remainder; and the wrongs that may injure isolated individuals are forgotten in the general contentment that prevails. (p. 68)

The absence of a highly centralized bureaucracy in America was also due, of course, to the favorable birthplace of American democracy:

> The Americans have no [powerful] neighbors and consequently they have no great wars, or financial crises, or inroads or conquest to dread; they require neither great taxes, nor large armies, nor great generals; and they have nothing to fear from a scourge which is more formidable to republics than all these evils combined; namely, military glory. (p. 289)

The absence of those conditions accounted for the unobtrusive and unoppressive character of the American State. Throughout the *Democracy* Tocqueville's praise of decentralization is polemical, directed against the partisans in his own country of the highly centralized State. The history of France had taught him that however it might begin, a centralized bureaucracy inevitably becomes the absolute master of liberty and life. In America, in contrast, the people accomplish their tasks by and for themselves. The autonomous local and provincial institutions allow for unfettered individual initiative and private enterprise. That such institutions are essential for the preservation of liberty was clear from the history of his own country. France was a society especially vulnerable to despotism because organized local powers, capable of resisting a despot, had been severely weakened first by the absolute monarchy and then by the democratic revolution, which continued to concentrate power in the hands of the State bureaucracy. As the State thus gathered unto itself virtually all power, nothing stood between it and the atomized populace, which, therefore, could be manipulated by a charismatic political leader like Napoleon. This special vulnerability of French democracy to despotism had been overlooked by those who favored a strong centralized State as a bulwark of freedom.

If the existence of provincial and local autonomy is essential for the prevention of despotism and the preservation of liberty, so is the development of political checks and balances, constitutionalism and other safeguards. Tocqueville united both principles in his theory of good government, for only both together could prevent the domination of the whole society from the center. A plurality of autonomous social bases of power was as essential as the division of powers among the respective branches of government: the executive, legislative and judicial. In America both principles appeared to have been realized without hampering the federal government's ability to serve the general interests of the nation. In addition to these principles Tocqueville recognized that the only alternative to freedom of the press, speech and assembly was despotism.

THE THREE RACES OF THE UNITED STATES

There is perhaps no better evidence of Tocqueville's humanistic outlook than his rejection of racism in the chapters on the Afro-Americans and native peoples of the United States. Additional evidence is found in the lengthy correspondence he carried on with his friend Count Gobineau. The latter had sought in four copious volumes to demonstrate the thesis implicit in the title of his book, *The Inequality of Human Races.* This book, in turn, later exercised considerable influence, through H.S. Chamberlain, on the Nazi racial theorists. To Tocqueville, the races appeared "distinct" not so much due to their outward characteristics as to their culture and education. The "Indians" and the blacks had been forced into inferior positions and subjected to tyranny and worse at the hands of the whites. None of the dehumanizing consequences of slavery escaped Tocqueville's notice. Blacks were deprived of all privileges of humanity—of their historic memories, of something as fundamental as the family, of their language and customs without, however, having acquired "any claim to European privileges" (p. 322).

Similarly, Tocqueville fully recognized the tragic disorders white tyranny had caused among the aboriginal peoples. Forced from their native lands, their whole way of life was undermined. Tribe after tribe was expelled from its land, which the whites soon appropriated, obtaining in that manner vast territories. There could be no doubt that despite the virtuous and high-minded rhetoric of official policy, the real aim of the government was expulsion. "The rapacity of the settlers was usually backed by the tyranny of the government" (p. 350). The federal and the state governments were alike deficient in good faith. Again and again they broke the treaties they had made with the Indian tribes.

As for slavery and its implications, Tocqueville prophetically observed:

> The most formidable of all the ills that threaten the future of the Union arises from the presence of a black population upon its territory, and in contemplating the cause of the present embarrassments, or the future dangers of the United States, the observer is invariably led to this as a primary fact. (p. 356)

And later, in Volume II of *Democracy,* he states:

> If ever America undergoes great revolutions, they will be brought about by the presence of the black population on the soil of the United States; that is to say, they will owe their origin . . . to the inequality of condition. (II, p. 256)

Throughout, one is impressed with Tocqueville's sensitive grasp of the slave's condition. He observes, for example, how different in its consequences was slavery in the United States as compared with the slavery of antiquity, where master and slave were of the same color and where the latter was often superior to his master in education and culture. To confer freedom upon a slave in antiquity it was enough to enfranchise him, since he carried no permanent sign of his formerly servile status. In the United States, in contrast, even when a slave was set free, he could never shed the badge of his ignominy which he inevitably transmitted to "all his descendants." In America, there was so much more "to conquer than the mere fact of servitude: the prejudice of the master, the prejudice of the race, and the prejudice of color" (p. 358).

Tocqueville also perceived that prejudice was often stronger in the North than in the South. In the North, where blacks lived officially as free individuals, whites shunned them anyway lest they be "confounded together." But there were still other, far-reaching consequences of slavery. Almost like a controlled experiment, the obvious differences between the border states, Kentucky and Ohio, demonstrated that the institution of slavery had retarded economic development in the slave states. Slavery destroyed the dignity of labor. Thus Tocqueville proposed that the presence or absence of this pivotal, master-slave relationship had much to do with the fact that the North had developed commercially and industrially while the South had not. Furthermore, the basic differences between the northern and southern socioeconomic systems accounted for the fact that new European immigrants went only to the free states, fearing a country where labor had no honor. For the black, however, being formally free and residing in the North made little difference, since he continued to perform his labor in the meanest and most degrading status. Sensing the coming crisis, Tocqueville predicted "the most horrible of civil wars" (p. 379).

Although Tocqueville generally stressed the egalitarian character of American society, he recognized that even among whites there existed class divisions between those who owned property and those who owned little or none and labored for the former. In his view, however, these divisions were temporary and destined to disappear. As a rule, when he spoke of workers he did not distinguish between those of agriculture and those of manufacturing industry. When he wrote, therefore, that it appears to be a great social law that wages will rise with the further advance of equality, he referred to the wages of agricultural laborers

> who are themselves owners of certain plots of ground, which just enable them to subsist without working for anyone else. When these laborers come to offer their services to a neighboring landowner or farmer, if he refuses them a certain rate of wages they retire to their own small property and await another opportunity.[3]

When, however, Tocqueville turned from agriculture to manufacturing industry, he observed "a great and gloomy exception" to his general social law: a new "aristocracy," he notes, has emerged in "productive industry and has established its sway there . . ." (II, p. 190).

THE "ARISTOCRACY OF MANUFACTURES"

Tocqueville discerned in democratic societies an emerging relationship comparable to that between master and slave. This was a new form of servitude in which the workers are "almost at the mercy of the master." They "soon contract habits of body and mind which unfit them for any other toil." The masters can unite in order to reduce wages; and if and when the workers strike:

> The master, who is a rich man, can very well wait, without being ruined, until necessity brings them back to him; but they [the workers] must work day by day or they die, for their only property is in their hands. They have long been impoverished by oppression, and the poorer they become, the more easily they may be oppressed; they can never escape from this fatal circle of cause and consequence. (II, p. 190)

Tocqueville thus observed a new form of dependence, accompanied by great human wretchedness, emerging among the manufacturing populations of the democratic societies of his time.

In his discussion of the "aristocracy of manufactures," he describes the two classes most characteristic of the industrial system—the system Karl Marx later called "capitalism." Tocqueville recognized the technical advantages of the industrial division of labor: goods are produced in large quantities with greater speed and economy; and production costs per unit diminish as the amount of capital and the scale of production grow larger. But it was strikingly evident to Tocqueville that such gains in productivity degraded the worker as a human being. Tocqueville grasped the phenomenon that Marx later described as *alienation*: a process over which the worker has no control and in which he has little or no need for creativity, knowledge, judgment or will; a process in which he is chained to one debilitating task in the division of labor. "When a worker is unceasingly and exclusively engaged in the fabrication of one thing," Tocqueville wrote,

> he ultimately does his work with singular dexterity; but at the same time he loses the general faculty of applying his mind to the direction of the work. He every day becomes more adroit and less industrious; so that it may be said that in proportion as the worker improves, the man is degraded. What can be expected of a man who has spent twenty years of his life in making heads for pins? (II, p. 158)

Marx, as we shall see, also described the dehumanizing consequences of the industrial division of labor. Its higher productivity is made possible by dividing, classifying and grouping the workers according to narrow and specific functions. What is taken away from the individual worker in artistic skill, creativity and reflective powers is imparted to the organization. The deficiencies of the former become the virtues of the latter. The entire organization is enriched by alienating the worker from his human powers. Tocqueville viewed the consequences of the division of labor in much the same way:

> In proportion as the principle of the division of labor is more extensively applied, the workman becomes more weak, more narrow-minded, and more dependent. The art advances, the artisan recedes. On the other hand, in proportion as it becomes more manifest that the productions of manufactures are by so much the cheaper and better as the manufacture is larger and the amount of capital employed more considerable, wealthy and educated men come forward to embark in manufactures, which were heretofore abandoned to poor or ignorant handicraftsmen. The magnitude of the efforts required and the importance of the results to be obtained attract them. Thus at the very time at which the science of manufactures lowers the class of workmen, it raises the class of masters. (II, p. 159)

And further describing the emerging social dichotomy of the new productive system, Tocqueville continues:

> While the worker concentrates his faculties more and more upon the study of a single detail, the master surveys an extensive whole, and the mind of the latter is enlarged in proportion as that of the former is narrowed. In a short time the one will require nothing but physical strength without intelligence; the other stands in need of science, and almost of genius, to ensure success. This man resembles more and more the administrator of a vast empire; that man, a brute.
>
> The master and the worker have then here no similarity, and their differences increase every day. . . . Each of them fills the station which is made for him, and which he does not leave; the one is continually, closely, and necessarily dependent upon the other and seems as much born to obey as that other is to command. What is this but aristocracy? (II, p. 159)

Tocqueville thus recognized some of the chief characteristics of the new industrial serfdom. However, although he had personally witnessed the harshness of the new system, "one of the harshest that ever existed in the world," he believed it was "one of the most confined and least dangerous." He had already seen the most advanced industry of his time in Manchester, England, and he had also visited the industrial cities of the United States. But he continued to regard manufacturing industry as an "exceptional" phenomenon. He thus failed to grasp what Saint-Simon had fully recognized, namely, that the new mode of production would increasingly supersede the old and become the rule. For Tocqueville, the growth and dominance of capitalist industry was only a remote possibility. He did, however, urge all those who cherished democracy to keep their eyes fixed on the manufacturing aristocracy "for if ever a permanent inequality of conditions and aristocracy again penetrates into the world, it may be predicted that this is the gate by which they will enter" (II, p. 161).

SOCIOLOGY OF IDEAS, CULTURE, AND RELIGION

Tocqueville, following the cues of Montesquieu, attempted to explain the nature of ideas by situating them in their social context. As applied to America this proposition suggested that if the American consciousness is eminently democratic, practical and experimental, those qualities reflected the general social conditions of the nation. In America it was believed that ". . . the greater truth should go with the greater number" (II, p. 10). Accordingly, great faith was placed in public opinion. Tocqueville's sociological approach to the origin and nature of ideas enabled him to propose how inequality and equality affect the beliefs people hold. Where inequalities are great and of long duration, the members of different social classes tend to regard one another as if they were members of distinct races. Inequality, therefore, militates against a general view. In democratic-egalitarian societies, in contrast, people tend to recognize their common humanity. Such societies also prompt individuals to investigate the truth for themselves, because no class of intellectual superiors exists which can set an example or show them the way. In democratic societies the individual has great curiosity but little leisure; his life is active, practical and excited and he craves quick success. Americans being a practical people, their pragmatic, empirical attitude inclines them less to theory and more to practice even where science is concerned. Americans mistrust abstract systems and "visionary speculation." They do not easily defer to authority, precedent or "schools"; and "they adhere closely to facts and study facts with their own senses" (II, p. 41). Not that they altogether ignore theory in science; they pay the most careful attention "to the theoretical portion which is immediately requisite to application" (II, p. 42).

The primary reason for the pronounced practicality of American science and knowledge may be found in the American way of life and the structure of American society. The restlessness, the ceaseless quest for gain, for power and for fortune, tend to preclude the leisure and calm so necessary for meditation. In America—and to a lesser extent in other democratic societies—agitation is constant; there is an "incessant jostling of men, which annoys and disturbs the mind without stimulating or elevating it" (II, p. 43). Men rarely sit and meditate and have little esteem for those who do. The American is a man of action, so though he is certainly interested in the truth and accuracy of ideas, he prefers to act, using the information at hand, rather than to research every idea to the bottom. Tocqueville linked the active, practical, experimental attitude to the love of physical well-being. To men living in the democratic era

> every new method that leads by a shorter road to wealth, every machine that spares labor, every instrument that facilitates pleasures or augments them, seems to be the grandest effort of the human intellect. (II, p. 45)

In democracies it is materialistic motives such as these that guide and shape science. Material interest draws the mind away from the loftier spheres down to the middle zone, for science, in democracies, is predominantly practical and applied. In aristocracies, in contrast, science is cultivated for its own sake and highly theoretical but often confined "to the arrogant and sterile search for abstract truths" (II, p. 46).

Aristocracies stress the beautiful, quality being the highest virtue of a manufactured product, as was the case in the craft guilds. The customers being the aristocratic few, the craftsman strives for perfection in his workmanship to appeal to their refined tastes. Even a peasant would rather go without the objects he covets than procure them in a state of poor quality. In democracies, on the other hand, the middle- and lower-class customers, the great multitude, cannot afford real *objets d'art* and would rather have a poor imitation than none at all. Accordingly, the manufacturer seeks to produce as many such items as possible at the lowest cost. Hence, a middling standard, mediocrity, becomes the rule in the arts. Although Tocqueville's analysis of the "mass" or "popular" culture in democracies may be construed as a critique of that tendency from an aristocratic standpoint, it is important to note that he was no less critical of art and literature dominated by aristocratic values. In aristocracies, he observes, because the members of the literary class often live among themselves, and speak and write for themselves and the very few, their art is often infected with a "false and labored style." In their effort to keep themselves separate from the lower classes, they create

> a sort of aristocratic jargon which is hardly less remote from pure language than is the coarse dialect of the people. Such are the natural perils of literature in aristocracies. Every aristocracy that keeps itself aloof from the people becomes impotent, a fact which is as true in literature as it is in politics. (II, p. 58)

Literature and art, then, are profoundly influenced by the social and political conditions of a nation. Democracy also changes the character of language as many new words appear, borrowed mostly from industry and trade. The majority lays down the law in language as it does in everything else. The general tendency of democracy to lower class barriers results in lowering linguistic barriers as well, so that mutually unintelligible dialects disappear.

The character of historiography and social science is also transformed in the transition from an aristocratic to a democratic system. The aristocratic historian tends to see a few prominent actors, a few great individuals, who occupy the entire historical stage and who, presumably, make history. The democratic historian sees large social forces and general causes, corresponding to the new situation in which the people have a greater role to play. There is, however, a dangerous tendency among the historians of the democratic age: they tend to divorce actions from the actors. They reify actions and organize them into formal systems. In that way they not only deny the influence on history of the few, they also "deprive the people themselves of the power of modifying their own condition," thus subjecting them to a blind and inflexible necessity (II, p. 87).

Finally, Tocqueville proposed that religion can also be analyzed in relation to social, economic and political conditions. In America, for instance, he discerned a connection between religion and worldly interests: American preachers, be observes, were always "referring to the earth, and it is only with great difficulty that they can divert their attention from it" (II, p. 127). Describing their discourses, Tocqueville continues:

> . . . it is often difficult to ascertain . . . whether the principle object of religion is to procure eternal felicity in the other world or prosperity in this. (II, p. 127)

Anticipating Max Weber's thesis concerning the protestant ethic and the spirit of capitalism, Tocqueville notes the preponderantly Puritanical background of the independent entrepreneurs and merchants. The values of Puritanism on the one hand, and of commerce and industry on the other, appeared to be not only compatible but mutually reinforcing. Although Tocqueville includes other elements that contributed to the peculiarly practical temperament of the Americans he mentions first their "strictly puritanical origin [and] their exclusively commercial habits . . ." (II, pp. 36–37). They spend "every day in the week in making money, and Sunday in going to Church . . ." (II, p. 83).

In the light of this all-too-brief exposition of Tocqueville's analysis of democracy in America, one can easily appreciate his importance as a social theorist and comparative historical-sociologist. His final work has also stood the test of time. Indeed, it stands alone as the most succinct and masterful analysis of the conditions that led to the revolution of 1789, and to the subsequent French revolutions as well.

THE OLD REGIME AND THE FRENCH REVOLUTION

The central idea of this work, as of Tocqueville's first great book, is still the struggle between aristocracy and democracy. In the *Old Regime,* however, the concept of social class becomes a more salient analytical element. In the light of his own political experiences during the 1848 revolutions and their aftermath, he now maintained that an adequate grasp of French historical developments required a knowledge of "the exact relations that obtained among the various classes."[4] And in another passage he pauses to remind the reader that "undoubtedly one could produce individuals as evidence against my generalization; however I am discussing classes which alone ought to concern the historian" (p. 179). In place, then, of the rather ambiguous terms, "aristocracy" and "democracy," which dominated his early works, one finds in the *Old Regime* analyses of specific classes and the relations between them. Equally important is the fact that Tocqueville continues to employ a comparative, historical-sociological method: to understand French developments, one had to compare and contrast them with those of other European societies.

The Revolution of 1789 was the violent culmination of a long historical process, and at the same time the explosive beginning of a revolutionary movement that continued throughout the nineteenth century. If the explosion of 1789 had never occurred, Tocqueville argued, the old order would in any case have crumbled, but slowly instead of collapsing all at once. The key question for Tocqueville was this: Given the fact that before the Revolution feudal conditions had prevailed throughout continental Europe, often in more oppressive forms than in France, why were those conditions so much more detested in France? If the main aim and effect of the Revolution was to destroy feudalism, why did it not break out elsewhere, in those countries in which feudalism was a much heavier yoke? In Germany, for instance, serfdom, strictly speaking, was still in effect at the time of the Revolution. The German peasant was subject to many harsh constraints, including *corvée*, which "in certain districts compelled him to give not less than three days of [unpaid] labor a week" (p. 99). In France, in contrast, such conditions had long since disappeared, and "the peasant could come and go, buy and sell, enter into contracts and work as he pleased" (p. 100). Serfdom had been abolished in France so far in the past that its very date was forgotten. Moreover, the French peasant had early become something of a landowner. Splitting up the giant estates was not the exclusive work of the Revolution. Much earlier—Tocqueville argues against the commonly accepted view—there had existed a comparatively large class of peasant proprietors; and in this respect France was unique.

The records Tocqueville had examined clearly demonstrated that in France a petit-bourgeois stratum of peasants had long owned land and that it was their descendants who bought the land of the Church and nobility parcelled out during the Revolution. So the main effect of 1789 and the Napoleonic aftermath was not to create for the first time a class of free peasant proprietors, but rather to increase the size of their holdings, and to transfer the land officially from feudal to bourgeois hands. Under the old regime, however, these peasant proprietors were greatly impeded in deriving the full benefits of ownership because they were forced by the monarchy to shoulder numerous charges and imposts which they greatly resented and from which they could not free themselves. It was, therefore, not the heaviness but the comparative lightness of the feudal burden in France which, for Tocqueville, needed to be taken into account in explaining the cataclysm of 1789.

Equally indicative of the distinctiveness of French feudalism prior to the Revolution is the fact that the nobility did not rule the countryside. The parish was administered either by locally elected officials or, more frequently, by officials of the monarchy. The noble had lost all real authority in the community; yet he retained certain privileges which added considerably to the peasants' resentment. The peasants detested the monarchy for the taxes it imposed upon them and detested the nobility for its exemption from taxes, a privilege which appeared wholly unjustified since this class now provided none of the useful services it had once provided. Unlike their English and German counterparts, the French nobles had ceased to have anything to do with service to their communities, save the administration of justice. Even there, however, the State had largely taken over this function as well. The French nobles had thus lost their authority but retained their privileges; and it was their retention of privileges, while making no useful contribution to their communities, which became increasingly offensive in the eyes of the people.

The Church had also retained feudal privileges; and it was precisely its political alliance with the absolute monarchy that engendered the hatred of the people. It was primarily as a political and not as a religious institution that Christianity had provoked so violent a reaction. And yet, throughout Europe the same feudal rights were in force, and in most countries of the Continent they weighed more heavily than in France. Why, then, did the same feudal rights, which were more oppressive elsewhere, generate in the French people so strong a hostility towards the monarchy, the nobility, and the Church? So we come to the heart of Tocqueville's thesis: paradoxically, it was the relative emancipation of the French cultivator which made him so bitterly resentful of the much lighter feudal prerogatives. If the French peasant had not become a landowner and had remained fully under the lord's control, feudal rights would have seemed quite natural and, therefore, much less onerous. Tocqueville's explanation, then, rests on an analysis of the changing relations of the two classes of rural France, and the consequent social psychology of the peasants who sank their very being into their small parcels of land but who met on every side with the feudal rights to tolls, dues, and taxes which remained in force long after the lords had ceased to fulfill useful obligations, such as protection and the administration of justice. Great hatred and envy thus accumulated in the peasant's heart. Feudalism was now hated more than in its heyday because "the very destruction of some of the institutions of the Middle Ages made those that remained a hundred times more odious" (p. 106).

THE MONARCHY'S CENTRALIZATION OF POWER

In another of his original contributions Tocqueville demonstrates, contrary to prevailing opinion, that the immense concentration of administrative power in France was the creation neither of the Revolution nor of the Napoleonic era, but rather of the monarchy. The power the nobility lost was acquired by the monarchy and its bourgeois officials. The center of power, the Royal Council, Tocqueville observed, "was composed not of great seigniorial lords but of persons of middle-class or even low extraction . . ." (p. 109). This powerful but inconspicuous council, staffed by the bourgeoisie, controlled "everything that had to do with money, that is almost the entire administration of the country . . ." (p. 109). The central power administered either directly or indirectly every aspect of provincial and local life, including public order and even public works of a purely local concern. Thus what had earlier been the lord's obligation to the peasant, contributing to the orderly relationship of the two classes, now came under the authority of the central government. By its expanding encroachment upon the life of the local communities the State not only usurped the lord's traditional functions, thereby undermining his rapport with the peasant, but also increased substantially the fiscal burden upon the people.

Even under the old order the towns continued to govern themselves long after the lords had lost their powers and responsibilities. With time, however, municipal autonomy also succumbed to the central government. In 1692, free elections were abolished by royal edict and the "King now sold to some of the inhabitants of each town the right to govern in perpetuity all the others" (p. 115). In the fifteenth century the *corps de ville,* or executive, was elected by all the townsfolk. By the eighteenth century it was no longer the whole people but an assembly of officials who elected the executive, officials who were neither elected by the people nor in sympathy with them. "These assemblies," Tocqueville notes,

> soon became almost exclusively bourgeois, admitting virtually no artisans. As a result the people, not so easily deceived as one might imagine, ceased to interest themselves in local government and became estranged from the affairs of the commune. (p. 117)

What began as municipal democracy thus degenerated into oligarchy. Parallel to the early municipal autonomy there had also existed a form of village autonomy in the Middle Ages. The villages, however, suffered the same fate and eventually fell under the sway of the central power. By the eighteenth century village autonomy had disappeared and the parish officials had become agents of the royal bureaucracy. By now, not only had the seigniorial lord lost his administrative role in the community, but his privileges alienated him from the rest of its inhabitants. Long before the Revolution the nobility had thus become a "former ruling class" which retained only its titles and privileges. The immense royal bureaucracy, which had developed as a function of the struggle for power, acted quite naturally in gathering unto itself as much power as possible. The bureaucracy in Paris now supervised every detail of provincial and local government. "At least a year would elapse," Tocqueville notes, "before a parish obtained authorization from Paris to repair a church steeple or the priest's house; and more often than not it would take two or three years to honor local requests" (pp. 130–131). When the government recognized this and the justice of the complaints, it nevertheless insisted that all the administrative formalities were indispensable. Tocqueville rejected the bureaucratic ideology in the following terms:

> The administrative functionaries, almost all bourgeois, already formed a class with its own particular spirit and traditions, code of honor and pride. Indeed, this was the new aristocracy of the new and thriving social order which had already formed and waited only for the Revolution to assure it of its place. (p. 132)

The bureaucratic machine, staffed by the bourgeoisie, had already succeeded by the eighteenth century in eliminating all intermediate forms of authority between the centralized State and the individual.

The old order had exhibited contradictory aspects. There appeared to be a growing social and cultural homogeneity between the upper and middle classes: nobleman and bourgeois came very much to resemble each other. This came about as nobles lost their traditional form of wealth to the Third Estate, selling their land "plot by plot to the peasants, retaining only their seigniorial dues which preserved the appearance rather than the reality of their former condition" (p. 145). As for the bourgeois, he not only became wealthier than the noble, his wealth often included substantial tracts of land. And yet, class differences and cleavages became greater than before. While noble and bourgeois appeared to be drawing closer, they were actually drawing apart, with the bourgeoisie growing more and more hostile toward the nobility. To explain this phenomenon, Tocqueville compares and contrasts the French and English social structures. Whereas in France and elsewhere on the Continent feudalism had led to the formation of an aristocracy of birth and blood—a closed and rigid caste—feudalism in England evolved into an open and flexible aristocracy. In England, nobles and commoners had not only joined forces in business and politics, but they also intermarried, which was even more consequential. Tocqueville illustrates the difference between the English and French social structures by showing how the words "gentleman" and "*gentilhomme,*" perhaps of a common origin, were now worlds apart—as far apart as their respective social worlds. The connotation of "gentleman" grew steadily wider in England as classes drew nearer and intermingled. In America, "gentleman" was applicable to all male citizens. The history of the word is thus the history of democracy itself. In France, however,

> the word *gentilhomme* has always remained confined to its primitive meaning. Since the Revolution it has dropped out of usage but has never altered its meaning. The word has been preserved intact to designate the members of a caste because the caste itself is as exclusive today as it has ever been. (pp. 148–149)

Paradoxically, this caste-like tendency became even more pronounced in France after the bourgeoisie had penetrated the noble ranks and taken over much of their wealth. The gulf between these classes grew steadily wider despite the similarities between them. They became not mere rivals, but enemies. The major source of this enmity was the retention of noble privileges; and the privilege most resented was the nobility's exemption from taxes, which became more and more valuable from the fifteenth century on. The value of the tax exemptions to the nobility was as great as the resulting financial burden imposed exclusively on the common people. The taxation policy was an especially flagrant form of class discrimination, stressing class differences and creating a clear line of demarcation between those who gained from the policy and those who suffered from it. Each member of the privileged class saw clearly the real material interest he had in not being confounded with the masses and in remaining firmly set apart from them. The "ennobling of commoners" thus increased class hostility, not because barriers between noble and commoner were insuperable, but because the barriers were always visible and

> once a man crossed them he was cut off from all outside the pale by privileges which were as onerous and humiliating to the commoners as they were profitable and honorific to him. (p. 152)

As the wealth and power of the nobility diminished, resentment and hostility towards it increased. To avoid the dreaded dues and taxes the bourgeoisie fled to the towns where, acting as a unified class, they could reduce the impact of the tax and occasionally escape it altogether. This made for a large number of towns in France but not to any great upsurge in business and industry; for place-hunting in the bureaucracy had become a widespread disease, and the typical bourgeois therefore bought an official post instead of investing his money in an industrial enterprise, as did his English counterpart. While the English aristocracy took upon itself the heaviest public charges in order that it should be allowed to govern, the French nobility retained to the very end its exemption from taxes to console itself, as it were, for having lost control of the government. And the French kings continued to grant tax-exemption privileges to the nobility simply because it was the most effective means of reducing the likelihood of conflict between the nobility and the Crown.

The pre-Revolutionary social structure of France was therefore characterized by interclass estrangement and hostility. The peasant, although something of a landowner and no longer subject to a feudal lord, felt himself to be worse off than before and left behind by the other classes. Most of the wealthy elements, whether noble or bourgeois, had abandoned the countryside while the few who remained, having nothing of the old *noblesse oblige* but retaining their privileges, treated the peasant with the utmost disdain. The peasant, in turn, developed a deep-seated resentment toward all other classes, including the priests who

> by attaching themselves firmly and visibly to the political hierarchy and sharing its privileges, came unavoidably to share the hatred inspired by the temporal elites. (p. 180)

On all sides the peasant was cold-shouldered and looked down upon, while he alone bore the real burdens—taxes, military service and *corvée*. The economic and social advancement which was enriching the upper and middle classes thus drove the peasants to despair. Though formally free and in a small way landowners, they felt themselves more miserable than their forefathers, the serfs (p. 187).

THE PHILOSOPHES

For Tocqueville, then, the reasons why France had moved almost inexorably to the social cataclysm of 1789 could best be understood by analyzing the class relations of the old order. However, another element of the old order had also to be taken into consideration, namely, a group of French intellectuals who were very different from both their English and German counterparts. Although the *Philosophes,* the French men of letters of the eighteenth century, were apparently removed from practical, political issues, they nevertheless probed the foundations of society, often savagely criticizing "its general plan" (p. 193). The *Philosophes* proposed profoundly critical and revolutionary ideals. Their ideas, moreover, far from being confined to intellectual circles, were diffused throughout the society from the highest to the lowest classes, gripping finally the minds of the masses. Under the influence of the *Philosophes* everyone now seemed to be pointing to the unreasonableness of existing institutions while demanding that they be abolished and replaced by new social forms based on the rule of reason and natural laws.

It is not difficult to understand why such radical ideas caught on in France at the time. With the prevailing abuses, the mutual hostility of the classes, the absence on the part of the people of any real participation in politics, the only choices before the Frenchmen seemed to be either to support everything or to destroy the whole system. This general frame of mind was one more consequence of the degeneration of the French nobility into a caste. Having lost their authority, they lost also their ability to guide public opinion. The *Philosophes* therefore filled the gap with ease, and no one challenged them in this role they had taken upon themselves. On the contrary, the nobility regarded the doctrines of these intellectuals which were "most inimical to their privileges and even to their very existence as ingenious *jeux d'esprit*" (p. 196). Neither the nobility nor the Crown, those destined to be the chief victims of the coming democratic upheaval, had any presentiment of it. Even the unfortunate Louis XVI continued to view the nobility as the main enemy of the throne, while believing that the bourgeoisie and the people were his staunchest supporters. The King and the upper classes, having lost touch with the people, had no realization of the people's radical estrangement from the status quo, nor of their determination to seek "the ideal world which the *Philosophes* had constructed" (p. 199).

The people had become equally estranged from religion and the Church owing to its political alignment with the oppressive upper classes. With the decline of religion, the new secular ideals took its place. In effect, the doctrines of the *Philosophes*—fundamentally transforming the entire social order and regenerating the human species—soon became the new worldly faith of the masses. For the first time in history both temporal and religious authorities were attacked and destroyed at once. This Tocqueville attributed not only to the doctrines of the *Philosophes* and to the mood of the masses, but also to the emergence of a new phenomenon: *professional revolutionaries*. Their appearance, Tocqueville cautions his readers, must not be regarded as an isolated or ephemeral development:

> They have formed a new race of men who have perpetuated themselves and have spread out in all countries, everywhere retaining the same characteristics and passions. They were with us then and are still with us today. (p. 208)

PROSPERITY AND THE REVOLUTION

One of Tocqueville's central theses in the Old Regime is that "the reign of Louis XVI was the most prosperous period of the monarchy" and that "this very prosperity hastened the coming of the Revolution" (p. 218). Tocqueville shows that by 1780, the administration, through the Intendants—the bourgeois officials of the royal bureaucracy—concerned itself with increasing the wealth of the provinces by building roads and canals and encouraging trade and industry. Tocqueville also shows that although the laws were just as harsh as earlier, they were applied with leniency, as were the methods of collecting taxes. Concern for the poor was also now greater, as evidenced in the establishment of charity workshops and the allocation of huge sums for poor relief. So again we have a paradox: It was precisely in this period, Tocqueville observes, that discontent seemed to grow. Prosperity appeared to promote unrest. When one looked over the various provinces of the country, one found that where freedom, wealth and reforms were greatest, so was the revolutionary movement. Conversely, where the old regime was firmly entrenched, one witnessed the "fiercest and most prolonged resistance to the Revolution" (p. 223). In spite of the expanding wealth of the bourgeoisie, its relation with its erstwhile ally, the monarchy, was undermined. The monarchy's unlimited budgetary needs were met by borrowing immense sums from the bourgeoisie; but now that the interest on the debt was not paid on time or not paid at all, this class grew more and more indignant. The taste for comfortable living which accompanied the expansion of commerce and industry now made the bourgeoisie's grievances intolerable. Thus it happened that *rentiers,* merchants, manufacturers and financiers lost their patience and became the strongest advocates of reform.

Ironically, it was the upper classes and the monarchy itself that imparted to the masses a revolutionary consciousness. The powerful and privileged elements of the society behaved as if the masses were deaf and dumb. It was those who had the most to fear from the lower classes who employed a highly colored rhetoric to describe the poverty of the people. Thirteen years before the Revolution the King himself sounded like a revolutionary when he described the consequences of *corvée:*

> By forcing the poor man alone to maintain the roads and to give his time and labor without compensation, one is depriving him of the sole means he has of avoiding poverty and hunger and, therefore, compelling him to work for the profit of the rich. (p. 226)

While the *Intendants* denounced the rich "who owe to the labor of the poor all they possess," the King proclaimed:

> His majesty will defend the people against all maneuvers designed to deprive them of the barest necessities by forcing them to work for any wage that the employers see fit to give. The King will not tolerate a situation in which one part of the nation suffers as a consequence of the greed of the other. (p. 227)

And when the King attempted to abolish the restrictions of the guild system, he declared:

> . . . the right to work is a man's most sacred possession and any law that violates this natural right should be considered null and void. The existing trade and craft corporations are artificial and tyrannical institutions, the products of egoism, cupidity and violence. (p. 227)

And Tocqueville observes that the masses soon came to see the disparity between the rhetoric and the practice. Such words were perilous indeed, but especially so as they were uttered in vain; for a few months later both the guilds and *corvée* were reinstated.

Thus trying to convince itself of the expediency of reform, the political elite succeeded in teaching the people that their social superiors were responsible for the evils they were suffering, while the most objectionable features of the system remained intact. Worse, the elite continued to show its contempt for the lower classes. Tocqueville cites the example of Madame Duchatelet, who felt no embarrassment while undressing in the presence of her menservants, being unable to convince herself that valets were real men. In this way the dominant classes conducted themselves with a curious mixture of sympathy and contempt. They themselves exposed the abuses of their rule but continued to rule abusively. They talked of reforms but made none.

This was the great folly of the privileged and powerful who thought they were talking to themselves and that no one else was listening, but who, in actuality, were creating their own grave diggers.

The Revolution was therefore a foregone conclusion. Little tangible had been done by the privileged classes to diminish inequalities or abolish the worst abuses. The nobility retained its privileges to the very end and thus effectively isolated itself. The bourgeoisie became increasingly ambitious and impatient; and the monarchy brought centralization to such an extreme that he who captured Paris could dominate all of France. When, finally, the old order was destroyed, even the most feeble checks on the central bureaucracy were demolished with it. The new, post-Revolutionary State became more absolute than that of any French King; and ultimately, Tocqueville believed, this centralized State was the condition that made despotism possible in France.

What we have, then, in *Democracy in America* and *The Old Regime and the French Revolution* are two classical examples of historical-sociological analysis. We learn much from Tocqueville, both substantively and methodologically.

NOTES

1. These words of the fiery Jacksonian senator, Thomas Hart Benton, are quoted in Arthur M. Schlesinger, Jr., *The Age of Jackson* (Boston: Little, Brown, 1946), p. 125.
2. *Democracy in America*, vol. I, The Henry Reeve text, revised by Frances Bowen, and further corrected and edited with an introduction, editorial notes and bibliographies, by Phillip Bradley (New York: Knopf, 1948) p. 7. (Hereafter, page references to this volume will appear in parentheses immediately following the quoted passage.)
3. Ibid., vol. II, pp. 189–190. (Hereafter, page references to this volume will appear in parentheses immediately following the quoted passage.)
4. Alexis de Tocqueville, *Oeuvres Complètes*, edited by J.P. Mayer, tome II, part I, *L'Ancien Régime et la Revolution* (Paris: Gallimard, 1952). (References to this volume are hereafter indicated by the page number in parentheses immediately following the quoted passage. The translations are mine.)

11

Harriet Martineau (1802–1876)

As a true heir of the Enlightenment, Harriet Martineau promoted the values of that movement throughout her life. Sister of James Martineau, the Unitarian leader, she was a member of the distinguished literary circle which included such luminaries as John Stuart Mill, Thomas Carlyle, and Harriet Taylor who, as we shall see in the next chapter, profoundly influenced Mill's views. Afflicted at the age of 12 with a substantial loss of hearing, Martineau was compelled thereafter to converse with the aid of a large ear trumpet. In a run of additional bad luck, her father, brother, and lover all died before her twenty-fourth birthday, leaving her impoverished and totally dependent for her livelihood on the facility of her pen. She resolved to become a writer and in fact became the first English woman journalist writing for a living under her own name. She began contributing articles to the *Monthly Repository,* the Unitarian journal, in 1821 when she was 19 and by 1832 she had established her reputation with a series of stories illustrating principles of political economy.

Her *Autobiography,* in three volumes, represents only a fraction of her total output, but she is best known to social philosophers and scientists for her superb translation and abridgement of Auguste Comte's *Cours de Philosophie Positive* which appeared in English as *The Positive Philosophy.* However, even before her encounter with Comte, who had coined the term "sociology," Martineau had come to believe that the study of society ought to become a methodologically rigorous discipline in its own right. Martineau's concern with method is evident from the fact that on her way to America in 1834, she produced on shipboard the first draft of *How to Observe Manners and Morals,* a volume instructing travelers how to study foreign cultures. Together with her young traveling companion, Louisa Jeffrey, Martineau departed from Liverpool on August 9, 1834, and after a voyage of 42 days commenced her travels throughout the United States, interviewing key informants. Devoting in this way two intensive years to her studies of the American republic, she sailed for England on August 1, 1836. The fruit of her studies was a major treatise called *Society in America* in which Martineau largely succeeded in gaining some reliable glimpses of the first new nation.

What prompted Martineau to undertake this project was her strong desire to witness firsthand the actual workings of democratic institutions. She preferred and admired democracy, and she was eager to learn whether the people of the United States lived up to their own theory of government and social life. After landing in New York City, she toured New York state, New Jersey, Pennsylvania, Massachusetts, and Maryland. She stayed in Baltimore three weeks and in Washington five. Congress was in session at the time, and she witnessed the proceedings of both houses and of the Supreme Court. She personally met the president, almost every senator and representative, and several Supreme Court members. Indeed, she had prolonged conversations with Chief Justice John Marshall and James Madison. In Virginia she visited with professors at the University of Virginia, founded by Jefferson, and then proceeded to Richmond, where the state legislature was in session. A long wintry journey took her through North and South Carolina and then to Georgia, Alabama, and Louisiana. After ten days in New Orleans, she went up the Mississippi and Ohio Rivers to the mouth of the Cumberland River and ascended to Nashville, Tennessee. She spent three weeks in Lexington, Kentucky, and then descended the Ohio River to Cincinnati. Another steamboat trip on the Ohio took her back to Virginia. She returned to New York City in mid-July 1835. She spent the autumn in New England and then turning west, she toured Niagara, Detroit, Chicago, and Cleveland. Her final journey took her through the interior of Ohio and then through Pennsylvania to New York.

In the course of this tour, Martineau visited almost every type of institution: prisons, insane asylums, hospitals, literary and scientific associations, the factories of the North, the plantations of the South, and the farms of the West. She lived in the palatial residences of the well-to-do and in log cabins and farm houses. She traveled in wagons, stagecoaches and on horseback, and in the best and worst of the steamboats. She witnessed the weddings and christenings of the rich and the country festivals of the poor. She was present at orations, land sales, and the slave market. She met personally nearly every eminent person in politics, science, and literature, and members of the many diverse religious denominations. She held lengthy interviews with farmers, merchants, lawyers, clergymen, professors, mechanics, abolitionists, and colonizationists. She visited several tribes of the native peoples and spent months in the Southern states where she addressed challenging questions to the slaveholders while observing carefully the condition of the black slaves. In a word, Martineau's impressions were based on an extraordinarily wide range of experiences and encounters with all elements of American society of the time.[1]

POLITICS

Martineau agreed with Madison that the United States was proving things that had long been regarded as impossible. Foreign skeptics and critics had asserted that it was still early in the life of the new republic and that the experiment would yet fail. For Martineau, however, as for Tocqueville, the American republic had demonstrated that a people can govern itself. The American people had in fact done so for a half century, and there was no sign anywhere on the horizon that they would fail to do so in the future. This suggested the sound principle that humanity is capable, in the right circumstances, of self-government. If earlier theories of government often assumed that human selfishness precluded self-government by the people, the new republic effectively refuted such views, replacing them with the immortal words of the Declaration of Independence:

> that all men are created equal; that they are endowed by their Creator with certain inalienable rights; that among them are life, liberty, and the pursuit of happiness; that to secure those rights, governments are instituted among men, deriving their just powers from the consent of the governed.

Martineau agreed that the Declaration of Independence embodied the great and timeless principles of universal justice—principles implicit in the Golden Rule; but, as we shall see in due course, she also recognized, as did Tocqueville, that those principles were blatantly contradicted by the institution of slavery.

Martineau also recognized that notwithstanding the commitment to equality, the new republic was not a classless society. In the United States there were two parties which she dubbed, respectively, the aristocratic and the democratic. Although America truly allowed an unprecedentedly high degree of equality of opportunity in the free states, even egalitarian America was divided by classes. On the one side were those who had gained considerable wealth, whose hopes were largely fulfilled and who feared the loss of their fortunes through political change. They were naturally the aristocratic class. Allied with them were the men of learning who, mistakenly equating learning with wisdom, feared the ascendancy of the uneducated multitude. Men of talent also feared that where the majoritarian principle prevailed, merit would be neither recognized nor rewarded. To the wealthy, learned, and talented, Martineau added many other individuals who out of ignorance and prejudice despised the multitude and dreaded yielding to them.

On the other side there existed the larger class consisting of the hopeful and rising, but not yet risen. This class comprised all those citizens who had the most to gain and the least to lose. They were the "people"—those who gained their knowledge from actual life, not from books. They were the artisans, the craftsmen, the unskilled workers, and the poor farmers who supported the Democratic party, which had made appreciable gains under the Constitution. The gains were so substantial that, as Martineau remarked, it is no wonder that there is panic in many aristocratic hearts, "and that I heard from so many tongues of the desolations of the 'levelling spirit,' and the approaching ruin of political institutions"(63). Another way to distinguish the two classes, Martineau suggests, is found in Jefferson's description of the Federal and Republican parties of 1799 which, in her opinion, applied equally to the Federal and Democratic parties of the Jacksonian era. One party, said Jefferson, "fears most the ignorance of the people, the other, the selfishness of rulers independent of them." Like Tocqueville, however, Martineau recognized that the class divisions of the new republic bore no real resemblance to the class divisions of the old countries. In the New World there was no massive, degraded, injured, and politically dangerous white class. Even the poorer citizens of the United States evinced as strong an interest in the security of property as the richest merchant of Salem, or planter of Louisiana. Law and order were as important to the family holding a small plot of land for subsistence, or to the wage earner hoping to acquire land of his own, as to the wealthier members of society.

In these terms America was different and exceptional. From the time of her arrival to the time of her departure, Martineau was in a state of awe at the prevalance of practical energy, intelligence, and competence and the absence of abject poverty and gross ignorance. Strikingly absent too, as compared with the Old World, was any sign of servility on the part of employees and insolence on the part of employers. Every man in the towns conducted himself as a thoughtful, free citizen, and every man in the countryside seemed to own a small plot of his own. Even villages had their newspapers, and factories had their libraries. Public debates between candidates for office addressed real, substantive issues, and the people seemed well enough informed to judge the merits of the respective arguments. With the contrasting conditions of her homeland in mind, Martineau could not but be impressed with the evidence of prosperity in the comfortable homesteads which every turn of the road brought into view.

And yet, poverty did, of course, exist. Paupers could occasionally be seen in both towns and the countryside. And at the opposite pole were the very rich who flaunted their wealth. Given such divisions between the well-to-do on the one side and the working people and small farmers on the other, it came as no surprise to Martineau that the central political issues in

Jacksonian America were so often framed as a struggle between aristocracy and democracy. She frequently heard that the grand question of the time was whether the people should be encouraged to govern themselves, or whether the rich, who were presumably also the wise, should save the people from themselves. The wealthy and privileged, fearing the people, looked upon the "will of the majority" as a basic "flaw" of the new republic. The democrats recognized that rulers in general are prone to use their power for selfish purposes, and the aristocrats feared that the people would overtax the rich. Democracy implied a government by the people; aristocracy implied a government of the rich. The central political issue, then, was whether the people or the large property holders should govern.

Southern planters, blind to the fundamental flaw of their own social system, had sanctimoniously remarked to Martineau that it was the destiny of their Northern fellow citizens to be subjected to an unending struggle between pauperism and property. Northern citizens replied effectively, however, that a perpetual struggle between pauperism and property exists everywhere. The important question is: Which succeeds? In the old countries, property succeeds. Indeed, it most often becomes despotic. In America, however, both the people and the wealthy succeed. Paupers characteristically rise out of poverty, and proprietors keep what they have. The people recognize that it is shorter and easier to obtain property by enterprise and labor than by pulling down the wealthy. Martineau observed that even those of her well-to-do Northern informants who were most fearful of the possible excesses of the people felt no urgency. One such informant predicted that in 30 years his children would be living under a popular despotism. When Martineau asked him why he did not therefore emigrate, he replied: "Where could I be better off?" (70). This reply further confirmed Martineau's strong impression that the new republic promised and delivered better material conditions than one could expect elsewhere. The fact that so many citizens of the free states possessed moderate property, constituting a great middle class, as it were, suggested to Martineau that neither revolution nor despotism were real potential threats to the American republic. The extremes of great wealth and pauperism existing in America at the time were numerically negligible in proportion to the rest of the populace and, hence, too insignificant to destabilize the political system.

In the free states, then, Martineau foresaw no fundamental political crisis. She did, however, discern a disparity between the theory and practice of republican government in one important respect. The great theory of the democratic republic is that the majority not only wills the best measures but also chooses the best men to represent it. This, Martineau believed, was far from true in practice. The Golden Age of the Revolutionary period had raised up leaders and public servants of a truly extraordinary stature. The Revolutionary era seemed to have inspired the people with a romantic faith in men who professed a strong attachment to the high ideals of the republic.

From Martineau's observation of the workings of the political system and from her many discussions of the subject with a wide range of informants, she arrived at the view that from the time of the Revolution to the time of her stay in America, it was the Federal party that had furnished a far superior set of men to the public service than the Democratic party. There seemed to be a shortage of honest and able friends of the people willing to serve them. The people thus faced a dilemma: They had to take either a somewhat better sort of men whose politics they disapproved, or a somewhat worse sort of men whose politics they approved. Given this dilemma, the people treated politicians as temporary and disposable tools. The people used the tool and then threw it away as the politician's lack of ability or corrupt practices became known. On balance, however, Martineau regarded this as a not too serious problem, since American democracy had a self-correcting capability. Corrupt practices and factions were discovered sooner or later, and the people pulled down the betrayer of public trust and replaced him with another. And even if the people were fooled again, and the replacement were no better than his predecessor, this was a rectifiable condition. For it was generally recognized, that if the people were deceived, it was out of naiveté or ignorance, and ignorance was a temporary evil which could be overcome through education. As the citizenry becomes more educated, vigilant, and active, it is bound to gain a more effective control over its public servants. America, Martineau appreciated, cherished a high democratic hope and a profound respect for the basic principle, that its "rulers derive their just powers from the consent of the governed." And it was this hope and respect which contrasted so sharply with certain societies of the Old World in which the people were despised.

MORALITY AND POLITICS

For all her praise of the American republic and her appreciation of its strengths and virtues, Martineau was fully aware that a democratic republic half slave and half free is a contradiction in terms. Like Tocqueville, she anticipated that this contradiction would eventually lead to civil strife of crisis proportions; but she also discerned the threat to freedom and the attendant moral corruption that the institution of slavery caused not only in the Southern states but in the Northern free states as well. It came as no surprise to Martineau that Southern newspapers took no notice of the outrages perpetrated against blacks by mobs. Two men had been burned alive in Mobile, and no newspaper even alluded to the event until many months later when a Northern publication treated it as a matter of hearsay in a brief and obscure paragraph. Similarly, several months before Martineau's departure from the United States, a black man was burned alive in St. Louis, with a large crowd of "respectable" people standing by. The majority of the state's newspaper editors implicated themselves in the responsibility for this outrage by refusing, out of fear or other motives, to condemn it. Martineau was informed that the newspaper men of St. Louis dared not give conspicuous coverage to the event for fear of retaliation by the murderers. The journalists merely made brief reference to the deed as something to be regretted. They had hoped that the newspapers throughout the Union would give due attention to the deed and generate a movement demanding that the murderers be brought to justice. But the newspapers of the North also refrained from commenting at length on the outrage. They saw the example of the St. Louis editors, and also feared reprisals if they were to headline the crime and bring it to the attention of the wide public.

Martineau also observed a striking difference between the mobs of Europe and those of the United States. Several notorious mobbing events had occurred: abolitionist riots in New York, Boston, and Cincinnati; the burning of a convent in Charleston and also of the mails in that city; bank riots in Baltimore; hangings by lynch-law at Vicksburg; and the burning of black men. In Europe, Martineau observes, mobs and riots are typically an expression of the exasperated misery of workers and impoverished peasants rebelling against oppression and insults to their humanity. When, therefore, Europeans read about mobbing in the United States, they naturally assume that there, too, it is the poor who create the social disturbances and the gentry is their target. In fact, however, the opposite was true in the United States: the Boston mob was wholly composed of gentlemen of social status. The only working man in it was a trucker who saved the victim. It was the gentlemen of St. Louis who burned the black man, and who forcibly ejected the students of Marion College; it was the gentlemen of Cincinnati who rioted against the abolitionists; it was the judges and gentlemen of Vicksburg who lynched vagrants, gamblers, and slaves in a long row; it was the gentlemen of Charleston who broke open the post office and burned the mails.

Martineau also observed how Northerners were becoming morally compromised where the issue of slavery was concerned. Merchants and professional men of Boston and other New England cities were fond of Charleston because of their commercial relations. This fondness was carried to such an extreme that it threatened the liberties of some of the leading citizens of the Northern cities. They learned that their brothers were dismissed from pastoral posts, their sons expelled from colleges, their friends excluded from professorships, and they themselves were ostracized if they expressed opinions critical of the "peculiar institution." Citizens of Boston encountered persecutions of almost every conceivable kind for having formed associations to oppose the institution which violated the first principles of morality and justice. There was, of course, no law in Massachusetts abridging the expression of opinion on moral and political subjects. But Martineau heard many regrets at the absence of such a law, and, indeed, no effort was spared to compensate for the absence. Persons writing to oppose slavery were so thoroughly denounced that people feared to purchase their books; clergymen holding abolitionist views were no longer invited to preach; proprietors of public rooms would not rent them out to members of abolitionist associations; even churches were closed to them; abolitionist notices of public meetings were torn in the pulpits; and newspapers poured contempt upon the abolitionist movement unrelentingly.

Martineau, who long before her arrival in the United States had been a staunch abolitionist, provides an example of how she herself was temporarily taken in by the antiabolitionist propaganda. Often she had been told in the South that the abolitionists of Boston and New York continually distributed incendiary tracts among the slaves, inciting them to rebellion. At first she never questioned the allegation, although she had never seen any such tracts nor met anyone who had. Nor at first had it occurred to her that such tracts would be utterly useless since slaves were never taught to read. She heard the allegation from every slaveholder and Southern merchant, and also from such notables as Madison, Clay, and Calhoun. However, Martineau soon discovered that the charge was wholly groundless. No abolitionist association of Boston or New York had ever sent any antislavery literature south of Washington, except for certain circulars addressed to public officers of several Southern states. The circulars, moreover, were burnt at Charleston immediately upon arrival.

No effort was spared to prevent the abolitionists from being heard. They were denied by the municipal authority the use of Faneuil Hall, called in memory of the Revolutionary era, the "Cradle of Liberty." Certain influential merchants and lawyers had organized a meeting there in August 1835. Acting upon the misleading information of Southern propaganda, the assembled approved the principles of the abolitionists but denounced their so-called incendiary measures. Martineau recognized that whenever such meetings took place they were the prelude to violence. Meetings held in support of the abolitionist movement were invariably followed by mobbing and rioting. And ironically, it was the abolitionists, not the mobs, who were blamed for the violence and warned, that if they continued to meet publicly, they would be held responsible for any disorders that might ensue. The abolitionists correctly viewed this warning as an abridgement of their fundamental civil liberties—freedom of speech and freedom of assembly. They therefore resolved that threats of illegal violence would not deter them from meeting publicly and conducting their business.

Women played a central role in carrying out this policy. Martineau describes in detail the events she herself had witnessed. On October 21, 1835 the women met at their association office. Anticipating trouble, and planning, therefore, to arrive three quarters of an hour early, 25 women got there safely. A crowd had already begun to gather outside, and 5 more women made their way to the hall with difficulty, but 100 more prospective participants were turned back by the mob. Due to advance publicity, the crowd, consisting exclusively of "gentlemen," knew that the well-known English, antislavery orator George Thompson was to address the meeting. He, however, was forewarned that a monetary reward was being offered to anyone who would apprehend him and bring him to the tar kettle before dark. Thompson had a narrow escape. The women themselves had been warned that if they showed themselves on their own premises that day, they were liable to be severely injured or killed. When they asked for police protection, the city marshall replied that they were a troublesome lot. The meeting of the women began, as usual, with a prayer, but they were surrounded by a growing mob of howling men, some of whom hurled missiles at the woman presiding. Soon the partition yielded to the pressure of the crowd, and the mayor himself arrived urging the women to go home to save their lives.

The women did in fact leave and headed for the home of one of their members, where they learned the shocking news that William Lloyd Garrison—the chief apostle of abolition in the United States—had fallen into the hands of the mob. Like Thompson, Garrison had come to the meeting prepared to address the women but was turned down out of concern for his safety and urged to leave the premises immediately. However, having remained in the house when the women left it, he was hunted down by the mob, bound with a rope and dragged through the streets as brickbats were hurled at his head. He was saved by the trucker mentioned earlier, who had made his way into the crowd as if to attack the victim, but who actually protected Garrison's head and ushered him into a coach. Unrelenting, the mob tried to upset the coach, but with the help of police Garrison was safely lodged in jail for his own protection. When Martineau later asked certain respectable persons why there were such violent reactions to the meetings of the abolitionists, she was told there was no mob: They were all gentlemen dressed in fine broadcloth. Even those who acknowledged that the violent mob actions had taken place refused to prosecute the leaders and main offenders. When Martineau asked a prominent judge why the offenders were not being prosecuted for breach of the peace and the assault on Garrison, he replied that he had advised against it, because the "feeling was so strong against the abolitionists,—the rioters were so respectable in the city,—it was better to let the whole affair pass over without notice"(116).

As an ardent representative of the antislavery cause long before she had arrived in the United States, Martineau was naturally sympathetic to the American antislavery movement. But it took her a while to understand the concrete circumstances which divided the movement in the North and which even engendered extreme hostility toward individuals like William Lloyd Garrison. Garrison began his antislavery career by assisting in the edition of *The Genius of Universal Emancipation,* for which he was thrown into jail for libel. When he was released with the financial help of a friend, he founded the *Liberator* in 1831. The language of this journal was so violent that Garrison effectively alienated himself from other antislavery enthusiasts. He was distrusted as a leader and had only a small personal following. With a subscription list of only about 400 white individuals, but many free blacks, Garrison became the symbol of antislavery and the target of proslavery attacks. Thwarted more and more by opposition within the ranks of the antislavery movement, Garrison adopted additional unorthodox causes—feminism, anticlericalism, anarchism—thus further estranging himself from the mainstream and earning the reputation among the general public as one who undermined his own cause. But his friends and followers viewed him differently. They knew that the harshness of his language was derived from his "righteous absolutes of faith, never from vindictiveness. . . . For all his 'I-ness'—his obsessive self-importance—Garrison was truly what his followers believed him to be, the embodiment of devotion to a cause."[2] As R.K. Webb remarks, "And those were precisely the qualities which committed Miss Martineau to his service. With her lively admiration of martyrs for principle, she could not easily forget that Garrison had been dragged through the streets in 1835 by a Boston mob."[3]

When Martineau visited the South, she deliberately fostered a courteous demeanor. Her antislavery views were known there, and she worked hard at trying to understand the Southern planters as they understood themselves. She was determined to educate herself where their attitudes were concerned. She soon learned that "opposition to slavery and support of the abolitionists—a term which meant Garrison to the enraged South—were not the same thing. Miss Martineau's tact in questioning brought such a unanimity of response on the latter subject that she assumed that Garrison and the abolitionists were an unfortunate and retarding influence."[4]

As we shall see, Martineau provides a penetrating analysis of the consequences of slavery, but she also gives us a clear view of the life conditions of free blacks in the North. Although she was assured by some of the notables of New England that black American citizens were perfectly well treated, she soon learned that racial segregation and discrimination were facts of life in the North. Worse, even segregated black schools were not tolerated in New England, where they were often closed down. Blacks were forbidden to frequent restaurants where they might eat with their fellow white citizens; they were assigned to separate galleries in the churches; they were excluded from colleges, from municipal office, from the liberal professions, and from scientific and literary associations. In a word, they were excluded from all areas of society except the menial and servile.

SOCIOLOGY OF SLAVERY

By the time of Martineau's visit to the United States, the indentured servitude of white immigrants had been abolished, and the introduction of any form of servitude had been prohibited in the Northern and Western regions of the country. The institution of slavery was therefore confined to 13 Southern states that grew tobacco, rice, cotton, and sugar. The slave population at the time numbered two-and-a-half million. Some states, possessing more slave labor than their exhausted soils required, sold to those which suffered from a shortage of labor for their still rich soils. The agricultural economy of Virginia, for example, being in a depressed condition, found that its chief source of revenue was the rearing of slaves as stock to be sent to Alabama, Mississippi, and Louisiana. Martineau observed how work had acquired a moral significance in the North and, in contrast, how work and labor had become stigmatized among the whites of the slave states. In the North, children learned to work early and were taught the dignity of labor. Youths worked hard not only for their daily bread, but also for their future. Whether they aspired to the liberal professions, to business, manufacturing, or farming, they had to provide for themselves. Typically, there was much manual labor in the country colleges, and many a successful man had spent his boyhood and youth doing the numerous, daily manual chores, without which their families could not have sustained themselves.

In the slave states, there were two classes, the servile and the imperious. The fundamental, white moral value of the slave system was that labor is demeaning and disgraceful. Very young children were indoctrinated with this view, so much so that they considered it a loss of honor to do the basic chores for themselves. Martineau heard utterances of the following kind: "Do you think *I* shall work?" "O, you must not touch the poker here." "You must not do those things for yourself. . . it won't do for a lady to do so." "Poor thing! She has to teach: If she had come here, she might have married a rich man, perhaps." "Mamma has so much a year now, so we have not to do our work at home, or any trouble. 'Tis such a comfort!'"(217). Children grow up pitying all white folks who have to work and dreading the degraded status that a life of manual labor would bring upon them. One result of this value system was to produce a degraded class among the whites themselves, those who had come to be called "mean whites," signifying whites who worked with their hands. Martineau aptly remarked in this regard that where there is a black servile class, whose color has become a stigma due to their servitude, two consequences are unavoidable: Those who have the color without the servitude are despised by the whites; and those who have the servitude without the color are despised among the blacks.

For Martineau, the primary characteristic of a slave system is injustice. It is an illusion to suppose that there can be justice where a society is divided into two classes: Those who command and those who serve. Where there is no justice, Martineau asks, what other social virtues are possible? Mercy, she replies, is the most obvious. The affection that slaveholders often showed for their slaves was a form of mercy, which the slaveholders mistakenly regarded as an adequate substitute for justice. Being merciful, patient, and indulgent, the imperious masters pleaded that those virtues make their society a good and just one. The masters, moreover, berated their intractable slaves for failing to appreciate the treatment they received at the hands of the virtuous masters. Martineau's informants often found it difficult to see the gross fallacy of their outlook. She became weary of explaining that indulgence can never atone for injury: "that the extremest pampering, for a life-time, is no equivalent for rights withheld, no reparation for irreparable injustice"(221).

Nor did the corrupting and destructive influence of slavery on the planter's own family escape Martineau's attention. Every white master had his own harem; and since the law stipulated that the children of slaves were to follow the fortunes of the mother, there was the widespread practice of planters selling and bequeathing their own children. The Quadroon girls of New Orleans, for instance, were brought up by their mothers to be what the white male masters had made of them: the mistresses of white gentlemen. When the offspring of the planters' black mistresses were boys, they were sent to France for illicit sexual purposes or sold on the slave market. The girls were educated to be refined, attractive, and accomplished; and every white young planter or wealthy merchant selected one and established her in one of those pretty and peculiar houses, whole rows of which could be seen in the city and its environs. The liaison often lasted for life or for several years. When the time came for the man to take a white wife, he apprised his Quadroon partner of the news she had dreaded, either by means of a letter transferring to her ownership of the house and furniture, or by a newspaper announcement of his marriage. Abandoned Quadroon ladies rarely formed a second relationship. Many, Martineau learned, committed suicide, and many more died broken hearted. Frequently, however, men continued the relationship clandestinely after marriage. Every Quadroon woman lived in the hope that her partner would prove an exception, and remain loyal to her; and every white lady believed that her husband was an exception, who would take no mistress. Fairly typical, then, was the state of affairs in which every white man had two sexual relationships, one of which had to be concealed, and two families, the existence of which had to be hidden from one another.

Conjugal relations between white masters and black slave women were not uncommon on the plantations themselves. Female slaves were reared on certain estates where the object was to produce them for the slave market. This led to a licentiousness which prompted the wife of a planter to acknowledge bitterly that a planter's wife was only "the chief slave of the harem." James Madison informed Martineau that the licentious practices in many Virginian plantations "stopped just short of destruction; and that it was understood that female slaves were to become mothers at fifteen"(226). The new laws enacted to make the emancipation of slaves more difficult were a direct response to the widespread relations between white masters and their female slaves. The prevalence of such relations introduced a category of mulattos so numerous that if their white parents had been permitted, out of affection, to set them free, that would have made a dangerous breach in the slave system. The law therefore prohibited their emancipation while permitting their sale. Martineau remarks sardonically, that it was the very same planters who engaged in sexual relations with their female slaves and who sold their offspring to fill their purses, who falsely accused the Northern abolitionists of wanting to mix the races.

The slave system inevitably bred a mutual hatred between the planter and his slaves, a hatred that led to the perpetration of savage violence against them. During her stay in the United States, Martineau knew of the burning alive of four black men and other heinous crimes. For Martineau, the cause of such unspeakable crimes lay not only in the general oppressiveness of the system, but also in the licentiousness of the masters. The black man's resentment rose to a very high pitch at being deprived of his wife—at being sent out of the way so his master could take possession of her. Often, therefore, black men sought revenge in violent acts and thus became objects of vengeance in return and destined for a cruel fate. Martineau had no doubt that much of the blacks' intense resentment flowed naturally from their subjection to toil and the lash, but she also recognized that the sexual exploitation of black women by white masters was the proximate cause of the mutual hatred between the planters and their slaves. Martineau recognized, however, that black resentment was not likely to produce insurrection: The slaves were too scattered to act in concert, and the planters had total control of the most effective means of violence.

The "mind" or ideology of the South suggested to Martineau that the planters as a class failed to grasp realistically the nature of their relationship with the slaves. She relates that a Southern acquaintance was conveying all kinds of information about her family's slaves, in the field and in the house, and self-righteously asserting that she fed, clothed, and indulged them. While the conversation was taking place, one of the female house slaves passed by and Martineau remarked that she appeared superior to the others, and the acquaintance agreed. Martineau then asked, whether she was A's wife and the acquaintance replied that they call her A's wife, but the couple had never actually married. They had approached the planter some five years earlier requesting permission to marry, but the planter refused because he had not made up his mind whether or not to sell A. The couple now had four children, and the planter still refused to let them marry because, although he would never have sold her, he was still undecided about selling A.

Another example of an unconscious, self-justification of the planters' ways: A Southern lady owned a pretty mulatto girl whom she claimed she was very fond of. A young man came to visit and soon fell in love with the girl but was not allowed to court her. He went away disappointed, but returned weeks later saying he was so in love with the girl that he could not live without her. "I pitied the young man," concluded the lady, "so I sold the girl to him for 1500 dollars"(230). The hypocritical brand of religion with which the whites attempted to indoctrinate the blacks also evoked

Martineau's contempt. A liberal Southern minister preached a sermon on the text, "cast all your care upon him, for He careth for you." Martineau was present when the minister, pointing to the gallery where the blacks sat segregated from the rest of the congregants, stated: "He cares for that colored person as well as for the wisest and best of you whites." And Martineau comments that this "was the most wanton insult I had ever seen offered to a human being . . . yet no one present to whom I afterwards spoke of it seemed able to comprehend the wrong. 'Well!' said they: 'does not God care for the colored people?' Of course, in a society where things like these are said and done by its choicest members, there is a prevalent unconsciousness of the existing wrong"(230).

THE POLITICAL CONDITION OF WOMEN

It is a fundamental principle of the Declaration of Independence that the government of the American republic derives its just powers from the consent of the governed. How, then, Martineau asks, can the political condition of American women be reconciled with that principle? Government had the power to tax women who owned property, to divorce women from their husbands, and to fine, imprison, and even execute them for certain crimes. Why should women obey laws to which they have never given their consent? What Martineau found particularly disgraceful in this regard was that some of the most distinguished liberal-democratic writers on government advocated, in effect, a despotic rule over women. Jefferson, for example, in his *Correspondence* (vol. IV, p. 295), excluded from full citizenship in a democracy infants, women, and slaves. And James Mill, in his *Essays on Government,* excluded women on the ground that their interests were adequately represented by their fathers and husbands.

In response, Martineau asks why women should be denied the authority to represent their own interests. It is a sure sign, she avers, that a society is lacking in justice when one-half rules the other on the cynical principle, "might is right." Indeed, Martineau discerned certain parallels between the status of women and the status of slaves. Women were given indulgence instead of justice. On public occasions and in literature, men sang the praise of women, motherhood, and the home. But at the same time men deliberately excluded women from all of the most significant spheres of economic, cultural, and political life. Because women were denied the education required for participation in those spheres, their intellectual and other creative capacities remained undeveloped. The result: Philosophy, science, art, and musical composition were the exclusive domains of men. Literature stood out as an exception, as a realm in which women had in fact demonstrated greatness, for women could write in the privacy of their homes. In order to write they had no need to break into a professional guild or into some other exclusive, male association. Even there, however, male prejudice against women writers was such that they occasionally resorted to masculine pseudonyms (e.g., George Eliot and George Sand).

On the other hand, Martineau acknowledged that notwithstanding the sexual inequalities of American society, women enjoyed certain advantages there as compared with the status of women in the Old World. America was exceptional in that true love ran smoother there. Marriage in America was more universal, safe, tranquil, and fortunate than, say, in Britain—more universal owing to the general prosperity of the country; safer owing to the greater freedom of divorce and the protection this affords women against abuse; more tranquil and fortunate owing to several additional circumstances: Marriage vows were absolutely reciprocal; property arrangements were generally more favorable to the wife; and the wife was not made, in effect, the property of her husband as she was in Britain. But while Martineau readily acknowledged the advantages of American women, she stressed that they would remain victims of injustice as long as they were subjected to systematic subordination. The emancipation of any class, Martineau averred, takes place primarily through the efforts of the individuals of that class; and so it would have to be with women too. Martineau confidently anticipated that as women gained consciousness of the many ways in which their sex is subordinated, they would come to exert a moral and political power strong enough to burst the bonds of their subjection (307).

NOTES

1. The present discussion is based on Harriet Martineau, *Society in America*, edited with an Introduction by S.M. Lipset, (Garden City, N.Y.: Anchor Books, 1962.) (All quotations from this volume will be indicated by the page number in parentheses immediately following the cited passage.)

   For biographical information I have relied on Martineau's *Autobiography*, ed. by Maria Weston Chapman, 3 vols. (Boston: James R. Osgood and Company, 1877.) See also R.K. Webb, *Harriet Martineau: A Radical Victorian*, (London: Heinemann, 1960).
2. See Webb, p. 153, where he cites G.H. Barnes.
3. Ibid.
4. Ibid., p. 154.

12

Harriet Taylor
(1807–1858)
and
John Stuart Mill
(1806–1873)

In his *Autobiography*, John Stuart Mill drew a literary portrait of the woman who eventually became his wife. He described Harriet Taylor's extraordinary intellectual gifts and credited her with having made a major contribution to his own scholarly work. When Mill wrote his high praise of Taylor after her death, many readers of the *Autobiography* discounted much of what he had to say about her as kind and gracious hyperbole, an exaggerated tribute to the great love of his life. F.A. Hayek, however, was among the first to recognize that there was no exaggeration in Mill's portrait and that Harriet Taylor may properly be regarded as one of the major figures who shaped the thinking of the later Victorian era. Indeed, after studying the available evidence, Hayek proposed that Taylor's influence on Mill's thought and outlook was quite as great as he had asserted, but that the influence was somewhat different from the common view. Far from the influence having been sentimental, Hayek concluded, "it was the rationalist element in Mill's thought which was mainly strengthened by her influence."[1] Hayek acknowledged that even before he had recognized the true nature of her influence, a Swedish writer, Knut Hagberg, had correctly discerned her impact. "It is obvious," wrote Hagberg, "that it was this woman who made him [Mill] into a radical rationalist. She gave the impress of her personality to all his greater works; to all her opinions Mill gave the form of philosophic maxims."[2] To understand the intellectual product of the Taylor-Mill relationship, we need to review aspects of their respective biographies and the circumstances in which they intertwined.

Born Harriet Hardy, the daughter of a surgeon, she was one of seven children. It was perhaps her less than happy home life which drove her into early marriage in 1826 with John Taylor, a prosperous wholesale druggist. Both families were Unitarians and Dissenters. In addition to their common religio-moral background, the couple shared a liberal political outlook. Their hospitable doors were always open to the many foreign refugees who sought asylum from tyranny in London. The Unitarians, in contrast to the other principal Dissenting sects, were almost entirely free from bigotry. Drawing their membership largely from the scientific professions, they lived on a more intellectual level than the others, evincing a rational, individualistic, unregimented outlook.

At the time of Harriet's marriage, William John Fox was the most prominent of the Unitarians. Unimpressive in appearance, he nevertheless possessed a most unusual gift for preaching—a soft and melodious but compelling voice. Characteristically, Fox's interests were more worldly than divine. Aware that the written word diffused far more widely than the spoken among the literate classes to whom the Unitarian faith appealed, he sought to enlarge his flock more as a journalist than as a clergyman. For years he had contributed faithfully to the existing Unitarian organ, the *Monthly Repository*. Then, as he became dissatisfied with its parochial flavor, he bought the journal and sought to introduce articles of a more general interest by well-known writers and thus bring the Unitarian gospel into the homes of the educated and open-minded. The *Repository* came into his hands in 1831, but even earlier he had already attracted a small and intimate circle of personal devotees. Introduced to this circle on her marriage in 1826, Harriet lived and moved among its members almost exclusively until she met Mill four years later. From a literary point of view, Harriet Martineau was a leading member of the group. As we noted in the preceding chapter, she became the first woman journalist writing for a living under her own name. She had written for the *Repository* since 1821, when she was 19 and her first essays had been accepted.

In the spring or summer of 1830, as soon as Harriet Taylor had recovered from the birth of her second son, she went to Fox and told him that she was perplexed by a number of philosophical problems, and that since her husband lacked intellectual competence in such matters, she had no one with whom to discuss them. At that point Fox resolved to introduce her to John Mill, a well-known Radical, rightly suspected of free-thinking tendencies. During the first quarter of the nineteenth century the Dissenters and the Radicals had drawn closer, and the Unitarians were becoming linked with the Utilitarians. Fox had known the Mills personally for several years, and the Mills and Taylors were old acquaintances. And so it came about that Mill, escorted by two friends, went to dine with Harriet and John Taylor in their home. Also present at the dinner party were Fox himself and Harriet Martineau. Mill found he had much in common with the Taylors. He shared John Taylor's sympathy and enthusiasm for aiding political refugees; and he formed a warm sentiment for Harriet Taylor that certainly went beyond their common intellectual interests, though he immediately recognized the superior capacities of her mind.

Harriet, for her part, found Mill a first-rate teacher who would help her realize her great ambition of becoming a writer like Harriet Martineau. Mill advised her constantly, and in May 1832, soon after the birth of her third child, Helen, Harriet's reviews, poems and articles began to flow regularly into the *Monthly Repository*. At about the same time Mill composed for the *Repository* his first article, "Genius," a powerful plea for originality that looked longingly back to the glories of Athenian democracy. The Greeks, he said, considered wisdom a political instrument of daily life available to all. Hence, the aim of their education was *how* to think, not what to think. Socrates laid down no dogma but rather gave us a method by which to develop a clear-thinking mind. In contrast, Mill sadly observed, modern education was a matter of cramming ready-made "truths" into the heads of the multitude. With such practices, Mill argued, there was little likelihood of producing mental giants and creative geniuses. This view of modern democracy, as tending in some circumstances to produce mediocrity, was quite different from the views Mill had held before, and it is almost certain that Mill's new view was the elaboration of a principle stated by Harriet in a paper written at the time but never published. In that paper Harriet had exposed the dangers of social conformity, thus anticipating the danger Tocqueville later called a "tyranny of the majority." In a similar vein Harriet Taylor had written that

> whether it be religious conformity, political conformity, moral conformity or social conformity, no matter what the species, the spirit is the same: All kinds agree on this one point, of hostility to individual character . . . . What is called the opinion of society is . . . a combination of the many weak, against the few strong: an association of the mentally listless to punish any manifestation of mental independence. The remedy is, to make all strong enough to stand alone; and whoever has once known the pleasure of self-dependence, will be in no danger of relapsing into subserviency.[3]

It is clear that just as Harriet Taylor's fragment on marriage had inspired Mill's great essay on *The Subjection of Women*, her article on conformity, calling for a toleration of diversity, provided the leading ideas of Mill's other great essay, *On Liberty*. Indeed, Mill gave Taylor full credit for her contribution to both great works, maintaining that both works should be regarded as products of their joint effort and collaboration. If there were two missions in the lives of Taylor and Mill, they were the emancipation of women and the enhancement of liberty for all. How to free the many without repressing the extraordinary few was the central moral, intellectual, and political question throughout the 28 years of the Taylor-Mill union. And the main elements of the two missions were outlined during the first two years of their friendship.

When Mill completed the first draft of his *Political Economy*, he spent from March to December 1847 rewriting it. Harriet took a keen interest in his revision, scrutinizing every line. Although she favored the socialist form of society as an ideal, she agreed with Mill's assessment of socialism as being impractical, at least for the immediate future. She critically observed, however, that Mill's description of the ultimate utopia had a distinctively bourgeois character: Mansions were allowed for the businessmen and bankers in the financial arcady, which, realistically, the poor could never reach. She therefore insisted that he append an additional chapter, taken almost verbatim from her, proposing the means for improving the conditions of the working classes. Throughout this chapter she laid emphasis upon the development of strong character by means of personal self-help, and she opposed paternalism in the relation between rich and poor. At her bidding, Mill wrote:

> The poor have come out of their leading strings, and cannot any longer be governed or treated like children. To their own qualities must now be commended the care of their destiny . . . . Whatever advice, exhortation or guidance is held out to the laboring classes, must henceforth be tendered to them as equals, and accepted by them with their eyes open. The prospect of the future depends on the degree in which they can be made rational beings.
>
> The aim of government should be not solely to place human beings in a condition in which they will be able to do without one another, but to enable them to work with or for one another in relations not involving dependence.[4]

With Harriet's substantial additions, the book was sent to press in December 1847, and Mill, in gratitude, proposed to preface it with a high tribute to her:

> To Mrs. John Taylor
>
> as the most eminently qualified of all persons known to the author either to originate or appreciate speculations on social improvement, this attempt to explain and diffuse ideas many of which were first learned from herself, is with the highest respect and regard dedicated.[5]

Harriet felt immensely honored. She recognized, however, that this was a matter about which she ought to consult her husband who, being already quite embarrassed at the closeness of her relationship with Mill, urged her to reject Mill's offer so as to prevent talk that would be extremely unpleasant. In the end, a compromise unsatisfactory to all was reached: The dedication was confined to a few gift copies. This practice was repeated in the second edition, but in the third edition of 1852 the inscription was omitted altogether. By that time, John Taylor had died and Harriet had married Mill, so the dedication, she believed, was no longer appropriate.

For some two years after their marriage Mill became overwhelmed by feelings of intellectual inadequacy. It appeared to him that he had exhausted his creative capacities. He now believed and often repeated in different ways what he wrote to Harriet:

> I am but fit to be one wheel in an engine not to be the self-moving engine itself—a real majestic intellect, not to say moral nature, like yours, I can only look up to and admire.[6]

With her love and encouragement, however, he recovered his self-confidence sufficiently to produce a series of newspaper articles about specific injustices inflicted by society on its weaker members: "corporal punishment," "punishment of children," "wife-murder," and more. All these concerns were far removed from Mill's usual concerns with political and economic theory. In his manuscripts he scrupulously acknowledged that these creations were "very little mine"; and eventually he described them as "a joint production with my wife, like all my newspaper articles on similar subjects, and most of my articles on all subjects."[7]

For some time Mill had been experiencing certain disquieting symptoms: His chronic cough was worse, his pulse was high, he lay awake at night perspiring profusely, and he found traces of blood in his sputa. In March 1854, after trying for some time to shield Mill from the truth, the doctor confessed that Mill was suffering from tuberculosis. At first he tried to keep the news from Harriet, for she had had similar symptoms and was trying to heal herself in the warm Mediterranean air. When she returned to England in April, they both recognized the possibility of an early death for either of them, and he resolved to accomplish as much as possible with her help. For many years now she had repressed her own early ambitions, devoting herself totally to his career. In spite of his illness, he worked constantly, and the worse his symptoms became, the more furiously he wrote. Together with Harriet he outlined a list of subjects for a book of essays, which became with very little change the foundation for most of his later publications, notably, *On Liberty, Utilitarianism, Representative Government*, the unfinished *Chapters on Socialism*, and the posthumous *Three Essays on Religion*. Moreover, the first draft of the *Autobiography*, which they both regarded as a sacred project, and which was, in effect, a summary of their whole intellectual life, was completed. Mill now wrote to Harriet:

> I shall never be satisfied unless you allow our best book, the book which is to come, to have our *two* names on the title page. It ought to be so with everything I publish, for the better half of it all is yours, but the book which will contain our best thoughts, if it has only one name in it, that should be yours.[8]

In the same spirit, Mill informed her that

> The fact is that there is about as much written as I *can* write without your help and we must go through this together . . . . But of what particularly concerns *our* life there is nothing yet written, except the descriptions of you and . . . of what I owe to you intellectually.[9]

In the light of the *Autobiography* and the correspondence between Mill and Harriet, it is certain that every major work published after the *Political Economy* was drafted or planned during the first few years of their married life. And though Harriet did not actually write those works, she suggested, advised, approved, and even dictated whole portions which were written down verbatim. This implies that where Mill's accomplishments are concerned, Harriet Taylor deserves equal credit in bringing them to fruition. Mill himself stated that principle in the *Autobiography*:

> when two persons have their thoughts and speculations completely in common . . . it is of little consequence in respect to the question of originality, which of them holds the pen.[10]

As both Mill and Harriet were seriously ill and their symptoms growing progressively worse, they were often separated by convalescent holidays on the Continent. However, when Mill retired from his post at India House in 1858, they went together to the south of France where Harriet died at Avignon on November 3. On November 30 Mill, in a painful mourning state, wrote to his publisher informing him that his "little book," *On Liberty*, was ready for publication. In fact it had been ready for 18 months during which time he and Harriet had discussed and weighed every word, written and rewritten every sentence. Now that Harriet was gone, no further revisions were possible. Both Mill and Harriet's daughter, Helen, affirm that in this classical essay in particular, the ideas were mostly Harriet's, having originated in her early paper on toleration of individualism and diversity, which she continued to elaborate throughout her life and which Mill finally formulated in his graceful prose. As both knew they had not long to live, they intended this essay as the consummation of their intellectual collaboration, a joint statement of the moral and political values they held dearly.

In certain important respects, *On Liberty* was an effective rebuttal to Comte's despotic "positive polity" in which an intellectual and industrial élite rule, and the people merely do what they are told; in which society is everything and the individual nothing; in which individuals become capable of bettering themselves only at a certain stage determined solely by the élite. Comte, we recall, despised intellectual "anarchy" and regarded it as the main cause of moral disunity. He had nothing but disdain for what he called the prevalent "vagabond liberty" in which laymen expressed themselves about complex social and political issues. Indeed, Mill and Harriet were very upset with Harriet Martineau, not so much for having translated Comte's work as for having been taken in, apparently, by some of his ideas.[11]

In contrast, then, to Comte's view of the good society, Mill and Harriet Taylor severely circumscribed the sphere of government. They were inspired by Wilhelm von Humboldt's famous dictum that "the true aim of man . . . is the highest and most harmonious development of his powers to a complete and consistent whole. Freedom is the ground and indispensable condition which the possibility of such a development presupposes."[12] It followed for the Mills that the *only* ground on which government may rightfully exercise power over a citizen, against his will, is to prevent harm to others. Comte's philosophy had alerted the Mills to the danger of a general system in which the free agency of the individual is reduced to zero, and political democracy is out of the question. But even political democracy may fail to guarantee individual freedom. The Utilitarians, in combatting the tyranny of the few, posited the just rule of the many. But Tocqueville proposed that the majority may also become tyrannical in certain circumstances. The Mills therefore insisted that society, in its own best interest, must encourage minority opinions. The good of the human race depends on the power of original thought, on the rediscovery of old truths and the discovery of new. Original minds have one thing in common: They are always in the minority. Only the encouragement and stimulation of diversity can break the hold of despotic institutions.

On Liberty came out in February 1859. Mill's dedication to Harriet on the opening page is too long to quote in its entirety, but the opening sentence sufficiently conveys the spirit of the whole:

> To the beloved and deplored memory of her who was the inspirer, and in part the author, of all that is best in my writings—the friend and wife whose exalted sense of truth and right was my strongest incitement, and whose approbation was my chief reward—I dedicate this volume . . . .

With the foregoing background in mind, we can turn to an exposition of two works, in particular, which were the product of Harriet Taylor's mind no less than they were of John Mill's: *The Subjection of Women* and *On Liberty.*

THE SUBJECTION OF WOMEN

The object of this innovative essay was to explain why the age-old principle regulating the relations of the sexes was not only morally wrong, but also a chief obstacle to the betterment of the human condition; and also to explain, therefore, why the old principle must be replaced by a new one of perfect sexual equality. The Mills recognized that the attainment of their aim would be no easy task, because the old principle was strongly rooted and almost universally accepted. They recognized, too, that even if they had successfully refuted all arguments in favor of the old principle, they would have accomplished little, since people seldom abandon their prejudices in response to the cogency of a reasonable argument. What made matters even more difficult for the Mills was the nineteenth-century romantic-conservative reaction to the Enlightenment in which reason was dethroned and instinct and emotion reigned in its place. In spite of the difficulty, the Mills were determined to demonstrate that if one reflects honestly on the existing condition, one can see that it is based on the worse rather than the better parts of human nature.

How did the subjection of women originate? Was it based on the lessons of experience, showing that it led to the greatest happiness and well-being of both sexes and of the whole society? Did human beings in primordial times experiment with a variety of forms, in which they first tried men's authority over women, then women's authority over men, and, finally, equality between the two, deciding after all this that male dominance is the best? If they had, then perhaps one could say that the existing relations are based on sound principles and the lessons of experience. But, of course, such experiments have never been made, and the truth is that the subordination of the physically weaker sex by the stronger, rests on a "theory" that has never been tested in the light of alternatives. Worse, it rests on the morally despicable notion that might is right. For it is clear that the subordination of women first arose from the fact that men desired and attached great importance to women who, however, due to their inferior muscular strength, found themselves in a state of bondage to men. Historically, laws and political systems first emerged by recognizing the prevailing relations between individuals. A social fact was thus converted into a legal right, giving it the sanction of society. In that way those who were already forced to obey became legally bound to do so. Slavery is a case in point: The power of the masters over their slaves became "legitimized" through a compact among the masters who bound themselves to one another for their common protection. And the Mills observe that the institution of slavery was once regarded as just, and that many ages elapsed before any thinker had the courage to question either its rightfulness or its necessity. In time such thinkers did arise and the institution was abolished—or, more accurately, the enslavement of men was abolished. The Mills propose that the condition of women is a primitive form of slavery lasting on, albeit in a milder form.

Apologists for existing institutions claimed that the mere persistence of an institution proved that it was a proper adaptation of human nature and conducive to the general good. What such apologists failed to understand, the Mills underscored, is the great capacity for endurance enjoyed by an institution "legitimized" by those with superior might. Throughout history, legal power was obtained by those who first possessed the material means of realizing their will against the resistance of others. Those who controlled such means seldom relinquished their hold upon them until they were compelled to do so by a more powerful adversary. How, for example, were limitations imposed on the power of kings and nobles? It was only with the growth of a wealthy and war-like bourgeoisie in the fortified towns, the Mills remind their readers, that an infantry of commoners was able to curtail the insolent tyranny of the nobles over the townspeople and the peasantry. In England, fewer than 40 years before the Mills had written this essay, it was legal to hold human beings in bondage as salable property; and in half of the American states slavery, the slave trade, and the breeding of slaves existed until recently and was abolished only after a civil war, the human cost of which was hundreds of thousands of casualties. Similarly, it was a civil war in England that had put an end to absolute monarchy. In a word, overcoming oppression has always required resistance and, ultimately, rebellion.

But the condition of women is such, the Mills argued, that it is highly unlikely that they will organize themselves collectively to rebel against the power of men. The position of women is quite different from that of other subject classes. The masters of women demand something more from them than mere service. Men want not only obedience of women, but also their love and affection. All men, except the most brutish, desire that the women most closely associated with them should be not forced slaves, but willing ones. This has been accomplished through an enslavement of women's minds. The masters of other slaves instill fear in order to maintain obedience. The masters of women, however, wanting more than mere obedience, have devised a system of indoctrination with which to accomplish their purpose. All women are brought up from their earliest years to believe that the virtues of feminine character are submission, yielding to the control of men. It is the duty of women, they are told from early childhood, to live for others and to have no aspirations but for their loved ones—the men with whom they are connected and their children. In Victorian England, a wife was entirely dependent on her husband, and all her objects of social ambition were obtainable only through him. Given, then, the natural attraction of the sexes and the subservient status of wives, it is no wonder, the Mills remark, that being attractive to men was the polar star of feminine education and character. Meekness, submissiveness, and resignation of self-will were the cardinal feminine virtues enabling men to hold women in subjection.

As societies experienced increasing democratization, more and more positions in the business and professional worlds became open to the common people. Wealth, for example, could be striven for by anyone and was actually obtained by men of the humblest origins. Indeed, the principle emerged that no full-grown citizen of the male sex was to be legally excluded from competition for the highest and most coveted social, economic, and political positions. The legal and social subordination of women stood out, therefore, as the sole exception to the democratic principle, a vestige of the old, predemocratic world. Not surprisingly, there were men who justified the exceptional status of women by proposing that it is women's nature which makes them ineligible to participate in the world outside the home. In response to such views, the Mills adopted a thorough-going sociological perspective to show that one cannot even begin to speak intelligently about the natural differences of the sexes until women have acquired absolute equality of opportunity in all respects. For it is clear that any sound analytical study of the differences between the sexes would have to take into account the influence of circumstances on character. Only such characteristics could then be inferred to be natural, as could not possibly be due to education and other conditions in the social environment.

Moreover, the Mills rightly observed, the argument from nature is self-contradictory. If something were contrary to women's nature, they would fail to accomplish it no matter how much freedom and equality they possessed. What women, by nature, cannot allegedly do, it is quite superfluous to prohibit them from doing. In an open society founded on the principles of liberty and equality, competition would suffice to exclude the less capable persons.

The legal subordination of women not only precluded such competition, but it also often subjected wives to outrages. Although a husband may have treated his wife with contempt, he could nevertheless claim and enforce her degradation as a human being: He could make her a sexual object against her will. In every social class one found that the legal powers of a husband allowed outrages. Even a most vile, cruel, and vicious man managed to tie some hopeless and sorrowful woman to him and to commit against her any atrocity without fear of legal penalty. In the lowest classes, too, there were countless thousands of husbands who, unable to vent their frustrations at work, indulged in extremes of physical violence against their wives.

The only way, then, in which marriage can be made consistent with justice to both parties—the Mills argued—is to institute the equality of married persons before the law and to allow either party to sue for divorce if and when he or she experiences a persistent injustice. A good marriage is one in which husband and wife live together as equals, a condition in which neither party claims anything for himself that he will not concede to the other. A good marriage therefore presupposes not only equality before the law, but also equality in all respects. Marriage is a relationship based on mutual love and respect, without power on one side and obedience on the other. This means that even in a sexual division of labor in which the husband earns the income and the wife assumes responsibility for the home economy, the notion is unacceptable that the earner is somehow privileged with more authority.

In spite of the subjection experienced by women in the nineteenth century, it became evident that women had proved themselves capable of fulfilling any social function of which men were capable. It is therefore inconsistent with elementary principles of justice, the Mills maintained, to refuse women their fair share of honor and distinction, or to deny them the equal moral right to choose their occupation according to their own preferences and at their own risk. Furthermore, denying women such basic rights is not only unjust to them, but also to all those who might have benefited from their services. To decree that any category of persons shall not be physicians, lawyers, or members of parliament, is to injure not only them, but also all those who need good doctors, lawyers, or political representatives. That is not all. Such a decree deprives everyone of the stimulating and beneficial effects of competition and reduces drastically the pool of those who, if they were admitted to the competition, would demonstrate excellence. If the professions, for example, were entirely open, any woman who succeeded would prove by that fact that she is qualified for it.

The Mills nevertheless recognized that an unavoidable question remained: How come no truly great production in philosophy, science, or art has been the work of a woman? Is there any intelligent way to account for this without supposing that women are naturally inferior in those areas? The Mills reply by questioning whether time has afforded to women enough experience to prove themselves in philosophy, science, and art. At the time of the Mills' writing of this essay, scarcely three generations had elapsed from the time that those cultural areas had been opened to women. And it had become quite clear that in those cultural realms in which women had longer experience—literature, for instance, both prose and poetry—women had distinguished themselves as outstanding writers. Among the best novelists of the time were George Sand and George Eliot, and the fact that they felt compelled to write under male pseudonyms showed how much resistance remained to women entering the field of literature. Mill then makes an additional observation: Given the obstacles standing before a woman's entry into the academic professions and other intellectually creative realms, what right do we have to suppose that original and important thoughts do not occur to women? "They occur," Mill writes, reflecting on his own relationship with Harriet Taylor,

> by hundreds to every woman of intellect. But they are mostly lost, for want of a husband or friend who has the other knowledge which can enable him to estimate them properly and bring them before the world: and even when they are brought before it, they generally appear as his ideas, not their real author's. Who can tell how many of the most original thoughts put forth by male writers, belong to a woman by suggestion, to themselves only by verifying and working out? *If I may judge by my own case, a very large proportion indeed.*[13]

Plato, in the *Republic*, opened the ranks of the philosopher-guardians to all women who qualified by meeting the rigorous mental and physical requirements. He observed that it would be sheer folly to reduce by half the eligible candidates for the class of wise rulers. Similarly, the Mills also underscored the great benefit to be derived from granting women the free use of their capacities and opening to them all social functions and occupations. Such a policy would double "the mass of mental faculties available for the higher services of humanity."[14] The demand for mental excellence everywhere exceeds the supply, and the shortage of persons capable of achieving excellence is such, "that the loss to the world, by refusing to make use of one-half of the whole quantity of talent it possesses, is extremely serious."[15]

Finally, the Mills convincingly argue, women, who are most likely to be the victims of violence, naturally tend, as much as they can, to limit and prevent it. Women, who in modern times are not taught to fight, are, accordingly, in favor of any other method of settling disputes rather than fighting.

Insofar, then, as women gain full equality, their increasing political influence and their aversion to war may strengthen the general ability to avoid it. In sum, there is everything to be gained and nothing to be lost from eradicating sexual inequality, for the imposition of jealous and prejudiced restrictions on one-half of the human race is an evil from which everyone suffers. This is the note on which the Mills ended their future-piercing statement on the status of women.

ON LIBERTY

The key question addressed in this classical essay is the nature and limits of power, which may be legitimately exercised by society over the individual. As the Mills reflected on the past, it became clear that the struggle between liberty and power has been a central feature of the history of society. In antiquity the rulers were most often considered to be antagonistic to the people they ruled. Liberty therefore meant protection from the tyranny of the rulers, who derived their authority through conquest or inheritance, and almost never with the consent of the governed. From the people's standpoint the power of the rulers was a dangerous weapon which they often used against the ruled. To prevent the stronger members of society from preying upon the weaker, a central power was instituted, stronger than all others in the society. Soon it was discovered, however, that the central power was frequently no less bent upon preying on the weaker. After a protracted struggle, the nobles and the people succeeded in setting limits on the ruler's power, and that became the meaning of liberty. Subjects thereby acquired certain political rights which the ruler was prohibited from infringing; and if he attempted to infringe those rights, that justified resistance and rebellion on the part of the subjects. Later, further limits were successfully imposed: Constitutional checks were established by the community or by a representative body, and royal absolutism thus gave way to constitutional monarchy. The struggle for liberty continued everywhere, and in time political thinking went even farther, to propose that the magistrates of the state should be representatives of the people, revocable at their pleasure. What was now demanded was the sovereignty of the people, so that magistrates would no longer be rulers, but rather servants of the people. Various versions of liberalism and democracy thus became common in Europe and America.

Earlier we saw that Harriet Taylor's essay on toleration, stressing the need to protect minorities in a democracy, had a profound impact on John Mill's thinking. On the matter of protecting minorities and preserving diversity in a democracy, Taylor's view converged with that of Tocqueville, whose reflections on France and America persuaded him that the "tyranny of the majority" was a real danger. In *On Liberty* the Mills alert us to the fact that phrases such as "self-government" or "the power of the people over themselves" may be misleading insofar as they fail to reflect the political reality. The people who exercise power are not always the same people over whom it is exercised. Besides, the "will of the people" in practical terms means the will of the majority—those who succeed in making themselves the majority. It can therefore happen that the more numerous part of the people may wish to oppress the less numerous. For the Mills, then, precautions against such abuse are as much needed as against any other abuse of power.

The danger of the "tyranny of the majority" emanates not only from the acts of the political authorities, but also from Society itself, for Society as a collectivity can become tyrannical by imposing the dominant and prevalent opinion on minorities and by punishing dissenters. Mill was writing *On Liberty* at a time when all sorts of collectivist doctrines were on the rise: Tories, trade unionists, Comtists, and Christian Socialists all preached greater social solidarity. All seemed to agree that the individual had no significance apart from the group or society of which he or she happened to be a part. The Mills, considering it urgent to expose the danger of such ideas, therefore advanced a principle which ought to govern the relations of society and the individual:

> the only purpose for which power can be rightfully exercised over any member of a civilized community, against his will, is to prevent harm to others. His own good, either physical or moral, is not a sufficient warrant. He cannot rightfully be compelled to do or forbear because it will be better for him to do so, because it will make him happier, because, in the opinions of others, to do so would be wise, or even right.[16]

As observed earlier, the Mills were especially disturbed by the fact that some of the most influential of the collectivist notions, such as Auguste Comte's, were advanced in the name of "progress." The Mills recognized that some of their contemporary "reformers," who strongly opposed the religious oppression of the past, were as adamant as the churches and sects in their assertion of the right of spiritual domination. Comte in particular, Mill wrote, "whose social system, as unfolded in his *Système Politique de Positive,* aims at establishing . . . a despotism of society over the individual, surpassing anything contemplated in the political ideal of the most rigid disciplinarian among the ancient philosophers."[17] In opposition, then, to all ideologies which exalt society over the individual, the Mills emphasize that human liberty must comprise the inner domain of consciousness: freedom of conscience in the most comprehensive sense; freedom of thought, feeling, opinion and sentiment on all subjects, whether political, philosophical, theological, moral, or scientific.

Because the Mills perceived the growing influence of collectivist ideologies in the liberal democracies—a general intolerance on the part of the public that threatened basic civil liberties—they were determined to present the best theoretical defense of fundamental freedoms. Even if one were to suppose that a government is entirely at one with the people, the Mills would still deny the right of the people to exercise coercion over the minds of a dissenting minority. If only one person dissents, the majority is no more justified in silencing that one person than he would be in silencing the rest if he had the power. The Mills ground this principle on sound reasoning: We can never be sure the opinion we wish to stifle is false; and even if we were sure, stifling it would still be an evil. All attempts to silence discussion is an assumption of infallibility on the part of the silencer, but no one is infallible, and hence the opinion one attempts to suppress may be true. For the Mills, one may presume an opinion to be true only after it has been sufficiently contested and has remained unrefuted. Full opportunity for contesting opinion is essential. To rectify mistakes one needs both experience and discussion. Experience is not enough. Discussion is necessary to clarify how an experience is to be interpreted. If every opportunity to contest the prevalent opinion is granted, wrong opinions and practices will eventually yield to argument. Moreover, the Mills saw through the presumptuous notion that there exists a positive social science that can inform us with certainty whether an opinion is useful. The usefulness of an opinion is itself a matter of opinion, as open to critical discussion as the opinion itself. To forestall misunderstanding, the Mills explain that the assumption of infallibility refers not to one's own feeling sure of a doctrine, but rather trying to decide that question for others, without permitting them to hear what can be said in opposition to it. Furthermore, social intolerance actually fails to root out dissenting views and merely prompts individuals to disguise them or refrain from expressing them openly. But such repression of one's own views in the face of intolerance leads to the loss of moral courage. Even long-held truths need to be frequently and fearlessly discussed if they are to be living truths and not mere dogma.

Liberty refers not only to the free expression of opinion, but also to the freedom of individuals to act upon their opinions. Society has no right to hinder the actions of individuals or groups as long as they act at their own risk or peril. This is an essential proviso, since it is clear that actions cannot be as free as opinions. Actions, therefore, which harm others without justification, do in fact require the interference of society. And here the Mills introduce another fundamental principle: Just as an open society requires that there should be diverse opinions, it requires equally that there should be a variety of experiments in living. Free scope should be given to varieties in ways of life as long, again, as no injury is done to one another. It is in this context that *On Liberty* cites the writings of Wilhelm von Humboldt who taught that the aim of humanity ought to be the highest and most harmonious development of its creative powers; and, therefore, that the object

> towards which every human being must ceaselessly direct his efforts, and on which especially those who design to influence their fellow men must ever keep their eyes, is the individuality of power and development.[18]

And for that, there are two preconditions: "freedom, and variety of situations"; from the union of these emerge "individual vigor and manifold diversity," which unite themselves in "originality."[19]

Diversity in ways of living is no less essential to an open society than diversity in opinion. Both are the preconditions of originality in thought and action. This proposition complements the arguments in the essay *The Subjection of Women*. "In proportion to the development of his individuality," Mill writes in *On Liberty*, "each person becomes more valuable to himself, and is therefore capable of being more valuable to others."[20] This necessarily implies that as a woman develops her individuality, she becomes more valuable not only to herself, but also to others as well; and for that, the emancipation of women is indispensable.

It is precisely manifold diversity, the Mills insisted, which makes possible the flourishing of originality and the emergence of genius. Where dissenting opinions are stifled and diversity in the ways of life are discouraged or suppressed, mediocrity tends to prevail. The Mills noted the frightening tendency in contemporary society which allows dissenting persons to be judicially declared unfit for the management of their own affairs. All the minute details of a person's life are pried into, and if he deviates only slightly from commonplace views or acts, it is presented to the jury as evidence of his insanity. Such trials, Mill observed,

> speak volumes as to the state of feeling and opinion among the vulgar with regard to human liberty. So far from setting any value on individuality—so far from respecting the right of each individual to act, in things indifferent, as seems good to his own judgment and inclination, judges and juries cannot even conceive that a person in a state of sanity can desire such freedom.[21]

Such cases were regarded by the Mills as flagrant violations of an individual's rights and liberties; for according to the principle they have laid down, only when there is a definite damage or definite risk of damage either to an individual or to the public, is a case taken out of the realm of liberty and placed in that of the law.

On Liberty also addresses the question of whether government interference in the lives of citizens should be limited when there is no infringement of their liberties. This question is not about restraining individuals, but about helping them. Should government do things for the benefit of citizens, or should such things be left for the citizens to do for themselves, either individually or in voluntary associations? In addressing this question, the Mills raise three objections to government interference: (1) When citizens need something to be done for their own benefit, it is likely to be better accomplished by individuals than by government. The reason is that speaking generally, the people most directly and personally interested in a matter are best fit to deal with it. (2) Although individuals may not accomplish a particular task as well as officers of government, it is still desirable that it be done by individuals ". . . as a means to their own mental education—a mode of strengthening their active faculties, exercising their judgment, and giving them a familiar knowledge of the subjects with which they are thus left to deal."[22] (3) The most important reason for limiting the interference of government "is the great evil of adding unnecessarily to its power."[23]

Another central question that has policy implications today is whether government should interfere in situations where the legitimate competition for goals causes pain to the losers. For example, conflicts of interest between individuals are most often unavoidable when they compete for positions in an overcrowded profession or occupation. Whoever is hired over others in such situations gains a benefit from the loss of others, from their wasted effort and disappointment. For the Mills, it is better for the general interest of society to avoid government interference in such cases, because society admits no right, either legal or moral, on the part of the disappointed competitors, "to immunity from this kind of suffering; and feels called on to interfere, only when means of success have been employed which it is contrary to the general interest to permit— namely, fraud or teachery, and force."[24]

Now the Mills were perfectly aware that in any social competition, some are likely to have advantages over others for environmental reasons—social class background, education, and so on. So the important question arises: Did the "disappointed competitors" lose the contest due to some environmental condition or other, and what would the Mills propose as social policy in this regard? As Gail Tulloch has observed, "though Mill did not use the term 'equality of opportunity,' what he constantly invoked was what we now term an equality of access interpretation of equal opportunity."[25] This is especially evident in the Mills' concern to remove all legal and ideological obstacles preventing women from entering and competing in the contest for professional and other occupational positions. We have seen that the Mills denounced discriminatory practices against women on the basis of a principle: Discrimination excludes people not because of their competence, but in spite of it. The only way to discover the natural capacities of the sexes is to put the question to experience, which presupposes absolute equality of opportunity. For the Mills, all forms of discrimination should therefore be made illegal, and that would necessarily include so-called "reverse discrimination"—discrimination in favor of women. As Gail Tulloch, again, has argued, "if race or sex should not be given a negative weighting, they should not be given a positive weighting either; in themselves they do not constitute a competence qualification."[26]

However, Tulloch then goes on to favor a certain form of "affirmative action," which in her view avoids injustice, "namely through *ceteris paribus* discrimination, that is, using sex or race as a tie-breaking bonus factor, other things being equal, where the candidates are equally qualified."[27] The problem with this proposal, however, is that it is in fact a form of discrimination. Note that Tulloch uses that very term in her proposal. In Tulloch's proposal the breaking of the tie would in fact be based on race or sex, which she herself has rightfully maintained should be given neither negative nor positive weighting, since race and sex are not competence qualifications. Moreover, the notion of a tie, in which two contestants are equally qualified, is an unrealistic and self-serving hypothesis in this case. If there were only one available position, but two candidates of the *same* sex, there could be no tie; one would have to be chosen over the other strictly on the ground of merit. And on the basis of Mill's writings reviewed here, it is clear that he and Harriet Taylor would have opposed any hiring policy based on factors other than competence and merit.

The Mills zealously defended the ideal of equality of opportunity; and they understood that if any affirmative action is to be taken toward the realization of that ideal, it must come long before individuals compete for desirable positions in their adulthood. If a society is concerned to remove the socially inherited disabilities due to past discrimination or oppression, the Mills would have urged that such a project must begin in early childhood. In Mill's words:

> If the government would make up its mind to *require* for every child a good education, it might save itself the trouble of *providing* one. It might leave to parents to obtain the education where and how they pleased, and content itself with helping to pay the school fees of the poorer classes of children, and defraying the entire school expenses of those who have no one else to pay for them.[28]

Clearly, the Mills have given us much to think about where the relationship of government to liberty is concerned.

NOTES

1. F.A. Hayek, ed., *John Stuart Mill and Harriet Taylor: Their Correspondence and Subsequent Marriage* (London: Routledge & Kegan Paul Ltd., 1951).
2. Ibid., p. 18, fn. 6.
3. Ibid., p. 275.
4. Michael St. John Packe, *The Life of John Stuart Mill,* with a preface by F.A. Hayek (London: Secker and Warburg, 1954, p. 307). I rely on Packe's splendid work for biographical details about both Mill and Harriet Taylor.
5. Hayek, op. cit., p. 122.
6. Ibid., p. 165.
7. *The Mill-Taylor Collection,* 36, cited in Packe, p. 346.
8. Hayek, op. cit., p. 185.
9. Ibid., p. 190.
10. John Stuart Mill, *Autobiography* (New York: Columbia University Press, 1924), p. 171.
11. Packe, op. cit., p. 399.

12. Humboldt, *The Sphere and Duties of Government,* 1791, translated by Coulthard, 1854, cited in Packe, p. 401.
13. John Stuart Mill, *The Subjection of Women,* in Alice S. Rossi, ed., *Essays on Sex Equality: J.S. Mill and Harriet Taylor Mill* (Chicago and London: The University of Chicago Press, 1970), p. 206, italics added.
14. Ibid., p. 221.
15. Ibid.
16. J.S. Mill, *On Liberty,* ed. Albury Castell (New York: Appleton-Century-Crofts, 1947), p. 9.
17. Ibid., pp. 13–14.
18. Wilhelm von Humboldt, *The Sphere and Duties of Government,* tr. from the German by Mill and cited in *On Liberty,* p. 57.
19. Ibid.
20. Ibid., p.63.
21. Ibid., p. 69, fn. 1.
22. Ibid., p. 111.
23. Ibid., p. 112.
24. Ibid., p. 96.
25. Gail Tulloch, *Mill and Sexual Equality,* (Hertfordshire, England: Harvester Wheatsheaf, 1989), p. 185.
26. Ibid., p. 191.
27. Ibid., p. 193.
28. *On Liberty,* pp. 107–108.

13

The Philosophical Orientations of Karl Marx (1818–1883)

Comte's positive philosophy, as we have seen, was a conscious attempt to discredit and repudiate what he had termed "negative" philosophy. The negative-critical philosophy that emerged and took shape with the Enlightenment had proved itself a formidable weapon in the hands of the rising bourgeoisie in its struggle against the older classes of the theological-feudal order. Ultimately, that struggle resulted in the French Revolution and the dissolution of the old order. In those terms, negative philosophy, even for Comte, had fulfilled a useful historical function. Now, however, with the establishment of the bourgeois order, Comte believed negative philosophy, the legacy of the Enlightenment, had outlived its usefulness. Now, when the major task had become consolidation of the new bourgeois-industrial order and creation of a truly organic and integrated society, negative philosophy led only to divisiveness, conflict, and disorder. It stirred the imagination and hopes of the proletariat and encouraged class conflict. The proletarians, instead of finding their place in the new organic society and adjusting peacefully to it, as Comte desired, were being agitated to struggle for the transformation of the existing society.

Each stage in the evolution of the new organic society was viewed by him as a necessary one; therefore, the working class must adjust to the present stage. Improvement would come about organically as the society progressed harmoniously from stage to stage. Revolution—that is, a total transformation of the social system—was out of the question. Revolution could have only negative consequences; it would only shatter the existing order without bringing in its wake any fundamental change in the condition of the vast majority of the people. Progress was best assured not by criticism, class conflict, and revolutionary activity, but by reconciling the conflicting tendencies and classes; by educating all classes of society—and especially the lower classes—to take their proper place in the new, hierarchically organized society and to resign themselves to their condition. This is what the new positive science taught and this was to be its chief function: to achieve an organic and conflict-free social order.

If with Comte, then, there is a complete renunciation of the legacy of the Enlightenment (and the French Revolution), with Marx we return full circle to a whole-hearted reaffirmation of that legacy. Marx restores, and skillfully employs, the very philosophical premises Comte so intensely detested.

First among those premises was the perfectibility of man. Marx had a conception of "natural man"—the individual human being, his needs, and his potential for development—not unlike that of Rousseau and, more generally, of the Enlightenment thinkers. Although Marx's conception is expressed most explicitly in his early writings, it remains throughout his life the basis of his analysis and criticism of the capitalist system, and of his hopes for the attainment of a truly *human* society.

Man, Marx believed, is infinitely perfectible. Man's *essential* powers—his latent and potential human powers—are unlimited in their capacity for development. If man is now no more than a laboring beast, he need not remain in that condition; he can attain the highest forms of creativity, thought, and action. This is the underlying conception by which Marx assessed and evaluated social systems. Man's latent creative powers were stifled and repressed under the social conditions of all class societies. The existing system, capitalism, was not only preventing the fulfillment of his potential, it was even depriving him of his animal needs—fresh air, food, sex, and so on. Hunger, for example, was a condition of deprivation imposed by other men. Marx thus condemned the capitalist system for its effect on individual human beings. That view finds its clearest and most consistent expression in one of Marx's early philosophical works, *Economic and Philosophic Manuscripts of 1844,* to which we now turn.

It offended Marx's conception of man that the capitalist-industrial system had reduced him to an *animal laborans,* "a beast reduced to the strictest bodily needs."[1] The workers' "needs" were now at the "barest and most miserable level of physical subsistence" and their activity for the better part of their waking day was a tedious and repetitive mechanical movement. The lowest possible level of life and activity had become the general standard—one in which men were deprived not only of their human needs but of their animal needs as well:

> Even the need for fresh air ceases for the worker. Man returns to living in a cave, which is now, however, contaminated with the mephitic breath of plague given off by civilization, and which he continues to occupy only *precariously*, it being for him an alien habitation which can be withdrawn from him any day—a place from which, if he does not pay, he can be thrown out any day. For this mortuary he has to *pay*. A dwelling in the *light*, which Prometheus in Aeschylus designated as one of the greatest boons, by means of which he made the savage into a human being, ceases to exist for the worker. Light, air, etc.—the simplest *animal* cleanliness—ceases to be a need for man. *Dirt*—this stagnation and putrefaction of man—the *sewage* of civilization (speaking quite literally)—comes to be the *element of life* for him. Utter, unnatural neglect, putrefied nature, comes to be his *life-element*. None of his senses exist any longer, and not only in his human fashion, but in an *inhuman* fashion, and therefore, not even in an animal fashion. (p. 117)

Clearly, Marx had an image of man as he could be and hence ought to be, and what he saw and described was a far cry from that image. For instead of developing his essential human powers, man was being debased and deformed and thus becoming something less than an animal.

In these philosophical writings, the dehumanization of man was viewed by Marx as a consequence of *alienation*. That idea, though Hegelian in origin, was fundamentally transformed in Marx's hands. Alienation for Hegel, like his other constructs, was exclusively a phenomenon of the mind. With the Young- or Left-Hegelians, the concept was significantly altered but remained primarily a philosophical notion—that is, a condition in which man's own powers appear as independent forces or entities controlling his actions.

One of the Left-Hegelians, Ludwig Feuerbach, had elaborated the Enlightenment view of religion as an "illusion." For the French *Philosophes*, "God" was simply a symbolic expression of humanity's yearnings for perfection. Feuerbach, in a book called *The Essence of Christianity*, presented a view of religion quite similar to that of the Enlightenment. God, he maintained, is a creation of the human imagination. The Divine is a symbolic expression of humanity's unfulfilled promises and aspirations. Humans unconsciously project their ideals unto hypothetical beings, which they then treat as sacred and divine. They thus come to worship the product of their own minds.

When Marx was a young university student, such atheistic ideas were quite fashionable in radical circles. He found them convincing as far as they went. In his judgment, however, they did not go far enough. Existing theories remained on the psychological level and ignored what he regarded as the key sociological question: *Why* do people project the best part of themselves unto the cosmos? What are the social conditions that prompt people to externalize their own powers and values and to attribute them to hypothetical, superhuman beings? Marx's reply was, in a word, that religion is the product of *social alienation*. That meant that, historically, humanity has been divided against itself by the social-class cleavages of society. It is the domination, oppression, and exploitation of man by man that has given rise to religion. Religious ideas are an expression of human suffering and a protest against it as well. In the words of the young Marx:

> Religion is the sigh of the oppressed creature, the sentiment of a heartless world, and the soul of soulless conditions. It is the opium of the people.
>
> The abolition of religion as the *illusory* happiness of men, is a demand for their real happiness. The call to abandon their illusions about their condition is a call to abandon a condition which requires illusions.[2]

Reflecting on the degraded condition of the industrial proletariat and other oppressed classes, Marx concluded that, by itself, a demonstration of the illusory character of religion was not likely to have liberating effects. So long as oppression and sharp inequalities prevail, people will continue to create comforting illusions. The main task, therefore, is to change the social order and to eliminate the circumstances that require illusions. For Marx, it was industrial capitalism in particular which imposed great suffering on the majority of the people, diminishing their humanity and distorting their self-understanding. Religion is an "opium" because it so often leads people to seek meaning and happiness not in the human world but in the divine hereafter.

In that light we can more readily grasp Marx's meaning when he writes that religious criticism

> has plucked the imaginary flowers from the chain, not in order that man shall bear the chain without . . . consolation but so that he shall cast off the chain and pluck the living flower. The criticism of religion disillusions man so that he will think, act and fashion his reality as a man who has lost his illusions and regained his reason. . . .[3]

It is only through the rational reconstruction of society, so that it may meet the human needs of each and every member, that alienation can be overcome.

There are several senses in which Marx employed the term *alienation*, and the meanings he assigned to the concept may best be grasped from the two German words he used to describe the phenomenon he had in mind: (1) *entäussern* (verb) or, in its noun form, *Entäusserung*, and (2) *entfremden* (verb) and *Entfremdung* (noun). The first of these means "to part with," "to give up," "to deprive one's self of," and "to divest one's self of," and, as noted by the translator of these manuscripts, it also implies "making external to one's self." The noun *Entäusserung* is also explicitly defined as alienation (of property). The second German word, also rendered in English as "to alienate," connotes primarily two people becoming estranged from each other. Thus, the term "alienation" refers to a complex process with several aspects. As will be seen in a later discussion of *Capital*, Marx described the process and its consequences in great detail. Here it may be summarized in general terms.

The process begins with the separation of men from their means of production and subsistence (as was the case in England when the yeomen were driven from their land following passage of the various Enclosure Acts). Men are alienated from their property and therefore compelled, if they are to avoid starving and becoming vagabonds, to sell their labor power to the capitalist entrepreneurs awaiting them. The two parties, capitalist as well as laborer, thus enter into an essentially instrumental relationship with each other. Forming that relationship is and remains an act of expediency, and the two parties remain estranged from each other because the relationship is based on conflicting interests and fundamentally different conditions of life.

Immediately upon entering the relationship, the worker begins to consume his energies in the production of things; his labor power becomes objectified in commodities over which he has no control. In that sense, the more he produces, the poorer he becomes.

> All these consequences are contained in the definition that the worker is related to the *product of his labor* as an *alien* object. For on this premise it is clear that the more the worker spends himself, the more powerful the alien objective world becomes which he creates over against himself, the poorer he himself—his inner world—becomes, the less belongs to him as his own. . . . The worker puts his life into the object; but now his life no longer belongs to him but to the object. Hence, the greater this activity, the greater is the worker's lack of objects. Whatever the product of his labor is, he is not. Therefore the greater this product, the less is he himself. The *alienation* of the worker from his product means not only that his labor becomes an object, an *external existence,* but that it exists *outside him,* independently, as something alien to him, and that it becomes a power on its own confronting him; it means that the life which he has conferred on the object confronts him as something hostile and alien. (p. 70)

The worker has no control over the process of production or its results; his labor is an alienating activity, not only because he loses the product in which he has reified a part of himself, but because the whole productive process is external to him and his human needs. In

> his work, therefore, he does not affirm himself but denies himself, does not feel content but unhappy, does not develop freely his physical and mental energy but mortifies his body and ruins his mind. The worker therefore only feels himself outside his work, and in his work feels outside himself. He is at home when he is not working, and when he is working he is not at home. His labor is therefore not voluntary, but coerced; it is *forced labor*. It is therefore not the satisfaction of a need; it is merely a *means* to satisfy needs external to it. Its alien character emerges clearly in the fact that as soon as no physical or other compulsion exists, labor is shunned like the plague. (p. 72)

Consequently, he experiences the process of production as an oppressive activity, as a loss of freedom. He

> no longer feels himself to be freely active in any but his animal functions—eating, drinking, procreating. . . . And in his human functions he no longer feels himself to be anything but an animal. . . . Certainly eating, drinking, procreating, etc., are also genuinely human functions. But in the abstraction which sep-

> arates them from the sphere of all other human activity and turns them into sole and ultimate ends, they are animal. (p. 73)

Man, as worker, has become something less than human, because he is separated from his potential human qualities. The animal, Marx says, is immediately identical with its life activity; man, on the other hand, has the ability to make his life activity the object of his will and consciousness. That is what makes it possible for man to attain ever greater degrees of freedom. The animal produces only when dominated by his immediate physical needs; man, however, can produce "even when he is free from physical need and only truly produces in freedom therefrom" (p. 75). This is reversed under conditions of alienated labor where man's whole conscious being and life activity, "his essential being [becomes] a mere means to his existence."

Thus we have an initial alienation from his means of production that forces an individual (the worker) to form an estranged relationship with another individual (the employer). The activity itself, which he now performs for the means of existence, is an alienating activity, for the product remains alien to the worker and the process of production itself remains external to his consciousness and to his human needs and desires. Man becomes increasingly alienated from himself, a fact that expresses itself in his estrangement from others. One can then see why Marx remained unimpressed with the "forcing-up of wages" and other such ameliorative measures that would not alter the basic relationships underlying the conditions of alienation and "would therefore be nothing but *better payment for the slave,* and would not conquer either for the worker or for labor their human status and dignity" (p. 81).

It is not the worker alone, however, but the nonworker as well (albeit in a different form and in differing degrees) who is subject to the condition of alienation. Everything ". . . which appears in the worker as an *activity of alienation, of estrangement,* appears in the nonworker as a *state of alienation, of estrangement*" (p. 83). The capitalist who regards as luxury everything the worker desires above his barest physical needs is himself subject, though to a lesser extent than the worker, to denial and want. For political economy, denial and want, or thrift and saving, were major virtues for both the capitalist and the worker:

> This science of marvelous industry is simultaneously the science of *asceticism,* and its true ideal is the *ascetic* but *extortionate* miser and the ascetic but *productive* slave. . . . The political economy—despite its worldly and wanton appearance—is a true moral science, the most moral of all the sciences. Self-denial, the denial of life and of all human needs, is its cardinal doctrine. The less you eat, drink, and read books; the less you go to the theatre, the dance hall, the public house; the less you think, love, theorize, sing, paint, fence, etc., the more you *save*—the *greater* becomes your treasure which neither moths nor dust will devour—your *capital.* The less you *are,* the more you *have;* the less you express your own life, the greater is your *alienated* life—the greater is the store of your estranged being. (p. 119)

This general condition, then, a consequence of specific social relationships and processes, was one that had to be abolished if men were to elevate themselves to a truly *human* status. For Marx, that was possible only *"in a practical way,* by virtue of the practical energy of men" (p. 109). If men were to develop their essential human powers, if they were to perfect themselves, they had first of all to abolish the conditions of their present malaise. That was to be a process, a movement. Therefore, the establishment of what Marx called "communism" was not an end but a means to man's greater freedom and hence to man's greater humanity. "Communism," wrote Marx in another early work, *German Ideology,* "is for us not a stable state which is to be established, an *ideal* to which reality will have to adjust itself. We call communism the *real* movement which abolishes the present state of things. The conditions of this movement result from the premises now in existence."[4] Communism is no static utopia toward which men should strive; it is a critical and revolutionary movement. "Communism . . . is the *actual* phase necessary for the next stage of historical development in the process of human emancipation and recovery" (p. 114). As we shall see, Marx's conception of "communism" presupposed and entailed the enhancement of human rights and civil liberties.

It is clear, then, that Marx had a conception of what the human individual could become and that this was his measure of the existing social system. Man's creative powers, his capacity for self-perfection and self-realization, are practically unlimited—given the abolition of those relationships and conditions which until now have so drastically impeded his development. Man is a creature of the very social conditions he himself has created, but *he need not remain a prisoner of those conditions.* To understand how, in Marx's view, men could make their history more consciously than ever before, we must examine another aspect of the Enlightenment legacy—negative-critical thinking—the dialectical form of which Marx learned directly from Hegel but fundamentally transformed.

NOTES

1. Karl Marx, *Economic and Philosophic Manuscripts of 1844* (Moscow: Foreign Languages Publishing House, 1961), p. 30. (Hereafter all page references to this work will be indicated in parentheses immediately following the quoted passage.)
2. Karl Marx, *Early Writings,* trans. and ed. T. B. Bottomore (London: C. A. Watts, 1963), pp. 43–44.
3. Ibid.
4. Karl Marx and Frederick Engles, *The German Ideology* (New York: International Publishers, 1960), p. 26.

14

Marx's Relation to Hegel and Feuerbach

For Hegel, it will be recalled, reason embraced the total universe; all of its realms, the inorganic as well as the organic, nature as well as society, were governed by the Idea and its dialectical logic. Reason was an immanent force that expressed itself in the unfolding of reality. In the natural realm, development and change—things becoming actually what they always were potentially—took place in "a direct, unopposed, unhindered manner." It was both a peaceful process and one of blind necessity. Not so in the human realm, where history had shown that development was a conflictive process dependent on human consciousness and will. The rational structure of being could be comprehended by the human mind and that was a necessary condition of freedom: the actualization of the potentialities inherent in reality. "Truth" was not merely a function of formal propositions; the criterion of truth was reality in process. Herbert Marcuse has explained Hegel's view rather well: "Something is true if it is what it can be, fulfilling all its objective possibilities."[1]

For Hegel, the form in which a thing immediately appears is not yet its true form. What one sees at first is a negative condition, not the real potentialities of a thing. Something becomes true "only in the process of overcoming this negativity, so that the birth of the truth requires the death of the given state of being. . . . All forms are seized by the dissolving movement of reason which cancels and alters them until they are adequate to their notion."[2] In those terms, there is a revolutionary side to Hegel's philosophy. The given facts as they appear can never be more than a temporary and partial truth, because they represent only one negative phase in the unfolding of truth which reveals itself precisely by the destruction and supersession of that phase.

This dialectical conception of reality which can be traced to Aristotle and even to certain pre-Socratic philosophers profoundly influenced Marx's thinking about social phenomena.[3] The realm of the "is" must always be challenged to reveal the possibilities within it. The existing factual order is a transient negativity that can be transcended. One cannot even comprehend the existing order, let alone free its potentialities, unless it is critically opposed and ultimately transcended. The data are not "positives," nor is the existing factual order inviolable. On the contrary, since that order imposes a subhuman condition of existence upon men, since they are therefore less than they can be, men must strive to change that order.

This approach is directly opposed to that of positivism, which treats facts *in their immediately given form* as truth. By their rejection of universal concepts and their reduction of truth to the immediately observable and verifiable, the positivists exclude "from the domain of knowledge everything that may not yet be a fact."[4] Marx, like Hegel—at least up to a given point in the latter's system—refused to limit truth to a particular "given"; he firmly believed "that the potentialities of men and things are not exhausted in the given forms and relations in which they may actually appear. . . ."[5]

Of course, all this should not be taken to mean that Marx had no use or regard for "the facts"; that would be patently false and absurd. The point is, rather, that he was always conscious of the transient character of any given facts, which are but negative moments in a ceaseless historical process. The existing factual order of capitalism, for instance, had to be studied carefully, if only to learn how to negate it. The possibility of revolution rested on certain objective economic and political conditions, which could be grasped through an analysis of the structure and tendencies of capitalism. Only with factual knowledge could Marx develop (as was his intention) a theory to guide the revolutionary action of the working class. Moreover, once he arrived at an empirical generalization or theoretical proposition that he regarded as true, he always pointed to the historically specific conditions to which it applied. The proposition, for example, that the "relations of production" tend to determine the character of men, including their consciousness, is regarded by Marx as a sociohistorical fact; but that fact is precisely what he regards as man's alienated condition. At the same time, therefore, that he describes that fact, he exposes the materialistic nature of the prevailing order in which relations of production are fundamental in forming and *deforming* human relations and in divesting man of his human character. Thus,

> Marx's proposition is a *critical* one, implying that the prevailing relation between consciousness and social existence is a false one that must be overcome before the true relation can come to light. The truth of the materialistic thesis is thus to be fulfilled in its negation.
>
> Marx emphasizes time and again that his materialistic starting point is forced upon him by the materialistic quality of the society he analyzes.[6]

Misunderstanding of that point has led to the worst distortions of Marx's theory, in which the very opposite of what he believed is attributed to him—namely, that his ideal was a materialistic society. Actually, his ideal was to invert the prevalent relationship between social being and social consciousness. Precisely what Marx meant by leaving the domain of "necessity" and entering the domain of "freedom" was that men would now begin *consciously* to determine their future. That is the view Marx held not only in his early philosophical writings but in his maturity as well. In *Capital,* he wrote: "The life-process of society, which is based on the process of material production, does not strip off its mystical veil until it is treated as production by freely associated men, and is consciously regulated by them in accordance with a settled plan."[7]

In those terms, as was pointed out earlier, Marx viewed socialism and/or communism not as ends in themselves. The abolition of private property and the socialization of the means of production are the first steps in the abolition of alienated labor. That this will lead to "an association, in which the free development of each is the condition for the free development of all" is *not* at all inevitable. Everything will depend on what men do with the socialized resources. If men do not associate freely and utilize those resources to fulfill their human needs and to further their human development, then the socialization of the means of production has merely substituted one form of subjugation for another. Marx foresaw that danger and warned against reifying "society" and setting it up against the individual. "What is to be avoided above all is the establishing of 'Society' as an abstraction *vis-à-vis* the individual. The individual is *the social being.* His life . . . is therefore an expression and confirmation of *social life.*"[8]

The needs and freedom of the individual thus remain paramount in Marx's ideal; he therefore condemns any society that imposes a division of labor without considering the need for well-being and for maximum self-realization of each and every individual. This is his main criticism of class society: It is a situation in which an individual's entire fate tends to be determined by his class position and the function assigned him in the system of production. The difference between this condition and the one he envisioned in the future, Marx made clear in a famous passage:

> The division of labor offers us the first example of how, as long as man remains in natural society [i.e., governed by laws which are inexorable, like natural laws over which men have no control], that is as long as a cleavage exists between the particular and the common interest, as long therefore as activity is not voluntar-

> ily, but naturally, divided, man's own deed becomes an alien power opposed to him, which enslaves him instead of being controlled by him. For as soon as labor is distributed, each man has a particular, exclusive sphere of activity, which is forced upon him and from which he cannot escape. He is a hunter, a fisherman, a shepherd, or a critical critic, and must remain so if he does not want to lose his means of livelihood; while in communist society, where nobody has one exclusive sphere of activity, but each man can become accomplished in any branch he wishes, society regulates the general production and thus makes it possible for me to do one thing to-day and another to-morrow, to hunt in the morning, fish in the afternoon, rear cattle in the evening, criticize after dinner, just as I have a mind, without ever becoming hunter, fisherman, shepherd or critic.[9]

From Hegel, then, Marx took the emphasis on negative critical thinking, which he integrated into his intellectual consciousness.[10] With Marx, however, dialectical thinking is not only critical and revolutionary but empirical and sociological as well. Conflict, for example, is explained not abstractly but in terms of concrete and specific social relationships. One class owns the means of production whereas the other does not; that is the basis of the various forms of conflict between them. Marx views the entire capitalist system as resting on conflicting principles and tendencies: "Contradictions" exist between the social character of production and the institution of private property, or between the growth of the "productive forces" and the existing "relations of production"; between production for use and production for profit; between production and consumption, and still others. For Marx, those conflicting principles are rooted in definite social relationships, and his dialectical reasoning is therefore quite the opposite of Hegel's closed ontological system. Marx's thought is in all respects a different order of truth from Hegel's, and not to be interpreted in terms of the latter's philosophical concepts. That can only be appreciated by a further examination of Marx's work.

Marx worked out his own theory of the relationship between social existence and social consciousness—the so-called materialist conception of history—in direct opposition to Hegel's idealistic conception of that relationship. Throughout his life Marx continued to honor his intellectual debt to that "mighty thinker" by coquetting with the Hegelian mode of expression. Nevertheless, he believed that dialectical thinking had suffered from mystification in Hegel's hands. "With him it is standing on its head. It must be turned right side up again, if you would discover the rational kernel within the mystical shell."[11] What was that rational kernel? "In its rational form," Marx wrote,

> It [the dialectic] is a scandal and abomination to bourgeoisdom and its doctrinaire professors, because it includes in its comprehension and affirmative recognition of the existing state of things, at the same time also, the recognition of the negation of that state, of its inevitable breaking up; because it regards every historically developed social form as in fluid movement, and therefore takes into account its transient nature not less than its momentary existence; because it lets nothing impose upon it, and is in its essence critical and revolutionary.[12]

In Hegel, moreover, the "existing state of things" appeared as an expression of the Idea or Spirit; he had held, apparently, to an inverted conception of the relationship between existence and consciousness. That prompted Marx to state once more in his maturity what he had already repeatedly insisted upon in his youth:

> My dialectical method is not only different from the Hegelian, but its direct opposite. To Hegel, the life-process of the human brain, i.e., the process of thinking, which, under the name of "the Idea," he even transforms into an independent subject, is the demiurgos of the real world, and the real world is only the external, phenomenal form of "the Idea." With me, on the contrary, the ideal is nothing else than the material world reflected by the human mind, and translated into forms of thought.[13]

Marx thus dissociated himself from the metaphysical premises of Hegel's philosophy, in which thinking was separated from the life-process. At the same time, however, Marx rejected the prevailing form of materialism. He vehemently opposed the mechanistic and reductionist standpoint according to which man's mental activity was nothing more than matter in motion. Chemical bodily processes, according to that doctrine, were sufficient to explain men's ideas and emotions. Materialists of that kind contended that "Ideas stand in the same relation to the brain as bile does to the liver or urine to the kidneys."[14]

The *locus classicus* of Marx's critique of mechanistic materialism is his famous "Theses on Feuerbach."[15] There Marx rejects any doctrine that ignores the active, creative, and determining side of man. In his first thesis, Marx acknowledges that the active side was in fact recognized by idealism—that is, by such great idealistic philosophers as Kant and Hegel. In the same thesis, Marx repudiates all previous materialistic philosophies, including Feuerbach's, for treating humans as if they were no more than passive, determined objects. What emerges from Marx's critique is his own conception of humanity as actively constituting itself. The external world is a humanly created world that is molded and changed by means of man's theoretical-practical activity. Man creates the world in the sense that he produces his tools and external objects with the materials of nature, thus modifying nature, his means of acting upon it, and his relations with his fellow man.

Thus Marx developed his own distinctive view in opposition to idealism and materialism alike. With the exception of Feuerbach, whose notable achievement Marx believed was to make the social relation of man to man the basic principle of his theory, none of the Young Hegelians had advanced much beyond Hegel conceptually. But Feuerbach had committed the basic error of the mechanistic materialists: He had overlooked the creative, determining side of practical human activity. Marx's theory and method (the so-called "materialist conception of history," which he also described as "dialectical" because it took into account both the active and the passive sides) cannot therefore be adequately grasped as materialism in the traditional sense. Marx's view, as he himself characterized it, was to be distinguished from both idealism *and* materialism. Marx sought to overcome the one-sidedness of both philosophical traditions and to preserve their elements of truth. That must always be borne in mind when we hear Marx and Engels speak of their "materialist conception"; for gross misunderstandings of Marx's theory persist to this very day.

NOTES

1. Herbert Marcuse, *Reason and Revolution*, 2nd ed. (Boston: Beacon Press, 1954), p. 25.
2. Ibid., p. 26.
3. In this connection, Hannah Arendt has remarked that "the influence of Aristotle on the style of Marx's thought seems to me almost as characteristic and decisive as the influence of Hegel's philosophy," *The Human Condition* (Garden City, N.Y.: Anchor Books, 1959), p. 365.
4. Marcuse, *Reason and Revolution*, p. 113.
5. Ibid., p. 113.
6. Ibid., pp. 273–74.
7. Karl Marx, *Capital* (Moscow: Foreign Languages Publishing House, 1954), Vol. I, p. 80.
8. Karl Marx, *Economic and Philosophic Manuscripts of 1844* (Moscow: Foreign Language Publishing House, 1961), p. 105.
9. Karl Marx and Frederick Engels, *German Ideology* (New York: International Publishers, 1960), p. 22.
10. However, unlike his friend and colleague, Frederick Engels, Marx made no attempt to codify dialectical reasoning into a rigid system equally applicable to nature and society. A critique of Engels's view of the dialectic and his vacillation between Hegelianism and Positivism may be found in George Lichtheim's *Marxism: An Historical and Critical Study* (New York: Frederick A. Praeger, 1962), and in Sidney Hook's *Reason, Social Myths and Democracy* (New York: Harper & Row, 1940).
11. Marx, *Capital*, p. 20.
12. Ibid., p. 20.
13. Ibid., p. 19.
14. Franz Mehring, *Karl Marx* (Ann Arbor: University of Michigan Press, 1962), p. 280.
15. See T. B. Bottomore and M. Rubel, eds., *Karl Marx: Selected Writings in Sociology and Social Philosophy* (London: C. A. Watts, 1961), pp. 67–69.

15

Marx's Historical Sociology

Marx died in 1883. Soon after, "Marxism" came to stand for a theory in which economic and other "material" factors explained the structure of society and the course of history. That was the dominant view among Marxists and critics of Marxism alike. Marx and Engels, it was widely believed, had proposed that callous self-interest governs individuals, classes, and nations, driving the world forward. The history of people throughout the centuries is to be explained by a changing, complex interplay of strictly material causes. Economics is everything! Marxism was thus reduced to a one-factor theory.

At the same time, Marx's theory was transformed by his followers in another respect. Marx's focus on the connections between economic development and social-class formation was reduced to a form of technological determinism. Economic and historical changes were thus made to depend directly on technical changes in the instruments of work. Changes in some important element of production—the discovery of a new raw material or fuel—was said to determine the movement of history.

In time, both economic and technological determinism came to be regarded as one-sided and misleading. Prominent Marxists, often under the influence of outstanding non-Marxist thinkers, assailed these forms of "vulgar Marxism" and exposed them as basic distortions of the founder's ideas. The efforts of these critics were largely successful, for they convincingly reconstituted the original complexity of Marx's conception of history. Under their influence, Marxism came to be regarded as an "open," nondogmatic theoretical approach. Adherents of this view stressed the relative autonomy of the noneconomic spheres of society and underscored the role of human consciousness and will in the making of history.

In recent years, however, the "open" view has itself come under attack. There has been a reversion to the older, deterministic versions of Marx's ideas. Indeed, several recent studies of Marx's social thought have attributed to him a narrow, technological and "productive force" determinism.

Recent interpretations, like those of the late nineteenth and early twentieth centuries, base themselves on the presumed centrality of Marx's "Preface" of 1859—a text that we shall later examine in some detail. W. H. Shaw declares openly for a "technological-determinist interpretation," while G. A. Cohen adopts the "technological" label but eschews the "determinist" one.[1] Yet, Cohen alleges that for Marx,"... history is the development of human power, but the course of its development is not subject to human will" (p. 148). In Marx's "Preface," as we shall see, he speaks of "forces of production" and "relations of production" and refers to the economic structure of society as the real "foundation" (or "base") on which there arise legal and political "superstructures." Both Shaw and Cohen subscribe to the simple, mechanistic "primacy thesis," in which the "foundation" is the cause of historical development and "superstructure" the effect. Primacy, for Cohen, means "unidirectional/ity/" (p. 137); he thus rejects any "dialectical" (pp. 138, 145) or interactive relationship between "forces of production" and "relations of production." Cohen concedes, however, that the "relations" do condition the "forces." Hence Shaw and Cohen believe that for an explanation of social change and revolution, an objective analysis of base-superstructure relations will suffice.

Such reversions to a mechanistic Marxism suggest that it is necessary to take still another look at the original texts and to address the key questions systematically.

MARX'S FAMOUS "PREFACE"

In 1859 Marx wrote a preface to *A Contribution to the Critique of Political Economy.* The preface has long been regarded as Marx's most succinct formulation of his theory, and recent interpreters of Marx have treated the preface as the *locus classicus* of Marx's conception of history. The text therefore deserves to be quoted in its entirety:

> I was led by my studies to the conclusion that legal relations as well as forms of State could neither be understood by themselves, nor explained by the so-called general progress of the human mind, but that they are rooted in the material conditions of life, which are summed up by Hegel after the fashion of the

> English and French writers of the eighteenth century under the name *civil society,* and that the anatomy of civil society is to be sought in political economy. The study of the latter which I had begun in Paris, I continued in Brussels where I had emigrated on account of an expulsion order issued by M. Guizot. The general conclusion at which I arrived and which, once reached, continued to serve as the guiding thread in my studies, may be formulated briefly as follows: In the social production which men carry on they enter into definite relations that are indispensable and independent of their will; these relations of production correspond to a definite stage of development of their material powers of production. The totality of these relations of production constitutes the economic structure of society—the real foundation, on which legal and political superstructures arise and to which definite forms of social consciousness correspond. The mode of production of material life determines the general character of the social, political and spiritual processes of life. It is not the consciousness of men that determines their being, but, on the contrary, their social being determines their consciousness. At a certain stage of their development, the material forces of production in society come in conflict with the existing relations of production, or—what is but a legal expression for the same thing—with the property relations within which they they had been at work before. From forms of development of the forces of production these relations turn into their fetters. Then occurs a period of social revolution. With the change of the economic foundation the entire immense superstructure is more or less rapidly transformed. In considering such transformations the distinction should always be made between the material transformation of the economic conditions of production which can be determined with the precision of natural science, and the legal, political, religious, aesthetic or philosophical—in short ideological, forms in which men become conscious of this conflict and fight it out. Just as our opinion of an individual is not based on what he thinks of himself, so can we not judge of such a period of transformation by its own consciousness; on the contrary, this consciousness must rather be explained from the contradictions of material life, from the existing conflict between the social forces of production and the relations of production. No social order ever disappears before all the productive forces for which there is room in it have been developed; and new, higher relations of production never appear before the material conditions of their existence have matured in the womb of the old society. Therefore, mankind always sets itself only such problems as it can solve; since, on closer examination, it will always be found that the problem itself arises only when the material conditions necessary for its solution already exist or are at least in the process of formation. In broad outline we can designate the Asiatic, the ancient, the feudal, and the modern bourgeois modes of production as progressive epochs in the economic formation of society. The bourgeois relations of production are the last antagonistic form of the social process of production; not in the sense of individual antagonisms, but of conflict arising from conditions surrounding the life of individuals in society. At the same time the productive forces developing in the womb of bourgeois society create the material conditions for the solution of that antagonism. With this social formation, therefore, the pre-history of human society comes to an end.[2]

As the reader will note, Marx here speaks of an economic "foundation" and of legal and political "superstructures." He goes on to say that the "mode of production" ". . . determines the general character of the social, political and spiritual processes of life" and in a most unequivocal way he asserts that it is social existence that determines social consciousness. It also appears that Marx assigns causal priority to the "forces of production" in bringing about social change. Little wonder, then, that both his followers and critics have continued to labor under the misapprehension that Marx had advocated a form of economic determinism in which the "foundation" is the cause, and the "superstructure" the effect.

Frederick Engels, Marx's colleague and friend who coauthored many of their writings, also contributed to the misapprehension of their views. When Engels discovered after Marx's death that their so-called "materialist conception of history" was widely misunderstood, he undertook to clarify their position in several letters that are by now quite well known among Marx scholars. To J. Bloch, Engels wrote,

> The economic situation is the basis, but the various elements of the superstructure . . . also exercise their influence upon the course of historical struggles and in many cases preponderate in determining their *form*. There is an interaction of all these elements [of the superstructure] in which, amid all the endless host of accidents (that is, of things and events, whose inner connection is so remote or so impossible of proof that we can regard it as nonexistent, as negligible) the economic movement finally asserts itself as necessary.[3]

And to H. Starkenburg, Engels wrote in a similar vein,

> Political, juridical, philosophical, religious, literary, artistic, etc., development is based on economic development. But all these react upon one another and also upon the economic basis. It is not that the economic condition is the cause and alone active, while everything else only has a passive effect. There is, rather, interaction on the basis of economic necessity, which *ultimately* always asserts itself.[4]

Here we see that while Engels allows for some interaction between "base" and "superstructure," he insists in both letters that economic conditions ultimately assert themselves. The effect of these letters was to reaffirm the causal priority of economic conditions.

In the light of Engels's letters (which are representative of his many other pronouncements on the subject) and Marx's own formulation in the "Preface," we are justified in saying that Marx and Engels must share responsibility for the widespread and persistent misunderstanding of their views. That is not all. Engels and Marx must also share responsibility for the impression that they were social evolutionists and that the only difference between them and other nineteenth-century evolutionists was that Marx and Engels designated the "mode of production" as the motor of evolutionary change. In the "Preface" Marx states that the " . . . Asiatic, ancient [slave], feudal, and modern bourgeois modes of production can be designated as progressive epochs in the economic foundation of society." Hence we have the additional question of whether Marx and Engels were in fact evolutionists.

Of course, one cannot simply dismiss either the "Preface" or Engels's letters; neither must we take the centrality of the "Preface" for granted, as a host of commentators have done. The only reliable way of assessing the importance of the "Preface" and thus ferreting out its true meaning, is to place it in the context of Marx's total scholarly output. Only by this method will we learn why Marx expressed himself as he did in the "Preface"; only by such a method will we learn whether or not Marx proposed some sort of suprahistorical theory in which economic conditions and "productive forces" constitute everywhere and always the prime mover of history. Our procedure therefore will be to examine the texts in which Marx and Engels discussed the major modes of production, or socioeconomic epochs, in history. We will then ask what those texts imply for an adequate interpretation of the "Preface."

TRIBAL OWNERSHIP

In *The German Ideology*, one of their earliest coauthored works, Marx and Engels introduced the concept "mode of production." In that work, as in the "Preface," the concept "mode of production" embraces both "productive forces" and "relations of production." A society's "productive forces" may be analyzed into several components:

a. the social cooperation of the producers themselves, as it is conditioned by,
b. the existing instruments of production,
c. the available technical knowhow and, finally,
d. the society's natural habitat.

"Relations of production," on the other hand, refers to property relations or forms of ownership. If, therefore, *productive forces* speaks to the question of how a society produces its means of livelihood and goods, *relations of production* addresses the question of who owns and/or controls a society's productive resources.

Now, from the "Preface" one may gain the impression that Marx sought the key to social change solely in the internal dynamic of the productive forces pressing upon the existing relations of production. But Marx's other writings make it quite clear that that is not at all what he had intended. In *The German Ideology*, for example, Marx writes that the entire internal structure of a society ". . . depends on the stage of development reached by its production and its internal and *external* intercourse."[5] Moreover, Marx designates the first form of ownership as "tribal," a form coinciding with an elementary division of labor. "The social structure," he continues,

> is therefore limited to an extension of the family; patriarchal family chieftains; below them the members of the tribe; finally slaves. The slavery latent in the

> family only develops gradually with the increase of population, the growth of wants, *and with the extension of external relations of war or of trade.*[6]

The italicized passage makes the point we are after. It leaves no doubt that for Marx and Engels a significant social change, such as the development of slavery, could not be explained solely as a result of the growth of "productive forces"—or of any other solely internal factor.

Marx did not somehow change his mind about this matter between the time of writing *The German Ideology* (1846) and the "Preface" (1859). Throughout the *Grundrisse* (1857–58), a large draft of his chief work, *Das Kapital (Capital)*, Marx pays due regard to external relations. His discussion of nomadic and pastoral peoples, whether in the Asiatic steppes or among the Indian tribes of America, is a case in point. "The only barrier," writes Marx,

> which the community can encounter in relating to the natural conditions of production—the earth—as to its own property (if we jump ahead to the settled peoples) is *another community*, which already claims it as its own inorganic body. *Warfare* is therefore one of the earliest occupations of each of these naturally arisen communities, both for the defense of their property and for obtaining new property.[7]

And Marx continues,

> If human beings themselves are conquered along with the land and soil as its organic accessories, then they are equally conquered as one of the conditions of production, *and in this way arises slavery and serfdom*, which soon corrupts and modifies the original forms of all communities, and then itself becomes their basis.[8]

Of course, Marx does not mean to suggest that war and pillaging are sufficient explanations of slavery. In fact, he vehemently rejects a received opinion to that effect and reminds his reader that slavery presupposes economic conditions of a certain kind. For "pillage to be possible," he writes,

> there must be something to be pillaged, hence production. And the mode of pillage is itself in turn determined by the mode of production . . . . To steal a slave is to steal the instrument of production directly. But then the production of the country for which the slave is stolen must be structured to allow of slave labour, or (as in the southern part of America, etc.), a mode of production corresponding to the slave must be created.[9]

So the "mode of production" is an essential element in an analysis of how and why slavery has appeared in a given society, or why other significant changes have occurred within it. But even the fullest examination of the "mode of production" will fail to provide the whole answer. When, for instance, a pastoral people finally settles down, ". . . the extent to which this original community is modified will depend on various external, climatic, geographic, physical, etc., conditions as well as their particular natural disposition—their clan character."[10] This is surely as far from one-factor determinism as one can get.

We have only scratched the surface. For there exists a mountain of evidence with which to demonstrate that in their actual analyses of societies and institutions Marx and Engels never confined themselves to economic conditions. In his well-known essay called "The Mark," Engels provided a historical sketch of the agrarian conditions of the ancient Germanic peoples. Basing himself on the writings of Caesar and Tacitus, Engels describes the earliest known forms of communal landed property among the German tribes. A large portion of these migratory peoples cultivated their fields in common when they temporarily settled down. Nevertheless, hereditary, private property existed among them from earliest times. How does Engels explain that fact? "The first piece of ground," he writes,

> that passed into the private property of individuals was that on which the house stood. The inviolability of the dwelling, that basis of all personal freedom, was transferred from the caravan of the nomadic train to the log house of the stationary peasant, and gradually was transformed into a complete right of property in the homestead.[11]

The free German's homestead had from earliest times been excluded from the common property of the mark. Inaccessible to officials, the homestead was a refuge for fugitives. The inviolability of the dwelling was firmly rooted in German tribal, customary law. The sacredness of the dwelling, Engels concludes,

> . . . *was not the effect but the cause of its transformation into private property.*[12]

So much for the allegation that Marx and Engels always considered ideas as derivative from economic or other "material" conditions.

Moreover, kingship soon arose among the Germans, a tendency favored by the existence of *retinues.* In earliest times, leaders among the Germanic tribes were elected for their military prowess. At the same time, however, leading men organized retinues, that is, private associations of warriors recruited on the basis of their military skills. Recruited from diverse clans and tribes, young men joined a retinue eager for the booty they would gain in raids upon neighboring groups. The spoils—primarily cattle, slaves, and jewelry—remained the private property of the retinue members, and never became communal clan property. Differences of wealth thus increased inside the clans, severely weakening the democratic-communal character of Germanic society as it existed at the time. Hence the retinues, Engels observed, were

> the beginnings of the decay of the old freedom of the people and showed themselves to be such during and after the migrations. For in the first place they favored the rise of monarchic power. In the second place, as Tacitus already notes, they could only be kept together by continual wars and plundering expeditions. Plunder became an end in itself. If the leader of the retinue found nothing to do in the neighborhood, he set out with his men to other peoples

> where there was war and the prospect of booty. . . . When the Roman empire had been conquered, these retinues of the kings formed the second main stock, after the unfree and the Roman courtiers, from which the later nobility was drawn.[13]

For Engels private property among the Germanic peoples developed out of several conditions. There was first the old Germanic tradition of treating the family dwelling as sacred and inviolable. This custom, originating in the Germanic migratory culture, led to private homesteads once they settled down. Second was the Roman influence. In their conquests of Roman territory, where the soil had been private property for centuries, the Germans "borrowed" this institution. Finally, there were the retinues, which had become permanent, and of mixed clan composition. When the retinues went to war, it was increasingly the case that the men fought not side by side with their own kinsmen, but with their fellow retinue warriors. Retinues followed and obeyed their own leaders rather than the duly elected military chieftains of the people, which led to very significant social changes.

Among the early Germans, as among many primitive agricultural societies, tillage was typically the work of the women, while men hunted and looked after the domesticated animals, such as cattle. But with the introduction of the horse-drawn plough, tillage and other forms of heavy work in the fields was transferred to men. The growth of the retinues, however, caused a reversion to the old practice. The young men engaged in wars and forays while the women, old men, and children tended to the fields and to the running of the homes. The young men had an increasingly tenuous connection with production, and *war* became a major method of appropriation. By Tacitus' time, retinue members had acquired substantial herds of cattle and received the produce of the fields worked by their slaves. Growing dependence on booty as a source of wealth gave rise among the retinues to contempt for agricultural labor, which was left more and more to women, children, and slaves. Thus what the retinues had become in the 150-year period between Caesar and Tacitus served to undermine the older communal institutions in several ways:

- Retinue leaders became largely independent of the discipline of their kinsmen and even of the tribal assembly of warriors.
- Retinue leaders became monarchs and nobles whose accumulated wealth and power raised them above their kinsmen.
- Retinues became "international," that is, they cut across the boundaries of the various tribes and peoples.
- Retinue leaders and members alike bequeathed their property to their own children rather than to their entire kindred, thus undermining the clan and elevating the family at the clan's expense.

We see that Engels's analysis of early Germanic society was quite complex. The developments leading to the emergence of private property as an institution, to the crystallization of socioeconomic classes and to the rise of a monarchical state, were partly economic and partly noneconomic. An understanding of these changes required a study of the history of the Germanic peoples from the time of *Caesar's Memoirs of the Gallic Wars* (51 B.C.) to the time of Tacitus' *Germania* (98 A.D.). The structural changes that Germanic society had undergone in that 150-year period, Engels clearly understood, could never be adequately grasped by any theoretical formula. No economic or "productive force" determinism could ever explain why the highly communal Germanic people were transformed into a class society.

Indeed, what is striking about Engels's analysis is the prominent role he assigns not to "productive forces," but to "force" in general. The decline of the "mark," that is, German communal institutions and the prevalence of the retinues, was accompanied by the formation of feudalism. The constant wars of the early Middle Ages, wrote Engels,

> . . . whose regular consequences were confiscations of land, ruined a great number of peasants, so that even during the Merovingian dynasty, there were very many free men owning no land. The incessant wars of Charlemagne broke down the mainstay of the free peasantry. . . . [The] eternal wars between kings, and feuds between nobles, compelled one free peasant after another to seek the protection of some lord . . . ; by fraud, by promises, threats, violence, they forced more and more peasants and peasants' land under their yoke. . . . [The] peasants' land was added to the lord's manor, and was, at best, only given back for the use of the peasant in return for tribute and service. Thus the peasant, from a free owner of the land, was turned into a tribute-paying, service-rendering appanage of it, into a serf.[14]

For Marx and Engels, it is clear, feudal serfdom was an outgrowth of war and military conquest which disrupted the old tribal pattern by turning retinue leaders and other military chieftains into sovereigns and lords.

PRODUCTIVE FORCES: DID MARX IN FACT ASSIGN THEM CAUSAL PRIORITY?

Earlier we observed that some commentators ascribe to Marx a form of "productive force" or technological determinism. So before we examine other modes of production, we should pause to ask this question: Are "productive forces," for Marx, some kind of inexorable, prime mover of history?

It is true that not only in the "Preface" but elsewhere as well, Marx occasionally expressed himself in a manner that lends support to a technological interpretation of his theory. There is, for instance, that famous passage in *The Poverty of Philosophy* (1847), where Marx remarks

> The hand-mill gives you a society with the feudal lord; the steam-mill, a society with the industrial capitalist.[15]

Many commentators have taken this aphorism literally. They have ignored the more careful formulation Marx introduced some twenty pages later in the same book:

> Labour is organized, is divided differently according to the instruments it disposes over. The hand-mill presupposes a different division of labour from the steam-mill.[16]

Here we see clearly the meaning Marx had intended; as the instruments of production vary, so does the *division of labor*—but not necessarily the nature of the society as a whole, or even its class structure.
Similarly, in *Capital,* Vol. I, Marx wrote:

> Relics of bygone instruments of labour possess the same importance for the investigation of extinct economical forms of society, as do fossil bones for the determination of extinct species of animals. It is not the articles made, but how they are made, and by what instruments, that enables us to distinguish different economical epochs. Instruments of labour not only supply a standard of degree of development to which human labour has attained, but they are also indicators of the social conditions under which that labour is carried on.[17]

Thus Marx proposes a kind of "archeology" based on changing forms of instruments of labor. But, as we shall see, Marx understood, as does every good archeologist, that from tools alone only limited inferences can be made about social forms.

"Productive forces" are fundamental for Marx in this sense: The level of their development is the necessary but not sufficient condition for the emergence of certain social formations. If a laborer needs all of his time to produce the necessary means of subsistence for himself and his dependents,

> . . . he has no time left to work gratis for others. Without a certain degree of productiveness of his labour, he has no such superfluous time at his disposal; without such superfluous time, no surplus labour, and therefore no capitalists, no slave-owners, no feudal lords, in a word, no class of large proprietors.[18]

Production, writes Marx, the rudimentary process of producing use-values,

> is the necessary condition for effecting exchange of matter between man and Nature; it is the everlasting Nature-imposed condition of human existence, and therefore is independent of every social phase of that existence, or rather, is common to every such phase.[19]

But in the very same paragraph Marx adds:

> as the taste of porridge does not tell you who grew the oats, *no more does this simple process [i.e., production] tell you of itself what are the social conditions under which it is taking place, whether under the slave-owner's brutal lash, or the anxious eye of the capitalist. . . .*

This last passage speaks loudly, for it demonstrates that though the hand-mill presupposes a division of labor different from the steam-mill, neither type of mill, in and of itself, tells us anything about the "property relations" under which it is being employed.

For a proper understanding of the concept "productive forces," we must remember that Marx makes a fundamental distinction between capitalist and precapitalist modes of production. Modern capitalist industry, Marx writes,

> . . . never looks upon and treats the existing form of a process as final. The technical basis of that industry is therefore revolutionary, while all earlier modes of production were *conservative.*[20]

This is the same point Marx made in the *Communist Manifesto*, where he stated that whereas the bourgeoisie could not exist without revolutionizing the instruments of production:

> Conservation, in an unaltered form, of the old modes of production was, on the contrary, the first condition of existence of all earlier industrial classes.[21]

An example of such earlier classes would be the guilds of the Middle Ages where traditional ways of producing were highly valued and preserved.

The conclusion is beyond doubt. If, for Marx, precapitalist modes of production were *conservative,* he never could have intended his formulation in the "Preface" to mean that "productive forces" are a constantly and invincibly expanding force in history—the major cause of the historical changes that societies have undergone. And, of course, more direct evidence is plentiful that Marx and Engels never proposed such an untenable notion. In *The German Ideology*, in their discussion of the conditions of emerging feudalism, Marx and Engels wrote:

> The last centuries of the declining Roman Empire and its conquest by the barbarians *destroyed a number of productive forces;* agriculture had declined, industry had decayed for want of a market, trade had died out or been violently suspended, the rural and urban population had decreased. From these conditions and the mode of organization of the conquest determined by them, feudal property developed under the influence of the Germanic military constitution.[22]

And in a later context they wrote:

> *It depends purely on the extension of commerce whether the productive forces achieved in a locality, especially inventions, are lost for later development or not.* As long as there exists no commerce transcending the immediate neighborhood, every invention must be made separately in each locality, and mere chances such as irruptions of barbaric peoples, even ordinary wars, are sufficient to cause a country with advanced productive forces and needs to have to start right over again from the beginning. In primitive history every invention had to be made daily anew and in each locality independently. That highly productive forces are little safe from complete destruction, given even a very extensive commerce, is proved by the Phoenicians, whose inventions were for the most part lost for a long time to come through the ousting of this nation from commerce, its con-

> quest by Alexander and its consequent decline. . . . *Only when commerce has become world-commerce and has as its basis big industry,* when all nations are drawn into the competitive struggle, is the permanence of the acquired productive forces assured.[23]

A similar point is made by Engels while describing the conditions of the declining Roman Empire:

> . . . the level of production had neither risen nor fallen significantly during the following four centuries and had therefore with equal necessity again produced the same distribution of property and the same classes in the population.[24]

In light of such evidence we can see that there are no good grounds for believing that Marx viewed productive forces as a universal, ever-expanding lever of social change. Only in the epoch of modern capitalist industry and world commerce was there a consolidated growth of productive forces. Furthermore, there is a good deal more evidence with which to support this interpretation.

THE FEUDAL MODE OF PRODUCTION

Whether it was a matter of explaining the rise of the ancient slave systems of Greece and Rome or the feudal order of medieval Europe, Marx and Engels considered a variety of factors. Nowhere did they attempt to explain historical change by means of economic or technological factors alone.

In the history of European society, the chattel slavery of antiquity eventually gave way to a different type of organization called "feudalism." With the decline of the Roman Empire, the seminomadic cultivators were tied down to the soil. Although ultimately that may have increased the productivity of the temperate forest zone, Marx nowhere attempts to explain the establishment of feudalism as a result of the growing "productive forces." On the contrary, he sees the origins of feudalism in several closely connected circumstances—the disintegration of the Roman Empire into a multiplicity of military chieftainships, a process accompanied by the barbarian invasions and the decline of the towns. Originally the mode of production in many of the empire's provinces was based on common possession or access to the soil. "Part of the land," Marx notes,

> was cultivated in severalty as freehold by the members of the community, another part—*ager publicus*—was cultivated by them in common. The products of this common labour served partly as a public store for providing costs of war, religion, and other common expenses. In the course of time military and clerical dignitaries usurped, along with the common land, the labour spent upon it. The labour of the free peasants on their common land was transformed into corvée for the thieves of the common land.[25]

Corvée gave rise to the servile relationship called serfdom. The corvée rarely arose from serfdom. On the contrary, "serfdom much more frequently . . . took origin from the corvée."[26]

Throughout their scattered remarks on the formation of feudalism, Marx and Engels stress the role of force and violence. Not only that, they also criticize others for neglecting the role of force and for interpreting the transition from slavery to serfdom as unambiguous evolutionary progress. In 1882 Engels published his essay, "The Mark," basing his analysis largely on the work of the eminent German historian Georg Ludwig Maurer (1790–1872). Although Engels much admired Maurer and acknowledged his debt to him, he nevertheless criticized him in a letter to Marx. Maurer's errors, Engels argued, were a consequence of the

> . . . insufficient importance which he attaches to *force* and the part it plays [and] from his enlightened prejudice that since the dark Middle Ages a steady progress to a better state of things must simply have taken place; *this prevents him [Maurer] from seeing not only the antagonistic character of real progress, but also the individual retrogressions.*[27]

Unlike Maurer, then, Engels gave due attention to *force,* and to antagonisms and retrogressions. If the conditions of the peasants improved in the middle of the thirteenth century, it was thanks to the consequences of the Crusades. "Many of the lords," writes Engels,

> when they set out to the East, explicitly set their peasant serfs free. Others were killed and never returned. Hundreds of noble families vanished, whose peasant serfs frequently gained their freedom.[28]

Yet the rise of towns in the fourteenth and fifteenth centuries had the opposite effect on the peasants. The luxurious life of the town patricians aroused the envy of the coarsely fed and clothed country lords in their roughly furnished dwellings. Engels continued:

> Lying in wait for traveling merchants became more and more dangerous and unprofitable. But to buy them [the goods the merchants had to sell], money was requisite. And that the peasants alone could furnish. Hence, renewed oppression of the peasants, higher tributes, and more corvée; hence renewed and always increasing eagerness to force the free peasants to become bondmen, the bondmen to become serfs, and to turn the common mark land into land belonging to the lord.[29]

In that way the flourishing towns gave the manorial lords an interest in the expanding market economy and prompted them to intensify the exploitation of their peasants—that is, to squeeze larger surpluses out of them.

Despite the widespread usurpation of the peasant's common lands in the earlier feudal period, there remained for common use uncultivated soil as well as forest and pasture land in many parts of Germany. When the lords moved to usurp those common lands, they provoked the great peasant uprisings of the early sixteenth century.[30] With the defeat of the peasants by the princes and lords, a renewed serfdom became prevalent. "In those places where the fighting raged," writes Engels,

> all remaining rights of the peasants were now shamelessly trodden under foot, their common land turned into the property of the lord, and themselves into serfs.[31]

Then came the devastations of the Thirty Years' War breaking the peasants' last power of resistance; unlimited corvée was introduced anew and serfdom became general until it was shattered from without by the French Revolution.

For Marx and Engels the establishment and development of feudal serfdom are complex processes to which war and other historical events contributed. And the emergence of the market economy, instead of alleviating the peasant's burden, accomplished the exact opposite. In any event, it is indisputable that for these thinkers there certainly was no straight line of progress from the ancient society to that of feudal serfdom.

Historically, feudalism has been associated with simple instruments of production, with production for the immediate needs of the household or village community and with a politically decentralized system. The lord of each manor rendered the juridical function for the dependent population. In the earliest period, production for the market was either nonexistent or minimal. Hence the feudal mode of production as a pure type, was not an exchange economy. That is to say that what was produced on the manor had not yet become a "commodity." For Marx, the term "commodity" refers to an article produced for exchange, for the market. Only when the peasant family began to produce more than enough for its own wants and for the dues payments to the lord, did exchange begin. The surplus products were offered for sale. These products became commodities, thus providing the manorial lords with money income. It is true that in the towns the artisans produced for the market from the very beginning. As Engels observed, however, even the artisans:

> supplied the greatest part of their own individual wants. They had gardens and plots of land. They turned their cattle out into the communal forest, which also yielded them timber and firing. The women spun flax, wool, and so forth. Production for the purpose of exchange, production of commodities, was only in its infancy. Hence exchange was restricted, the market narrow, *the methods of production stable. . . .*[32]

Under feudalism the methods of production were stable. In time, however, the "natural economy," producing for self-subsistent village communities, gave way to an exchange economy. In Marx's vocabulary, products that earlier had only "use-value," now acquired "exchange-value" as well. Commodity production became a growing tendency. It was only with respect to this epoch and the emergence of capitalism that one could justifiably speak of growing "productive forces" coming into conflict with the existing "relations of production." For it was capitalism, as we have seen, that Marx regarded as the first revolutionary mode of production in history. But before we turn our attention to that revolutionary mode, we must explore another conservative mode of production.

THE ASIATIC MODE OF PRODUCTION: ITS SIGNIFICANCE FOR MARX'S THEORY

In developing his conception of the Asiatic mode of production, Marx relied heavily on English classical economics. Adam Smith had already noted that similarities among several governments in Asia appeared to be related to the complex irrigation and water-regulation projects of those societies, and he commented upon the extraordinary power of the rulers in ancient Egypt, China, and India.[33] James Mill viewed the "Asiatic model of government" as a distinct institutional type not to be confused with European feudalism.[34] Richard Jones provided a general portrait of Asiatic society,[35] and John Stuart Mill placed that society in a comparative framework.[36]

Other thinkers had noted the peculiarities of Asiatic society and government, even earlier than the English economists. Montesquieu, for example, in his classification of societies, included a type he called Asiatic "despotism." That was a type in which all groups in society were so weak that organized resistance to the despot was impossible. Everyone was equal in his condition of servitude to the ruler. Machiavelli contrasted two different types of government exemplified by the Turkish empire and the kingdom of France. Though he made no explicit use of the term despotism, his discussion shows that he understood the basic *political* differences between oriental despotism and feudalism.[37]

It was in 1853 that Marx and Engels began, for the first time, to give more sustained attention to Asia. Their interest was prompted by British colonial behavior in China and India. From that time on, Marx employed not only the concept "Asiatic mode," but, in addition, the terms "Oriental despotism," "Asiatic society," and other such designations. The Marx–Engels conception of the Asiatic mode must be constructed from their correspondence, from several articles that Marx wrote for the *New York Daily Tribune,* and from numerous remarks scattered throughout the writings of both men.

In a letter to Engels dated June 2, 1853, Marx relates how informative and insightful he found François Bernier's *Travels Containing a Description of the Dominions of the Great Moguls.* Quoting several passages from Bernier's work, which he describes as "brilliant," Marx notes the distinctive condition of Eastern society, ". . . namely, that the *king is the one and only proprietor of all the land* in the kingdom. . . ." Marx then goes on to say that "Bernier rightly considered the basis of all phenomena in the East—he refers to Turkey, Persia, Hindustan—to be the *absence of private property in land.* This is the real key, even to the Oriental heaven. . . . "[38]

In his reply (June 6, 1853), Engels agreed that the ". . . absence of property in land is indeed the key to the whole of the East," but he then went on to ask how it came about that the Orientals never arrived ". . . at landed property, even in its feudal form?" Here is Engels's explanation:

> I think it is mainly due to the climate, taken in connection with the nature of the soil, especially with the great stretches of desert which extend from the Sahara straight across Arabia, Persia, India and Tatary up to the highest Asiatic plateau. *Artificial irrigation is here the first condition of agriculture* and this is a matter either for the communes, the provinces or the central government. . . . The artificial fertilization of the land, which immediately ceased when the irrigation system fell into decay, explains the otherwise curious fact that whole stretches which were once brilliantly cultivated are now waste and bare (Palmyra, Petra, the ruins in the Yemen, districts in Egypt, Persia and Hindustan); it explains the fact that one single devastating war could depopulate a country for centuries and strip it of its whole civilization.[39]

Marx took the analysis further in his response to Engels on June 14, 1853. In that letter Marx stressed the *stationary* character, economically speaking, of that part of Asia, and suggested that it is to be explained by two related facts:

1. that the public water and other works were under the control of the central government; and
2. that the entire empire ". . . was divided into *villages,* each of which possessed a completely separate organization and formed a little world in itself."[40]

Every village was a *self-sufficient* community, almost identical to every other. At the head of each village stood a representative of the central government. He was a kind of superintendant of affairs who settled the disputes of inhabitants, supervised the police, and collected the village taxes. The economic organization of the village typically included a record keeper, a watchman of the village crops, an official who ensured that irrigation water was justly distributed to the several fields, and an astrologer who determined the planting and harvest times. In addition, every village had its own craftsmen and artisans: a smith, carpenter, potter, washerman, barber, and a silversmith, who often also served as poet and schoolmaster. Finally, there was the Brahmin for worship.

Marx quoted a parliamentary report describing this village structure in which:

> the inhabitants of the country have lived from time immemorial. . . . The inhabitants give themselves no trouble about the breaking up and division of kingdoms; while the village remains entire, they care not to what power it is transferred, or to what sovereign it devolves; its internal economy remains unchanged.

And Marx comments,

> I do not think anyone could imagine a more solid foundation for stagnant Asiatic despotism.[41]

For Marx and Engels Oriental despotism was a system in which all power was centralized in the hands of the emperor, the political sovereign *and* the absolute landlord. The absolute power of the emperor rested on the fact that the myriad villages were like so many disunited atoms incapable of offering resistance to the central government. Villages had no real property in land and depended totally on the central government and its officials for the proper and adequate irrigation of the soil.

All governments associated with the Asiatic mode of production performed the economic function of providing public works, mainly irrigation and drainage or, in a word, the artificial fertilization of the soil. Those are the distinctive circumstances that account for the fact, writes Marx, that

> However changing the political aspect of India's past must appear, its social condition has remained unaltered since its remotest antiquity, until the first decennium of the nineteenth century.[42]

It was only under British colonial rule that the Asiatic mode was undermined. For the British, unlike previous rulers, had entirely neglected the public water works of India, thus causing a fateful deterioration of agriculture.

For Marx, the Asiatic form thus hung on so tenaciously for so long a time owing to its ". . . presupposition that the individual does not become independent *vis-à-vis* the commune; that there is a self-sustaining circle of production, unity of agriculture and manufactures. . . ."[43] Engels, in his book *Anti-Dühring,* made similar points. The self-sufficiency of the Asian village communities was such that for

> . . . thousands of years Oriental despotism and the changing rule of conquering nomad peoples were unable to injure the old communities. . . .[44] However great the number of despotisms [Engels continues in another context] which arose and fell in Persia and India, each was fully aware that above all it was the entrepreneur responsible for the collective maintenance of irrigation throughout the river valleys, without which no agriculture was possible there. It was reserved for the enlightened English to lose sight of this in India; they let the irrigation canals and sluices fall into decay, and now at last are discovering, through the regularly recurring famines, that they have neglected the one activity which might have made their rule in India at least as legitimate as that of their predecessors.[45]

The Asiatic mode of production thus formed the basis for thousands of years of ". . . the cruelest form of state, Oriental despotism, from India to Russia."[46]

It is important to emphasize that for Marx and Engels there was a sharp contrast between the Asiatic and feudal modes of production. The dominance of the Oriental despot precluded genuine, private ownership of land, the precondition of feudalism. If anything distinguished the Orient, it was the absolute supremacy of the State, so that even the advantaged and privileged elements were never genuine land *lords.* No real feudalism had existed in India and China, the two Asian countries that received the most attention from Marx and Engels.

THEORETICAL IMPLICATIONS

It follows from everything that has been said so far that Marx's conception of the Asiatic mode of production has definite implications for an understanding of his theory and method. If the Asiatic mode was above all a *stationary* one from time immemorial until the nineteenth century, that can only mean that the "productive forces" were stable and unchanging. That fact alone is sufficient to refute the erroneous but widespread view that Marx, in the "Preface," had set forth a theory that growing "productive forces" are the *universal* source of social change.

It also follows from Marx's conception of the Asiatic mode that he never proposed a theory of *unilinear* development. Even if one insists that Marx did in fact propose a theory of social evolution or development—a view that we shall later challenge—the Asiatic mode allows for only one inference: Marx and Engels discerned at least *two* lines of development, the Western and the Eastern.

Our rejection of the universal, unilinear interpretation of Marx's conception of history may appear to be irreconcilable with one statement in particular that he made in the "Preface." There, we will recall, Marx wrote, "In broad outline we can designate the Asiatic, the ancient, the feudal, and the modern bourgeois modes of production as progressive epochs in the economic formation of society." This statement has traditionally reinforced the impression that Marx perceived only one line of development. To attain a full understanding of why such an impression is quite mistaken, we must first consider Marx's view of capitalism, its origin, and its development.

THE CAPITALIST MODE OF PRODUCTION

One cannot, of course, date the beginnings of a historical process with precision. Marx relied on the historians of the time who largely agreed that it was from the thirteenth and fourteenth centuries on that the "natural economy" of Europe, producing for self-subsistent manorial villages, was increasingly replaced by an exchange economy. In Marx's vocabulary, products that earlier had only "use-value" now acquired "exchange-value" as well. Commodity production, or production for the market, became a growing tendency. Yet this was not capitalism, as yet, but rather a preparatory stage for it.

For Marx, money and commodities were transformed into *capital* under specific historical circumstances. Capitalism requires that ". . . two very different kinds of commodity-possessors must come face to face and into contact; on the one hand, the owners of money, means of production, means of subsistence, who are eager to increase the sum of values they possess, by buying other people's labor power; on the other hand, free laborers, the sellers of their own labor-power and therefore the sellers of labor."[47] The laborers are free in two senses, the first literal and the second ironic. The typical laborers of capitalism are neither a part of the means of production, as are slaves and bondmen; nor do they possess means of production of their own, as do peasant proprietors. Laborers under capitalism have been "freed" or *separated* from their means of production, and are now entirely dependent for their survival on the sale of their labor. In the absence of "free labor" in the double meaning of the term, capitalism never could have arisen.

The origins of the capitalist mode of production may therefore be traced to the process that separates the producer from his means of production and means of subsistence, while placing those means under the exclusive control of the capitalist. Capitalism thus required the proletarianization of the agricultural population. A "proletarian" possesses nothing but the labor of his hands. How, then, did such a socioeconomic class emerge for the first time?

By the end of the fourteenth century, serfdom was almost nonexistent in England. The vast majority of the population consisted of free peasant proprietors. They worked with their own instruments of production and provided for their own subsistence. These peasant proprietors also enjoyed the usufruct of the common lands that provided them with timber and firewood, and provided their cattle with pasture. A century later, however, that state of affairs had begun to change. The power of the feudal lords had been so greatly reduced by the monarchy that it was not difficult for the Crown to break up the feudal retainers and to confiscate their estates. As a result, a mass of peasants and yeomen were driven from the soil. At the same time the more powerful feudal lords created an even larger proletariat by the forcible eviction of their peasants and by the usurpation of the common lands.

The forceful evictions were economically motivated. The continental wool manufacturers were prospering, which led, in turn, to a marked rise in the price of English wool. Marx describes the new nobility as a child of its time, for whom ". . . money was the power of all powers. Transformation of arable land into sheepwalks was, therefore, its cry."[48] Humans were displaced by sheep. Describing the tragic spectacle in his book *Utopia,* Thomas More wrote: "Your shepe that were wont to be so meek and tame, and so small eaters, now, as I hear saye, be become so great devourers and so wylde that they eate up, and swallow downe, the very men themselves."[49] The evicted became vagabonds helplessly roaming the countryside; their descendants eventually became wage-laborers.

Thus what was formerly the peasant's means of production now became *capital* in the hands of the new commercial lords and big farmers, and what was formerly produced by the peasants for their own use and consumption, now became means of subsistence that the new proletarians could acquire only by selling their labor for wages. Labor had become a commodity subject to market forces. The expropriation of the self-supporting peasants necessarily led to the destruction of their distinctive rural domestic industry. As a consequence, Marx writes,

> The spindles and looms, formerly scattered over the face of the country, are now crowded together in a few great labor-barracks, together with the laborers and the raw material. And spindles, looms, raw materials, are now transformed from means of independent existence for the spinners and weavers, into means for commanding them. . . .[50]

Manufacture was thus separated from agriculture, and in time the new class of proletarians created an internal market for the emerging capitalist mode of production.

The first phase of capitalism was "manufacture" quite literally, that is, hand production. Capitalist production at this stage is distinguished from handicraft production in the guilds only by the greater number of workers simultaneously employed by one and the same capitalist. Capitalist manufacture thus arose out of handicrafts, in some cases uniting the formerly distinct crafts and in other uniting the members of the same craft. In this increasingly complex division of labor, each worker is forced to engage in one simple operation. He is therefore alienated from the creative prerogatives he enjoyed as a craftsman. His entire body now becomes an "automatic, specialized implement of that operation."[51] What the worker loses in creativity, the organization gains in efficiency. The worker now takes less time in performing a specific operation than the craftsman who performed the entire series of operations in succession. The division of labor among many workers, each with his specialized operation, is the basis of capitalist manufacture, a new organization of labor under which *the socially productive power of labor is greatly enhanced*. Manufacture produces the detail laborer ". . . by reproducing, and systematically driving to an extreme within the workshop, the . . . differentiation of trades which it found ready to hand in society at large."[52]

The concentration of the various skills and trades in one workshop, entailed changes in the tools employed. Unlike the craftsman who used a few tools for many operations, the worker employed one tool in a specialized operation. Radical changes were taking place in the world of work. The transformation of the worker into a detail laborer, Marx believed, had far-reaching consequences. The new industrial division of labor effectively alienated the worker from his creative powers, thus diminishing him as a human being. The higher productivity of the new organization of labor was made possible by classifying and grouping workers according to their specific functions. What was taken away from the individual worker in artistic skill, creativity, and reflective powers was imparted to the organization. The organization as a whole was enriched by alienating the worker from his individual human gifts.

With machine production, a later stage of capitalist development, the individual worker pays an even bigger price for his increased productivity. If manufacture was somewhat adapted to the skills of the worker, the machine system compelled the worker to adapt to it. Production is analyzed into a sequence of phases, each of which is solved by means of machinery. The capitalist now strives for a productive process that is continuous and uninterrupted in its various phases; shifts from one phase to another are made not by hand, but by machinery. "The life-long specialty," wrote Marx, "of handling one and the same tool, now becomes the life-long specialty of serving one and the same machine."[53] In manufacture the worker used the tool; in the factory the machine uses the worker. Under such circumstances the intellectual and creative powers of the worker become superfluous.

Machine production greatly accelerated the concentration of capital and led to the prominence of the factory system. Older forms of production were increasingly displaced by the modern capitalist form and by the power of capital. Hence, the expansion of productive forces under capitalism was accompanied by growing alienation. For it was only by forfeiting his creative human faculties that the worker contributed to the growth of the productive organization. He had lost all control over the productive process. Marx's revolutionary reply to that condition is well known: while labor itself could never be abolished—it being the process by which human beings produce and reproduce their very life—*alienated* labor, exploitation, and oppression could be eliminated from human experience. Those who suffered most directly from those conditions would sooner or later find them intolerable and wrest all power from their oppressors. With that as a beginning, and with the gradual abolition of classes and class conflicts, humanity might some day create a society in which "the free development of each is the condition for the free development of all."[54]

Marx's conception of the genesis and development of capitalism is therefore essential for a clarification of his theory: *Only in the capitalist epoch and in the transition to it, do "productive forces" become a dynamic element. Precapitalist modes of production in the West were "conservative," and the Asiatic mode of production was "stationary."*

Therefore when Marx, in the "Preface," speaks of the Asiatic, ancient, feudal, and modern bourgeois modes of production as "progressive epochs," all he means to convey by that phrase is that those have been the major epochs in the history of human civilization. "Progressive," in the context of the "Preface," simply refers to the chronological sequence of epochs beginning with the Asiatic mode of production in ancient Mesopotamia and Egypt, and culminating in the capitalism of nineteenth-century Europe. Marx was *not*, as we shall see from additional evidence, proposing that the Asiatic mode evolved stage by stage into capitalism; nor was he proposing that the "progressive epochs" were necessary stages through which every society was fated to pass.

So we are now ready to confront the central question: Did Marx subscribe to social evolutionism or to any other *suprahistorical* theory?[55]

WAS MARX A SOCIAL EVOLUTIONIST?

To answer this question, we need first to have a look at some of the typical nineteenth-century theories of social evolution. The nineteenth century was the heyday of social evolutionism. Edward Burnett Tylor, Lewis Henry Morgan, Auguste Comte, Herbert Spencer, and numerous others all subscribed to a doctrine according to which the human race has progressed from lower to higher stages. Doubtless we owe an immense intellectual debt to those extraordinary thinkers, for we have acquired from them a large body of substantive knowledge about a wide range of human societies and cultures. The question remains, however, whether their conception of social evolution was scientifically sound.

Most nineteenth-century evolutionary schemes had in common certain stated and unstated premises that may be summed up in the following statement: Change is natural, directional, immanent, continuous, and derived from uniform causes.[56] These premises were shared by such otherwise diverse thinkers as Hegel, Saint-Simon (and his pupil Comte), Tocqueville, Spencer, Morgan, and Durkheim. For Hegel the developmental idea expressed itself in his view of the spirit of freedom, which grew from its modest beginnings in the ancient Orient until it attained its highest form in the Prussia of his day. In Saint-Simon and Comte the idea is evident in their law of three stages: Knowledge evolves from the religious through the metaphysical to the positive (or scientific) stage. In Tocqueville we find societies increasingly embodying the spirit of equality, thus proceeding from aristocracy to democracy. For Spencer the direction of evolution was from the relatively homogeneous "military" society to the complex "industrial" one. Morgan perceived three main stages of societal development: "savagery," "barbarism," and "civilization." And Durkheim, finally, placed the subject of social solidarity into an evolutionary framework, arguing that society normally progresses from a mechanical to an organic stage of solidarity. Many more thinkers could be mentioned to illustrate the prevalence in the nineteenth century of evolutionary schemes. As Robert A. Nisbet has stressed in his illuminating monograph *Social Change and History*, all such schemes are drawn "from the metaphor of growth, from the analogy of change in society to change in the growth-processes of the individual organism."[57]

How did the idea of growth, development, and evolution become so pervasive in the nineteenth century? Historians have sought the answer to that question in the Romantic-Conservative Reaction to the French Revolution, which we already have explored in previous chapters of this book. Conservatives throughout Europe deplored the consequences of that great social upheaval. They looked upon it as a disaster resulting from the folly of the revolutionaries who, intoxicated with Enlightenment ideas, attempted to reorder society according to mechanistically rational principles. In opposition to the eighteenth-century exaltation of the individual, conservatives elevated the *group* the *community,* and the *nation* to paramountcy. Eighteenth-century thought had been dominated by mechanistic metaphors: The Newtonian universe was "spring and wire," and even the human being was likened to a machine. Nineteenth-century thought, in contrast, adopted organic metaphors. This is exemplified in the political philosophy of Edmund Burke who insisted that society was a living organism.

Burke was only one among numerous other nineteenth-century thinkers whose categories of analysis had become thoroughly dominated by evolutionary metaphors or by what J. B. Bury called "the idea of progress." Bury identified that idea as a distinctively modern product which emerged in its earliest forms in the seventeenth century and reached its fullest expression in the nineteenth.[58] The idea of progress stands in sharp contrast to the idea of cycles in Greco-Roman antiquity.

With knowledge of the historical grounds of the evolutionary idea, we are better prepared to address this question: Are nineteenth-century evolutionary theories to be regarded as objective and scientific accounts of social change? If, following Robert A. Nisbet, we define social change "as a succession of differences in time in a persisting (social) entity," then we have to answer that question in the negative. For the theories with which we are concerned have failed to demonstrate a series of developmental steps in the transformation of a single social entity. Typically, evolutionists selected their evidence for stages from diverse societies and from various historical periods. The great anthropologist Lewis Henry Morgan, for example, illustrated "savagery" with one society, "barbarism" with a second, and "civilization" with a third. Selecting their data from divergent cultural areas and historical periods, the evolutionists then arranged them in a series resembling the actual historical series in the West. Thus this school of thought has given us, Nisbet has convincingly noted, not a theory of the actual course of development of a single social entity, but rather a

> series of "stills" as in a movie film. It is the eye—or rather in this instance, the disposition to believe—that creates the illusion of actual development, growth, or change.
>
> It is all much like a museum exhibit. (It might be observed in passing that the principles of museum arrangement of cultural artifacts have not been without considerable influence on the principles of cultural evolution.) The last one I saw was an exhibit of "the development of warfare." At the beginning were shown examples of primitive war-making—spears, bows and arrows, and the like. At the far end of the exhibit were examples (constructed miniatures) of the latest and most awful forms of warfare. In between, constructed in fullest accord with the principles of logical continuity, was the whole spectrum or range of weapons that have been found or written about anywhere on the

> earth's surface at whatever time. All of this, observers were assured, represented the development of warfare. But the development of warfare where? Not, certainly, in the United States, or in Tasmania, or in China, or in Tierra del Fuego, or in any other concrete, geographically identifiable, historically delimited, area. What "develops" is in fact no substantive, empirical entity but a hypostatized, constructed entity that is called the "art of war."[59]

That is a telling criticism. The social evolutionists, far from having proved the validity of their theories, have merely given expression to the dominant intellectual and cultural ideas of their time. The entire evolutionary theory and method rested on the prior acceptance of the idea of progressive development. Thus evolutionary theory has suffered from an inherent circularity that it has never overcome. Robert Nisbet and other scholars have included Marx among the evolutionists. As we shall see, however, the view that Marx belongs in that category is quite erroneous.

It would not be surprising at all if Marx and Engels, for all their originality, had been influenced by the evolutionary ideas of their time. Indeed, scholars who classify Marx and Engels with the evolutionists support their claim by pointing to apparent signs of evolutionary thinking throughout their writings. Here are some of those apparent signs: In their early coauthored book, *The German Ideology,* Marx and Engels described several stages of ownership forms—tribal, ancient, feudal, and capitalist. In the "Preface," to which we have referred throughout this study, Marx again speaks of "progressive epochs." That Marx and Engels had viewed society as developing in stages is further suggested by their enthusiastic reception of Lewis Henry Morgan's *Ancient Society*, and by Engels' heavy reliance on that work in his *Origin of the Family, Private Property, and the State.* In addition, the argument continues, Marx and Engels frequently employed progressivist-evolutionary language and apparently saw some parallels between organic and social evolution. In his funeral oration over Marx's grave in 1883, Engels stated ". . . just as Darwin discovered the law of evolution in organic nature, so Marx discovered the law of evolution in human history."[60] In 1888, in his preface to the English edition of the *Communist Manifesto,* Engels prophesied that Marx's ideas are "destined to do for history what Darwin's theory has done for biology." Analogies between historical processes and evolutionary biology may be found in *Capital.* In Marx's own preface to the second edition of *Capital* in 1873, he states that capitalism is ". . . a passing historical phase" and quotes from a Russian review of the first edition. The review praises Marx's work for demonstrating that the unfolding processes of economic life are analogous with biological evolution; and for ". . . disclosing the special laws that regulate the origins, existence, development, and death of a given social organism and its replacement by another and higher one." And Marx approvingly comments that the reviewer has accurately portrayed his "dialectical method."[61] Marx's study of England as the most advanced capitalism of his time has also suggested that for him the "less developed" societies were ultimately destined to mirror the conditions of the "more developed."

In light of such utterances it is clear that Marx and Engels must bear some responsibility for the widespread and persistent misapprehension of their theory. As we have seen, however, a careful and open-minded examination of their writings demonstrates that it would be a gross error to take their evolutionary metaphors as anything more than rhetoric. For this much is incontrovertible as a result of our study thus far: For Marx and Engels there was no unambiguous, unilinear progress from lower to higher stages. Even in terms of technology and "productive forces," there was no such pattern of onward and upward. Instead, there were ups and downs and zigzags in the precapitalist epochs, which were predominantly *conservative* modes of production.

Furthermore, the Asiatic mode of production decisively foils any attempt to foist a unilinear evolutionism upon Marx and Engels. For, as we have seen,

1. their conception of the Asiatic mode implies not one but at least two major lines of development, a Western and an Eastern; and,
2. the Asiatic mode was *stationary*, which is to say that it had undergone no socioeconomic development at all.

And in point of fact, we have rather direct evidence that Marx never intended to set forth a universal-unilinear conception of history. In a letter to N. K. Mikhailovsky, a Russian author of an article discussing *Capital*, Marx emphasizes that the chapter on Primitive Accumulation of Capital (in which Marx describes the separation of the peasant producers from their means of production) ". . . does not pretend to do more than trace the path by which, *in Western Europe*, the capitalist order of economy emerged from the womb of the feudal order of economy." Marx then goes on vehemently to reject Mikhailovsky's attempt to transform Marx's sketch of the origins of capitalism in *Western Europe* into a universal theory ". . . of the general path every people is fated to tread, whatever the historical circumstances in which it finds itself. . . . " And Marx concludes the letter by dissociating himself from all attempts to turn his economic emphasis, which he applied to specific historical circumstances, into a universal generalization.[62]

Marx made the same point in a letter to Vera Zasulitch, another Russian who had queried him about his theory. She had asked him what implications his theory had for the vitality of the *Mir*, the Russian rural community and, in particular, its institution of common property. In his reply Marx reminded her, as he had Mikhailovsky, that his sketch in *Capital* of the genesis of capitalism ". . . is expressly limited to the countries of *western Europe*;" and that his analysis in *Capital* therefore had no necessary implications either ". . . for or against the vitality of the [Russian] rural community. . . . " Moreover, he added, in Western Europe the genesis of capitalism entailed the transformation of one form of private property (the peasant's or yeoman's) into another form of private property (the capitalist's); while in Russia, capitalism would require the transformation of the Russian peasants' common property into private property.[63]

If one examines Marx's writings in the light of the foregoing qualifications, it becomes perfectly evident that he always had intended his emphasis on socioeconomic processes as a *historically specific* proposition relating to the West European origin of capitalism, and not to societies in general. Marx subscribed neither to social evolutionism nor to any other suprahistorical doctrine. That Marx had no dogmatic commitment to "economic determinism" is further evident in such writings as the "Class Struggles in France" and "The 18th Brumaire of Louis Bonaparte," where Marx's analysis is almost exclusively concerned with political struggles and political events. In fact, Marx's preface to the second edition of "The 18th Brumaire of Louis Bonaparte" demonstrates that he rejected rigid determinisms of all kinds. To clarify the purpose of his essay on the *coup d'état* of Louis Napoleon, Marx compares his own treatment with that of Victor Hugo and Pierre-Joseph Proudhon. Bonaparte's *coup*, says Marx, appears in Hugo's work as a

> . . . bolt from the blue. He sees in it only the violent act of a single individual. He does not notice that he makes this individual great instead of little[64] by ascribing to him a personal power of initiative such as would be without parallel in world history. Proudhon, for his part, seeks to represent the *coup d'état* as the result of an antecedent historical development. Unnoticeably, however, his historical construction of the *coup d'état* turns into a historical *apologia* for its hero. Thus he falls into the error of our so-called *objective* historians. I, on the contrary, demonstrate how the class struggle in France created circumstances and relationships that made it *possible* for a grotesque mediocrity to play a hero's part.[65]

In other words, while Hugo made the error of turning Louis Napoleon into a "great man," who presumably made history quite by himself, Proudhon committed the opposite error of interpreting the *coup* as if it had been fatalistically predetermined. Marx, in contrast to both Hugo and Proudhon, analyzed the social and historical circumstances that made it *possible* for a mediocrity to become the dictator of France.

In sum, the ups and downs of history, the conservative character of the precapitalist modes of production, the implications of the Asiatic mode of production, Marx's all-important repudiation of suprahistorical theory and fatalistically determined historical processes—all of these facts make it quite impossible to argue that for Marx "productive forces" or economic processes more generally, determined everything else.

We may therefore safely conclude that Marx had never meant to propose a rigid determinism of any kind, that he had never intended to advance a universal theory, good for all times and all places. To be sure, his method enjoins the investigator to give due attention to the "mode of production." But nowhere does Marx assert that the mode of production is the universally decisive factor in determining the various forms of society. It is strictly a matter of empirical-historical investigation whether economics, politics, war, religion or ideology—or, indeed, any or all of these in combination—will be decisive for change or nonchange in any particular case.

In Marx's historical-sociological method, there is no universal "prime mover" of history; there are no "iron laws," no universally necessary stages. *The major scientific aim of Marx's method was to guide the exploration of the manifold and historically changing connections between the economy and all other facets of society.* It is such a reading of Marx that will enable contemporary social scientists to recover the fruitful elements, both methodological and substantive, of Marx's historical sociology.

NOTES

1. See William H. Shaw, *Marx's Theory of History* (Stanford, Calif.: Stanford University Press, 1978), and G. A. Cohen, *Karl Marx's Theory of History; A Defense* (Princeton, N.J.: Princeton University Press, 1978). The quoted terms may be found on p. 5 of Shaw's book and on p. 29 of Cohen's. (Hereafter all page references to these works will be indicated in parentheses immediately following the quoted passage.)
2. Karl Marx, *A Contribution to the Critique of Political Economy* (Chicago: Charles H. Kerr, 1904), pp. 11–12.
3. Karl Marx and Frederick Engels, *Selected Works*, 2 vols. (Moscow: Foreign Languages Publishing House, 1951), Vol. II, p. 443. These volumes are hereafter cited as *MESW*.
4. *MESW*, Vol. II, p. 457.
5. Karl Marx and Frederick Engels, *The German Ideology*, Parts I and III (New York: International Publishers, 1947), p. 8, italics added.
6. Ibid., p. 9, italics added.
7. Karl Marx, *Grundrisse*, trans. Martin Nicolaus (Middlesex, England: Penguin Books, 1973), p. 491, italics in original.
8. Loc. cit., italics added.
9. Ibid., p. 98.
10. Ibid., p. 472.
11. Frederick Engels, *The Peasant War in Germany* (Moscow: Foreign Languages Publishing House, 1956), p. 165. Engels's essay "The Mark" is in the appendix.
12. Loc. cit., italics added.
13. Frederick Engels, *The Origin of the Family, Private Property, and the State* (New York: International Publishers, 1942), p. 131.
14. Engels, *The Peasant War in Germany*, "The Mark," p. 173.
15. Karl Marx, *The Poverty of Philosophy* (Moscow: Foreign Languages Publishing House, n.d.), p. 105.
16. Ibid., p. 127.

17. Karl Marx, *Capital,* Vol. I (Moscow: Foreign Languages Publishing House, 1954), pp. 179–80.
18. Ibid., p. 511.
19. Ibid., pp. 183–184, italics added.
20. Ibid., p. 486, italics added.
21. *MESW,* Vol. I, p. 36.
22. Marx and Engels, *The German Ideology,* pp. 11–12.
23. Ibid., p. 141, italics added.
24. Engels, *The Origin of the Family,* p. 141.
25. Marx, *Capital,* Vol. I, p. 237.
26. Loc. cit.
27. Karl Marx and Frederick Engels, *Selected Correspondence* (Moscow: Foreign Languages Publishing House, 1953), p. 428, italics added.
28. Engels, "The Mark," pp. 174–75.
29. Ibid., pp. 175–76.
30. See Engels, *The Peasant Wars in Germany.*
31. Engels, "The Mark," p. 176.
32. Frederick Engels, *Anti-Dühring* (Moscow: Foreign Languages Publishing House, 1954), p. 377, italics added.
33. Adam Smith, *An Inquiry into the Nature and Causes of the Wealth of Nations* (New York: Modern Library, 1937), pp. 645ff., 687ff., 789.
34. James Mill, *The History of British India,* 2nd ed., 12 vols. (London: Baldwin, Cradock, and Joy, 1820), Vol. I, p. 175ff.
35. Richard Jones, *An Essay on the Distribution of Wealth, and on the Sources of Taxation,* (London: John Murray, 1831), pp. 7ff, 109ff.
36. John Stuart Mill, *Principles of Political Economy* (London: Longmans, Green, 1909), p. 12ff.
37. Niccolo Machiavelli, *The Prince,* trans. George Bull (Middlesex, England: Penguin Books, 1979), p. 44ff.
38. Marx and Engels, *Selected Correspondence,* pp. 98–99.
39. Ibid., p. 99.
40. Ibid., p. 102.
41. Ibid., pp. 102–103.
42. See Marx's article, "The British Rule in India," in *The New York Daily Tribune,* June 25, 1853; reprinted in Henry M. Christman, ed., *The American Journalism of Marx and Engels* (New York: The New American Library, 1966), p. 97.
43. Marx, *Grundrisse,* p. 486; see also pp. 473 and 493.
44. Engels, *Anti-Dühring,* p. 224.
45. Ibid., p. 249.
46. Ibid., p. 251.
47. Marx, *Capital,* Vol. I, p. 714.
48. Ibid., pp. 718–19.
49. Ibid., p. 720.
50. Ibid., p. 746.
51. Ibid., p. 339.
52. Loc. cit.

53. Ibid., p. 422.
54. Marx and Engels, "Communist Manifesto," *Selected Works,* Vol. I, p. 51.
55. By "suprahistorical" I mean a theory which, like social evolutionism, attempts to account for social change by means of laws of development that are immanent, objective, and inexorable.
56. See Robert A. Nisbet, *Social Change and History* (New York: Oxford University Press, 1969), p. 166ff.
57. Loc. cit.
58. J. B. Bury, *The Idea of Progress: An Inquiry into Its Origin and Growth* (London: Macmillan, 1928).
59. Nisbet, *Social Change and History,* p. 197.
60. Marx and Engels, *Selected Works,* Vol. II, p. 153.
61. Marx, *Capital,* Vol. I, p. 19.
62. Marx and Engels, *Selected Correspondence,* pp. 376–79, italics added.
63. Ibid., pp. 411–12, italics added.
64. Hugo called his study *Napoleon the Little.*
65. Marx and Engels, *Selected Works,* Vol. I, pp. 221–22, italics added.

16

Frederick Engels on the Origin of Patriarchy

In 1884, a year after Marx's death, Frederick Engels, his lifelong friend, colleague, and occasional coauthor, published a book entitled *The Origin of the Family, Private Property, and the State.* This book not only evoked considerable interest in its own time, but it also continues to stimulate discussion today, notably among those concerned with the issues raised by the feminist movement. What is especially striking about this work by Engels is that he tries to give due consideration to the *twofold* character of the production and reproduction of human life. On the one hand, there is the production of the means of existence and the tools required for that production, and on the other hand, the production of the human beings themselves, the propagation of the human species. The social organization in which people live in any given historical epoch is determined, Engels claimed, by both kinds of production: by the level reached in the productivity of labor and by the form of its family and kinship relations. There is a definite relationship between the socioeconomic structure of a society and the form and content of the family—in particular, the relation of the sexes. This is the central thesis of Engels's extraordinarily interesting book.

Although over a hundred years have passed since its publication, and many criticisms have been leveled against it, Engels's book continues to be either a starting point or a foil in many of the present-day analyses of the historically changing role of the woman in society. So Engels's work is fully deserving of a careful exposition.

A historical approach to the family is itself a comparatively recent phenomenon. Prior to the 1860s there was no such thing as a history of the family. The dominant conception of that institution was the one found in the five books of Moses. And it was widely assumed that the patriarchal form described there was the oldest and, indeed, largely identical with the one prevalent in the nineteenth century. The family, from this standpoint, had undergone no historical development at all. This state of affairs began to change with the publications of several outstanding, pioneering, nineteenth-century anthropologists: J. J. Bachofen, J. F. McLennan, E. B. Tylor and, most important, Lewis Henry Morgan. It was under the influence of Morgan, who had spent four decades of his life studying the Iroquois and other native peoples of North America, that Engels conceived and wrote his *Origin.* In fact, Morgan's comparative and evolutionary approach to society bore a marked resemblance to that of Marx and Engels. Morgan's central thesis, arrived at independently, captured a key element of the Marxian conception of history: Humanity has developed in accordance with the progress made in the methods of producing the necessaries of life.

Basing himself on Morgan's *Ancient Society, or Researches in the Lines of Human Progress from Savagery Through Barbarism to Civilization* (1877), Engels reviews the central features of each stage. In the lowest stage of savagery, human beings remained tree-dwellers, at least partially, in their original habitat, tropical forests. They subsisted on fruits, nuts, and roots and developed articulate speech. This stage is conjectural, there being no direct evidence to prove its existence. The middle stage of savagery is characterized by the utilization of fish for food (including crabs, mussels, and other aquatic animals) and the use of fire. With this new source of nourishment, humans became independent of particular localities, and they spread far and wide. Evidence of such migrations is the distribution over every continent of "paleoliths," crudely worked, unsharpened flint tools. The upper stage of savagery is inaugurated by the invention of the bow and arrow, a complex instrument implying long-accumulated experience and a sharpened intelligence. Here we also have the merest beginnings of settlement in villages. With the discovery of the uses of fire and the invention of the stone ax, dug-out canoes also became common, and beams and planks were occasionally used in the construction of houses. All this and more was present among the native North Americans.

For Morgan, the transition to the earliest stage of barbarism was made with the introduction of pottery. In all likelihood this craft began with the habit of covering baskets or wooden vessels with clay to make them fireproof, and discovering in due course that the clay mold served the desired purpose without any inner vessel. The chief characteristic of the middle stage of barbarism is the domestication and breeding of animals and the cultivation of plants. This originally emerged in the Eastern Hemisphere, which possessed nearly all the animals suited for domestication and all the varieties of cultivable cereals except one. In the Western Hemisphere, in contrast, the llama was the only domesticable animal, and maize was the only cultivable cereal. By the time the Europeans arrived in North America, the native people east of the Mississippi were already practicing some horticulture of maize, and perhaps also of gourds, melons, and other garden plants. Finally, the upper stage of barbarism begins with the smelting of iron ore and passes into civilization with the invention of alphabetic writing and its use for the keeping of records and for other literary purposes. This stage, first reached independently in the Eastern Hemisphere, used iron plowshares drawn by cattle. This made the cultivation of large fields possible, thus leading to a remarkable increase in the productivity of labor and large surpluses. The nineteenth-century categories of "savagery" and "barbarism" employed by Morgan are roughly equivalent to the modern anthropological concepts of "paleolithic" and "neolithic," respectively. The former refers to the gathering-hunting stage and the latter to the agricultural revolution.

THE FAMILY

The "consanguine family" is Morgan's term for the earliest stage of this social institution. In this stage only parents and children are proscribed marriage partners. Brothers and sisters and male and female cousins are all potential husbands and wives for one another. There is no direct evidence for the existence of such a stage. It was inferred by Morgan from the fact that the kinship terms employed by the Iroquois failed to describe the actual kinship patterns prevailing among them. This suggested that the current terms were vestiges of an earlier marriage pattern. And, indeed, Morgan believed he had found the earlier pattern in Hawaii and other Polynesian islands.

The next stage Morgan dubbed the "*punaluan* family," which went on to exclude not only parents and children, but also brothers and sisters from sexual intercourse. This stage is also conjectural. It was inferred by Morgan from Hawaiian kinship terms pointing to a custom in which a number of women were the common wives of their common husbands, from among whom the women's own brothers were excluded. The husbands no longer called themselves brothers, as they presumably had in the consanguine stage, for they were no longer necessarily brothers. Instead they called themselves *punalua*, that is, companions. Similarly, the common wives called themselves *punalua*. This implied some form of *group marriage*. The aborigines of South Australia, for instance, were organized into two rather large exogamous categories, or "moieties." Sexual intercourse within a moiety was strictly prohibited. On the other hand, every man in one moiety was the husband by birth of every woman in the other moiety, and she was by birth his wife. This did not necessarily imply that any man from one group could have sexual relations with any woman of the other. Although both Morgan and Engels consider the possibility of an earlier stage of sexual promiscuity from which the *punaluan* form may have evolved, they found no indications of such a state of affairs. Moreover, they emphasize that already in the so-called group marriage stage and even earlier, there existed a certain frequency of "pairing." The man had a chief wife for whom he was the chief husband—whence the next stage emerged, called by Morgan the "pairing family." But this early pairing family was too weak and unstable to form its own household. It remained embedded in the communal household inherited from earlier times.

It is here that Engels, following Morgan, begins to develop his thesis concerning the role and status of women in such a communal context:

> Communistic housekeeping . . . means the supremacy of women in the house; just as the exclusive recognition of the female parent, owing to the impossibility of recognizing the male parent with certainty means that the women—the mothers—are held in high respect. . . . Among all savages and barbarians . . . the position of women is not only free but honorable.[1]

The authority and respected status of women was witnessed by both Morgan and Ashur Wright who was for many years a missionary among the Iroquois Senecas. The women from one clan took in husbands from another and lived together in "long-houses" comprising several families. Usually, Wright observed,

> the female portion ruled the house. . . . The stores were in common; but woe to the luckless husband or lover who was too shiftless to do his share of the providing. No matter how many children or whatever goods he might have in the house, he might at any time be ordered to pick up his blanket and budge; and after such orders it would not be healthful for him to attempt to disobey. The house would be too hot for him; and . . . he must retreat to his own clan; or, as was often done, go and start a new matrimonial alliance in some other location. The women were the great power among the clans, as everywhere else. They did not hesitate, when occasion required, "to knock off the horns," as it was technically called, from the head of a chief, and send him back to the rank of warrior. (p. 43)

Now the all-important question arises: If up to the time of "barbarism" women held so high a position of honor and authority, how did they lose it with the dawn of "civilization"? The New World, never having gone beyond this stage, could provide no answer. Engels therefore turns to the East to reconstruct the chain of events that presumably led to that result.

Up to a certain stage of "barbarism" the wealth of the community consisted of house, clothing, tools, crude ornaments, boat, weapons, and utensils. Food had to be acquired afresh every day. But with the domestication of herds of horses, camels, asses, cattle, sheep, goats, and pigs, the advancing pastoral peoples "had acquired property which only needed supervision and the rudest care to reproduce itself in steadily increasing quantities and to supply the most abundant food in the form of milk and meat" (p. 47). "But to whom did this new wealth belong?" asks Engels.

Originally, Engels surmised, it must have belonged to the whole clan community. Our earliest *historical* records, however, reveal that private property in herds had already emerged in the oldest civilizations. How did this come about? According to the sexual division of labor within the pairing family, it was the man's responsibility to obtain food and to produce the instruments of labor necessary for that purpose.

> He therefore also owned the instruments of labor, and in the event of husband and wife separating, he took them with him, just as she retained her household goods. Therefore, according to the social custom of the time, the man was also the owner of the new source of subsistence, the cattle, and later of the new instruments of labor, the slaves. But according to the custom of the same society, his children would not inherit from him. (p. 49)

Why not? Because under the rules of clan exogamy and matrilinear descent he had to bequeath his herds and other goods to his clan brothers and sisters and to their children. But since his own children were the offspring of a woman of a different clan, his own biological children were disinherited. As wealth increased, then, and as the man's role in generating that wealth increased correspondingly, it strengthened his resolve to change the traditional order of inheritance. "Mother-right" or matrilinear descent had to be overthrown and overthrown it was. This was a peaceful revolution brought about by a simple decree that hereafter a man's children will belong to his clan and inherit from him. "The reckoning of descent in the female line and the matriarchal law of inheritance were thereby abolished, and the male line of descent and the paternal law of inheritance were substituted for them" (p. 49). This constituted the *"world historical defeat of the female sex"* (p. 50). The classic example of this decisive transfer of power was the Roman *pater familias,* in which the male head of the household had life-and-death control, at least theoretically, over his wife, children, and slaves. However, the patriarchal family is already evident in our earliest historical records of the ancient Near East.

THE MONOGAMOUS FAMILY

It is out of the pairing family and the growing importance of the man's role in the economy that the monogamous family emerged. Monogamy, accompanying or following patrilinear descent, was instituted by man for the express purpose of producing children of undisputed paternity, which was necessary if fathers were to bequeath their property to their natural heirs. For Engels, then, though there may have been an element of individual sexual love and chastity in the selection of a wife under monogamy, the monogamous family as an institution came about as the victory of private property over primitive, communal property.

Under capitalism, moreover, and most notably among the propertied classes, Engels proposed that the monogamous family often originates as a marriage of convenience. Marriage, in such circumstances, is conditioned by the class position of the parties concerned and frequently turns into a form of prostitution. Most often, it is the woman who lets out her body not for wages, as does a worker, but once and for all, as does the slave. In bourgeois marriage, a chief motive behind the liaison on the part of one or another of the individuals and families concerned is the enhancement of their economic position. As a rule, concerns about wealth and property become the salient consideration while true love is the exception. Hence a genuine love relationship between man and woman can only become the rule, says Engels, within the proletariat. For here there is no property to be concerned with, no wealth to be preserved and passed on to the next generation, for which monogamy and male supremacy were established. Among working men, Engels discerned no incentive to make male dominance effective. Furthermore, he argues, now that large-scale industry has taken the woman out of the home and onto the labor market and into the factory, and made her a bread-winner of the family, ". . . no basis of any kind for male-supremacy is left in the proletarian household—except, perhaps, for something of the brutality towards women that has spread since the introduction of monogamy" (p. 64).

Engels then goes on to observe that with the emergence of the patriarchal, monogamous family, household management lost its public character and became a private service. The wife became the head servant at home, but was excluded from social production. "Not until the coming of modern, large-scale industry," writes Engels,

> was the road to social production opened to her again—and then only to the proletarian wife. But it was opened in such a manner that, if she carries out her duties in the private service of her family, she remains excluded from public production and unable to earn; and if she wants to take part in public production and earn independently, she cannot carry on her family duties. And the wife's position in the factory is the position of women in all branches of business, right up to medicine and law. . . .
>
> In the great majority of cases today, at least in the possessing classes, the husband is obliged to earn a living and support his family, and that in itself gives him a position of supremacy, without any need for special legal titles and privileges. Within the family he is the bourgeois and the wife represents the proletariat. (pp. 65–66)

How did Engels envision the resolution of the woman's dilemma in which her service to her family and to the larger society conflict? Engels, being a Socialist, saw the solution in the transfer of the means of production into common ownership. The family household would thus also transfer one of its major functions to society, and housekeeping would become a social industry. "The care and education of the children becomes a public affair: society looks after all children alike . . . " (p. 67). Only in such a social system can real love and freedom of choice in marriage partners be generally established. The abolition of capitalist property relations would also remove all those accompanying economic considerations which traditionally have exerted so powerful an influence on the choice of a marriage partner. Under socialism there would be no other motive left except mutual inclination. What can we now conjecture, asks Engels, about how man-woman relations will appear in the new society? "That will be answered," he writes,

> when a new generation has grown up: a new generation of men who never in their lives have known what it is to buy a woman's surrender with money or any other instrument of power; a generation of women who have never known what it is to give themselves to a man from any other consideration than real love, or what it is to refuse to give themselves to their lovers from fear of the economic consequences. (p. 73)

THE FAMILY, PRIVATE PROPERTY, AND THE STATE

As we remarked earlier, what makes Engels's work especially interesting is his effort to provide a theoretical and historical analysis that ties together the origins of male supremacy, private property, socioeconomic classes, and the State. Morgan's work was germane in that it systematically analyzed a society, the Iroquois, which was essentially egalitarian and democratic. The members of the clan community elected both their peacetime and wartime leaders, and they could depose these leaders at will. The property of deceased persons was passed on to other members of the clan and remained in the community. All the members of an Iroquois clan were personally free and owed one another mutual aid and protection. Morgan's work thus had extraordinary scientific importance because it provided an opportunity to study a society which had none of the institutions so characteristic of all civilizations, East and West. Iroquois society had no patriarchy, no private property in land or other resources, no classes, no state. No masters, no slaves, no kings or nobles, no gendarmes or police, no prisons, no lawsuits. Of course, there was a dark side, and neither Morgan nor Engels shy away from acknowledging that democracy, equality, and peace prevailed only within the tribe but not outside. Wherever there was no explicit peace treaty, "tribe was at war with tribe, and wars were waged with the cruelty which distinguishes man from other animals . . ." (p. 87).

Both Morgan and Engels surmised that other peoples in their early history had organized their societies in ways similar to those of the Iroquois. The key question for Engels was this: How did the communal-democratic structure break down? What were the historical processes that led to the emergence of private property, classes, and the state? The Iroquois case could provide no answer, since it had not in fact transformed itself prior to the arrival of the Europeans. But there were other societies in which a communal stage appears to have broken down to produce class antagonisms. Engels therefore reviews the histories of the Greeks, Romans, Celts, and Germans with the aim of shedding light on the processes that brought about such momentous changes. The case of the early Germanic tribes was most useful in this regard because historical evidence on the transition was plentiful.

That the early Germans were organized in clans is evident from the work of Julius Caesar. And about 150 years later the Roman historian Tacitus stated that the maternal uncle looked upon his nephew as his own son and that some even looked upon the kinship between maternal uncle and nephew as more sacred and binding than that between father and son. This strongly suggests a matrilinear clan organization very similar to that of the Iroquois. But the Germanic tribes had already undergone something of a transition, for Tacitus also observes that mother-right had already given way to father-right. The children now inherited from the father, although the fact that the nephew could still, on occasion, inherit from his maternal uncle shows how recent father-right was among the Germans at the time. That father-right was associated with a significant economic change was discernible in the works of Caesar and Tacitus. Whereas Caesar had described land as communally owned and collectively cultivated by the German clans, Tacitus, writing some 150 years later, stated that the land was individually cultivated. While in Caesar's time the tribes were still largely on the move, looking for settled abodes, in Tacitus' time they already had many years of settled life behind them.

These changes were accompanied by still another that yields real insight into the concrete process by which the monarchical-type state arose among the Germanic tribes. Even the American native peoples, Morgan had shown, formed, side by side with the clan community, quasi-private and private associations for the purpose of carrying on wars independently. Among the Germans there were similar associations. A military leader, whose courage and skill had become evident in battle, gathered to himself a band of young men eager for booty, who pledged personal loyalty to him. This gave rise to the institution of the *retinues.*

In Caesar's time these retinues were still subordinate to the clan and tribal community. It was with the authority of the community that the retinue went out on its forays, and when the retinue returned with booty, it was turned over to the community. The young men in the retinue were only part-time warriors who, when they returned from battle, took up their agricultural duties alongside the other community members. But by Tacitus' time all this had changed. Now the retinues had become, in effect, independent of the community. Typically they were "international" in that young warriors were now recruited not only from their own tribe but also from others. When they returned from a plundering expedition, they no longer turned over the booty to the community, but kept it for themselves. They now became full-time warriors who disdained agricultural labor, leaving it for the women, children, and old men. As Tacitus notes, these retinues could only be kept together by frequent wars and plundering expeditions. Plunder became an end in itself. In time the leader became a king who organized his followers on a hierarchical basis: a bodyguard, a standing army of troops, and a regular corps of officers. When the Roman Empire disintegrated, it was from these retinues and from the Roman courtiers that the later nobility was drawn. The longer the clan remained settled in its village, and the more the Germans and the Romans merged, the more the unity among the people became territorial. And the territory now became the domain of the king, with sad consequences for the people.

Engels had thus traced the process from primitive communal society to a society based on classes and on rulers and ruled. As a general proposition his theory may be stated thus: With the agricultural revolution and the marked increase in production in all branches—field crops, cattle raising, and handicrafts—human labor began to produce more than was necessary for its own maintenance. The daily amount of work to be done by clan members increased correspondingly. Additional sources of labor were needed and provided by war: prisoners of war were turned into slaves. The growth in the productivity of labor and, therefore, wealth, brought in its train the first great cleavage of society into two classes: masters and slaves. Accompanying this change was another: A revolution came over the family. In the primitive communal context the sexual division of labor was such that the woman was in charge of the household while the man was responsible for hunting and procuring the other necessities of life. With the domestication of animals and the expansion of the herds, the taming and tending of the animals became the man's work. The "savage" warrior and hunter had been content to take second place in the household, but the "gentler" shepherd, having gained a new source of wealth, pushed himself ahead of the woman in order to preserve that wealth and transmit it to his own offspring. The inequalities of property among the individual heads of families broke up the old communal organization, and the transition to full private ownership and control of the land was gradually accomplished, creating rich and poor, masters and slaves, rulers and ruled. What we call civilization, then, emerged as a society divided against itself.

Engels believed that socialism—public ownership of the means of production and national planning of the economy in the interest of society as a whole—would lead to the end of patriarchy. The emancipation of the woman would come about as she came to play an increasingly important role in the public sphere and as her domestic work, with the aid of child care facilities, declined to an insignificant amount of time.

CRITICAL OBSERVATIONS

There have been many criticisms of Engels's book, some of them pertaining to ethnographic details and others to his central thesis. Concentrating on the latter, we may begin with his explanation of the origins of monogamy. For Engels, as we have seen, it was the emergence of transferrable wealth in the form of herds of domesticated animals that strengthened the relative position of men within the family, leading to the overthrow of matrilinearity. But some students of Engels's work find this unconvincing. Why should herds, they ask, have been distinguished from other forms of property? Why did men automatically gain control of the herds, as Engels suggests, if women in fact played a significant role in gathering and producing the society's means of subsistence? If it was the enormous increase in wealth brought about by the herds that prompted men to wrest this wealth from women's control, then men must already have held the power necessary to accomplish this. Although this criticism is well taken, it tends to overlook Engels's discussion of the growing independence of the retinues, in which their property was separated from that of the community and the power of the young men grew commensurately. It is the phenomenon of the retinues which helps us to understand better how some young men established themselves in power and changed the patterns of descent and inheritance. However, Engels is partially to blame for the apparent weakness of his explanation, for although he discusses the retinues, he fails to bring their role into relief. He does not tie together the changing character of the retinues and the general appropriation of herds by men. Nevertheless, as a distinguished scholar has remarked,

> Engels made major contributions to our understanding of women's position in society and history: (1) He pointed to the connection between structural changes in kinship relations and changes in the division of labor on the one hand and women's position in society on the other. (2) He showed a connection between the establishment of private property, monogamous marriage, and prostitution. (3) He showed the connection between economic and political dominance by men and their control over female sexuality. (4) By locating "the world historical defeat of the female sex" in the period of the formation of archaic states, based on the dominance of propertied elites, he gave the event historicity. Although he was unable to prove any of these propositions, he defined the major theoretical questions for the next hundred years.[2]

Feminists[3] have challenged Engels's central assumption that the key to women's emancipation lies largely in the gaining of their economic independence. This assumption was certainly not borne out by the experience of socialism in the former Soviet bloc countries and in China. But there is also a more general criticism that has been made of Engels's theoretical approach.

ENGELS'S SCIENTIFIC SOCIALISM

When Marx died in 1883, Engels became the chief representative of what eventually became known as "orthodox Marxism." And it was in fact during the dozen years separating the death of Marx from that of Engels (1895) that "Marxism" came into being as a coherent and influential system. Engels was the founder of the Social Democratic movement organized around Marxian theories. But it seems clear that during those dozen years Engels introduced into Marx's ideas a significant modification that may be summed up in the new term Engels coined to describe his view, namely, "scientific socialism." For Engels and his followers, socialism was to be above all "scientific," in contrast to pre-Marxian ideas of socialism which were dubbed "utopian."

This new emphasis on the "scientific" was not, however, entirely foreign to Marx's own conception, since a close reading of *Capital* and other mature writings reveals that he placed considerable stress on the scientific study of social processes that were independent of human will and, therefore, "historically necessary." A definite tension may be discerned in Marx's theorizing: On the one hand, going back to his earliest work and persisting in his maturity, there was the emphasis on the creative potential of human consciousness and will in changing the world. But, on the other hand, there was also a highly deterministic conception of social and historical processes. Yet Marx himself managed to discharge this tension and to prevent it from exploding his system. He managed this by positing a class-conscious, working people's movement that was, in principle, capable of gaining control over historical processes and redirecting them so as to widen the boundaries of human freedom.

Engels, however, appears to have transformed Marx's more complex view into a causally determined process of *social* evolution parallel to the scheme of Darwinian evolution. Engels's view is best exemplified in his "speech at the graveside of Karl Marx," where he said: "Just as Darwin discovered the law of development of organic nature, so Marx discovered the law of development of human history."[4] Engels's earliest steps in this direction were taken in a bulky volume entitled *Anti-Dühring*, a polemical rejoinder to a positivist-socialist named Eugen Dühring. The fact that Engels wrote this book while Marx was still alive, and, evidently, with his approval, has made it difficult to claim that Engels deviated significantly from their jointly held theory. One plausible explanation of Marx's approval is that he viewed the determinist emphasis in *Anti-Dühring* as more effective in countering Dühring's influence on the socialist movement. Be that as it may, the unanticipated result of this book by Engels as well as his *The Origin of the Family,*

Private Property, and the State was to lay the foundations for a new system of "laws," on the basis of which the inevitability of socialism could be predicted with scientific precision. Socialism would emerge out of capitalism in much the same way that capitalism evolved out of feudalism. The evolution of capitalism into socialism was governed by inexorable laws.

As we have seen in our discussion of Marx's historical sociology, it is doubtful in the extreme that Marx ever subscribed to a theory of social evolution. It is even more doubtful that he viewed human history as an aspect of the general evolution of nature and subject to the same "laws." Engels, however, and the succession of leading Marxists who followed him, all shared a common world-view which came to be called "dialectical materialism," a term characterizing Marxism as a universal science of the "laws" of nature *and* history. In this way Marx's critical theory of society and history, which left room for human creative activity, was turned into the very form of "mechanical materialism" that he had fought against in his theses on Feuerbach and other early writings.

All this has a definite bearing on Engels's thesis in his *The Origin of the Family, Private Property, and the State.* The overwhelming impression made by that work is that male supremacy was the automatic consequence of economic developments, just as women's emancipation will be the necessary and inevitable fruit of the evolution of capitalism into socialism. We are thus presented with a one-sided economic determinism that ignores the role of will and consciousness, as well as the relative autonomy of the family, religion, and other institutions. Take religion as just one example. In Genesis 2:22 we read that "the rib which the Lord God had taken from the man he made into a woman. . . . " And in St. Paul's letters we read that wives should be subject to their husbands, as to the Lord (Eph. 5:22–24), and "Let a woman learn in silence with all submissiveness. I permit no woman to teach or to have authority over men; she is to keep silent. For Adam was formed first, then Eve; and Adam was not deceived, but the woman was deceived and became a transgressor" (1 Tim. 2:11–14). One can hardly exaggerate the influence of this religious ideology in perpetuating the subordination of women. This ideology was not the product of economic developments, so there is no good reason to assume that it will automatically cease to have an effect if certain economic changes are brought about. And insofar as Engels failed to acknowledge the autonomy and influence of religious doctrines, treating them as mere epiphenomena, his prognosis remains unconvincing.

Both Marx and Engels believed that socialism would be humanly and morally superior to capitalism. But, today, as the twentieth century draws to a close, it seems clear that socialism has yet to demonstrate such superiority. And even if such superiority were in fact demonstrated, it is doubtful that women would want to wait patiently for the new era to grant them the rights they have been calling for since the time of Mary Wollstonecraft, if not earlier.

All this said, however, it is a fine tribute to Engels that his *The Origin of the Family,* more than one hundred years after its publication, still occupies a central place in discussions of feminist issues. He would have been pleased and honored, no doubt, to learn this fact.

In the decades following the deaths of Marx and Engels, and largely as a result of the latter's new doctrine of "scientific socialism," the ideas of these two founders were transformed into a variety of "Marxisms," some of them quite vulgar and mechanistic. This brings us to the second major theme of this book: the critical response to Marx and Marxism in the intellectual circles of Europe in the early decades of the twentieth century. For it is clear that much of twentieth-century sociology took shape in a critical encounter with the Marxian legacy.

NOTES

1. Frederick Engels, *The Origin of the Family, Private Property, and the State* (New York: International Publishers, 1942). (Hereafter all page references to this work will be cited in parentheses immediately following the quoted passage.)
2. Gerda Lerner, *The Creation of Patriarchy* (New York: Oxford University Press, 1986), p. 23.
3. See Janet Sayers et al., eds., *Engels Revisited: New Feminist Essays* (London: Tavistock, 1987), and Jane Slaughter and Robert Kern, *European Women on the Left: Socialism, Feminism, and the Problems Faced by Political Women, 1880 to the Present* (Westport, Conn.: Greenwood Press, 1981).
4. Karl Marx and Frederick Engels, *Selected Works* (Moscow: Foreign Languages Publishing House, 1951), Vol. II, pp. 153–154.

17

Max Weber[1]

(1864–1920)

INTRODUCTION

Talcott Parsons, who was among the first to introduce Weber's writings to English readers, declared in 1929 that *The Protestant Ethic and the Spirit of Capitalism* was intended by Weber as a ". . . refutation of the Marxian thesis in a particular historical case."[2] In the late 1940s, in his translation of parts of Weber's *Economy and Society,* Parsons again declared that after an early contact with the Marxian position Weber ". . . soon recoiled from this, becoming convinced of the indispensability of an important role of `ideas' in the explanation of great historical processes."[3] Parsons thus implied that Marx and his followers had somehow failed to understand that ideas are important in history. Soon it became common opinion in the American social sciences that much of Weber's work had been intended as a refutation of Marxian theoretical and methodological principles.

That view still prevails. In a recent textbook on the history of social thought, the authors make the following allegations:

> Like all his works, Weber's essays on social stratification are an attempt at refuting Marxist thought.
>
> The originality of Max Weber's sociology lies in its dual rejection of both Marxism and theory that is modeled after the natural sciences.

> Thus, as in the *Protestant Ethic*, Weber's analysis of social stratification also showed how cultural phenomena circumscribe social action and, in so doing, refuted the Marxist emphasis on economic factors as the primary causal agents in history.[4]

Although this view of Weber's relation to Marx remains dominant, it has not gone unchallenged. In a 1945 essay on German sociology, Albert Salomon stated that Weber ". . . became a sociologist in a long and intense debate with the ghost of Karl Marx," and that Weber's *Economy and Society* was a reexamination of the Marxian thesis.[5] At about the same time Hans Gerth and C. Wright Mills wrote " . . . throughout his life, Max Weber was engaged in a fruitful battle with historical materialism."[6] And somewhat later George Lichtheim observed ". . . the whole of Weber's sociology of religion fits without difficulty into the Marxian scheme."[7] Such interpretations of Weber became the starting point for the present author's 1968 essay in which he attempted to substantiate the thesis that Weber's work ". . . must be read not as a repudiation of Marx's methodological principles but rather as a `rounding out' and supplementing of his method."[8] In the present discussion of sociology and history in Max Weber fuller documentation will be provided to support this thesis. In their respective conceptions of history, it will be argued, Weber and Marx are compatible and complementary; this is true in spite of the obvious political and ideological differences that exist between the two thinkers.

Before we begin to consider the evidence, however, a word must be said about an objection that has been raised against the complementarity thesis. Guenther Roth has insisted "Weber and Marx were further apart" than proponents of the complementary view have suggested. Roth, primarily interested in the question of whether Weber's work was in fact influenced by Marx, contends that Weber's concern with social classes, strata and interests emanated from August Meitzen, the scholar under whom Weber wrote his second dissertation. Meitzen had also been interested in the historical antagonism between property and labor, and it was under his direction that Weber wrote his *Roman Agrarian History* Roth agrees that one may discern in that work a "quasi-Marxist approach," but he maintains that "it was adopted from Meitzen, not Marx."[9] It is beyond doubt, however, that Weber knew Marx's writings quite well, and that he took them into account. That is a fact we shall demonstrate in due course and, indeed, a fact acknowledged by Roth when he writes that Weber ". . . accepted the heuristic utility of historical materialism. . . . "[10]

Roth has highlighted certain criticisms that Weber made of the Marxism of his time. In his remarks to the first meeting of the German Sociological Association in 1910, Weber said:

> I would like to protest the statement by one of the speakers that some one factor, be it technology or economy, can be the "ultimate" or "true" cause of another. If

> we look at the causal lines, we see them run, at one time, from technical to economic and political matters, at another from political to religious and economic ones, etc. There is no resting point. In my opinion, the view of historical materialism, frequently espoused, that the economic is in some sense the ultimate point in the chain of causes is completely finished as a scientific proposition.[11]

Weber also criticized Marxism for confusing technological with economic conditions:

> To my knowledge, Marx has not defined technology. There are many things in Marx that not only appear contradictory but actually are found contrary to fact if we undertake a thorough and pedantic analysis, as indeed we must. Among other things, there is an oft-quoted passage: The hand-mill results in feudalism, the steam-mill in capitalism. That is a technological, not an economic construction, and as an assertion it is simply false, as we can clearly prove. For the age of the hand-mill, which extended up to modern times, had cultural "superstructures" of all conceivable kinds in all fields.[12]

Weber was among the first to raise such objections against Marxism. And it is true, of course, that in Marx's and Engels's copious writings one can find such ill-fated aphorisms as the one about the hand- and steam-mills. Yet a careful examination of the context shows that Marx had never intended this statement as a form of technological determinism, in which one could infer feudalism from the hand-mill. As we have seen (p. 164), Marx's real meaning is that

> Labour is organized, is divided differently according to the instruments it disposes over. The hand-mill presupposes a different *division of labour* from the steam-mill.[13]

So we see that it was not Marx himself, but rather some of his followers and critics who wrongly attributed to him a form of technological determinism. To be sure, one finds ambiguous statements in the writings of Marx and Engels; one finds formulations apparently lending credence to the view that they proposed a form of economic and even "productive-force" determinism. But as we have seen, such interpretations have ignored important pieces of evidence. And it is precisely because the so-called "materialist conception of history" is *not* a rigid, deterministic, suprahistorical theory, but rather a methodological approach, that we insist on the compatibility and complementarity of Marx and Weber.

Before we begin to substantiate this thesis, one more point needs to be made. Roth's primary interest is ". . . with the way in which certain ideas were transmitted and transformed in a particular intellectual and institutional setting. . . ."[14] We, in contrast, shall focus attention primarily on the methodological and substantive affinities between Marx and Weber. Nothing in our interpretation is intended to detract from Weber's originality and greatness; least of all is our interpretation intended to reduce Weber to a mere elaborator of Marx. Our sole objective is to extract the most fruitful analytical elements from both of these extraordinary thinkers, and thus to lay firm foundations for a historical sociology.

WEBER'S DIALOGUE WITH MARXISM

It is not at all difficult to show that Weber did in fact carry on such a dialogue. We have already cited Albert Salomon's remark that Weber became a sociologist in the course of a "debate with Marx's ghost." Dialogue is a better word for our purposes because at times Weber criticizes either Marx himself or his followers; at other times Weber affirms the correctness of Marx's economic emphasis and of his substantive analyses; and at still other times he applies Marx's concepts, extending his analysis and rounding it out.

The title of one of Weber's chief works, *Economy and Society,* his concern with the Protestant ethic, and with the religions of East and West, all attest to his sustained interest in the questions and issues Marx had raised. Weber's lifelong intellectual preoccupation was with the origin and nature of modern capitalism and with the question of why it emerged first in the West. Ultimately, the answer to that question became a matter of grasping the distinctive nature of Western civilization and its fundamental contrasts with the civilizations of the East. In his investigations of that complex problem, Weber employed a historical-sociological method wholly compatible with Marx's. Marx's major scientific aim, as we have seen, was not to prove that economics everywhere always determined all other facets of society. His aim was rather to guide the exploration of the manifold and historically changing connections between the economy and other social institutions. That was also Weber's scientific aim. He was not concerned with refuting Marx, as is still widely believed, nor did he see himself as having bested Marx. On the contrary, he looked upon Marx's major analytical concepts as extraordinarily fruitful. Insofar as any refutation of Marxism was intended by Weber, it was of the dogmatic, vulgar, and mechanistic varieties that had become common in his day.

The "economic" for Weber as for Marx, referred to the ". . . material struggle for existence."[15] How economics conditioned other institutions and how they, in turn, affected economic processes, was the lifelong focus of Weber's intellectual work. As an editor of the *Archiv fur Sozialwissenschaft und Sozialpolitik,* an important social science journal, Weber decided ". . . the scientific investigation of the general cultural significance of the social-economic structure of the human community and its historical forms of organization" was to be the journal's central aim. Why the journal adopted that editorial policy Weber explained this way: "the analysis of social and cultural phenomena with special reference to their economic conditioning and ramifications was a scientific principle of creative fruitfulness and, with careful application and freedom from dogmatic restrictions, will remain such for a very long time to come. The so-called "materialistic conception of history" as a *Weltanschauung* or as a formula for the causal explanation of historical reality is to be rejected most emphatically. The advancement of the economic *interpretation* of history is one of the most important aims of our journal."[16]

For Weber, then, the reaction against the dogmatic and vulgar types of Marxism had brought with it the danger of underestimating the fecundity of Marx's method conceived as a heuristic principle, not as a key for unlocking all doors.

If, for example, one carefully examines Weber's *Protestant Ethic and the Spirit of Capitalism,* it becomes quite clear that he was by no stretch of the imagination attempting to refute Marx. Throughout these studies Weber acknowledges the fundamental importance of economic developments and insists that one must ". . . take account of the economic conditions."[17] In the *Protestant Ethic,* however, he set himself a special task, namely, to examine the economic relevance of a specific religious ethic which, in his judgment, had not been given the consideration it deserved. Hence he is deliberately examining "only one side of the causal chain," that is, the impact of religious values on economic conduct. Again and again Weber returns to remind the reader of his limited purpose: ". . . to clarify the part which religious forces have played in forming the developing web of our specifically worldly modern culture, in the complex interaction of innumerable different historical factors" (p. 90). Weber is fighting on two fronts. He wishes, on the one hand, to disprove the idea held by some Marxists, that the Reformation was a historically necessary consequence of economic developments. But, on the other hand, he has

> . . . no intention whatever of maintaining such a foolish and doctrinaire thesis as that the spirit of capitalism (in the provisional sense of the term explained above) could only have arisen as the result of certain effects of the Reformation, or even that capitalism as an economic system is a creation of the Reformation. In itself, the fact that certain important forms of capitalistic business organization are known to be considerably older than the Reformation is a sufficient refutation of such a claim. On the contrary, we only wish to ascertain whether and to what extent religious forces have taken part in the qualitative formation and the quantitative expansion of that spirit over the world. (p. 91)

It was Weber's intention to assess the contribution of the Protestant ethic to the shape of the modern economic system, and to shed light on the process by which "ideas become effective forces in history." Thus Weber is proposing to "round out" Marx's method by systematically exploring the role of religion. He is not denying or belittling the importance of economic processes; nor, on the other hand, is he arguing that Protestantism caused capitalism. In the last paragraph of his study Weber reminds his reader once again that he has been tracing influence in one direction, and that he has done only half a job since it is equally

> . . . necessary to investigate how Protestant asceticism was in turn influenced in its development and its character by the totality of social conditions, especially economic. The modern man is in general, even with the best will, unable to give religious ideas a significance for culture and national character which they deserve. But it is, of course, not my aim to substitute for a one-sided materialistic an equally one-sided spiritualistic causal interpretation of culture and of history. Each is equally possible, but each, if it does not serve as the preparation, but as the conclusion of an investigation, accomplishes equally little in the interest of historical truth. (p. 183)

Weber viewed capitalism as a modern phenomenon: a very complex system of institutions, characterized by a high degree of formal, or technical, rationality. Modern capitalism was not to be confused with the various forms of capitalistic activity (for example, speculative, commercial, adventurous, political) which were known in previous periods of history in the West and East alike. The new economic system had to fight its way to supremacy by overcoming a world of hostile traditional forces; its victory over those forces could not be viewed as "historically necessary" or "historically inevitable." When the capitalist economy first made its appearance in sixteenth- and seventeenth-century Europe, it entailed a sharp break with the past. It involved a new code of economic conduct and new social relations at odds with the accepted conventions and laws of Church and State. How did the pioneers of the capitalist system overcome the resistance of the old order and elbow their way to success?

The answer to that question typically given by the Marxists was roughly this: The successful emergence of the new system was made possible by changes in the economic world. The influx of precious metals from America, capital accumulated in commerce, expanding markets, the growth of population, and new technology resulting from the advance of natural science—those were the major factors.

Weber did not deny the importance of those conditions. He nevertheless believed that the Marxian answer was incomplete, for there were countries in which all of the enumerated conditions were present, but which failed to give birth to capitalist industry. France in the reign of Louis XIV, for example, commanded immense resources by the standards of the time, but dissipated them in luxury and war. Hence the economic explanation is insufficient and one must look outside economics for the supplementary factor. If the first entrepreneurs engaged in their economic pursuits with a special vigor and dedication, that fact may be traced to the Protestant ethic—to the new moral values that emerged with the religious changes of the sixteenth century, the Reformation. Let us follow Weber as he puts his thesis together step by step.

Weber begins by drawing attention to certain significant cultural differences between Protestants and Catholics. In their education Protestants were more inclined to study technical subjects; they were also more prominent as proprietors of industrial enterprises. Catholics, on the other hand, seemed to prefer more traditional humanistic studies and nonindustrial occupations such as crafts. Those differences remained evident even when one controlled for the social-class background of the two religious categories. Protestants, whether from upper or lower strata, "have shown a special tendency to develop *economic rationalism* which cannot be observed to the same extent among Catholics . . ." (p. 40, italics added). What is the source of the more pronounced economic rationalism among Protestants?

At first glance, it might appear that they have been more worldly and hedonistic than Catholics. But closer examination shows that that has not been the case. The "English, Dutch and American Protestants," writes Weber, "were characterized by the exact opposite of the joy of living . . ." (p. 41). Indeed, they adhered to a strict religious and moral code of self-denial. They were, in a word, *ascetic*. Ironically, it was their ascetic Protestant ethos that made them especially receptive to the rational spirit of capitalism.

To document his thesis, Weber employs the figure of Benjamin Franklin. From *Necessary Hints to Those That Would Be Rich* and *Advice to a Young Tradesman*, Weber selects some typical sayings that illustrate Franklin's commitment to industry, frugality, hard work, and punctuality. Franklin was important to Weber because, though he said, "Time is money," his attitude toward wealth was different from that of the rich man of earlier eras. Franklin's motives for making money, argues Weber, were devoid of hedonism. They were rooted in his strict Calvinist upbringing. Why should men make money and why should "money be made out of men?" To that, Ben Franklin replies by quoting the Bible: "Seest Thou a man diligent in his business? He shall stand before kings." Franklin's business interests were thus religiously motivated and justified. For Weber, Franklin was rather typical of the early entrepreneurs who found clear sanction for their business dealings in their new Protestant teachings. Not all Protestants, however, shared the emphasis on an ascetic way of life with the resulting stimulation of capitalistic spirit and enterprise. Asceticism was to be traced to Calvin, not Luther.

With Luther, Weber observed, a new concept had emerged, which heretofore had been absent from Christian theology. That concept, expressed in the German word *Beruf* and even more clearly in the English word *calling*, referred to the morally dutiful fulfillment of a task assigned by God. The concept with that connotation, first appearing in Protestant translations of the Bible and thereafter assuming special importance among Protestants, imparted for the first time in the West a religious significance to men's daily, worldly activities.

And yet, Luther's general doctrine, far from being favorable to the ethos of capitalism, was positively hostile to it. His attitude toward capitalistic activity was quite traditional and in some respects less accommodating than that of the medieval Scholastics. Moreover, after the peasant uprisings, when Luther had firmly aligned himself with the princes, he became a defender of the status quo. Hence, although Luther had introduced the idea of the "calling," that idea assumed a traditionalistic meaning and failed to provide a congenial environment for capitalistic activity. It is not in Luther's teachings, therefore, but in Calvinism that one must seek the ethical elements which fostered the capitalistic spirit. (Of course, the fostering of that spirit was an unforeseen and even unwished-for result of Calvin's labors.)

How, then, did Calvin's doctrine of predestination lead to worldly activity such as business? Actually, Weber explains, it was not the teachings of Calvin himself but rather of his followers that yielded that result. Calvin, though certain of his own election, rejected the principle that one could learn whether one was chosen or damned as an attempt to force God's secrets. But that doctrine proved to be too heavy a psychological burden for ordinary people who needed to know their fate and who required a "sign." Thus Calvin's followers increasingly gave way to the expressed need for ". . . infallible criteria by which membership in the *electi* could be known" (p. 110). The original doctrine was therefore modified, and now stressed the

> . . . absolute duty to consider oneself chosen, and to combat all doubts as temptations of the devil, since lack of self-confidence is the result of insufficient faith, hence of imperfect grace. The exhortation of the apostle to make fast one's own call is here interpreted as a duty to attain certainty of one's own election and justification in the daily struggle of life. In the place of the humble sinners to whom Luther promises grace if they trust themselves to God in penitent faith are bred those self-confident saints whom we can rediscover in the hard Puritan merchants of the heroic age of capitalism and in isolated instances down to the present. On the other hand, in order to attain that self-confidence, intense worldly activity is recommended as the most suitable means. It and it alone disperses religious doubts and gives the certainty of grace. (pp. 111–12)

Good works, then, though useless for the attainment of salvation, became a possible *sign* of election. They served to allay fear of damnation. Hard work in the morally dutiful pursuit of a worldly calling, and absolute avoidance of anything which detracts from an ascetic way of life—that was the Protestant ethic. It was embodied, in varying degrees, in Puritanism, Pietism, Methodism, and the Anabaptist sects, and it had the ". . . greatest significance for the development of the spirit of capitalism" (p. 151).

This brings us to the point at which Weber's method of presenting his thesis—the ideal-type—must be carefully examined if we are to understand the charges brought against him even by the most friendly of his critics. Just as earlier he had accentuated what he considered the characteristics of the new "spirit of capitalism" by employing Benjamin Franklin as its ideal representative, so now he treated ascetic Protestantism as a unified whole by placing one of its major representatives at the center of the discussion. For Weber, it was Richard Baxter, an English Puritan minister and writer, who "stands out above many other writers on Puritan ethics, both because of his eminently practical and realistic attitude, and, at the same time, because of the universal recognition accorded to his works . . ." (pp. 155–56). So, if Franklin epitomized at one and the same time the new capitalistic ethos as well as the Protestant conception of the pursuit of a calling in a morally dutiful manner, so Baxter expressed through his religious writings "a practical and realistic attitude." Baxter does not quite say "Time is money," but he does say the spiritual equivalent, Weber argues. A waste of time is "in principle the deadliest of sins." Every "hour lost is lost to labor for the glory of God." Out of strictly religious motives, Baxter preaches "hard, continuous, bodily or mental labor"; but unlike St. Paul or Thomas Aquinas, who exempted some from the rule that "He who will not work shall not eat," Baxter exempts no one—not even the wealthy. Weber grants that there are certain secular, utilitarian elements in Baxter's thought, as when he expresses himself on the division of labor. The manufacturing system tends to serve "the common good, which is identical with the good of the greatest possible number"; yet even that has a characteristic Puritan element that becomes perfectly clear in his insistence on the methodical and systematic pursuit of a calling—everyday and for everyone. Baxter's doctrine detests both the "superior indulgence of the *seigneur* and the parvenu ostentation of the *nouveau riche*," but "it has the highest ethical appreciation of the sober, middle-class, self-made man" (p. 163). Puritanism, Weber writes, carried with it "the ethos of the rational organization of capital and labor," and "turned with all its force against one thing: the spontaneous enjoyment of life and all it had to offer" (p. 166). Asceticism

> . . . looked upon the pursuit of wealth as an end in itself as highly reprehensible; but the attainment of it as a fruit of labor in a calling was a sign of God's blessing. And even more important: the religious valuation of restless, continuous, systematic work in a worldly calling, as the highest means to asceticism, and at the same time the surest and most evident proof of rebirth and genuine faith, must have been the most powerful conceivable lever for the expansion of that attitude toward life which we have here called the spirit of capitalism. (p. 172)

That becomes clear not only in Baxter's work, but also in the work of John Wesley, the founder of Methodism. The latter, Weber notes, even anticipated his own thesis, for he actually wrote that

> . . . the full economic effect of those great religious movements, whose significance for economic development lay above all in their ascetic educative influence, generally came only after the peak of the purely religious enthusiasm was past. Then the intensity of the search for the Kingdom of God commenced gradually to pass over into sober economic virtue; the religious roots died out slowly, giving way to utilitarian worldliness. (p. 176)

Protestant asceticism thus provided a positive religious sanction for the exploitation of the worker's willingness to labor; it eased the employer's conscience and at the same time provided the worker with religious motives for treating his labor as a calling. Weber therefore concludes:

> One of the fundamental elements of the spirit of modern capitalism, and not only of that but of all modern culture: rational conduct on the basis of the idea

> of the calling, was born—that is what this discussion has sought to demonstrate—from the spirit of Christian asceticism. (p. 180)

If we keep in mind the many qualifications Weber drew around his thesis—that in these essays he is tracing causal influence in only one direction, that he recognizes the fundamental importance of the economic conditions, and that in a subsequent essay he hoped to trace the influence in a reverse direction—then he is asserting on the basis of half-completed research that there was a mutually reinforcing convergence of the Protestant ethic and the capitalist ethos; and he is examining in this instance the degree to which the latter was derived from the former. Once the capitalist system had become established, however, the Protestant ethic was no longer a necessary ingredient for the maintenance of the system. Moreover, the ethic was not a necessary precondition for the emergence of the capitalist system per se, but rather for its markedly energetic character during the early phases of the system's development.

Whom did Weber select to illustrate the ethical injunctions of ascetic Protestantism? Never its founder!—which led some of his critics to wonder whether in Weber's view Calvin was a Calvinist. If indeed it were Weber's position—and some of his critics have thus wrongly interpreted him—that Calvin's religious teachings were of crucial causal importance in generating the capitalistic spirit, then it would have been methodologically impermissible to use anyone but Calvin as a representative of the new religious doctrine. But Weber does not do that; instead, as we have seen, he used Richard Baxter (1615–1691), John Wesley (1703–1791), Benjamin Franklin (1706–1790), and others, all of whom lived a hundred years after Calvin. Obviously, Weber was not employing them in order to show what Calvinism was in the middle of the sixteenth century, but rather to show what Calvinism became in the course of its development. Furthermore, he was showing what it became, not in isolation from other developments, but under the influence of economic and other developments. That is why the thinkers Weber cites embody elements of both Protestant asceticism and the capitalistic spirit. On the theoretical level, then, Weber is suggesting that two relatively autonomous developments intersected at a given historical point to contribute to the formation of the modern rational temperament: There was a great "elective affinity" between the norms of the new religious movement and the ethos of the new economic system.

It should be clear, then, that those commentators who describe the *Protestant Ethic* as a refutation of Marxism simply have not read the essay with sufficient care. Furthermore, insofar as such commentators claim that Weber's analysis stressed religious and other spiritual "factors" at the expense of economic conditions, they are quite wrong. No one had to persuade Max Weber, who was, among other things, an outstanding economic historian, of the importance of economics. The fact of the matter is that economic conditions remained central to his analyses of both capitalist and precapitalist formations. This statement is best documented by reviewing what Weber had to say about the several epochs that Marx called "modes of production."

ANCIENT SLAVE SOCIETY AND THE TRANSITION TO FEUDALISM: WEBER'S ANALYSIS

The centrality of economic conditions is evident in Weber's earliest writing, notably in his second dissertation, *Roman Agrarian History in Its Bearing on Public and Private Law* (1891); in an article entitled, "The Social Causes of the Decline of Ancient Civilization" (1896); and in his *The Agrarian Sociology of Ancient Civilizations* (1909). Let us begin with the article, a succinct, coherent and, indeed, fascinating attempt to lay bare the socioeconomic processes that fundamentally transformed the structure of ancient society.

Weber begins by defining the major characteristics of the ancient social structure. The civilization of antiquity was essentially urban, with the ancient urban economy resting on the exchange of manufactured goods for the agricultural products of the rural hinterland. Such local trade provided for all of a city's needs. In addition, from very early times there had existed an international trade centered in the coastal cities. Ancient European civilization was, above all, a coastal civilization with a well-developed commercial economy. But the rural interior was just the opposite in character, that is, a "natural economy" in which peasants lived in self-sufficient, tribal communities under the domination of quasi-feudal patriarchs. A truly international trade was confined to the sea routes and large rivers, whereas the volume of trade with the interior was insignificant compared with the Middle Ages. Such trade as existed between the towns and the interior was limited to a few expensive items of luxury that could be traded profitably in spite of the high costs of transport. Hence international trade was concerned not with the everyday needs of the masses, but with a slender stratum of the wealthy classes.

For Weber, the most salient feature of the ancient social structure was that it rested on slavery. From earliest times unfree labor in the countryside coexisted with free labor in the cities. While free craftsmen produced for the urban market, unfree laborers produced on and for estates not much different from those of the Middle Ages. Under conditions of free labor, Weber suggests, economic growth requires an expansion of the market, drawing new areas and more people into the exchange economy. In fact, there was an effort on the part of the ancient towns to break up the rural estates and to incorporate their laborers in the market. Under conditions of unfree labor, in contrast, economic growth can only be achieved by an increase in the number of laborers, "for the more slaves or serfs are assembled the more specialization of unfree occupations is possible."[18] The significant point here is that whereas free labor and the free market eventually prevailed in the late Middle Ages, the opposite occurred in antiquity. Why was that the case? "For the same reason," Weber explains,

> that technological development in antiquity was limited: human beings could be bought cheaply, because of the character of the chronic warfare of ancient civilization. Ancient wars were also slave hunts; they constantly supplied the slave markets and so promoted to an extraordinary degree the unfree labour sector of the economy and the accumulation of labour-power. The result was that the free sector ceased to expand . . . [And] no competition could arise between free entrepreneurs and free wage-labourers in production for the market, which would have set a premium on labour-saving inventions such as those induced by competition in modern times.[19]

In antiquity, it was predominantly the slaveowners who expanded production based on a division of labor. It was the slave enterprises that produced surpluses for the market. Slavery, then, explains why the ancient economy never developed into the kind of exchange system that emerged in the late Middle Ages. In that era the emerging modern economy rested on free labor, first in the putting-out system and later in manufactures. The modern economy created new forms of production by which to meet the expanding demand of the masses. In contrast, the ancient, urban, exchange economy was a frail and stagnant superstructure. For beneath it was a constantly expanding natural economy in which needs were met without exchange. "Thus trade in antiquity," Weber maintains,

> more and more became a thin net spread over a large natural economy, and as time passed the meshes of this net became finer and its threads became more tenuous.[20]

Slave labor became even more important under the Roman Empire with its incorporation of vast continental areas into the Roman socioeconomic system. As a result the meshes of the commercial net were stretched still further. A ". . . slave-labour system became the indispensable foundation of Roman society."[21]

The main features of the agricultural system based on unfree labor were these: The landowner, typically a city-dweller, turned over the management of his estate to *villici*, unfree overseers, and lived off of the cash rents. Because grain production for the market was, as a rule, unprofitable, and because slave-labor was unsuited to raising grain, it was not slaves but rather *coloni* who tended the cereal crops. *Coloni*, descendants of free peasants who had lost their land, rendered labor services under the supervision of the overseer. Seeds and tools were provided by the landlord. In time land was leased to *coloni* who became tenant-farmers struggling to raise grain on the least fertile soils. But *coloni* and slaves also worked side by side in another type of estate. Here the best land was turned over to the production of cash crops such as olive oil, wine, and other luxury items for the wealthy—all produced by the slave population. Slaves ate and slept in barracks under strict military discipline. Organized in squads, they performed their tasks under the command of slave drivers who maintained order with the whip. The typical slave in a plantation of this type was not only propertyless, but he also had no family, no monogamous relationship. A slave's sex life was a form of supervised prostitution in which slave women received bonuses and occasionally even their freedom if they reared children.

That state of affairs is especially vital to Weber's argument: Slaves condemned to live in barracks without monogamous family life failed to reproduce themselves. Hence slaves had to be continually purchased to replenish the barracks. The plantation system depended on a slave market that obtained regular supplies of human material. There came a time, however, when new slaves were no longer obtainable, thus creating a crisis in the entire system. The basic cause of the crisis Weber traced to the setbacks and defeats suffered by the Empire in its wars of expansion against the Germanic tribes and other "barbarians." Decisive in this regard was Tiberius' resolution

> to abandon the wars of conquest on the Rhine, a resolution later repeated on the Danube by Hadrian's evacuation of Dacia. These imperial policies meant that the Roman Empire ceased to expand. The entire area of ancient civilization was now pacified internally and (to a large extent) externally; but therewith the regular supply of human material for the slave markets ceased. As early as the reign of Tiberius the consequence seems to have become apparent: an acute shortage of labour.[22]

With the supply of slaves thus cut off, the slave barracks, together with the system resting upon it, were bound to decline.

What emerged in place of the slave plantations may be seen in the landed estates of Carolingian times. Under Charlemagne servile labor was also employed, as in antiquity. Slaves and plantations existed in both periods. But one aspect of slave life had been altered radically in the interim. Whereas Roman slaves lived together in common barracks, the typical slave of Carolingian times lived in his own cottage with his family on land he received from his lord in return for labor services. The reason for the change was that slaves in barracks under the late Empire had failed to reproduce themselves. In Weber's words,

> When slaveowners allowed their slaves to have their own families and made them hereditary dependents, they thereby assured themselves young slaves to take their parents' place and work the fields. This was now essential since workers could not be purchased on the slave market, which indeed disappeared completely in Carolingian times. Furthermore, whereas the plantation owner had to invest capital in maintaining his slaves, this burden was now shifted to the slaves themselves.[23]

Thus the lowest classes of society once again acquired the right to family life and to private property. The slave had risen in social status and become a serf.

As slave barracks gave way to peasant cottages, the "... thin net of commerce, which had covered the natural economy of antiquity, frayed and then snapped."[24] That occurred as the great estates increasingly provided for their own needs, including the products of smiths, cabinet-makers, masons, and carpenters. Urban craftsmen consequently lost their rural market. Now self-sufficient, the estates withdrew completely from the urban markets, thus destroying the economic foundation of small and medium towns. Exchange between the cities and the hinterland ceased. And since the State increasingly met its fiscal needs on a natural-economy basis, that policy further hastened the decline of the cities.

With the decline of commerce and the expansion of the natural economy, rural districts found it more difficult to provide what the State most needed: money (taxes) and men (recruits for the standing army). Given the closure of the slave market and the resulting shortage of labor, army recruitment among the *coloni* became especially ruinous for the estates, so much so that the landlords helped peasants evade the recruitment officers. Men even fled the cities knowing that the large landlords, in need of laborers, would aid them in avoiding conscription. Recruitment for the army became so difficult that from the time of the reign of Vespasian, Italy was exempted from conscription. Thus the State, compelled more and more to rely on mercenary services, recruited barbarians. For the expanding mercenary army the State required growing sums of money. But as the Empire reverted to a natural economy, the estate owners, who produced only for their own needs, were unable to pay taxes in the form of money. "It is clear, therefore," Weber concludes,

> that the disintegration of the Roman Empire *was the inevitable political consequence of a basic economic development:* the gradual disappearance of commerce and the expansion of a barter economy. *Essentially this disintegration simply meant that the monetarized [sic] administrative system and political superstructure of the Empire disappeared, for they were no longer adapted to the infrastructure of a natural economy.*[25]

The system that emerged out of the disintegration of the Empire had to be based on the institutions of the natural economy. And, indeed, that is precisely what we find under Charlemagne, whose entire fiscal administration was a matter of providing food for his table and supplies for the royal household. His empire had no standing army, no salaried bureaucracy, and no monetary taxes. All those features of the Roman Empire had disappeared, as had interlocal commerce and the cities. The manors were the units of the new society run by the manorial lords. Western civilization had become rural.

For Weber, then, this fundamental transformation was the result of the changing economic conditions. As the supplies of slaves dried up with the pacification of the Empire, the natural economy imposed itself throughout. The commercialized cities disappeared, and ". . . the intellectual life of

Western Europe sank into a long darkness."[26] With this socioeconomic transformation, a part of the formerly free or semifree *coloni* were subjected to serfdom, and the urban patricians of old were replaced by rural, barbarized feudal lords. Yet Weber sees something gained from the transformation. "For the great masses of unfree people regained family life and private property, and they themselves were elevated from the status of 'speaking tools' to the plane of humanity."[27]

Weber's analysis therefore leaves no doubt that he accorded extraordinary importance to economic conditions under definite historical circumstances. Whether the influence upon him in this instance was Marxian or not, is less important than recognizing the convergences between Weber and Marx in their explanations of the disintegration of the Roman Empire and the emergence of feudalism. Indeed, Weber's economic emphasis in this instance may be stronger than Marx's; for in Marx's scattered discussions of the rise of feudalism, he nowhere says, as does Weber, "that the disintegration of the Roman empire *was the inevitable political consequence of a basic economic development. . . .*" In any event, this article is entirely typical of Weber's concerns with economic institutions, and with classes, class interests, and class conflict in ancient societies.

CLASS AND CLASS CONFLICT IN ANCIENT SOCIETIES

In his *Agrarian Sociology of Ancient Civilizations*, the central problem with which Weber concerns himself is this: "What is the origin of the later medieval and modern economic system—in a word, of modern capitalism?"[28] This remained his lifelong intellectual preoccupation, the focal point of his intellectual labors. In probing the economic conditions of ancient civilization, Weber provides short, pithy essays on Mesopotamia, Egypt, Israel, Greece, the Hellenistic Age, the Roman Republic, and the Roman Empire. Weber's views of Mesopotamia and Egypt will be taken up later, while considering the parallels in his analysis with Marx's "Asiatic Mode of Production." For now it will suffice to illustrate the centrality of social class in Weber's discussion of ancient Israel and Greece.

The Ten Commandments and the Mosaic legislation as a whole, Weber argued, were designed for the protection of the mass of free persons against the consequences of social stratification in wealth and power. Some of the more important laws imposed limits on the enslavement of Hebrews for debt; extended protection to marriages between free persons and debt slaves; protected the Hebrew woman, bought as a wife, from the treatment accorded purchased slaves in general; protected slaves against physical injury by their masters; and protected persons from injury by cattle. The significance of the last provision, Weber explains, is that ". . . cattle formed the major element of the aristocracy's wealth, and so this is an ancient analogy to our contemporary controversies over damage done by game."[29]

In a large measure, then, the Mosaic legislation was designed to protect the poor and the weak against the wealthy and powerful. There were, however, other provisions prohibiting partiality either toward the rich or the poor. Such provisions, Weber convincingly suggests, reflect the legislator's

> aim to end class conflict through impartial arbitration, which was indeed the aim of the great legislators of antiquity. A significant feature is the exhortation not to oppress metics, reflecting the results of the commercial traffic which went by and in part through the homeland of the Hebrews.[30]

Hebrew law shared this basic principle with many other law codes of the West designed to "settle class conflicts."[31]

The most original and significant of the Mosaic provisions, Weber believed, was the injunction to keep the Sabbath rest—a law extended to laborers, slaves, and cattle. What Weber has to say about the Sabbath law illustrates how he distinguishes himself from some of his Marxist contemporaries who accorded religion and other elements of the so-called "superstructure" no real autonomy whatsoever. The Sabbath law, Weber writes,

> . . . cannot of course be explained on purely "socio-political" grounds, for it reflects most clearly the great power of religious motivations. Nevertheless this commandment clearly benefitted the debt slave as well as other classes.[32]

The methodological principle that Weber's interpretation exemplifies is this: One must give due consideration in all historical-sociological analyses not only to economic and economically conditioned phenomena, but to economically *relevant* phenomena as well.[33] Religion is an example of an institution that may have considerable economic relevance in some historical circumstances. Hence Weber concludes that the

> . . . Torah [the Pentateuch] was in part the result of purely religious forces, but mainly was meant to prevent the enslavement of the peasantry by the wealthy families, which had visibly occurred in the coastal towns, and to maintain the ancient freedom based on equality. This has more support from the evidence than many other theories now current. . . .[34]

Weber takes a similar approach to the changing social structure of ancient Greece. The growth of sea trade in the coastal cities led to a crisis owing to two conditions: the accumulation of wealth in money and land; and the increasing indebtedness of the peasantry. The money economy

> led to a differentiation in income and the creation of new classes: rich parvenus, poor free men without property, and impoverished aristocrats. From this sprang bitter class conflicts within the *polis*.[35]

The new commercial class made its money from the export and shipping businesses and therefore had little in common with the traditional landowning groups. The parvenus often formed political alliances with the free-born men who, having lost their land, were reduced to debt servitude. At times together and at other times alone, these groups formed social movements "aiming to overthrow the aristocratic regimes."[36] Indeed, writes Weber,

> all classical Greek history was characterized by the social contrasts between aristocracy and commons, and this itself was inextricably connected with the economic opposition which separated oligarchs from democrats.[37]

These are only a few examples of how Weber employs social-class analysis throughout.

COMMUNALISM IN ANTIQUITY

There is an important substantive question that Weber touches upon first in these earlier writings and again later in his *General Economic History*: What was the nature and extent of communalism in the earliest stages of these ancient societies? And were there actual "survivals" of these early communal forms in the modern era? Marx and Engels, as we have seen, speak of "tribal ownership" in their earliest writings, and Engels later posited some form of primitive communalism among the Germans, Greeks, and Celts.[38] Nevertheless Marx and Engels recognized that none of these cases was consistently communal. It was primarily access to the soil that was distributed in an egalitarian fashion, while cattle, slaves, and other goods acquired in forays and wars early became private property.

Weber questions whether the Greeks and Romans had a system quite similar to that of the Germans. He does maintain, however, that there cannot have been any unconditional appropriation of land as private property in Homeric times. A family's property was removed from the common lands, thus becoming royal land, only when the family was raised to monarchical status. "Even in the 4th century [B.C.]," writes Weber,

> Attic village communities (*dèmoi*) still owned considerable lands, and clearly they must have been commons for a very long time.[39]

In time, of course, the commons were first encroached upon and then eliminated entirely. In Rome, the state made a sharp distinction between *ager privatus* and *ager publicus* and the

> . . . communal forms of property ownership were deliberately put at a disadvantage, as the legal form of the private condominium shows. The ancient common lands (*ager compascuus*) were condemned to extinction, and the agrarian law of 111 B.C. (preserved in an inscription) prevented the creation of new commons.[40]

Weber rejects a view fashionable in his time that ancient Germanic institutions were ". . . the echo of an original agrarian communism uniformly valid for all peoples . . ."[41] After reviewing the evidence available for the Celts, South Slavs, Russians, and others, Weber concludes that the theory of a universal primitive communalism is untenable. Moreover, the view that forms of the original communalism continued to survive in the nineteenth and twentieth centuries was even more dubious.

The Russian *Mir*, for example, was regarded by some scholars as such a survival. The *Mir* held the land and distributed it, good and bad, in a patchwork intended to be as equitable as possible. The *Mir* fixed the times of ploughing, sowing, haymaking, and harvest.[42] Although Russian scholarship was divided on the question of the origin of the *Mir*, the more generally accepted view was that, far from being an ancient institution, it originated in recent times, in response to a specific system of taxation. Under the *Mir*, Weber explains, the community had unquestioned control over a village member's labor-power. The tax imposed a certain financial burden on the village community as a whole, and the community, in turn, ensured that each member paid his share of the common burden. Clearly, under such an arrangement, if some members left the village, the tax burden was correspondingly increased for all those who remained behind. The *Mir* therefore frequently forced members to return. "Consequently," Weber observes,

> the solidarity limited the individual member's freedom of movement and amounted merely to a continuation through the mir of the serfdom which had been abolished [in 1861]; the peasant was no longer a serf of the lord but a serf of the mir.[43]

The same principle of joint liability to the overlord or the state, accounts for the communal forms evident in the Far East in the late nineteenth and early twentieth centuries. In Indonesia, the Dutch East India Company made an entire community responsible for a tax in the form of rice and tobacco. The community therefore compelled the individual to remain in the village to shoulder his share of the common burden. In India there were also thought to exist vestiges of ancient communal forms. Here, again, however, Weber shows that such communal agrarian organizations originated in fairly recent times out of fiscal considerations.

In the light of what has been said so far, it should be quite clear that in his analyses of ancient civilizations, and the contrasts they exhibited with later epochs, Weber focused sharply on socioeconomic processes. Weber's main aim in these analyses of antiquity, was to explain why capitalism in the modern, formal-rational sense never developed in that epoch; and why manufacturing technique (Marx's "productive forces") failed to expand, though wealth increased. Industry in antiquity never acquired the commanding position that it attained in the late medieval cities.

How, in Weber's view, modern capitalism developed out of the late medieval cities will become clearer as we review his analyses first of feudalism and then of the Asiatic mode of production.

FEUDALISM: WEBER'S VIEW AND ITS AFFINITIES WITH THAT OF MARX

For Marx and Engels, as we have seen, it was the institution of *retinues* that eventually favored the rise of kingship. Among the Germanic tribes, for instance, such permanent associations had become evident in earliest times. A retinue was formed, wrote Engels, when

> a military leader who had made himself a name gathered around him a band of young men eager for booty, whom he pledged to personal loyalty, giving the same pledge to them.[44]

As the Roman Empire disintegrated, and Germanic and other groups conquered ever greater areas, the leaders of such retinues had already become kings, while the retinues themselves, together with the Roman chiefs and courtiers, formed the later feudal nobility. Even in earliest times the retinues had evaded the discipline of the community and had held their booty as private property. In due course the retinue became a firmly established institution—the major force that served to undermine communal property in land. The effects wrought by the powerful retinues may be illustrated with the history of the Frankish tribes that conquered Gaul. With victory, these West Germanic groups acquired possession of extensive Roman state domains. Large tracts of land were distributed to district and mark communities, while the rest, large forest areas, was designated as the commons, the land of the people as a whole. The land, however, did not remain in the people's hands for long. Engels writes:

> on his transformation from a plain military chief into a real sovereign of a country, the first thing which the king of Franks did was to transform this property of the people into crown lands, to steal it from the people and to give it, outright or in fief, to his retainers. This retinue, which originally consisted of his personal following of warriors and of other lesser military leaders, was presently increased not only by Romans . . . but also by [all those] who composed his court and from whom he chose his favorites. All these received their portions of the people's land, at first in the form of gifts, later of benefices, usually conferred, to begin with, for the king's life time. Thus at the expense of the people the foundation of a new nobility was laid.[45]

Like Marx and Engels, Weber also viewed feudalism as having emerged from the personal retinues of tribal chiefs. Both in antiquity and in the Middle Ages the followers of a chief soon became a royal retinue, the members of which, Weber observes,

> . . . were often regarded as foreign or, at least, as standing outside the regular law of the land and subject only to the royal ban. In both periods steps are taken to establish a royal storehouse system and to supply the army with it . . . In both periods, too, the royal retinue was the institution from which a knightly aristocracy developed (other institutions played a role too), and this became so

> powerful and indispensable as to make kings dependent, sometimes reducing them to elective status and so dominating the state completely.[46]

But there were, of course, basic differences between the royal retinues of antiquity and those of the Middle Ages. The medieval king was not an urban ruler just as the medieval nobility never became an urban aristocracy. To explain the divergent path taken by the royal retinues and manorial institutions of medieval times, Weber repeats the argument he had made in his "The Social Causes of the Decline of Ancient Civilization." In antiquity the manors remained the economic foundation of an *urban* rentier class. Ancient civilization was actually centered in the coastal cities and rested on their commercial economies. As one moved farther inland, one found a manorial organization similar to that of medieval times. In contrast to antiquity, a great change occurred in the Middle Ages:

> . . . throughout the great area linked by a continuous historical tradition stretching from pharaonic to modern times there was a great shift in the centre of gravity from the coastal to the inland areas. Most of the manors were not suburban but rural institutions, and they supported an agrarian ruling class—princes, free vassals, and their knightly ministeriales.[47]

For Weber, as for Marx, the "retinue" is a pivotal concept in explaining the origins of the feudal social structure. Everywhere military chieftainship was transformed into seignorial power, which became hereditary. The leader and his followers had a privileged claim in the distribution of booty and conquered land. They imposed their authority on the people, the occupiers of small holdings, who cultivated the seignorial land as well as their own. The transition from tribal ownership to seignorial and the growing internal differentiation of society developed with the establishment of a professional warrior class that monopolized the military means of violence. Neither the weapons, equipment, training, nor horses were available to men with ordinary holdings. There thus arose, writes Weber,

> a distinction between those classes which by virtue of their possessions were in a position to render military service and to equip themselves for the same, and those who could not do this and consequently were not able to maintain the full status of free men. The development of agricultural technique worked in the same direction. . . . The result was that the ordinary peasant was increasingly bound to his economic functions. Further differentiation came about through the fact that the upper classes, skilled in fighting, and providing their own equipment, accumulated booty in varying degrees through their military activity, while non-military who could not do this became more and more subject to various services and taxes.[48]

The internal differentiation of tribal society was also brought about by the conquest and subjugation of other societies and by the

> . . . voluntary submission of a defenseless man to the overlordship of a military leader. Because the former needed protection he recognized a lord as *patronus* (in Rome) or as a *senior*, among the Merovingian Franks.[49]

So for Weber as for Marx the development of feudal society reflected the growing wealth and power of the retinues.

Since the feudal lord was a professional warrior, not a farmer, he had nothing to do with agriculture. He received dues in kind from his dependents and, in return, guaranteed them protection. The resulting economy or "mode of production" was "conservative" in Marx's sense, and, indeed, Weber quotes Marx approvingly in this regard:

> The dues of the peasants originally served only to satisfy the requirements of the lord and were readily fixed by tradition. The peasants had no interest in making the soil yield more than was necessary for their own maintenance and for covering their obligatory payments, and the lord had as little interest in increasing the payments, as long as he did not produce for the market. The mode of life of the lord was but little different from that of the peasant. Thus "the walls of his stomach set the limits of his exploitation of the peasant," as Karl Marx observed.[50]

Lord and peasant had a common interest in maintaining the traditionally fixed dues.

The common interest in fixed dues came to an end, however, with the emergence of a market economy. Now kings, princes, and great lords all wanted to gain profit from commerce. The "natural economy" of the manor evinced a strong tendency to change in a capitalistic direction. Both the manorial lord and the peasant acquired a material interest in the emerging exchange economy, an interest that grew all the more intense as the market for agricultural products and the money economy expanded. Yet the internal changes in the manor, in the relations of lord to peasant, were insufficient to bring about the dissolution of the manor. For that to occur, other interests from without had to come into play, namely,

> the commercial interests of the newly established bourgeoisie of the towns, who promoted the weakening or dissolution of the manor because it limited their own market opportunities.[51]

Weber thus agrees with Marx that the town and the manor "were antagonistic" (Weber's words), and that feudal relations of production tended to "fetter" (Marx's term) and "set limits" (Weber's phrase) on capitalistic development. "Through the mere fact," writes Weber,

> of the compulsory services and payments of the tenants, the manorial system set limits to the purchasing power of the rural population because it prevented the peasants from devoting their entire labor power to production for the market and from developing their purchasing power. Thus the interests of the bourgeoisie of the towns were opposed to those of the landed proprietors. In addition, there was the interest on the part of the developing capitalism in the creation of a free labor market, to which obstacles were opposed by the manorial system through the attachment of the peasants to the soil. The first capitalistic industries were thrown back upon the exploitation of rural labor power in

> order to circumvent the guilds. The desire of the new capitalists to acquire land gave them a further interest antagonistic to the manorial system; the capitalistic classes wished to invest their newly acquired wealth in land in order to rise into the socially privileged landed class, and this required a liberation of the land from feudal ties. Finally, the fiscal interest of the state also took a hand, counting upon the dissolution of the manor to increase the taxpaying capacity of the farming country.[52]

It is therefore clear that Weber's analysis of declining feudalism converges strikingly with Marx's.

No less remarkable are the conceptual and substantive parallels that one finds in Weber's discussion of Eastern society. For it is indisputable, as we shall see, that Weber was familiar with Marx's characterization of the Asiatic mode of production and that he built on that concept in his own studies of Asiatic society and religion. Weber recognized that although landlords in all agrarian societies strove for independence from the political power above them, success in this endeavor was achieved only under feudalism. Feudalism was a decentralized political system in which the prince's officials were forbidden access to the lord's territory; or if permitted,

> . . . had to come directly to the lord himself for the performance of his mission on behalf of the political authority, such as collection of feudal dues or serving of military summons.[53]

Under feudalism, there was a "division of powers," a multiplicity of comparatively autonomous domains. The *locus classicus* of feudalism, thus understood, was Western Europe and Japan. Weber agreed with Marx that the East had exhibited a fundamentally different socioeconomic and political structure.

THE ASIATIC MODE OF PRODUCTION: WEBER'S FRUITFUL ELABORATION OF MARX'S CONCEPT

Weber had a lifelong concern with the question of why rational capitalism emerged first in the West and not in the East. This led him to a systematic exploration of the basic structural and cultural differences between the two civilizations. It is beyond doubt, as we shall see, that Weber recognized the distinctive character of the Asiatic mode of production and that he was familiar with Marx's ideas on the subject. In his study of the religions and social structure of India before it was subjected to British rule, Weber pauses to make this observation:

> Karl Marx has characterized the peculiar position of the artisan of the Indian village—his dependence upon fixed payments in kind instead of upon production for the market—as the reason for the specific "stability" of the Asiatic peoples. In this Marx was correct.[54]

Weber thus accepts Marx's characterization of the Asiatic mode, but expands and rounds out Marx's analysis by investigating religious as well as economic and political institutions.

Like Marx, Weber sees the roots of the Asiatic mode in the need to construct complex, artificial irrigation systems. Originating in the ancient Near East, riverine irrigation networks became the foundation of the entire economy in Mesopotamia and Egypt, the oldest centers of civilization.[55] "Every new settlement," writes Weber,

> demanded construction of a canal, so that the land was essentially a man-made product. Now canal construction is necessarily a large-scale operation, demanding some sort of collective social organization; . . . Here then is the fundamental economic cause for the overwhelmingly dominant position of the monarchy in Mesopotamia (and also in Egypt).[56]

That canals and irrigation networks had existed in the earliest historical centers, Sumer and Akkad, is evident from inscriptions. Building and maintaining the canals and dikes required the labor services of large numbers of people who labored ". . . under the direction of royal overseers, so that very soon the ancient city kingdom began to develop into a bureaucracy." The aggressive wars of Assyria and Babylonia were fought primarily with one aim in view: "to conquer subjects who would dig a new canal for a new city."[57]

In economic terms Weber likens the Mesopotamian monarchy to an *oikos*, a huge household. The royal *oikos* derived its revenue from bondsmen and serfs on the one hand and from royal subjects who rendered labor services and paid taxes in kind. Weber writes:

> Like the pharaohs, the kings of Sumer and Akkad regulated the labor services of their subjects, provided them with food and drink, and then saw to it that they received payment in kind. There were all sorts of royal warehouses—for wagons, grain, spice, treasure—and all sorts of royal workshops. . . . Above all, everything needed for official building projects was produced in the royal *oikos*.[58]

Sumerian kings also engaged in commerce and monopolized trade at the river mouths.

> Ancient Egyptian institutions were likewise shaped by the necessity, arising from geography and climate, to develop a somewhat sophisticated bureaucratic administration and to mobilize the population for large-scale work on the irrigation system. . . . [T]he individual was above all a servant of the state. Thus when the pharaohs boast that they have established order and have visited every city of their realms, it is clear from the context that they are thinking of the irrigation system and its demands.[59]

The ancient Egyptian economy, also an enormous royal *oikos*, mainly occupied itself with the construction of systems for distributing, channeling, draining, and raising the waters of the Nile. The entire society was therefore shaped by the basic requirement of regulating the great river, to ensure the provision of society's economic needs.

The resulting political-administrative structure was a highly centralized bureaucratic state, or what Weber calls a "liturgy-state." In such states, writes Weber,

> every individual is bound to the function assigned him within the social system, and therefore every individual is in principle unfree.[60]

Every individual was an instrument of pharaonic power; the individual and his possessions were no more than entries in the royal cadaster. The typical peasant of the time is depicted in inscriptions as paying little rent for his land, and always ready to evade taxes:

> . . . the officials arrived unexpectedly, the women began to cry, and soon a general flight and hunt began; those liable for taxes were hunted down, beaten, and tortured into paying what was demanded by the officials, who were themselves held responsible for quotas based on the official cadaster. This was the guise in which the state appeared to the peasants of the Near East. . . . The profound feeling of alienation from politics found among Near Eastern peoples had its origin in this repressive relationship.[61]

Thus Weber described the earliest forms of "Oriental despotism," based on forced labor and liturgies exacted from the population by a highly repressive, centralized bureaucracy. In the Near East, as elsewhere, the monarchy originally evolved with the expanding wealth and power of the military chieftain and his retinue. That the Egyptian monarch fed, equipped and led the army and became the absolute landlord and all powerful ruler, was causally bound up with the administrative requirements of river regulation and irrigation. The pharaoh's "retinue" was the entire army and bureaucracy. Little wonder that he was divinized.

In the East, then, political power belonged to no one but the Prince; for he, the ruler, had successfully "separated" the administrative officials from control over the key resources with which they worked. This Weber contrasted with a system in which the Prince granted land to the members of his retinue who paid their own costs and thus enjoyed considerable autonomy. "According to the dominance of one or the other of the systems," Weber observed,

> the political and social constitution of the state would be entirely different. *Economic considerations largely determine which form would win out.* The East and the West show in this respect the usual contrast. For oriental economy—China, Asia Minor, Egypt—irrigation husbandry became dominant, while in the West where settlements resulted from the clearing of land, forestry sets the type.[62]

To understand the fundamental structural differences between East and West, one must pay close attention to economic processes and how they conditioned other developments. For Weber, the differences between East and West extended to all the major institutions of the respective civilizations. The Asian "city," for instance, differed markedly from the Occidental one, for "Everywhere outside the West," writes Weber,

> the development of the city was prevented by the fact that the army of the Prince is older than the city.

And in an apparent dialogue with the Marxists, Weber observes,

> Whether the military organization is based on the principle of self-equipment or on that of equipment by a military overlord who furnishes horses, arms and provisions, is a distinction quite as fundamental for social history as is the question whether the means of economic production are the property of the worker or of a capitalistic entrepreneur. . . . In the west the army equipped by the war lord, and the separation of soldier from the paraphernalia of war, in a way analogous to the separation of the worker from the means of production, is a product of the modern era, while in Asia it stands at the beginning of historical development.[63]

The distinctiveness of the East rests on the fact that in Egypt, Western Asia, China, and India ". . . irrigation was crucial." The "water question," Weber continues,

> conditioned the existence of the bureaucracy, the compulsory service of the dependent classes, and the dependence of the subject classes upon the functioning of the bureaucracy of the king. That the king also expressed his power in the form of a military monopoly is the basis of the distinction between the military organization of Asia and that of the West.[64]

Thus Weber fully agrees that the requirements of water regulation and complex irrigation projects are crucial for an understanding of Asian social structure; just as he acknowledges that Marx was right in tracing the "stationary" character of Indian society to the peculiar position of the artisan in the Indian village. It is therefore undeniable that Weber's analyses of the East largely coincide with Marx's conception of the Asiatic mode of production.

What we find in Weber's analyses of Asian society is neither a belittling of economic conditions nor an attempt to refute Marx. On the contrary, what we find is a recognition of the centrality of economic conditions. Weber is nonetheless engaged in "rounding out" Marx's analysis by giving systematic attention to other salient conditions, notably the political, military, and religious. In Marx's and Engels's quite brief discussions of the Asiatic mode, they had little to say about Asian religions. But Weber wishes to show that in both China and India certain religious norms prevailed that positively precluded the spontaneous emergence of a western type of capitalism. In this case as in *all* others, Weber is certainly not arguing some sort of idealistic determination of history.

ASIAN RELIGIONS

The Religion of China

Here, as in his studies of India and ancient Israel, Weber is concerned with the question of why rational capitalism, as he defined it, emerged as an indigenous development only in the West. As he progressed in those studies, Weber came to view capitalism as an aspect of a much more comprehensive and general process, and he discovered fundamental differences between the civilizations of the East and the West.

Students of economic development in the West had stressed two factors that, among others, had contributed greatly to the rise of capitalism: the great influx of precious metals and a significant growth in population. Weber observes, however, that in the case of China, similar developments were evident. The great increase in the stock of precious metals led to a greater development of the money economy, particularly in state finance. Yet, that did not shatter traditionalism; if anything, it strengthened it. Likewise, the enormous growth in population "was neither stimulated by, nor did it stimulate, capitalist development. Rather, it was . . . associated with a stationary economy."[65]

In the West, Weber proffers, the cities of antiquity, the papal curia, the towns, and the emerging states of the Middle Ages "were vehicles of financial rationalization, of money economy, and of political capitalism" (p. 13). In China, in contrast, there were no cities like Florence, and the state failed to establish a money economy. The Chinese "city" was fundamentally different from the Occidental one; it did not become a center in which capitalist relations and institutions could germinate, for it lacked political autonomy. Unlike the *polis* of antiquity and the commune of the Middle Ages, it had neither political privileges nor military power of its own, no "self-equipped military estate such as existed in Occidental antiquity" (p. 13). The Occidental city became sufficiently strong to repel an army of knights and was not dependent for its survival on any centralized bureaucracy. Political associations of merchant and craft guilds were nonexistent in the Chinese "city," and legal contracts, either economic or political, could not be made. In short, there did not emerge in China an independent bourgeois class centered in autonomous towns—which, in the West, was the fruit of prolonged struggles and revolts. Revolts were indeed common in the Chinese city, but they were organized to remove specific officials or to change specific practices, not to guarantee the freedom of the city. One of the reasons was that the Chinese city dweller never became a citizen in the Western sense, for he "retained his relations to the native place of his sib, its ancestral land and temple. Hence, all ritually and personally important relations with the native village were maintained" (p. 14).

The differences between the Occidental and Oriental cities can be traced to their different origins. The *polis* of antiquity was an overseas trading city, whereas in China, trade was predominantly inland. In order to preserve tradition, foreign trade and contact were limited to a single port, Canton. Furthermore, industrial development was not centered in the city where it could, as in the West, escape the control of traditional groups and interests. Thus the economic, political, and formal-legal foundations of an autonomous and rational organization of industry and commerce were absent.

Control of the rivers, in China as in Egypt and other ancient civilizations, led to some rationalization of the economy, but was greatly limited due to religious and other conditions:

> [The] laws of nature and of rites were fused into the unity of *Tao*. Not a supramundane lord creator, but a supra-divine, impersonal, forever identical, and external existence was felt to be ultimate and supreme. This was to sanction the validity of eternal order and its timeless existence. The impersonal power of Heaven did not "speak" to man. It revealed itself in the regimen on earth, in the firm order of nature and tradition which were part of the cosmic order, and, as elsewhere, it revealed itself in what occurred to man. The welfare of the subjects documented heavenly contentment and the correct functioning of the order. All bad events were symptomatic of disturbance in the providential harmony of heaven and earth through magical forces. (p. 28)

River regulation, the basis of imperial authority, was assured not by empirical-rational means alone but by the conduct of the emperor who had to abide by the imperatives of the classical scriptures. If, for example, the dikes broke, this was evidence that the emperor did not have the qualities of charisma demanded by heaven and therefore had to do public penitence for his sins.

As in all large far-flung states with undeveloped systems of communication, administrative centralization remained relatively inefficient; nevertheless, that did not facilitate the growth of multiple centers of power. The central government employed various means to prevent officials from becoming independently powerful in their areas of assignment. The official was never assigned to his home province and had to shift every three years, either to another province or to another office. Not knowing the provincial dialect, he was dependent on interpreters, and not being familiar with the local laws and traditions, he became wholly dependent on assistants from the province, whom he paid from his own pocket.

> . . . this resulted in actual power being vested in the hands of the unofficial, native subordinates. And the higher the rank of the authorized official the less was he able to correct and control their management. Thus the local and central government officials were not sufficiently informed about local conditions to facilitate consistent and rational intervention. (p. 50)

Yet, that did not lead to a Western-type feudalism either, for appointment to office was based on educational qualifications rather than criteria of birth and rank.

The dependence of the central government on its officials, and of the officials, in turn, on provincial assistants, enhanced traditionalism; even the "money economy" contributed to the strengthening of traditional structures. The officials became in effect "tax farmers," who extracted what they could from their provincial subjects, gave as little as they dared to their superiors, and kept the rest. They were prebendaries who had a paramount interest in maintaining the existing socioeconomic conditions and hence the profits from their prebends. Thus, as the money economy expanded so did prebendalization, a great obstacle to attempts at internal change. To become prebendaries they were dependent on the central government; once they became officials and received their assignments, however, they acquired only a very limited power, for they remained dependent on the indigenous elements of the provinces in which they were strangers. That is in sharp contrast with the West where

> there were strong and independent forces. With these, princely power could ally itself in order to shatter traditional fetters; or, under very special conditions, these forces could use their own military power to throw off the bonds of patrimonial power. This was the case in the five great revolutions which decided the destiny of the Occident: the Italian revolution of the twelfth and thirteenth centuries, the Netherland revolution of the sixteenth century, the English revolution of the seventeenth century, and the American and French revolutions of the eighteenth century. We may ask: Were there no comparable forces in China? (p. 62)

The Chinese were no less acquisitive than the Europeans, and their capacity for work and industry was unsurpassed; there were even powerful and autonomous merchant guilds, though not concentrated in the towns; there was a tremendous growth in population since the eighteenth century, and, finally, there was a constant increase in precious metals. Yet, no capitalism. How does Weber explain that fact?

Though "private property" emerged, it never became truly private as in the West: The sib in China was so powerful that true alienation of land from it was impossible. Land was not unconditionally or permanently sold; rather, the sib always retained the right to repurchase. There were money lenders and various forms of commerce, but they did not lead to modern rational, capitalistic enterprise. "There was no rational depersonalization of business," Weber writes, "comparable to its unmistakable beginnings in the commercial law of Italian cities" (p. 85). In China, the growth of wealth in the form of money led to different results. When officials retired, for instance, they invested their money in landholdings which enabled some of their sons to study so as to pass the state examinations and thus become eligible for "tax-farming" careers of their own. In that way the whole familial community had a vested interest in the examination system and other traditional institutions. The community was held together by powerful and rigid kinship bonds.

The power of the sib rested to a large degree on the ancestor cult; ancestral spirits acted as mediators between their descendants and the deities. The "city," then, never became a "hometown" but remained "typically `a place away from home' for the majority of its inhabitants" (p. 90). Cities were mere urban settlements of farmers and "there remained only a technical administrative difference between city and village. A `city' was the seat of the mandarin and was not self-governing; a `village' was a self-governing settlement without a mandarin" (p. 91). The sib and other traditional elements were in the long run stronger than the rational bureaucracy. Illiterate old age, for example, carried a higher status and authority than the most learned mandarin, and Chinese justice, far from becoming formal, legal, and rational, remained patriarchal.

There were still other developments that contributed to the formation of capitalism in the West but were patently missing in China. After pacification of the empire, there was neither rational warfare nor even an "armed peace during which several competing autonomous states constantly prepared for war. Capitalist phenomena thus conditioned through war loans and commissions for war purposes did not appear" (p. 103). An additional handicap to capitalist development was the empire's lack of overseas colonies.

Administrative development in China also took a different form from that of the West. That is best seen in the bureaucracy composed of *literati*. To be sure, they had to qualify for office by passing examinations, which in turn required a certain education, but their education was based entirely upon the classical literature. They were therefore quite far from being bureaucrats in the Western sense, for their ideal, above all, was to be cultivated Confucian gentlemen.

> The Chinese examinations [writes Weber] did not test any special skills, as do our modern national and bureaucratic examination regulations for jurists, medical doctors, or technicians. . . . The examinations of China tested whether or not the candidate's mind was thoroughly steeped in literature and whether or not he possessed the *ways of thought* suitable to a cultured man and resulting from cultivation in literature. (p. 121)

Rational administration depended on subordinates who were skilled in the required technical and administrative tasks, for the *literati* themselves rejected the one-sided thoroughness and specialization characteristic of Western civilization from Plato to its restatement in the "calling" of ascetic Protestantism. Yet, although the *literati* viewed the examinations as tests of their cultivation and general humanistic knowledge, the popular view was different:

> In the eyes of the Chinese masses, a successfully examined candidate and official was by no means a mere applicant for office qualified by knowledge. He was a proved holder of magical qualities, which, as we shall see, were attached

> to the certified mandarin just as much as to an examined and ordained priest of an ecclesiastic institution of grace, or to a magician tried and proved by his guild. (p. 128)

Orthodox Confucianism had renounced the beyond and in so doing had ignored the religious needs of the masses. Magic and animism, always strong among the peasants,

> had come under the patronage of a priesthood which was tolerated because it claimed to have originated with a philosophical personage, Laotzu, and his doctrine. Originally the meaning of this doctrine did not differ in the main from that of Confucianism. Later it became antagonistic to Confucianism and was finally considered thoroughly heterodox. (p. 177)

There were repeated power struggles between the *literati* and the priests, in which the former were always victorious. Yet, ironically, the *literati* constantly availed themselves of the Taoist's priestly and magical services, affording Taoist heterodoxy a recognized place in religious practice. The "victorious Confucians . . . never seriously aimed at uprooting magic in general and Taoist magic in particular. They only sought to monopolize office prebends" (p. 194).

Not only were magic and animism tolerated, but they were also systematized so as to become highly significant forces in Chinese life. All sciences that had empirical and naturalistic beginnings were organized as magical and supernatural practices and rituals. The Chinese world, despite its secular, rational-empirical elements, remained enchanted—a magic garden. The *literati* were to a notable degree secular or "this worldly," but not consistently so. They not only tolerated magic as a means of taming the masses—they themselves believed in it. Under those circumstances it is understandable why they never waged war against magic, never strove to divest Chinese culture of magical beliefs and practices.

"Demagification" of religion, Weber believed, was carried out in the West most consistently and thoroughly by ascetic Protestantism, but the process had begun with the ancient Jewish prophets. That does not mean, Weber emphasizes, that the Puritans did not retain superstitious beliefs; that they did is obvious from their witch trials. Rather, it means that they came to regard "all magic as devilish." For Weber, then, one criterion of the rationalization of religion is the degree to which it has rid itself of magic. But there is still another criterion: "the degree to which it has systematically unified the relation between God and the world and therewith its own ethical relationship to the world" (p. 226). Whereas Puritanism resulted in a "tremendous and grandiose tension with the `world,'" Confucianism regarded this as the best of all possible worlds. Above all, the Confucian was to adjust to the world; his conduct had implications for cosmic harmony so he exercised rational self-control and repressed all irrational passions that might disturb his poise. But such conduct did not weaken the powers of magic; quite the contrary, it took the use of magic for granted, for though the educated Confucian adhered, or submitted, to magical practice with some skepticism, the masses were altogether steeped in it. And the *literati* (unlike the Old Testament prophets), far from having demanded that the masses abandon such practices, even connived in them—for material as well as spiritual reasons. "Tension toward the `world' had never arisen because, as far as is known, there had never been an ethical prophecy of a supramundane God who raised ethical demands" (p. 230). A true prophesy that raised such demands and which viewed the world as matter to be shaped according to ethical norms was unknown in Chinese history.

As we see, then, Weber counterbalances the conditions apparently favorable to the development of capitalism by other unfavorable conditions. As he repeatedly stresses, his treatment of an enormously complicated problem with innumerable conditions could hardly yield a simple answer. Yet his analysis strongly suggested that it was the prevailing religious mentality in China that constituted a major obstacle to the emergence of a rational capitalism of the European type. Now as earlier, however, Weber acknowledges that the religious mentality was codetermined by economic and political conditions.

The Religion of India

In India, too, Weber saw many social and cultural conditions which, it would seem, should have given rise to modern rational capitalism. Warfare, finance, and politics, for instance, had been rationalized, and the last of these even in quite "Machiavellian" terms. Many of the older type capitalist forms had at one time or another been in evidence: state creditors and contractors, tax farmers, and so on. Urban development also seemed to parallel that of the West at many points. In addition, what Weber called rationality was prominent in many aspects of Indian cultural life: the rational number system, arithmetic, algebra, rational science, and in general a rational consistency in many spheres, together with a high degree of tolerance toward philosophical and religious doctrines. The prevailing judicial forms appeared compatible with capitalist development; there existed an autonomous stratum of merchants; handicrafts as well as occupational specialization were developed, and, finally, a high degree of acquisitiveness and a high evaluation of wealth were notable aspects of Indian social life. "Yet," Weber writes,

> . . . modern capitalism did not develop indigenously before or during the English rule. It was taken over as a finished artifact without autonomous beginnings. Here we shall inquire as to the manner in which Indian religion, as one factor among many, may have prevented capitalistic development (in the Occidental sense).[66]

Here, again, we see Weber's distinctive methodological approach. He regards Indian religion as "one factor among many" which, "may have prevented capitalistic development. . . ." Because there was no way of quantifying or weighting the elements, all one could do was to make as strong and as cogent a case as possible. If Indian religion had taken another form—for example, equivalent to that of ascetic Protestantism—then, perhaps, a modern, rational type of capitalism might have developed there too. Because economic, urban, scientific, and other developments were somewhat equivalent in India and the West, and modern capitalism emerged autonomously only in the latter civilization, the different religious ethos that took shape there must have made a significant causal contribution to the origin of the modern economic system. Ultimately, however, Weber sees more operative there than just the Protestant ethic; what he sees as really crucial is that despite the rational, scientific elements in the East, and the existence there of economic strata and forms seemingly conducive to the emergence of a modern rational economy, the East remained an "enchanted garden." That meant that all aspects and institutions of Oriental civilization were permeated and even dominated by the magical mentality—which became a brake on economic developments in particular and on rationalization of the culture as a whole. In contrast, Occidental civilization, already in its early stages of development, had undergone significant *disenchantment*, which has increased almost as a unilinear development right to the present. Disenchantment or rationalization began with the scriptural prophets; but Christianity, Greek formal logic, Roman law, the medieval papal curia, cities and states, the Renaissance, the Reformation, the Enlightenment, and the various bourgeois revolutions all contributed to the process that has made Western civilization as a whole fundamentally different from that of the East.

Actually, Weber's studies of the world religions embrace much more than religious phenomena and institutions. In effect, he takes the entire social structure of the society in question into his purview. In the case of India, the caste system was clearly of fundamental importance. The origin of the four main castes or categories—Brahmans, Kshatriyas, Vaishyas, and Shudras—is shrouded in mystery; more, however, is known about the proliferation of groupings, so that literally thousands of subcastes crystallized in the course of Indian history. Basing himself on the best Indological sources, Weber sketches the process by which new castes form and others undergo schisms.

With the increasing wealth of some strata, numerous tasks were defined by them as "lower" and unclean so that eventually the native, resident population refused to engage in them. That made room for alien workers, whatever their origin, who moved into those occupations and became a "guest" people tolerated for the economic function they fulfilled. At first, they were not properly a part of the host village organization; they retained their own community organizations and had full jurisdiction over them. When, in addition, certain ritual barriers were raised against the guest peoples, Weber calls them a *pariah people*. (One example of this in the West was the Jews during the Middle Ages—except that in their case, as Weber shows, it was precisely the

Jews who brought with them certain ritual practices that they voluntarily maintained against the host people.) Eventually, through a variety of forms of transition, a *pariah people*, having established itself in some of the formerly native Hindu occupations, develops an interest in maintaining its hold over those occupations and demands and receives certain Brahmanical services. The members of the pariah group, underprivileged anyway, come to prefer a legitimate status to that of an alien people since "caste organizations, like quasi-trade unions, facilitate the legitimate defense of both internal and external interests of the lower castes" (p. 17). The hope and promise which Hinduism held out to these negatively privileged strata helps to explain "their relatively minor resistance in view of what one would expect of the abysmal distance Hinduism establishes between social strata" (p. 17).

The caste system, to be sure, had essentially negative consequences for economic development, but not, as one might at first expect, primarily because it imposed restrictions and prohibitions on social interaction. Rather, it was because the caste system became totally traditionalistic and antirational in its effects. It is here that Weber takes time to acknowledge an insight which reveals that in these studies, as in others, he took leads from Marx. "Karl Marx," writes Weber:

> . . . has characterized the peculiar position of the artisan in the Indian village—his dependence upon fixed payment in kind instead of upon production for the market—as the reason for the specific "stability" of the Asiatic peoples. In this, Marx was correct. (p. 111)

Weber adds, however, that "not only the position of the village artisan but also the caste order as a whole must be viewed as the bearer of stability" (p. 112). That order was quite flexible in the face of the requirements of the concentration of labor in large-scale enterprises; caste proscriptions on interaction with the ritually impure were not the main impediment to industrial development. All the great religions, he suggests, have placed such restrictions on modern economy. It was the traditional, antirational "spirit" of the whole social system which constituted the main obstruction; that, along with the "artisan's traditionalism, great in itself, was necessarily heightened to the extreme by the caste order" (p. 112).

The antirational spirit became manifest in the prevalence of magic and in the role of the Brahmans, whose very power was connected "with the increasing significance of magic in all spheres of life." This together with other religious developments had significantly modified the character of Indian economic strata. If, for example, there was an Indian "bourgeoisie," it was very weak for at least two reasons:

> . . . first, was the absolute pacifism of the salvation religions, Jainism and Buddhism, which were propagated, roughly, at the same time as the development of the cities. . . . Second, there was the undeveloped but established caste system. Both these factors blocked the development of the military power of the

> citizenry; pacifism blocked it in principle and the castes in practice, by hindering the establishment of a *polis* or *commune* in the European sense. (pp. 88–89)

The merchants as well as the guilds had no independent military organizations and therefore could be repressed whenever a prince found it expedient to do so. The Indian town enjoyed no true self-government or autonomy.

Also, apart from the implications that the sacred cow had for Indian animal husbandry, magico-religious practices retarded technical-industrial development. Often, "tools were worshipped as quasi-fetishes" and along with "other traditional traits, this stereotyping of tools was one of the strongest handicaps to all technical development" (p. 99).

Indian religions, including Buddhism, had attained a highly technical virtuosity that resulted in an extreme devaluation of the world; none of them enjoined the adherent to prove himself or his grace through action or work. Quite the contrary, the highest good was a contemplative flight from the world. Indian asceticism never translated itself into a methodical, rational way of life that tended in its effects to undermine traditionalism and to change the world.

Thus, India, like China, remained an "enchanted garden" with all sorts of fetishism, animistic and magical beliefs and practices—spirits in rivers, ponds, and mountains, highly developed word formulas, finger-pointing magic, and the like. In contrast to the Hebrew prophets, who never made peace with the magicians, the Brahmans (a distinguished, cultivated and genteel stratum like the Mandarins), in the interests of their power position, not only recognized the influence of magic but rationalized it and made numerous concessions to the unclassical magicians (p. 295)—despite the fact that ideally, according to the Classic Vedas, magic was to be suppressed, or at least merely tolerated among the masses.

The general character of Asiatic religion, Weber concluded (on the basis of his studies of China, India, Korea, Ceylon, and so on), was a particular form of gnosis—that is, positive knowledge in the spiritual realm, mystically acquired. Gnosis was the single path to the "highest holiness" and the "highest practice." Such "knowledge," far from becoming a "rational and empirical means by which man sought with increasing success to dominate nature," became instead "the means of mystical and magical domination over the self and the world . . . by an intensive training of body and spirit, either through asceticism or, and as a rule, through strict, methodologically ruled meditation" (p. 133). This gave rise to a redemption aristocracy, for such mystical knowledge was necessarily esoteric and charismatic, hence not accessible or communicable to everyone. The holy and godlike was attained by an "emptying" of experiences of this world. Psychic peace, not restlessness, was godlike; the latter, being specifically creaturelike, was illusory, transitory, and valueless.

Hence, in contrast to the soul-saving doctrines of Christianity, no emphasis was placed on "this life"; Asiatic religion led to an otherworldliness. "In Asia generally," writes Weber, "the power of a charismatic stratum grew." In sharp contrast to the Hebrew prophets, however, that stratum

> . . . succeeded in breaking the dominion of magic only occasionally and only with very temporary success.
>
> Not the "miracle" but the "magical spell" remained, therefore, the core substance of mass religiosity. This was true above all for peasants and laborers, but also for the middle class. (p. 335)

That this magical, antirational world had a profound impact on economic conduct and development could not be doubted. Magic was employed

> . . . for achieving all conceivable sorts of inner-earthly values—spells against enemies, erotic or economic competition, spells designed to win legal cases, spiritual spells of the believer for forced fulfillment against the debtor, spells for the securing of wealth, for the success of undertakings. (p. 336)

The depth and tenacity of the magical mentality created conditions in which the "lust for gain" never gave rise to the modern economic system Weber called rational capitalism. What was notably absent from Asiatic religion therefore was the development that in the Occident ultimately broke the hold of magic over the minds of men and gave rise to a "rational, innerworldly ethic." That historical process began

> . . . with the appearance of thinkers and prophets who developed a social structure on the basis of political problems which were foreign to Asiatic culture; these were the political problems of civic status groups of the city without which neither Judaism nor Christianity nor the development of Hellenic thought is conceivable. (p. 338)

The ancient Jewish prophets then were fundamental, since it was to them and to the early Greek thinkers that the roots of the *Rationalisierungsprozess* (that is, the "rationalization process") in the West could be traced.

Ancient Judaism

For Weber, the development of Judaism was important for the profound impact it had on the beginnings of Western civilization. According to the Jewish religious conception, God created the world and intervened in history; the world in its present form was a result of God's response to the actions of humanity and particularly the Jews. The present condition of toil, trouble, misery, and suffering, the opposite of that promised for the future, was temporary and would "give way again to the truly God-ordained order. The whole attitude toward life of ancient Jewry was determined by this conception of a future God-guided political and social revolution."[67] For the attainment of the future order, everything depended on the worldly actions of the Jews and their faithful devotion to the Commandments of God (Yahweh). In addition to ritual correctitude, there was

> . . . a highly rational religious ethic of social conduct; it was free of magic and all forms of irrational quest for salvation; it was inwardly worlds apart from the paths of salvation offered by Asiatic religions. To a large extent this ethic still underlies contemporary Mideastern and European ethic. World-historical interest in Jewry rests upon this fact. (p. 9)

The historical importance of Judaism, apart from its being the source of Christianity and Islam, lies in its rational-ethical character, and for this reason:

> Only the following phenomena can equal those of Jewry in historical significance: the development of Hellenic intellectual culture; for western Europe, the development of Roman law and of the Roman Catholic church resting on the Roman concept of office; the medieval order of estates; and finally, in the field of religion, Protestantism. (p. 5)

In this remarkably painstaking study, Weber defined the historical status of the Jews as that of a "pariah people"—a term that has been subject to considerable misunderstanding. The term refers primarily to the social segregation of the Jews that resulted to a large degree from the ritualistic requirements of their religion. Weber understands the segregation of the Jews in that sense as self-imposed and long antedating their forced ghettoization in medieval Europe for economic and other reasons. Weber is intent upon showing that general social and historical conditions, though important, were not sufficient to explain how Jewry developed into a people "with highly specific peculiarities," because Jewry's distinctiveness never would have come about in the absence of the specific Jewish ritual and religious commandments. Here again, Weber is exploring the influence of religious ideas on social existence and development—but always against the background of social, economic, and political structures which he examines fastidiously.

Weber shows, for instance, how the older stratification system in ancient Israel changed and how in its place there soon emerged a wealthy urban patriciate on the one hand and a number of impoverished and indebted strata on the other. Ancient Israel, situated as it was in the midst of the great and powerful states and along major trade routes, became a center of trade with many cities. Evidence of class conflict between "indebted peasants and urban creditors existed from the beginning of recorded history" (p. 61).

Conflict between the rich and the poor was exacerbated with the emergence of the monarchy, particularly under Solomon; Weber calls attention to the ambivalence with which Jewish tradition has regarded the third king of Israel. It was against the background of the basic transformation of Israelite society that the prophets of social justice emerged. Now, increasingly, the kings, whose oppressive consequences Samuel had prophesied, were making of Israel a *corveé* state, a "house of bondage" like the Egyptian state the Jews despised as an abomination. The prophets spoke out against this trend and voiced sharp criticism of the monarchs, their private sins as well as their public practices. The prophets, though not out of political motives per se, thus expressed the sentiments of the peasants and other oppressed groups who remembered that they had fought for freedom against the privileged strata, and that God had brought their forefathers out of the land of Egypt. Now the people saw themselves increasingly subject to debt bondage, taxes, and *corvée* duties.

It would be wrong to suppose, Weber emphasizes, that when the prophets rebuke the monarchs or speak out against the rich, they are direct ideological spokesmen of the oppressed. There is no doubt that the political content of their messages was drawn from the actual events of the day and from reflecting on the condition of the oppressed. But the real inspiration and meaning of their message, Weber insists, were purely religious. Yahweh and his Commandments were being foresaken and his Covenant violated. It was that primarily, if not exclusively, that motivated the prophets to say what they did and to foretell doom. They increasingly deprecated the patricians and their riches, and the kings and their chariots, and "hallowed the time when Yahweh himself as war leader led the peasant army, when the ass-riding prince did not rely on horses and chariots and alliances, but solely on the God of the Covenant and his help." (p. 111)

Here, we may pause to note how Weber conceives the relationship between religious ideas and socioeconomic conditions. The prophets were a relatively autonomous stratum in Israelite society; they were religious practitioners with strictly religious interests. However, their political orientation, which became evident in a specific period, was clearly related to changes in social stratification and to the institutionalization of the monarchy. "It is no accident," Weber writes,

> . . . that the first appearance of the independent, politically oriented seers, who were succeeded by these prophets, coincided almost exactly with that great transformation which kingship under David and Solomon brought about in the political and social structure of Israel. (p. 110)

Although the prophets were religious thinkers, and comprised a relatively autonomous stratum, their message, and the various forms it assumed, could not be explained in strictly immanent terms. There was a definite relationship between the prophetic movement and other aspects of the social structure, and the fact that prophecy acquired a political character in a given historical period can be understood only by viewing it in relation to the general social changes that had come about. The relative independence of the prophets was facilitated by the fact that in Israel the king was not a priestly dignitary at the apex of a hierocratic order and that the prophets received support and protection from wealthy and powerful Yahwistic families whom the monarchy could not suppress. However, if, in Weber's view, "rationalization" was a consequence of the prophets' unceasing war against magical and orgiastic practices, that was not out of any rational, secular, or political considerations on their part; rather, it had to be explained on the basis of their unswerving devotion to Yahweh.

This devotion was based on the unique relation of Israel to its God, expressed and guaranteed in a unique historical event—the conclusion of a covenant with Yahweh. The prophets and the antiroyalist Yahwistic nobles always hearkened back to that great and miraculous event in which God kept his promise, intervened in history, and liberated the Jews from Egyptian bondage. That was proof not only of God's power but of the absolute dependability of his promises. Israel, then, as the other party to the Covenant mediated by Moses, owed a lasting debt of gratitude to serve and worship Yahweh and to have no other gods before him. This rational relationship, unknown elsewhere, created an ethical obligation so binding that Jewish tradition regarded "defection" from Yahweh as an especially fatal abomination (p. 119). Moreover, the markedly rational nature of the relationship lay in the worldly character of God's promises to Israel; not some supernatural paradise or utopia was promised, but

> . . . that they would have numerous descendants, so that the people should become numerous as the sand of the seashore, and that they should triumph over all enemies, enjoy rain, rich harvests, and secure possessions. (p. 119)

To Moses was held out the hope of leading his people out of Egypt and into the Promised Land—here on Earth and, in fact, just across the border, despite the circuitous route required to reach it. "The god," writes Weber, ". . . offered salvation from Egyptian bondage, not from a senseless world out of joint. He promised not transcendent values but dominion over Canaan which one was out to conquer and a good life" (p. 126).

Of course, the conception of Yahweh, as well as the degree of devotion to him, varied through time and with the different social strata. The richness of Weber's analysis cannot be conveyed here. The main point is that the eminently rational character of Judaism could be explained by the convergence of a number of circumstances: (1) The Jews loathed everything that emanated from Egypt, including the cult of the dead; (2) Bedouin practices were also rejected, for Amalek was a traditional enemy of Israel; (3) as for Baal, once the Jews became a settled agricultural people in Canaan, the attributes of Baal and other functional deities were soon syncretized with those of Yahweh, so that he was no longer merely the "war god of the confederacy" but could bring rain and assure a good harvest. In addition, however, and perhaps most important, was Israel's peculiar relationship to God and his Covenant. When, in Weber's words,

> . . . [Yahweh] was angry and failed to help the nation or the individual, a violation of the *berith* with him had to be responsible for this. Hence, it was necessary for the authorities as well as for the individual from the outset to ask which commandment had been violated? Irrational divination means could not answer this question, only knowledge of the very commandments and soul searching. Thus, the idea of *berith* flourishing in the truly Yahwistic circles pushed all scrutiny of the divine will toward an at least relatively rational mode of raising and answering the question. Hence, the priestly exhortation under the influence of the intellectual strata turned with great sharpness against soothsayers, augurs, day-choosers, interpreters of signs, conjurors of the dead, defining their ways of consulting the deities as characteristically pagan. (p. 167)

In ancient Israel, the relation of priests to prophets was quite fluid so that the Levites, for example, gained their prestige less by their special skills in offering sacrifices than by their rational knowledge of Yahweh's Commandments. Oracular and magical means were systematically reduced to a minimum, and "became less and less important as against the rational case study of sins, until the theological rationalism of Deuteronomy (18:9–15) in substance discredited lot casting altogether or at least ceased to mention it" (p. 179). All forms of sexual and alcoholic orgiasticism were consistently opposed until they became anathema to the various advocates and defenders of Yahwism—the Levitical Torah teachers, the prophets, and the wealthy and politically influential, pious Yahwistic families. Thus, although magic was never eliminated from popular practice, it was dislodged from its position of dominance in ancient Judaism—a fact that contrasts with all other ancient religions.

In Weber's view, classical prophecy acquired its most characteristic form when the great powers of the area, Egypt and Mesopotamia, resumed their expansionist policy. The classical scriptural prophets—for example, Amos, Isaiah, Jeremiah, Ezekiel—despite their purely religious motives, were in effect political demagogues and even pamphleteers. It would be wrong, however, to view prophecy, exclusively or even primarily, as a response to internal developments and conflicts—as the expression of the interests and sentiments of the "people" who were now oppressed by the overlords and the monarchy. Prophecy in its classical form, Weber insists, never would have arisen in the absence of the great-power conflict that constituted a threat to the existence of Israel. When the monarchy was strong or protected by a great power, the prophets "remained silent—or rather [were] reduced to silence. With the decreasing prestige of the kings and the growing threat to the country, the significance of prophecy again increased and the scene of the prophet's activities moved closer and closer to Jerusalem" (p. 269).

They spoke in the streets and addressed their publics directly; their inspiration was spontaneous and their major concern was "the destiny of the state and the people. This concern always assumed the form of emotional invectives against the overlords" (p. 269). When they prophesied doom and a catastrophe actually befell the country, they showed no sign of personal jubilation; instead they mourned but also expressed hope for better times now that God's wrath had passed. Objectively, they were involved in conflicting political interests and party antagonisms, but they had no personal political interests or motives. They were mere mouthpieces through which Yahweh spoke. In Weber's words,

> . . . according to their manner of functioning, the prophets were objectively political and, above all, world-political demagogues and publicists, however, subjectively they were no political partisans. Primarily they pursued no political interests. Prophecy has never declared anything about a "best state" (disregarding Ezekiel's hierocratic construction in the Exile) nor has it ever sought, like the philosophical *aisymnete* or the academy, to help translate into reality social-ethically oriented political ideals through advice to power holders. The state and its doings were, by themselves, of no interest to them. Moreover, unlike the Hellenes they did not posit the problem: how can man be a good citizen? Their question was absolutely religious, oriented toward the fulfillment of Yahweh's commandments. (p. 275)

Thus Weber demonstrates the enormous complexity of prophecy in Israel and implicitly argues that no simple formula is sufficient for an understanding of the phenomenon. Their pronouncements on internal affairs must not be understood as direct ideological manifestations of class relationships and conflicts. The prophets did not stem from the oppressed and disadvantaged strata; most of them were wealthy and came from distinguished families. Even Amos, who was described as a poor stockbreeder, was an educated man; like Isaiah (who was wealthy and distinguished), he cursed the rich and the great but "yet pronounced the rule of the uneducated, undisciplined demos as the worst of all curses" (p. 277). They were therefore neither defenders of democratic ideals nor spokesmen for the "people," and their main support came not from the oppressed but from individual, pious, and distinguished families in Jerusalem. That their motives were purely religious becomes clear, in addition, from their condemnation at one and the same time of both debt slavery and the fertility cults and shrines of Baal "which meant much to the rural population for economic as well as ideal reasons" (p. 279).

The prophets and the Torah teachers were of major importance in the rationalization of Judaism. However, the documentation of the radical "disenchantment" of Judaism was only one of the tasks Weber set himself in this extraordinary study. Another important problem was how the Jews came to constitute a pariah community. That, Weber shows, must be viewed as the result of both prophecy and the special ritual requirements of Judaism that the Jews took with them into exile and held to stubbornly and tenaciously.

With the destruction of the Temple and the exile of the Jews, sacrifice, permissible only in Jerusalem, became impossible. Hence, it became all the more essential to preserve the tradition in other ways. Jews were to remain ritually pure and guard themselves against any and all pagan practices and worship. That was particularly important since the *Diaspora* was regarded as a temporary situation and the hope of returning to the homeland remained alive. Slowly, there emerged a distinctive religious community organization with new institutions peculiar to the Exile.[68]

Weber thus traced the "rationalization process" in the West to its roots in ancient Judaism. In his late writings on China, India, and Israel, in his posthumously published *General Economic History,* and in the introduction he wrote, just before he died, to the book edition of *The Protestant Ethic,* he views capitalism and Protestantism, as well as many other distinctive Western institutions, as the products of a long process of "rationalization." Weber's last pronouncements on the subject therefore reveal a wider and more complex conception than the earlier one conveyed in the *The Protestant Ethic.* It is Weber's illumination of the distinctive character of Western civilization as a whole that must be regarded as his most important substantive contribution.

The true importance of Weber's writings on religion should now be altogether clear. His fastidious examination of Asian religions (and the contrasts they present to Judaism and Christianity) may be viewed as a masterly analysis of what Marx might have called the religiocultural "superstructure" of the Asiatic mode of production. Nothing in Weber's analysis contradicts Marx's conception. On the contrary, Weber's penetrating insights provide a fuller grasp of the social totality—the "foundation" and the "superstructure."

Religion, for Weber, was neither an epiphenomenon nor a prime mover of history. Religion was rather a significant element in a complex constellation of factors. Moreover, Weber nowhere proposed a general theory of the relation of religion to other conditions. Weber's theories, like Marx's, were historically specific: if Eastern religion placed obstacles before the development of industrial capitalism, that was true only in a specific historical epoch. Weber observes that when the Western powers began to build railroads and factories in China, the geomancers demanded that in locating ". . . structures on certain mountains, forests, rivers, and cemetary hills, foresight should be exercised in order not to disturb the peace of the spirits."[69] Then in a footnote Weber adds this observation:

> as soon as the Mandarins realized the chances for gain open to them, these difficulties suddenly ceased to be insuperable; today [1920] they are the leading stockholders in the railways. In the long run, no religious-ethical conviction is capable of barring the way to the entry of capitalism, when it stands in full armor before the gate; but the fact that it is [now] able to leap over magical barriers does not prove that genuine capitalism could have originated in circumstances where magic played such a role.[70]

It remains for us to examine one more instance of Weber's convergence with Marx.

WESTERN CAPITALISM: WEBER'S COMPLEMENTARY ANALYSIS

A major presupposition of industrial capitalism, Weber agreed, is "free" labor in Marx's sense. Persons have to be free from bonds of servitude such as chattel slavery and serfdom and free, that is, separated, from their means of production. A large mass of free laborers had first emerged in the West, in England the classical land of peasant evictions. The Enclosure movement created a great mass of vagabonds, so that " . . . as early as the 16th century there was such an army of unemployed that England had to deal with the problem of poor relief."[71] This huge labor reservoir made the factory system possible. In the earliest phases of that system, the concentration of workers in shops was compulsory. The poor, the homeless and the criminals, writes Weber,

> were pressed into factories, and in the mines of Newcastle the labourers wore iron collars down into the 18th century. But in the 18th century itself the labour contract everywhere took the place of unfree work. It meant a saving in capital, since the capital requirement for purchasing the slaves disappeared; also a shifting of the capital risk onto the worker, since his death had previously meant a capital loss for the master. Again, it removed responsibility for the reproduction of the working class, whereas slave-manned industry was wrecked on the question of family life and reproduction of the slaves. It [the labour contract] made possible the rational division of labour on the basis of technical efficiency alone, and . . . freedom of contract first made concentration of labour in the workshop the general rule. Finally, it created the possibility of exact calculation, which again could only be carried out in connection with a combination of workshop and free worker.[72]

Like Marx, then, Weber stresses free labor as a precondition of the modern economic system. "Persons must be present," he writes,

> who are not only legally in the position, but are also economically compelled, to sell their labour on the market without restriction. . . . [T]he development of capitalism is impossible if such a propertyless stratum is absent, a class compelled to sell its labour services to live; and it is likewise impossible if only unfree labour is at hand. Rational capitalistic calculation is possible only on the basis of free labour; only where . . . workers who in the formal sense voluntarily but actually under the compulsion of the whip of hunger, offer themselve the costs of products may be unambiguously determined by agreement in advance.[73]

Industrial capitalism, as it emerged in eighteenth-century England, entailed ". . . *the concentration of all the means of production* in the hands of the entrepreneur. . . ."[74] Note the italicized phrase, the Marxian expression that Weber employs. For Weber, as for Marx, industrial capitalism rested on the ". . . appropriation of all physical means of production—land, apparatus, machinery, tools, etc., as disposable property of autonomous private industrial enterprises."[75]

Weber thus accepts the basic Marxian presuppositions of the capitalist mode of production. Now, however, as in the case of the Asiatic mode, Weber proceeds to supplement Marx's analysis by proposing an "elective affinity" between the ethos of ascetic Protestantism and the values (spirit) of modern, rational capitalism. Parenthetically, it is worth noting that both the "rational" dimension of capitalism in Weber's sense, and the "affinity" of capitalism with Protestantism were anticipated by Marx. The "boundless greed after riches," wrote Marx,

> this passionate chase after exchange-value, is common to the capitalist and the miser; but while the miser is merely a capitalist gone mad, the capitalist is a *rational* miser. The never-ending augmentation of exchange-value, which the miser strives after, by seeking to save his money from circulation, is attained by the more acute capitalist, by constantly throwing it afresh into circulation.[76]

And in another context Marx writes,

> [F]or a society based upon the production of commodities, in which the producers in general enter into social relations with one another by treating their products as commodities and values, whereby they reduce their individual private labour to the standard of homogeneous human labour—for such a society, Christianity with its *cultus* of abstract man, more especially in its bourgeois developments, Protestantism, Deism, etc., is the most fitting form of religion.[77]

From one of his last pronouncements on the subject of the relation of Protestantism to capitalism, it becomes certain that no so-called religious determinism was intended by Weber. That the *economic* and *political* interests of the Puritans had been salient could not be doubted. Weber reviews the situation in seventeenth-century England in which at first mercantilism prevailed, and the monarchy granted fiscal and colonial privileges and monopolies. This type of capitalism Weber describes as nonrational; it was *not* the system out of which modern industrial capitalism developed. Rather the modern form of capitalism was pioneered by

> a stratum of entrepreneurs which had developed in independence of the political administration [and] secured the systematic support of Parliament in the 18th century, after the collapse of the fiscal monopoly policy of the Stuarts.

The capitalism of these entrepreneurs, Weber continues, was oriented

> to market opportunities which were developed from within by business interests themselves on the basis of saleable services.

The two types of capitalism collided here for the last time, and the

> . . . point of collision of the two types was the Bank of England. The bank was founded by Paterson, a Scotchman, a capitalist adventurer of the type called forth by the Stuarts' policy of granting monopolies. But Puritan businessmen also belonged to the bank. . . . [W]e can trace step by step the process by which

> the influence of Paterson and his kind lost ground in favor of the rationalistic type of bank members who were all directly or indirectly of Puritan origin or influenced by Puritanism. . . .
>
> . . . In England it [mercantilism] finally disappeared when free trade was established, an achievement of the Puritan dissenters Cobden and Bright and their league with the industrial interests, which were now in a position to dispense with mercantilist support.[78]

So in this case too, it is undeniable that Weber took into account economic and political interests.

It is essential, in this connection, to understand what Weber is *not* asserting. Neither here nor anywhere else in his writings does Weber set forth a general theory of the relation of "religion" to "economics." Nor does he argue that the Puritan ethic is a permanent prerequisite or element of capitalism. On the contrary, just as his treatment of the influence of Eastern religion applied only to a specific epoch, so did his assessment of the impact of ascetic Protestantism. For once capitalism established itself, the religious roots of that system were dead. The Puritan concept of the "calling" became a *caput mortuum*.[79]

SOCIAL CLASS AND OTHER ASPECTS OF SOCIAL ORGANIZATION: WEBER'S REVISION OF MARX'S CLASS THEORY

In the last chapter of the third volume of *Capital*, Marx begins a very promising discussion of classes. That is one of the contexts in which Marx speaks of the wage laborers, capitalists, and landowners as the three big classes in England of his time. But Marx barely begins his analysis (it lasts a mere page and a half), when it is interrupted by the words: "[Here the manuscript breaks off]." Marx never completed what appears to have been intended as a systematic analysis of social classes. As a result, scholars have had to imagine how Marx might have completed that chapter by following his logic and piecing together the references to class scattered throughout his work.

It is quite evident that Weber developed his own conception of class in a critical dialogue with Marx. In *Economy and Society*, Weber notes, "The unfinished last part of Karl Marx's *Capital* apparently was intended to deal with the issue of class unity in the face of skill differentials."[80] Weber's highly sophisticated discussion may be regarded as an attempt to complete Marx's final chapter in the light of twentieth-century conditions.

Weber concurs in many essential respects with Marx's characterization of capitalism. Although capitalistic forms existed in premodern periods of history, Weber agrees that capitalism as described by Marx is a modern phenomenon, and that it has become the dominant mode of production since the middle of the nineteenth century. Weber also agrees that modern capitalism presupposes ". . . the appropriation of all physical means of production—land, apparatus, machinery, tools, etc., as disposable property of autonomous, private industrial enterprises."[81] Like Marx, Weber stresses, in addition, a free market and "free labor." "Persons must be present," he writes, "who are not only legally in the position, but are also economically compelled, to sell their labor on the market without restriction." On the face of it, workers hire themselves out voluntarily, but actually it is ". . . under the compulsion of the whip of hunger. . . . "[82] Thus "free labor," for Weber as for Marx, is precondition of modern industrial capitalism. For both thinkers "free labor" has a double meaning: It refers to the fact that workers are free of slavery and other forms of forced servitude, and it refers to the fact that they have been separated from any and all means of production.

Weber employs all of Marx's major class concepts: class consciousness, class conflict, class interest, and so on. For Weber, the main social classes were

1. the working class as a whole—the more so, the more automated the work process becomes;
2. the petty bourgeoisie;
3. the propertyless intelligentsia and specialists (technicians, various kinds of white-collar employees, civil servants—possibly with considerable social differences depending on the cost of their training);
4. the classes privileged through property and education.[83]

In that list, we can begin to see Weber's departure from Marx, and why he saw the need to revise Marx's theory. Earlier, we saw that Marx anticipated the "sinking" of the petty bourgeoisie (small producers and small businessmen) into the working class. But Weber and others, writing early in the present century, noted that that was not in fact happening as dramatically as Marx had supposed it would. At the same time, Weber witnessed the phenomenal growth of the "new middle class"—specialists, technicians, and other white-collar employees. That was a development that Marx never explicitly anticipated. Yet the remarkable growth of that class touched the very heart of Marx's theory, for in his scheme of things, the fact that the members of the new middle class were propertyless—that is, nonowners of the means of production—meant that they shared with the manual workers a common relationship to the means of production. At least, that is the way many Marxists after Marx looked at the matter. It followed that blue- and white-collar workers have common interests and that they would develop a common class consciousness. But it became increasingly clear in the early twentieth century that white-collar employees did not look upon manual workers as class brothers and sisters at all.

Under nineteenth-century conditions, Marx may have been justified in ignoring "status" distinctions among various types of workers, but for Weber, the theorist par excellence of growing bureaucratization, it was obvious that differences in education, training, and property other than means of production all played a considerable role in shaping social psychology and, hence, class identification.

Thus, what we find in Weber is a refinement of Marx's categories. Accordingly, he stressed that the control of all types of wealth—not only the means of production—was a source of power, and that social honor or prestige based upon property, education, or whatever, might also be transformed into power. For Weber, then, classes, status groups, and political parties "are phenomena of the distribution of power." "We may speak of a class," writes Weber,

> when (1) a number of people have in common a specific causal component of their *life-chances,* insofar as (2) this component is represented exclusively by economic interests in the possession of goods and opportunities for income, and (3) is represented under the conditions of the commodity or labor markets.[84]

Although Weber is intent upon analytically separating "class" from "status group," his intention is by no means a watering down of the class concept. Class situation, he emphasizes, tends to determine "life-chances"; members of a class tend to share a common fate. In those terms, Weber's view of class situation is not as remote from Marx's as some commentators have suggested. "It is the most elemental fact," writes Weber,

> that the way in which the disposition over material property is distributed among a plurality of people, meeting competitively in the market for the purpose of exchange, in itself creates specific life chances. According to the law of marginal utility, this mode of distribution excludes the non-owners from competing for highly valued goods; this favors the owners and, in fact, gives to them a monopoly to acquire such goods. Other things being equal, the mode of distribution monopolizes the opportunities for profitable deals for all those who, provided with goods, do not necessarily have to exchange them. It increases, at least generally, their power in the price struggle with those who, being propertyless, have nothing to offer but their services. . . . This mode of distribution gives to the propertied a monopoly on the possibility of transferring property from the sphere of use as a "fortune," to the sphere of "capital goods," that is, it gives them the entrepreneurial function and all chances to share directly or indirectly in returns on capital. All this holds true within the area in which pure market conditions prevail. *"Property" and "lack of property" are, therefore, the basic categories of all class situations.*[85]

At the same time Weber goes on to show that within the broad categories of propertied and propertyless, other important distinctions exist, not only in income, but in prestige, or social honor, as well. Prestige, for Weber, is associated with the *style of life* of a *status group. Within* any given class, one will find several status groups. The relative prestige accorded them may rest on the size and source of their income, their political positions in the community, their education, their specialized training, or other evaluated social characteristics. Among the wealthy and propertied, we find old and new rich and other status distinctions based on the source of one's wealth; among the propertyless, we find status gradations based upon occupation, education, skill, size of income, expertise, the color of one's collar, and so on. Status differences, Weber maintains, must be taken into account in class analysis because those differences give us an idea of how certain social groups within a class regard themselves and how they are regarded by others.

There is another facet of social structure Weber brought into relief. Marx had neglected noneconomic forms of power—power not directly derived from wealth and property. But Weber, living in the early twentieth century, saw more clearly the bureaucratization of modern society. Large, formally rational, complex organizations were becoming more and more common. "Power," for Weber, referred to the ability to realize one's will despite and against the resistance of others. It was crystal clear that those who occupied the command posts of bureaucratic organizations had little trouble in realizing their will, whether they were personally wealthy or not.

Thus Weber argued that the concentration of power was not confined to the economic sphere. There were several strategic areas of social life in which one could observe: (1) the concentration of the means of power in the hands of small minorities and (2) the consequent separation of the majority of the people from those means. Such was the inevitable meaning of advancing bureaucratization. For Marx and the Marxists, the essential question was: Who controls the means of production? For Weber, it was necessary to ask, in addition, Who disposes over the other strategic means of controlling and dominating human beings?

Weber does not deny that the control of key economic resources is decisive; but that in itself, he holds, is insufficient for an understanding of the structure of social power in general. He therefore elaborates Marx's theory, arguing that control of the means of political administration, means of violence, means of scientific research, and so on, are also major means of dominating men. He writes:

> Organized domination which calls for continuous administration, requires that human conduct be conditioned to obedience towards those masters who claim to be the bearers of legitimate power. On the other hand, . . . organized domination requires the control of those material goods which in a given case are necessary for the use of physical violence. Thus, organized domination requires control of the personal executive staff and the material implements of administration.[86]

In this way Weber convincingly observes that Marx's "separation" of the worker from the means of production is only one facet of a general social process. If "separation" is one side of the coin, concentration of power is the other. Marx's concentration of the means of production is generalized by Weber to other means of power—notably, the administrative, military, and scientific-technical. In that light Weber's analysis of bureaucracy is not so much a refutation as it is an adaptation of Marx's theory to twentieth-century conditions.

BUREAUCRACY

For Weber, bureaucracy was becoming more and more characteristic of twentieth-century society. Growing bureaucratization was one more powerful manifestation of formal and technical rationality, of the "rationalization process" in the West. Hence, it was essential, Weber believed, to understand the nature of bureaucracy.

Conceived as a pure type, the modern bureaucratic organization has several distinctive characteristics.[87] A "bureau," or office, is an official jurisdictional area regulated by definite administrative rules. The activities of a typical bureaucrat are regarded as duties for which he has been trained and which he is qualified to carry out thanks to his specialized training. Bureaus are arranged in a *hierarchy,* a system of superordinate and subordinate offices in which the lower have less authority than the higher, and are, accordingly, supervised by them. Each bureau or office contains a body of official records or "files." The underlying administrative rules of this type of organization are quite *general,* enabling the official to regulate matters abstractly. That is, the people outside the organization are not treated as individuals whose unique situations must be dealt with case by case, but rather as members of categories. The typical bureaucrat is supposed to be impartial and disinterested. That attitude is intended to ensure that all clients in a given category will be treated in the same manner.

Weber emphasized that office holding in a bureaucracy is not just a "job." Rather it is looked upon as a "vocation" or profession requiring specialized training and examinations. The official fulfills his tasks in a dutiful manner and owes his allegiance to the office, not to individuals. He obeys orders and follows the rules not as a personal servant of his superior, but because he is devoted to the organization.

Typically, such an official attains an elevated social esteem by virtue of his holding office. Historically, that has been more true in Europe than in the United States. In Europe, status conventions, the trained expertise of the incumbents, and the fact that they were drawn from the economically privileged strata all contributed to the high esteem associated with office holding in the State bureaucracy. In the United States, such status conventions were comparatively weak throughout its history. Since the end of World War II, however, the rapid growth of governmental bureaucracies has brought with it some "European" characteristics.

There are still other important features of a modern bureaucracy. Normally, the official, after a short qualifying period, acquires *tenure*— that is, he holds the position for life. Furthermore, he earns a salary, not a wage, and becomes entitled to an old-age pension. A wage is measured in terms of work done; but a salary is associated with one's status or rank in the organization. Officials aspire to move up from lower to higher positions and thus to earn a higher salary. Modern bureaucracy presupposes a money economy. Officials are compensated in money, not in kind. Salaries in the form of money tend to place officials in a state of extreme economic dependence.

The increasing expansion of bureaucracy in modern society may be accounted for by both the quantitative and qualitative development of administrative tasks. As Weber noted,

> The decisive reason for the advance of bureaucratic organization has always been its purely *technical* superiority over any other form of organization. The fully developed bureaucratic apparatus compares with other organizations exactly as does the machine with the non-mechanical modes of production. Precision, speed, unambiguity, knowledge of the files, continuity, discretion, unity, strict subordination, reduction of friction and of material and personal costs—these are raised to the optimum point in the strictly bureaucratic administration, and especially in its monocratic form.[88]

Speed, precision, and other forms of cost reduction are among the main reasons why we find that the typical, modern capitalist enterprise is a large, complex corporation. However, in both the private and the public spheres, it is not merely considerations of efficiency but rather of *power* that have accounted for growing bureaucratization. The bureaucratic tendency has been promoted by power politics, warfare, the creation of large standing armies, and by the immense budgets required for those purposes. At the same time, the social welfare policies of the modern state have also contributed to the enormity, complexity, and costliness of its administrative apparatus.

One of Weber's most illuminating observations with respect to modern bureaucracy was made by elaborating on a central idea of Marx's. Marx, it will be recalled, traced the roots of modern capitalism to the *separation* of the producers (peasant-proprietor) from their means of production. Marx was among the first to demonstrate that capital was becoming increasingly *concentrated* and *centralized*. His argument was, in brief, that the accumulation of capital in the economy as a whole assumed the form of competition among firms, with some winning and others losing. The latter were either destroyed or absorbed by the victors. The growth of capital in one enterprise was facilitated by the failure of others. Those who remained in the race had successfully reduced their production costs by making larger investments in machinery and the like. As the costs of investment increased, entry into the field of production was restricted to fewer and fewer, but larger, capitals. Capital thus became increasingly concentrated in large-scale corporate organizations.

Weber agreed that the concentration of economic power was, in fact, a powerful tendency of capitalism. But he hastened to add that Marx had centered attention on only one aspect of a much more general historical trend. That is, one could witness parallels to the separation of the producer from the means of production and the concentration of those means in several other social spheres. Thus, Weber argued that historically the soldier had been separated from the means of violence and the civil servant from the means of administration, while those means have also undergone continual concentration. At one time, fighting men owned their own weapons and were economically capable of equipping themselves. That was true of tribal levies, the armed citizens of the ancient city-states, the militias of early cities, and all feudal armies. But modern warfare is a "war of machines," writes Weber, "and this makes centralized provisioning technically necessary, just as the dominance of the machine in industry promotes the concentration of the means of production and management."[89] Historically, army service has shifted from the shoulders of the propertied to those of the propertyless.

Similar processes have occurred in other spheres as well, notably in scientific research. If, for example, we think of scientists and inventors as recently as the turn of this century, someone like Thomas Edison comes to mind. Edison was a "tinkerer" who worked alone in his cellar and produced a highly significant invention. Today's science is a different matter altogether. In order to become a "scientist," one must first successfully pass the examinations of a university or some other large educational organization, and obtain the required degrees. One is then enabled to engage in scientific activities by gaining employment in the laboratory of some governmental, corporate, or university organization, all of which are big bureaucratic enterprises. The means of research are large and expensive and they are controlled by the administrative heads of those organizations, not by scientists. Thus, as Weber observed, "Through the concentration of such means in the hands of the privileged head of the institute the mass of researchers and instructors are separated from their `means of production,' in the same way as the workers are separated from theirs by the capitalist enterprises."[90] The concentration of power is characteristic of several major institutional spheres of modern society and not just the economy. It is not just the blue-collar worker who has become "proletarianized." Almost everyone has become a paid laborer, working in a large complex organization, and depending upon it for a livelihood.

Once such bureaucratic structures are established, they are practically indestructible, Weber believed, because a bureaucracy is a power instrument of the first order for those who occupy its command posts. It facilitates the domination and control of large numbers of people. The individual bureaucrat is chained to his specialized activity and is only a small cog in the total operation. His entire mind and body have been trained for obedience and those who rule such organizations expect compliance as a matter of course. Thus Weber makes a strong argument for the inevitable growth of bureaucracy. The vested power interests in it, the social control and discipline it facilitates, the specialization of work and the accompanying requirements of expertise—all these factors would make the dismantling of bureaucracy extraordinarily difficult. Indeed, bureaucracies are rarely, if ever, dismantled; they are merely taken over. The bureaucratic state apparatus can be "made to work for anybody who knows how to gain control over it. A rationally ordered officialdom continues to function smoothly after the enemy has occupied the territory; he merely needs to change the top officials."[91] Weber's analysis therefore led him to the conclusion that "revolution," in the sense of transcending bureaucracy and creating a new, nonbureaucratic society, was becoming more and more unlikely.

Weber viewed the bureaucratization of modern society with apprehension. The immense concentration of power in fewer and fewer hands was bound to endanger liberal-democratic institutions and to diminish individual freedoms. Increasingly the individual was subjected to an organizational discipline that drastically reduced his initiative; increasingly he was subjected to a *formally* rational regimen that eliminated any opportunities for autonomous and genuinely rational conduct. In Weber's words, bureaucratic "discipline is nothing but the consistently rationalized, methodically prepared and exact execution of the received order, in which all personal criticism is unconditionally suspended and the actor is unswervingly and exclusively set for carrying out the command."[92] What all formally rational, large-scale organizations have in common are regimentation and discipline. A bureaucracy, no less than a factory, tends to mold a person's psychophysical being in an effort to adapt it to the demands of the organization. In short, bureaucracy "functionalizes" human beings. It is "horrible to think," wrote Weber "that the world could one day be filled with nothing but those little cogs, little men clinging to little jobs and striving towards bigger ones. . . ."[93]

THE CHARISMATIC POLITICAL LEADER: WEBER'S ERROR

The challenge that bureaucratization poses for democracy is a formidable one. To meet this challenge Weber placed his faith in "leaders." Whether in business, politics, or military affairs, great leaders had to be created as an antidote to bureaucracy. After the First World War he was asked by a student about his political plans and he replied that he had none "except to concentrate all my intellectual strength on one problem, how to get once more for Germany a great general staff."[94] It seems, therefore, that Weber's political concerns penetrated his scholarship in this important respect, and that his theoretical ideas on charismatic leadership crystallized in the course of his reflections on post-war Germany and the embattled Weimar Republic. In the debates of 1919–1920 on the new constitution, Weber vigorously supported provisions for a popularly elected president. Describing Weber's attitude in this regard, Wolfgang J. Mommsen writes:

> . . . by virtue of his direct links with the will of the masses the *Reichspräsident* was to be an opening for the rise of political leaders over and above party machines and parliaments. In this way Weber hoped to assist a "leader democracy" to come to the fore in Germany, in which charismatically qualified politicians with a sense of foresight but also with a sense of proportion are at the helm, instead of a "leaderless democracy of professional politicians without a calling."[95]

Like Nietzsche and most likely under his influence, Weber assigned considerable weight to the role of the outstanding individual in history. Only such individuals could make history by setting new goals and thus imparting new energy to the people. There was, however, no Nietzschean contempt for the masses here. "In contrast to Nietzsche's ethic of the Master," writes Mommsen, "which culminated in the outright rejection of all democratic politics, Weber adhered to the fundamental principles of liberalism which hold sacrosanct the dignity of the individual and aspire to see society organized in such a way that all individuals may preserve a maximum of free initiative" (p. 27). It was on the basis of such principles, and certainly not in opposition to them, that Weber formulated his ideas on charismatic leadership. What Weimar Germany needed in particular, Weber believed, were leaders of quality who could persuade the masses to follow them voluntarily. For Weber, great leaders emerged in response to an inner "calling"; they lived *for* politics, not off politics. In the competition of such leaders for mass followings, however, Weber approved of demagogy and emotional appeals designed to bind the masses to the leader.

A careful examination of Weber's writings reveals that he viewed charismatic leadership in a purely positive light. He was blind, somehow, to the anti-democratic and tyrannical potential of charismatic leadership. Only by keeping the charismatic principle alive could the world (Germany?) be saved from the mediocrity accompanying the inexorable advance of bureaucracy. Not too long after he died, however, the charismatic and bureaucratic principles were fused in his homeland into a horrendous synthesis. In that light Weber's concept of personal charisma, insofar as it was purely positive, was also misleadingly one-sided. Where Weimar Germany is concerned, it is easy to see why Weber recognized the need for strong leadership, but it is difficult to understand why he failed to anticipate the possibility of an anti-liberal fusion of the charismatic and bureaucratic principles, for he fully recognized the political immaturity and weakness of the German middle classes. Given their economic power, they should have supported the strengthening of liberal-democratic institutions. Instead, they sought the protection of the old-regime elements against the working classes. Yet, for Weber, the unrestrained will of the masses and their demands for equality were by far the greatest threat to the foundations of freedom in the Western world. "By contrast," writes Mommsen,

> he [Weber] regarded as comparatively negligible the danger that the rule of the *Führer*, legitimized through personal plebiscite, could turn into a dictatorial (or even fascist) regime, even though Weber himself had pointed out that in general "leader democracies" were characterized by a highly emotional type of devotion to and trust in the leader, and that this accounted for a tendency to follow as a leader the type of individual who is most unusual, who promises the most or who employs the most effective propaganda measures. (p. 34)

Under modern conditions, according to Weber, a "leader democracy" requires a bureaucratic administrative apparatus as well as a bureaucratic party organization. Their role is to serve as "obedient servants" ensuring that the leader's decisions are efficiently carried out. Here, again, it is noteworthy that the dangers and risks Weber perceived in this connection were the gradual undermining of a leader's charisma by the bureaucrats. The opposite danger, that the leader would succeed in wielding the entire State and Party apparatus as an instrument of cold-blooded tyranny and genocide, Weber failed altogether to foresee. So although Weber had never intended his theory of the charismatic political leader to be construed in an anti-democratic manner, his theory nevertheless lent itself to such an interpretation, for it gave pre-eminence to the political leader as opposed to the mass of citizens.

If one compares Weber with Robert Michels, a Weber disciple of sorts, one sees clearly that Weber's conception of the charismatic political leader was in fact construed in an anti-democratic fashion. Michels, as we shall see, decried the oligarchical tendency in democratic organizations in which leaders employed the administrative apparatus to preserve their own status and interests. The leaders of the German Social-Democratic Party, for example, behaved in a manner reminiscent of the Sun King, each thinking of himself, *"Le Parti c'est moi!"* As Mommsen reminds us, however, Weber

> drew very different conclusions from the evidence of an increasing bureaucratization within modern parties. Not only did he consider the trend towards "plebiscitarian democracy," which inevitably involved a substantial enhancement of the role of political leaders at the expense of the "ruled," to be irreversible; he saw it also as a *positive* development, in that it served as a counterweight to the bureaucratization of the apparatuses of power. (p. 100, italics added)

To support his contention that Weber's conception of leadership could be construed in an anti-democratic manner, Mommsen cites the fact that

> Michels justified his decision to support Mussolini and the Italian fascist *Füherstaat* by express reference to Max Weber. Among other things, Michels was able to invoke Weber's explicit claim that the emotional attachment of the broad masses to the leader constitutes the specific characteristic of charismatic authority, and that the leader determines the content of policy on his own ultimate authority alone, while the assent of his supporters resides purely in their trust in the leader's charismatic leadership-qualities as such, rather than in their concurrence with the particular objectives he lays down. (p. 102)

It seems indisputable, then, that a frank examination of Weber's theory of charismatic political leadership discloses the dangers to democracy that its one-sidedness entails.

SOCIAL SCIENCE AND VALUES

Weber demonstrated that the "disenchantment of the world" had been carried out more thoroughly in the West than elsewhere. Virtually all spheres of Western culture and social organization had undergone the rationalization process, so that now, in principle, there were no mysterious, unknowable, or inscrutable powers and humans could master all things through formal-technical rationalization. In its ideal-typical form, such rationalization was based on the assumption that both *things* and *humans* behave in predictable ways and that one could therefore use that knowledge for any given purpose.

Science, Weber believed, could provide us with *means* but not ends. Science can never show us the way to "true values." A conflict of values, or "gods," as he sometimes described it, is inevitable. Values can never be arranged through science or otherwise, in one universally agreed-upon scale. What, then, can science offer? *Clarity*, Weber replies, clarity with respect to our conduct, its motives, ends, means, and consequences. Science, and in our case social science, can provide insight into the value-oriented nature of human actions; it can afford insight into the means of attaining certain goals and some of the costs and consequences that it entails for other goals.

If clarity is the criterion, then we would have to conclude that Weber's contribution has extraordinary value, for his comparative analyses of religion and social structure have yielded genuinely penetrating insights into our civilization.

THE HISTORICAL-SOCIOLOGICAL METHOD

We have pointed out many substantive parallels in the writings of Marx and Weber. We have observed a wide area of convergence in their respective analyses of what Marx called the major modes of production in history, and where those analyses did not precisely converge, they proved to be complementary and compatible.

But there are methodological parallels as well. For we have seen that Marx's method, interpreted nondogmatically, makes no attempt to reconstruct history to fit some a priori conception. His method is revealed not as an effort to impute causal priority to economic conditions, but rather to determine the relationship between the economic and other orders of society. That being the case, we can see a definite methodological affinity between Marx and Weber, since much of the latter's work was also a study of "economy and society." Indeed, one might say that Weber took over Marx's method as a heuristic principle, and applied it with great skill.

So far as social science research is concerned, the really important lesson to be learned from Marx and Weber is the importance of history for an understanding of society. Though they were certainly interested in grasping the general and universal, they concerned themselves with the concrete circumstances of specific periods, and the similarities and contrasts of diverse geohistorical areas. They clearly recognized that an adequate explanation of social facts requires a historical account of how the facts came to be; they recognized that comparative-historical analysis is indispensable for the study of stability and change. In a word, it is these two extraordinary thinkers in particular who stand out as the architects of a historical sociology well worth emulating, for both of them subscribed to an open, historically grounded theory and method.

NOTES

1. The debate with the Marxian legacy includes Max Weber, Vilfredo Pareto, Gaetano Mosca, Robert Michels, Émile Durkheim, and Karl Mannheim (Chapters 18–22).
2. Talcott Parsons, "Capitalism in Recent German Literature," *Journal of Political Economy*, 37, 1929, p. 40.
3. See his introduction to *The Theory of Social and Economic Organization* (Glencoe, Ill.: The Free Press, 1947), p. 6.
4. Jonathan H. Turner and Leonard Beeghley, *The Emergence of Sociological Theory* (Homewood, Ill.: The Dorsey Press, 1981). The quoted passages may be found on pp. 257, 245, and 243, respectively.
5. See Albert Salomon's article in Georges Gurvitch and Wilbert E. Moore, *Twentieth-Century Sociology* (New York: The Philosophical Library, 1945), p. 596.
6. H. H. Gerth and C. Wright Mills, eds., *From Max Weber: Essays in Sociology* (New York: Oxford University Press, 1946), p. 63.
7. George Lichtheim, *Marxism: An Historical and Critical Study* (New York: Frederick A. Praeger, 1961), p. 385.
8. Irving M. Zeitlin, *Ideology and the Development of Sociological Theory* (Englewood Cliffs, N.J.: Prentice-Hall, 1968), p. 112.
9. Reinhard Bendix and Guenther Roth, *Scholarship and Partisanship: Essays on Max Weber* (Berkeley: The University of California Press, 1971), p. 238.
10. Ibid., p. 240.
11. *Verhandlungen des Ersten Deutschen Soziologentages* (Tübingen: Mohr, 1911), p. 101. Cited in Bendix and Roth, *Scholarship and Partisanship* p. 242–43.
12. Cited in Bendix and Roth, *Scholarship and Partisanship* pp. 242–43.
13. Marx, *The Poverty of Philosophy* (Moscow: Foreign Languages Publishing House, n.d.), p. 127.
14. Bendix and Roth, *Scholarship and Partisanship*, p. 227.

15. Max Weber, *The Methodology of the Social Sciences* (Glencoe, Ill.: The Free Press, 1949), p. 65.
16. Ibid., p. 68.
17. Max Weber, *The Protestant Ethic and the Spirit of Capitalism* (New York: Charles Scribner's Sons, 1958), p. 25. (Hereafter all page references to this work will be indicated in parentheses immediately following the quoted passage.)
18. Max Weber, *The Agrarian Sociology of Ancient Civilizations*, trans. R.I. Frank (London: NLB, 1976), p. 393. This volume is a translation of an essay published by Weber in 1909 called "Agrarverhältnisse im Altertum." See J. Conrad et al., *Handwörterbuch Der Staatswissenschaften*, 3rd ed., Vol. 1, (Jena: Verlag von Gustave Fisher, 1909), pp. 52–188. The article we are presently summarizing is included in the volume as an appendix. Hereafter the title of this book is abbreviated as *ASAC*.
19. Loc. cit.
20. Weber, *ASAC*, p. 394.
21. Ibid., p. 396.
22. Ibid., p. 399.
23. Ibid., p. 400.
24. Ibid., p. 403.
25. Ibid., p. 408.
26. Ibid., p. 410.
27. Loc. cit.
28. Weber, *ASAC*, p. 348.
29. Ibid., pp. 136–37.
30. Ibid., p. 137.
31. Ibid., p. 138.
32. Ibid., p. 136.
33. Max Weber, *The Methodology of the Social Sciences* (Glencoe, Ill.: The Free Press, 1949), p. 65ff.
34. Weber, *ASAC*, p. 138.
35. Ibid., p. 172.
36. Ibid., p. 173.
37. Ibid., p. 183.
38. In his *Origin of the Family, Private Property, and the State* (New York: International Publishers, 1942).
39. Weber, *ASAC*, p. 153.
40. Ibid., p. 309.
41. Max Weber, *General Economic History*, trans. Frank H. Knight (New York: Collier Books, 1961), p. 29. This volume is based on a series of lectures Weber delivered shortly before he died in 1920. The title of this book is hereafter abbreviated as *GEH*.
42. See John Maynard, *The Russian Peasant and Other Studies* (London: Gollancz, 1942); D. J. Male, *Russian Peasant Organization Before Collectivization* (Cambridge: At the University Press, 1971); and Richard Hennessy, *The Agrarian Question in Russia, 1905–1907* (Verlag in Geissen: Wilhelm Schmitz, 1977).
43. Weber, *GEH*, p. 33.
44. Engels, *The Origin of the Family, Private Property, and the State*, p. 131.

45. Ibid., p. 139.
46. Weber, *ASAC*, p. 349.
47. Ibid., pp. 349–50.
48. Weber, *GEH*, pp. 54–55.
49. Loc. cit.
50. Ibid., p. 67.
51. Ibid., p. 82.
52. Ibid., pp. 82–83.
53. Ibid., p. 63.
54. Max Weber, *The Religion of India*, trans. and ed. Hans H. Gerth and Don Martindale (Glencoe, Ill.: The Free Press, 1958), p. 111.
55. Weber, *ASAC*, p. 38.
56. Ibid., p. 84.
57. Loc. cit.
58. Ibid., p. 85.
59. Ibid., p. 106.
60. Ibid., p. 109.
61. Ibid., p. 131.
62. Weber, *GEH*, pp. 57–58, italics added.
63. Ibid., p. 237.
64. Loc. cit.
65. Max Weber, *The Religion of China*, trans. and ed. Hans H. Gerth (Glencoe, Ill.: The Free Press, 1951), p. 12. (Hereafter all page references of this work will be indicated in parentheses immediately following the quoted passage.)
66. Weber, *The Religion of India*, p. 4. (Hereafter all page references to this work will be cited in parentheses immediately following the quoted passage.)
67. Max Weber, *Ancient Judaism*, trans. and ed. Hans H. Gerth and Don Martindale (Glencoe, Ill.: The Free Press, 1952), p. 4. (Hereafter all page references to this work will be indicated in parentheses immediately following the quoted passage.)
68. A critical examination of the state of biblical scholarship since the publication of Weber's *Das Antike Judentum* (1921) may be found in Irving M. Zeitlin, *Ancient Judaism; Biblical Criticism from Max Weber to the Present* (Oxford: Basil Blackwell, 1984).
69. Weber, *GEH*, p. 265.
70. Ibid., p. 276, n. 4.
71. Ibid., p. 129.
72. Ibid., p. 137.
73. Ibid., pp. 208–09.
74. Ibid., p. 227.
75. Ibid., p. 208.
76. Karl Marx, *Capital*, Vol. I (Moscow: Foreign Languages Publishing House, 1954), p. 153, italics added.
77. Ibid., p. 79.
78. Weber, *GEH*, p. 258.
79. Ibid., p. 270.

80. Max Weber, *Economy and Society*, ed. Guenther Roth and Claus Wittich, 3 vols. (New York: Bedminster Press, 1968), I, 305.
81. Max Weber, *General Economic History* , trans. Frank H. Knight (New York: Collier Books, 1961), p. 208.
82. Ibid, pp. 208–09.
83. Weber, *Economy and Society*, I, p. 305.
84. Ibid., Vol. II, p. 927.
85. Ibid.
86. Max Weber, "Politics as a Vocation," in H. H. Gerth and C. W. Mills, eds., *From Max Weber: Essays in Sociology* (New York: Oxford University Press, 1958), p. 80.
87. The present discussion is based on Weber, *Economy and Society*, Vol. III, pp. 956–1005.
88. Ibid., p. 973.
89. Ibid., p. 981.
90. Ibid., p. 983.
91. Ibid., p. 989.
92. Ibid., p. 1149.
93. Cited by J. P. Mayer, *Max Weber and German Politics* (London: Faber and Faber, 1944), p. 127.
94. Mayer, *Max Weber and German Politics*, p 107.
95. Wolfgang J. Mommsen, *The Political and Social Theory of Max Weber* (Cambridge: The University of Chicago Press/Polity Press, 1989), p. 22. (Hereafter, references to this book are cited by page number immediately following the quoted passage.)

18

The New Machiavellians

Pareto, Mosca, and Michels

INTRODUCTION

Pareto, Mosca, and Michels have been called Neo-Machiavellians because their theories were profoundly influenced by the ideas of Niccolo Machiavelli (1469–1527), who viewed the human being as driven by self-interest and ruled by the insatiable desire for material gain. For Machiavelli, selfishness is an eternal trait of human nature which is constant and immutable. However, this rather negative view of human nature led Machiavelli to a positive assessment of human possibilities through the study of history. For if human actions are motivated by a selfish nature, and if that constant nature tends to produce similar and recurring types of action, then the actions of the past, as recorded in history, may be studied and used as a basis for anticipating the future. Hindsight provides a serviceable degree of foresight! The study of history supplies us with a vast reservoir of guidelines as we step into the future. Machiavelli thus rejected all utopias which envisioned a future radically different from the past. In this respect as in others Pareto, Mosca, and Michels followed in his footsteps.

Machiavelli never said that the end justifies the means. He did not argue that *all* means are justified in the pursuit of any end; nor did he completely separate moral standards from political actions, as some scholars have alleged. He did, however, maintain that the use of evil means, such as violence, is often necessary. When violence is clearly in the public interest, the prince, or political leader, should not shy away from using it. Force, as a last resort, is essential in some circumstances if the prince is to fulfill his two primary responsibilities of ensuring the State's internal stability and external independence.

Machiavelli proposed that violent conflict, invasions, and wars were permanent attributes of the human condition. But he stressed that conflict can produce beneficial results if it is dealt with by a properly organized and stable government which, for Machiavelli, is a mixed government. It was precisely the social strife between the plebeians and aristocrats of Rome that contributed to its greatness and liberty. One cannot get rid of conflict, and attempts to suppress it create only apparent stability. The wise prince will therefore strive to create a dynamic equilibrium between the diverse and competing social forces of his society.

Machiavelli has no sympathy for governments that fail to defend their societies with resoluteness and boldness. He prefers a free, republican form of government and insists that a citizens' militia is the strongest bulwark against tyranny. A militia of citizen-soldiers is always superior to standing professional armies or mercenary forces. The internal stability and external independence of a society demand of the wise prince that

> he should learn from the fox and the lion; because the lion is defenseless against traps and a fox is defenseless against wolves. Therefore one must be a fox in order to recognize traps, and a lion to frighten off wolves. Those who simply act like lions are stupid. (*The Prince,* chapter 18; and see *The Discourses,* II, 13)

As a fox the prince must be a skilful pretender. It is best if he possesses the virtues of good faith, charity, humanity, and religion; but if he lacks such virtues, he should certainly *appear* to possess them. As a lion he must be prepared to use force when necessary. Cruelty, employed economically, may be more merciful than clemency; for while the former injures only a few and restrains the rest by fear, the latter breeds disorder and rebellion, which injures the entire body politic.

The incidence of force could never be lessened in the international arena because it lacked a prince—a Leviathan, as Hobbes later argued. Domestic violence could, however, be reduced by means of law, appropriate political institutions, and civility. The greater the cruelty, the weaker the regime, since increased cruelty shows that the prince has lost the consent of the governed.

The aim of the wise prince, then, is to maintain the Republic by the force *of* the people; and this is best accomplished by fulfilling three basic responsibilities:

1. ensuring that the people's material needs are met;
2. protecting them and their possessions; and
3. eliminating dangerous inequalities.

The existence of conflicting interest groups and classes being inevitable, the prince must mediate between them so that order and justice and the overarching interests of the commonwealth as a whole are maintained. It is the well-being of the community as a whole, not merely of individuals and factions, that makes a State great. Moreover, the wise prince will foster the free and open pursuit of power, thus ensuring a continual supply of fresh political talent.

As we read the upcoming essays on Pareto, Mosca, and Michels, we will see how they adapted and applied Machiavelli's ideas to early twentieth-century conditions.

VILFREDO PARETO (1848–1923)

The work of Vilfredo Pareto is an exceedingly ambitious attempt at rebutting and discrediting the principles of the Enlightenment in both its eighteenth- and nineteenth-century forms. His voluminous writings may be viewed as a sustained onslaught upon liberal-democratic, socialistic, and Marxian theories. Whereas Marx had viewed man as a rational and perfectible creature, Pareto portrayed him as essentially nonrational and unchanging and advanced his theory of "residues" with the aim of demonstrating that proposition. And while Marx viewed class conflict in history as increasing man's potential for freedom, Pareto regarded history as essentially cyclical. As a direct antithesis to Marx's theory of class struggle, Pareto advanced his theory of élites. The circulation of élites, the real stuff of history, had few, or perhaps no, positive consequences for the "people."

Pareto had a strong background in French language and culture and knew French as well as or perhaps even better than Italian.[1] He was born in France and spent thirty years in French-speaking Switzerland. It was in Italy, however, that he received his secondary education. He studied primarily physics and mathematics at the University and Polytechnical School of Turin; it was there, in 1869, that he wrote his thesis, "The Fundamental Principles of the Equilibrium of Solid Bodies." Thus, "equilibrium," a concept which he was later to apply to social phenomena, first engaged his interest in the physical context.

As even a cursory glance at his illustrative material shows, Pareto knew Greek and Latin and had a great passion for Greek and Roman literature and history. But since there is no evidence of his having studied those subjects during his formal schooling, he must have acquired that knowledge well after his adolescence, as his interest in society and history grew. His general sociology is as much a study of antiquity as of contemporary society.

Although the intellectual influences on Pareto, particularly in sociology, were varied, he chooses for some reason never to acknowledge his debt to them. Not until he reaches the fourth and last volume of his general treatise on sociology does he acknowledge that he owes something to his antecedents, whom he nevertheless does not cite by name because, as he says, that is of no interest in the scientific study of social phenomena. That prompted his editor and translator, Arthur Livingston, to remark

> All the same, in a work of a million words with not a few asides and containing not a few strictures on great writers of past and present, a few hundred words more might not have come amiss to describe what Pareto in particular owed, for his general method to Auguste Comte, for his theory of derivations to Bentham (some of whose categories Pareto adopts verbatim), for his theory of class circulation to Gaetano Mosca, for his theory of residues to Frazer and others, and for a number of phrases and items of detail even to Hegel, William James, and many others.[2]

Obviously not a religious man, neither was he antireligious in the sense of desiring to suppress religious institutions. Pareto regards Christian and all other dogmas, for that matter, as nonsense, and Christian "miracles" have the same objective value as pagan "miracles." Eventually he would argue that as stupid and absurd as certain notions and practices may be, they may nonetheless have useful consequences for a given society. The aura of sanctity surrounding universal suffrage, democracy, socialism, or Christianity is foolish and "nonlogical," yet it may, perhaps, have some utility.

Religion, like other "sentiments" for Pareto, is constant and fundamental, regardless of the form it may assume. In 1907, for example, he writes that at the moment, the "religions" of socialism and humanitarianism are growing, while belief in a personal god is declining, but religion of some kind will always remain, for it is absolutely essential to society. The particular "theology" is not important, only its social effects. In an authoritarian situation the religion of freedom has "utility" and, conversely, where "anarchy" threatens, an authoritarian religion becomes indispensable to prevent the "dissolution" of society. "Fatherland," "honor," "virtue," and so on are manifestations of "sentiments," the prime movers of human conduct and the crucial factors determining the character and evolution of societies. As we shall see, however, he is far from consistent in his use of the concept "sentiment," which he sometimes treats as a synonym for cultural value but more often than not as an "instinct," that is, a biopsychic determinant of behavior that remains constant and, hence, does not vary with sociohistorical conditions. Pareto believes this despite the fact that his own "sentiments" changed conspicuously in the course of his intellectual development.

As a young man in Florence, for example, he was an active pacifist and humanitarian, a liberal in economic theory. In 1891, he wrote, "War and armed peace are the most costly luxuries which the ruling class offers at the expense of the nation."[3] He was also opposed to colonialism; in his opinion Tonkin cost France dearly and Tunisia would not benefit Italy except perhaps to provide some administrative positions for the sons of the bourgeoisie. Later, for some unknown reason, Pareto does a complete turnabout, to reveal an almost obsessive hatred and contempt for humanitarianism, a sentiment of the weak in the subject class and of the decadent in the governing élite.

Before the basic transformation in Pareto's outlook came about, however, he was a "democrat" and even, on occasion, favored the working class in its struggle with the bourgeoisie. In 1893 he deplored the violence committed by workers but blamed protectionism, corruption, and militarism. He was so convinced a liberal that he believed one day commercial treaties would appear as the peculiarities of a barbaric epoch in which free exchange was unknown. In the same period, he writes that the abuses and scandals of government then so evident provide a rough idea of "what awaits us when socialism will reign in all its glory."[4] But Pareto's early critique of socialism was quite different from what it was to become. As a young man he attacks the ruling bourgeoisie for not realizing its ideal of liberty; he supports temporary alliances with the socialists to resist oppression and comments that it is they who almost single-handedly fight the superstitions of "patriotism." And, finally, when they are persecuted by the government, he extends them aid—personal, moral, and intellectual. But all that was to change. Around the turn of the century there was a great transformation both in his daily habits and in his thought. He became what the intellectual world called "the hermit of Celigny," the adversary, as Bousquet has phrased it, of humanitarian democracy.

Pareto and Science

For Pareto, there were basically two independent and mutually exclusive domains of human conduct: that of science and logic on the one hand and of sentiment on the other. Science involves logic, observation, and objective experience, and "truth" rests on those processes. The other domain is "nonlogico-experimental"—which is just the beginning of Pareto's cumbersome vocabulary. There are two independent domains, and science has nothing to say about "reasoning" that leaves its realm. Pareto denies that rationality can ever replace the other realm or even make serious inroads upon it. In fact, *sentiment* is the fundamental and predominant force in society, *the determining factor* of human conduct (outside the very restricted sphere in which Pareto arbitrarily confined logico-experimental norms).

Pareto's first task as he saw it was to distinguish carefully between scientific and nonscientific propositions. Objective experience is the sole criterion of scientific theory, which is arrived at inductively by describing the relations among facts; in short, scientific theories are "logico-experimental." Other "theories," which he calls "nonlogico-experimental," add something to experience and seek to dominate the "facts." Pareto subscribed to the methodological view that treated "laws" as strictly heuristic devices, not necessarily as the workings of "reality." When uniformities, or relationships among phenomena, become evident, "law" is the name one gives to such patterns; "law" is not some *force* to which the facts are actually subject. The scientist selects certain observable phenomena and organizes them according to some scheme in which the phenomena appear to be subject to a certain "law." There are no "necessary" laws; rather, phenomena behave "as if" there were, and the scientist states the degree of probability with which the phenomena in question will follow a specified pattern. Scientific relativity, then, was for Pareto, as for others, such as Vaihinger, Mach, and Poincaré, a basic assumption.

Pareto's sole aim, he assures us again and again, is scientific truth, which can be attained in the social realm by applying the methods of the physical sciences. In all his works, he stresses that he is not interested in improving or changing the world; he is not concerned with providing theoretical guidance for practical affairs. Rather, he has one single and exclusive aim in view: to study the uniformities phenomena present, their "laws." Like many economists before him, Pareto advocated the method of successive approximations. Since no concrete phenomenon can be known in all its details, some sort of abstraction always becomes necessary. What aspect one singles out for study depends on one's interests. One begins with some simplifying assumptions, taking into account additional complicating factors as one proceeds—a method equally applicable to natural and social phenomena.

There is, however, an important characteristic of social phenomena Pareto is intent upon accentuating: The utility of an idea and its truth are not necessarily identical in the social sphere. As a matter of fact, they are often independent of each other. He reminds his reader periodically that when he argues for the absurdity of an idea, that does not necessarily mean that it is injurious to anyone; and when he argues that an idea has utility, the reader should not assume that it is experimentally true. Clearly, a great many ideas that are patently false, or whose relative truth is not known, have currency among men. Who holds those doctrines and why? What are the consequences of holding those beliefs and for whom? Those are the questions, Pareto tells us, that interest him and that he wants to answer by means of a scientific sociology.

Les Systèmes Socialistes

In this two-volume critique of socialist and communist doctrines, from the earliest schemes of antiquity through the so-called "utopian socialists" and concluding, finally, with the theories of Marx, one clearly perceives the outline of the theoretical framework that Pareto later elaborated in his general sociology. An examination of the *Systèmes* leaves no doubt as to the polemical nature of Pareto's "sociological" concepts and propositions. After examining the various socialist theories Marx himself had regarded as "prescientific" and finding them all wanting, Pareto is prepared for a scrutiny of so-called "scientific socialism." The last two chapters, in many respects the most interesting, deal with Marx's thought.

Pareto came to the study of sociology through his critique of socialism, which in effect contains all the ideas one later meets in his *Traité de Sociologie*. His explicit critique of Marx may be found first of all in the *Systèmes*, but also in a number of articles and in his introduction to *Capital*. In his *Systèmes* he promises us a rather interesting study:

> On the one hand, we shall inquire into the real facts which have favored the establishment of certain social systems, or the appearance of certain projects for social systems; in other words, what are the things or facts which reveal themselves to us in these forms; on the other hand, we shall examine the "reasonings" which have been employed to justify these systems or projects for systems and we shall see to what extent the premises are drawn from experience and from logical deductions.[5]

Pareto acknowledges, in passing, the limited validity of Marx's sociological theory: "This research will show us often that there are economic facts which modify social institutions and doctrines and which are thus reflected in the consciousness of men, as in the view of the `materialist conception of history'" (Vol. V, pp. 26–27). But he never uses its guidelines to assess its fruitfulness as an analytical tool and in fact never returns to it except to "refute" it by assertion. Socialism in general and Marxism in particular are regarded by Pareto as religions that emerged and gained popularity because they appealed to certain "sentiments" (a term, as previously mentioned, that has a special meaning in Pareto's system: a nonlogical principle of conduct). Never in this work does he relate doctrines and beliefs to social conditions, for that in effect would have taken him back to Marx's conception; nor does he ask whether and to what degree rational interests rather than blind sentiments might better explain the popularity in a given period of socialism or Marxism. Pareto rarely pauses to analyze the social conditions of men, but speculates instead about their sentiments and instincts.

Whereas classes and class conflict were transient historical phenomena for Marx, Pareto insists that class conflict is destined to continue forever. Its forms may change, but the substance remains the same. He writes:

> Suppose collectivism to be established, and that "capital" no longer exists; then only a particular form of class struggle will have disappeared and new ones will emerge to replace it. New conflicts will appear between the different kinds of workers and the socialist state, between the intellectuals and the non-intellectuals, between the various politicians, between the politicians and those they administer, between innovators and conservatives, etc. Are there really such people who imagine seriously that with the advent of socialism the sources of

> social innovation will be dried up? That men will no longer envision new projects, that interests will not push some men to adopt these projects in the hope of acquiring a dominant place in society? (Vol. II, p. 455)

Why, in Pareto's view, is class conflict destined to be an eternal human condition? Not so much because a complex, heterogeneous society is bound to have a variety of groups with different and conflicting interests; but rather because it is rooted in the nature of men and is a form of their struggle for life:

> The struggle for life or well-being is a general phenomenon for living things, and everything we know about this leads us to recognize it as one of the most powerful forces for the conservation and amelioration of the race. It is therefore extremely improbable that men will be able to transcend this condition. . . . All our efforts can never result in a fundamental change of this condition, only slight modifications of its forms. (Vol. II, p. 455)

Pareto thus views class conflict as an inseparable aspect of men's struggle with nature, and hence as inevitable and unending. Social conflicts are rooted in natural conditions, not least in the very nature of man, who is pushed into action by essentially "natural" and therefore "nonlogical" forces. That is the substance of Pareto's theory of human conduct as he later elaborates it in his "sociology."

As he develops his critique of socialism and shows us how one must "scientifically" analyze the phenomenon, he presents us with all the notions we shall later meet in the obscure and awkward terms of his sociological treatise. First, he discusses a number of concepts to illustrate that one cannot employ them logically. Take, for example, "liberty" and "constraint"; the first is associated with agreeable feelings and the second with disagreeable ones. All one has to do to get people to accept constraint is to give it the name of liberty. Why?—because those and similar concepts advanced by the socialists and optimistic liberals draw their force from sentiments and not from logic. Is there then anything salvageable in the general socialist idea? Any worthwhile elements?

Inheritance, he grants, is a very "imperfect" means of distributing the wealth of a society. The way is therefore open to reformers of goodwill, but they must take care not merely to criticize the existing system but rather to bring forth preferable alternatives. But Pareto still sees a number of problems—reformers ought to use clear and precise terms, and more important, the new social arrangement must be compatible with the character of men. "Every human society," argues Pareto, "includes some elements unadapted to the conditions of life of the particular society, and if the actions of these elements are not confined to certain limits, the society will be destroyed" (Vol. II, p. 131). This poses a difficult problem for socialists, because humanitarian sentiments (which he grants are "useful" up to a point) oppose the "necessity" of selecting and eliminating unadaptable elements. So Pareto sees two problems requiring solution: (1) Can the birth of unadaptable elements be reduced? (2) If not, can they be eliminated with a minimum of error in choice, with a minimum of suffering, and without violating humanitarian sentiments too much? Pareto thus offers us a "scientific" approach to the problem of selecting and eliminating the "poorly adapted," the "misfits."

Throughout his *Systèmes,* as in his later work, Pareto maintains that sentiment is the dominant and overwhelming force in social conduct, and that logic and rationality are of minimal significance. One must not stop at the "reasonings" of men—which are anything but reasonable—but go on to examine the underlying sentiments; sentiment for Pareto is an unchanging entity. Only the "reasonings" (or what he later calls "derivations") that justify and "explain" human conduct vary, not the sentiments. Just what are those sentiments or real forces, that are masked by, among other things, socialist rhetoric?

Pity, says Pareto, is one such prevalent sentiment, which impels men to sympathize with their fellows who suffer wrongs or pain and to seek a remedy. That is a very "useful" sentiment, he assures us, for it is the cement of society and the real basis of all ameliorative social doctrines. In the lower classes, there exists a sentiment that "has its sources in the suffering which those in these strata endure and in the desire to try to put an end to it by getting hold of the means which men in the higher strata enjoy, or quite simply by coveting what the other has" (Vol. I, p. 64). So, Pareto argues, "pity" manifests itself in socialist doctrine and men accept the doctrine for that "reason" and not for the "logico-experimental validity" of the doctrine. Why does socialism appeal mainly to the proletariat? Does the proletariat have a monopoly on the sentiment of pity? It has not escaped Pareto that socialist ideas have also appealed to individuals of the upper classes so he "explains" that fact as a result of the degeneration of the sentiment of pity, corresponding to a general degeneration of those classes (Vol. I, p. 65). In all epochs, humanitarian sentiments have given rise to sentimental reveries. When there is but a faint echo of that attitude in poetry or literature, that is a sign that the élite is strong, vigorous, and self-assured, but as the élite "decays," the expression of humanitarian sentiment grows. This, then, is Pareto's first major idea: the theory of sentiment, the manifestations of which he will later call "residues" and "derivations." His second major idea also appears for the first time in his *Systèmes.*

Sentiments change little or not at all. What does change is the form of appeal to certain sentiments and/or the justifications of certain actions motivated by sentiments. But here, to anticipate our later discussion somewhat, Pareto sees a distinction between the *élite* and the *nonélite.* The élite acts primarily on the basis of enlightened self-interest, whereas the lower, subject classes are moved largely by sentiment. To further its interests, the élite finds it expedient to appeal for support to the sentiments of the lower classes. Thus, the nonélite, the mass, is impelled into action by blind forces, while the élite conducts itself according to a rational understanding of its situation.

Élites and aristocracies do not last. They degenerate rather rapidly. Every élite therefore has the need to reinvigorate itself with reinforcements from the lower classes—its best elements. The decadence of the élite expresses itself in an outburst of sickly humanitarianism, while a new élite full of *strength* and *vigor* forms in the midst of the lower classes. "Every élite," writes Pareto, "that is not ready to fight to defend its position is in full decadence; there remains nothing for it to do but to vacate its place for another élite having the virile qualities which it lacks. It is by means of force that social institutions are established and it is by means of force that they are maintained" (Vol. I, p. 40). The struggle and circulation of élites is the stuff of history; therefore, popular uprisings are of no real consequence for the people. They serve merely to facilitate the fall of the old élite and the rise of the new. The élites use the lower classes, by paying lip service to their sentiments, in order to retain or to take power. "Most historians," writes Pareto, "do not see this movement. They describe the phenomenon as though it were the struggle of an aristocracy or oligarchy, always the same, against the people, always the same" (Vol. I, pp. 35–36). In reality, however, two aristocracies are struggling for power. The various revolutions of history, for example, the triumph of the bourgeoisie over the feudal aristocracy, achieved nothing for the people and neither will they do so in the future. There will be no definitive liberation of the human being.

Pareto's Sociology

Pareto defined sociology as the study of human society in general, and his declared aim in this work[6] was a general theory of society. More precisely, he wanted a theory of human conduct and chose as his point of departure an examination of the norms of scientific conduct, which is "logico-experimental," as is the typically rational conduct of *homo economicus*. Economic man acts on the basis of observation, experience, and logical reasoning. Do the logico-experimental norms so characteristic of scientific and economic conduct carry over into other areas? Do they guide man's other actions? There can be little doubt that Pareto had settled those questions in his own mind long before he undertook this copious study whose ostensible purpose was to answer them scientifically. His conclusions were not, contrary to what he would have us believe, the result of any inductive method.

Man's actions in general are nonlogical. That is the "hypothesis" Pareto wants to prove and account for in his sociology. How does he proceed? He does not ask whether, to what degree, and under what social circumstances man's general conduct is either logical or nonlogical. Rather, he defines logico-experimental conduct, confines it more or less exclusively to scientific and economic actions (though he might include certain military and political arts), and then by means of his residual definition classifies all other actions as nonlogical. He then proceeds to inundate us with illustrations of man's nonlogical or nonrational actions. Having convinced himself that all of man's acts that are "nonscientific" and "noneconomic" are also nonlogical, he needed a scientific explanation. Apparently he believed he was providing one in his concepts of "sentiments" and "residues," which he occasionally uses as synonyms for "values" but more often than not as unchanging, instinctual, biopsychic forces.[7]

The latter is also implied throughout Pareto's work in his treatment of residues (soon to be defined) as "constants." It makes no difference to Pareto whether it is a matter of worshipping fetishes or idols, saluting a flag, examining a creature's entrails to foretell the future, supporting universal suffrage, voting socialist, and so on—they are all manifestations of the unchanging psychic state of man. All those actions, different as they may appear, are motivated essentially by the same force, the same constant. What varies historically are the "explanations," "reasons," and theoretical justifications men provide for their actions. But those, the "derivations" as Pareto calls them (apparently because they are, in his view, derived from the sentiments), are to be regarded under all circumstances as the effects of the sentiment, *the ultimate cause* of both the nonlogical action and the nonlogical explanation. Only the action ("residue") and the rhetoric provided to justify it ("derivation") are observable, and both are the manifestations of a nonobservable, unchanging force—namely, the "sentiment." *How* the "constant" determines a variety of actions and how, according to any logic, constants can determine variables, Pareto never takes the pains to tell us. Furthermore, he does not attempt anywhere in his work to determine scientifically whether in fact man's conduct is predominantly nonrational but rather asserts it again and again, as he does his "purely scientific" intention. "We have no preconceptions, no a priori notions," he says somewhat naively and then proceeds, after he has distinguished the logical from the nonlogical, to give examples *only* of the latter. Logical or rational action is the appropriate linking of means to ends, appropriate not subjectively but objectively—that is, from the standpoint of an informed outside observer. Such rationality, Pareto would have us believe, is minimal if not altogether absent from most human conduct. He does occasionally grant somewhat inconsistently that logical actions are "very numerous" among "civilized" peoples, thereby implying that they are few and far between among the "noncivilized"; one is forced to wonder how man survived with little or no rationality and how the "primitives" survive if they have as little rational knowledge as Pareto suggests.

As for "logical actions," even among the civilized, Pareto drops them unceremoniously, never to weigh the proportion of them in man's total conduct. By means of the rather dubious "method" of citing examples of nonlogical conduct, Pareto believed that he had *demonstrated* the nonrationality of human conduct and that man is *by nature* nonrational and moved primarily, if not exclusively, by nonlogical forces. "Nonlogical actions," writes

Pareto, "originate chiefly in definite psychic states, and sentiments, subconscious feelings, and the like. It is the province of psychology to investigate such psychic states. Here we start with them as data of fact without going beyond that."[8]

In Pareto's system, A = sentiments, B = nonlogical conduct, and C = pseudological theory or rationale. People imagine that it is C that impelled them to act. In actuality, A determines both B and C, so that the causal relationship is AB, AC. Pareto is, however, prepared to assign some influence to C: The "existence of the theory C reacts upon the psychic state A and in many cases tends to reinforce it. The theory consequently influences B, following the line CAB" (Vol. I, p. 89). Actions can also have influence "upon the psychic state A and consequently upon the theory C, following the line BAC," and so on. A few paragraphs later, although he describes the psychic state very much as an effect of various social conditions, Pareto continues for some arbitrary reason to treat it as the main underlying cause of conduct:

> For example, C is the theory of free trade; D, the concrete adoption of free trade by a country; A, a psychic state that is in great part the product of individual interests, economic, political, and social, and of the circumstances under which people live. Direct relations between C and D are generally very tenuous. To work upon C in order to modify D leads to insignificant results. But any modification in A may react upon C and upon D. D and C will be seen to change simultaneously, and a superficial observer may think that D has changed because C has changed, whereas closer examination will reveal that D and C are not directly correlated, but depend both upon a common cause, A. (Vol. I, p. 91)

Here, clearly, social conditions, and economic, political, and other *interests* are assigned some importance. Do such interests and conditions conduce to rational conduct? Apparently not! In the very next paragraph, Pareto ignores the sociological implications of the previous one and proceeds as Pareto the psychologist to make a number of assertions that are never substantiated by the scientific empirical method he so celebrated:

> Theoretical discussions, C, are not, therefore, very serviceable directly for modifying D; indirectly they may be effective for modifying A. But to attain that objective, appeal must be made to sentiments rather than to logic and the results of experience. The situation may be stated, inexactly to be sure, because too absolutely, but nevertheless strikingly, by saying that in order to influence people thought has to be transformed into sentiment. (Vol. I, p. 91)

Inexact as the proposition is, Pareto nonetheless remains wedded to it: Sentiments, not rational interests, determine human conduct.

Throughout his exposition as, for example, in his discussion of magic and religion, he regards magical beliefs and practices as just so much nonsense. His approach is neither historical nor sociological, for he never stops to relate social conditions to certain beliefs and practices in various times and cultures. Since he is determined to show just how nonrational man is, he has nothing to say about the "scientific" knowledge and rational actions which play, no doubt, an essential role even in the most "primitive" of societies. Magic, religion, and so on, are regarded by Pareto as effects of "sentiments in which they originate (and which) are fairly common throughout the human race," not as correlates of the conditions under which men interact with each other and with the natural environment. The emphasis throughout is on institutionalized conduct as a manifestation of a psychic state, never vice versa. When he notes, for instance, the marked prominence of *law* in Roman culture, he "explains" it solely by reference to the prevailing *psychic state*. So important to him is that concept that he compares whole societies on that basis: "Among modern peoples, the English, at least down to last years of the nineteenth century, have more than any other people resembled the Romans in their *psychic state*" (Vol. I, p. 168, italics added). And that is all he has to say on the subject.

This, therefore, is the heart of the Paretian system, already adumbrated in his *Systèmes Socialistes*: Men are essentially nonlogical because they are impelled into action by nonlogical forces, namely, *sentiments*. But men also have a persistent "need" to "rationalize" their conduct, which they do by means of pseudological formulas. Together with his theory of élites, which occupies a very minor portion of his treatise, this constitutes the major theme of Pareto's work.

The Theory of Residues

In his one-volume discussion of "residues," Pareto focuses exclusively on what he has defined as nonlogical conduct and its alleged cause, which he labels "A." Element A, he now tells us, corresponds to "certain instincts of man, or more exactly men" and "is virtually constant in social phenomena."[9] Some instincts still remain outside his treatment. "Unaccounted for still," he adds, "would be simple appetites, tastes, inclinations, and in social relationships that very important class called `interests'". Pareto thus manufactures "instincts" as he requires them, and, moreover, always subsumes "interests" under his general rubric of nonlogical action. Why interests should be thus regarded and not as a relatively rational category, he does not say.

Pareto, who repeatedly calls for scientific precision, provides us with concepts that are anything but precise. Sometimes he really means "instinct" in the sense of a biological urge, such as sex. But at other times his use of the term either approximates the sociological concept of "value" or resolves itself into plain nonsense. In the United States, he writes, "the improvident instinct has fathered a theory that people ought to spend all they earn; and so analysis of that theory yields a quantum *a* which will be improvidence" (Vol. II, 853).

What Pareto himself never explains, but which becomes clear if one understands whom and what he is arguing *against*, is why "interests" should be conceived as nonrational. That social groups and classes have interests which are served by certain theories he readily acknowledges; but that the pursuit of interests is rational conduct he denies. "Interests" for Pareto are a nonlogical category, always subordinate to instinct and synonymous with sentiment. Animals have instincts *only*, but no theories, he assures us. Men, on the other hand, have instincts, "interests," and theories.

Now he introduces his peculiar terminology, simply, he says, to avoid embarrassing his exposition with symbols and letters and to make it easier to follow. Element A from now on will be called *residues*, what is left over, that is, when conduct is divested of its variable elements; residue is therefore the constant element and always reducible to the principle underlying nonlogical action or "reasoning." "Residues," writes Pareto, "correspond to certain instincts in human beings . . . " (Vol. II, 870). Element B in the Paretian system is called *derivations* and refers to the nonlogico-experimental theories. In addition, he introduces an element C, which he calls *derivatives;* apparently he regarded it as a kind of secondary theoretical manifestation of A, but never again uses the term.

No sooner does he introduce these terms than he cautions us about their use:

> The residues *a* must not be confused with the sentiments or instincts to which they correspond. The residues are the manifestations of sentiments and instincts just as the rising of the mercury in a thermometer is a manifestation of the rise in temperature. Only elliptically and for the sake of brevity do we say that residues, along with appetites, interests, etc., are the main factors in determining the social equilibrium. . . . The completed statement would be: "The sentiments or instincts that correspond to residues, along with those corresponding to appetites, interests, etc., are the main factors in determining the social equilibrium." (Vol. II, p. 975)

We are thus returned to the original simple formula: The underlying instinct or sentiment is the key force—in the strictest sense, the Paretian source or "principle" of nonlogical action. "Residue," then, refers to the overt conduct (verbal or nonverbal) that is a manifestation of the sentiment and/or instinct; and "derivation" is the strictly verbal "explanation," justification, or rationale one provides for one's act.

At times, sentiment is a fundamental individual property and at others a group characteristic. Pareto never settled in his own mind whether it was to be regarded as part and parcel of an individual's biopsychic drives or as a cultural belief acquired through tradition. Often he uses the term to refer to a nonlogical idea, or superstition, that has been perpetuated over so long a period of time as to become a residue: "The bad omen . . . that is associated with the presence of thirteen persons may be a derivative from the sentiment of horror at Judas' betrayal followed by his suicide; but that derivative has become a residue by this time, and people feel ill at ease at a table of thirteen without the least thought of Judas" (Vol. II, 877). That Pareto himself sensed his lack of clarity, consistency, and precision may be gathered from his periodic warnings to the effect that "all pointers just given must be kept in mind at all times in the investigations following. Anyone forgetting them will get everything askew" (Vol. II, 878).

Instincts or sentiments (residues) differ among themselves and Pareto distinguishes six types:

1. *Instinct for combinations.* A term he uses synonymously with "ability to think," "inventiveness," "imagination," "ingenuity," "originality," and so on. In terms of consequences, this residue has led to human "progress," a term Pareto does not define.

2. *Instinct of group persistence, or persistence of aggregates.* Persistence of relations between a person and other persons or places:

- Relationships of family and kindred groups
- Relations with places
- Relations of social class
- Persistence of relations between the living and the dead
- Persistence of relations between a dead person and the things that belonged to him in life
- Persistence of abstractions
- Persistence of uniformities
- Sentiments transformed into objective realities
- Personifications
- Need of new abstractions

As we see, relationships of social class are included here and thus summarily *defined* as nonrational; his "proof" consists of examples of nonrational conduct among workers.

3. *Need of expressing sentiments by external acts.* Need of "doing something" expressing itself in combinations:

- Religious ecstasies

4. *"Residues connected with sociality."* This refers to the "need" for uniformity and conformity. Neophobia, self-pity, repugnance to suffering, and so on, are also included, as are "risking one's life," "sharing one's property with others," "sentiments of superiors," and "sentiments of inferiors," "need of group approbation," and "asceticism."

5. *"Integrity of the individual and his appurtenances."* Here Pareto includes "resistance to the social equilibrium" (always nonrational by definition), "sentiments of equality in inferiors," the restoration of individual integrity, and so on.

6. *The sex residue.* Though he has given us six types of residue, he employs primarily the first two and rarely has anything to say about the remaining four.

Class I Residues

"Taking Class I as a whole," Pareto writes, "one notes: (1) a propensity for combinations; (2) a search for the combinations that are deemed best; (3) a propensity to believe that they actually do what is expected of them" (Vol. II, 889). This class is "experimental" not in the sense of "logico-experimental" but in the sense of playfully trying all sorts of combinations, toying with things, making unexpected discoveries, and doing things having unexpected consequences. All that, says Pareto, has led to "progress." The combinations residue is the common basis of theology, metaphysics, *and* experimental science. "Those three kinds of activity are probably manifestations of one same psychic state, on the extinction of which they would vanish simultaneously" (Vol. II, 974).

Though derived from the same psychic condition, there is an insuperable barrier between the logical and the nonlogical. If A is always seen in conjunction with B, logico-experimental science infers that it is highly probable that they will continue to appear together. No "necessity" is ascribed to this proposition, for then one is superimposing something nonexperimental on the proposition—an act of faith. The scientist adds something too; he "imagines" and "invents" and is guided by preconceptions, guesses, and assumptions. But in his case, Pareto avers, "Experience will be there to rectify any error that may develop from the sentiment he feels" (Vol. II, 977). For the nonscientist, in contrast, sentiment plays a key role, and propositions are accepted on faith. That is the rule among the majority of humans, and the more intimate the contact between the scientist and the population at large, the greater the likelihood that the scientist will succumb to popular conceptions and be blinded to the conflict between experience and beliefs based on sentiment. "That is why the study of the social sciences finds it more difficult to adhere to the logico-experimental method than, for instance, the chemist or the physicist" (Vol. II, 979).

Occasionally, we are surprised to learn that despite the "constant" sentiments, superstition has declined among the masses, which can be attributed to the advance of science and the "enormous development of industrial life." Recognizing, however, that he is thereby opening the door to the possibility of growing rationality—even among the "people"—he drops the point and never treats as an empirical question whether, to what degree, and in which areas of social life, Everyman is guided by rational norms. By and large, rationality remains for Pareto the exclusive province of the scientific, economic, political, and military élites, and nonrationality, the province of the "masses."

Class II Residues

This brings us to class II residues, the persistence of aggregates—habits, customs, traditions, and other beliefs and practices that persist through time. Basic to Pareto's theory of social equilibrium and circulation of élites, and to his conception of society and history, these "persistences" reside primarily in the masses—or more correctly in the individuals making up the mass. Livingston offers the following interpretation:

> The tendency of the mind (the instinct, sentiment, impulse) that creates such units is the force now of first, now of second, importance in determining the social equilibrium. The intensity of the impulse or sentiment in individuals determines what we ordinarily call "character." In society at large it determines the type of civilization or culture. (Vol. II, 991n)

The aggregate of persistent elements may refer to beliefs in the "devil," in "Santa Claus," in "democracy," and so on. For Pareto they are all substantially the same—nonlogical elements, passively received, accepted, and tenaciously held. This again is traced by Pareto to an "instinct." "After the group has been constituted," he writes, "an instinct very often comes into play that tends with varying energy to prevent the things so combined from being disjoined. . . . This instinct may be compared roughly to mechanical inertia: it tends to resist the movement imparted by other instincts."

It is among the "masses" at large that this residue is most active; the social equilibrium and the decline of one élite and the rise of another depend on the degree of success with which an élite can invent formulas that appeal to the dominant sentiments of the masses. The mass is passive in its reception and retention of virtually unchanging sentiments and the élite is active in exploiting those sentiments by means of its ingenious formulas. Just as the sentiments remain unchanged, so do the conditions of the masses regardless of how often élites change positions. In the final analysis, it is not the social conditions of the masses that determine their sentiments, but quite the reverse. The mass always remains blindly nonrational because it is controlled or moved by sub- or unconscious "forces," "impulses," "instincts," or "sentiments."

Nowhere in his exposition does Pareto systematically consider any causal forces outside his residues, the prime mover to which he returns again and again. There is no attempt anywhere to relate the contrasting character and conduct of the "élite" and the "mass" to their respective cultural conditions. The "stupidity" of the mass is an eternal trait because it is the result of those constant residues. There will always be an élite and always a mass—and all this follows from Pareto's "method" and ultimately from his own sentiments. Despite his admonishments about the need for "objectivity," he transforms what may be a tenable proposition under certain sociohistorical conditions into a suprahistorical philosophy, and provides us with a new theory of "historical inevitability." There is nothing metaphysical, he apparently believed, in the assertion that "forms" change but the "thing in itself" (sentiment) remains constant. It is only a change in form, he insists, if yesterday "witches" were burned and thieves hanged, and today "sex heretics and thieves alike get off with mere terms in prison" (Vol. II, 1010).

In almost every case, the "sentiment" is employed as the chief explanatory principle; then, suddenly, as an aside, Pareto injects a remark that is supposed presumably to refute simultaneously the idealistic and "materialistic" viewpoints. "Erroneous the idealistic theory that regards the residue as the cause of facts. Likewise erroneous, but at times less so, is the materialistic theory that regards the facts as the cause of the residue. In reality, the facts reinforce the residue, and the residue the facts. Changes occur because new forces came into play to affect either the facts or the residue or both—new circumstances occasion changes in modes of life" (Vol. II, 1014). Thus he almost, but not quite, makes a concession to the Marxian view: *"New circumstances,"* he says, *"occasion changes in modes of life."* What are those "new circumstances"? Are they new social facts? If so, does not that tend to undermine the theory of residues particularly if the new facts lead to changes in the mode of life? At best, this formulation is an equivocal "theory," in which everything interacts with everything else and nothing is quite determinable. But the "interactionist" view, presumably superior to any one-sided view, is never developed. He continually reverts to the causal priority of sentiments and believes, apparently, that he is confirming the proposition by piling up hundreds of cases of ostensibly nonrational behavior—*substantially* the same everywhere and at all times because they are the product of the underlying, unchanging sentiments.

Classes III and IV

Pareto now argues that acts not only manifest and strengthen sentiments but "may even arouse them." People have a "need" to do something, "to act"; but then "doing something" can engender the "need." He proliferates "needs" as required to "explain" the various phenomena that have caught his eye. So now, as he presents his class IV—Residues Connected with Sociality—he says: "This class is made up of residues connected with life in society"—whatever that is supposed to mean—and adds: "A need for particular associations is observable among the majority of peoples. They are of many different kinds. Some are for purposes of mere amusement, others for purposes of individual advantage. Still others have religious, political, literary, or other purposes" (Vol. II, 1114). There is a "need" for particular associations and whether one joins a church, political party, social club, or what have you, it is all the same, since it is determined by the single common underlying need. Pareto goes on to enumerate still other subcategories of this residue—the need for uniformity, conformity, and imitation. Especially interesting is the residue called Self-Pity Extended to Others. That, we are told, accounts for the phenomenon of humanitarianism, as does the Instinctive Repugnance to Suffering:

> This is a sentiment of disgust at the sight of all suffering, regardless of whether it be beneficial or otherwise. . . . The sentiment is often observable in weak, submissive, spineless individuals. If they chance to succeed in overcoming it, they are likely to show themselves exceedingly cruel. That explains a remark one sometimes hears to the effect that women are more tender-hearted and at the same time more cruel than men. (Vol. II, 1142)

Here as elsewhere, one cannot help wondering in what sense Pareto fancies this to be science.

We learn, in addition, that there are sentiments of social ranking—of superiors and inferiors, of group approbation and asceticism, that he views as a uniquely human phenomenon and explores at some length. Though he attributes varying "utilities" to ascetic practices, he treats them all, not surprisingly, as effects of the same residue and, of course, as nonrational conduct. But he fails here as elsewhere to give even passing attention to the possibility that certain forms of asceticism may be very rational indeed—as Max Weber had argued in his thesis regarding the Protestant ethic and the spirit of capitalism.

Class V: The Integrity of the Individual, His Appurtenances, and Possessions

This class is a complement of the previous one and refers to sentiment (whether natural or learned Pareto does not say) which prompts one "to defend one's own things and strive to increase their quantity." This he relates to what he calls the "social equilibrium."

In a slave system, as, for example, in ancient Greece, even if one is not himself a slave owner, he may feel that the slave owner is wronged by having the slave taken from him. That, we are told, flows from "sentiments of resistance to alterations in the [prevailing] social equilibrium." A partially ideal equilibrium would be one in which another citizen would make all Greeks free men and all barbarians slaves. An altogether ideal equilibrium, for the times, would be the demand for the total abolition of slavery. If the existing equilibrium is disturbed or altered, "forces" come into play which tend to reestablish it. Those forces are, of course, the sentiments which manifest themselves in the various types of residues, themselves in turn masked by derivations. The masses know nothing of "equilibrium," "forces," and so on, which, we are told, are "scientific" terms utilized only by the scientist. "Just" and "unjust," "right" and "wrong" are the words plain people use to express whether they approve of something or whether it offends their sentiments. Pareto tells us little or nothing more about his concept of social equilibrium, but the illustrations he employs fit into his total picture of man as a nonrational being. Man is "not inspired by any `ideal of justice,' but by his instinct of self-preservation, an instinct that he shares with animals and which has nothing to do with any `ideal' of `justice'" (Vol. II, 1213).

Self-preservation, a quasi-biological concept, suits Pareto's purposes, for it serves to accentuate the animal-like character of human action in general. Again he seeks to eliminate from the question of "social equilibrium" anything remotely resembling interest in the rational sense. He studiously avoids looking at social acts in any way which might disclose some degree of rationality. His own example, however, lends itself to rational interpretation, for when individuals feel threatened, physically or otherwise, the course they adopt to protect and defend themselves may be altogether rational. Whether, and to what degree, reactions to "threats" are rational ought to be an empirical question for Pareto; but he never treats it as such. If, to pursue another of his own examples, slaveholders respond to the slave uprising by repressing it harshly, that may or may not be to their "interest," but if Pareto's "objective outside observer" determines that the success of the uprising would have adversely affected the wealth and power of the slaveholders, then their reaction was, at least in part, rational. Similarly, there is no good reason why the uprising should be regarded as nonrational from the standpoint of the slaves. Of course, the problem is complicated by short- and long-run interests and the like, but if the concept of rationality is to have any meaning at all, then there is no sound reason why either the uprising or its suppression should be viewed as inherently nonrational, which, in effect, is Pareto's position.

Pareto consistently views "sentimental" and rational conduct as mutually exclusive. If his intention had been as scientific as he claimed, he would have adopted a different methodological approach designed to measure the degree of rationality of the acts in question, and, equally important, he would have distinguished types of rational conduct. That Pareto did not regard the degree to which interests and acts are rational as an empirical question is evident from his many illustrations. Here one will suffice to show that his polemical aim led him to deny dogmatically the rational character of certain acts.

Discussing the sentiment of equality in social inferiors, he says that it "is often a defense of integrity on the part of an individual belonging to a lower class and a means of lifting him to a higher one." If the demand for equality is indeed a means of lifting an individual from a lower to a higher social position, why is that nonrational? Because Pareto prefers to see the demand taking place "without any awareness, on the part of the individual experiencing the sentiment, of the difference between his real and apparent purposes. He talks of the interest of his social class instead of his own personal interest simply because that is a fashionable mode of expression" (Vol. II, 1220). For Pareto, it is inconceivable, apparently, that an individual from the lower class might arrive at the rational conclusion that he could further his personal interests by furthering those of his social class. Sensing that he might have gone too far, that he has, in effect, emptied social life of *all* rational content, Pareto returns now and again to say that "nonlogical actions play a great part in social life." And if that is all he meant, who would disagree?

Even when he himself has provided an example of eminently rational conduct, he refuses to view it as such. The following, for instance, is for some reason nonrational for Pareto: The "tendency is to admit to the advantages all whose cooperation helps one toward obtaining them so that their introduction yields more in profit than in cost; and to exclude all who do not help, or help less effectively, so that their participation costs more than it yields" (Vol. II, 1221). What, one wonders, could be more rational than that? And even if, as Pareto insists, the demand for equality on the part of the socially disadvantaged is really a demand for inequality, but this time in their favor, that only illustrates the possible deception of self and others but does not diminish the rationality of the demand.

Pareto's dichotomy of rational/nonrational allows for no gradations between polar opposites; acts are always either one or the other. Since the effectiveness of his polemic rests on "proving" that it is the nonrational that dominates social life, and must continue to do so, he ignores the subtle mixtures of rational and nonrational one encounters in any society. The fact that some human associations may rest predominantly on a "sentimental" and affective basis, and others on a cognitive-rational one, is not given any consideration. For Pareto, cognitive-rational man is *always* and *everywhere* subordinate to and dominated by sentimental-affective man. The very "method" he employed—defining logico-experimental conduct, arbitrarily assigning it to very narrow spheres, and then proceeding to examine the other spheres of conduct, a priori *defined* as nonlogical—led him unswervingly to the very conclusion he had as a hypothesis: Human conduct is so thoroughly nonrational as to preclude any possibility of consciously and rationally altering the social order. Man acts as a result of sentimental causes, which are so pervasive and powerful that they cannot be counteracted or overcome by his weak, insignificant, and occasional efforts at conscious, rational action. Thus Pareto's work, its title notwithstanding, can hardly be regarded as sociology, for he virtually ignores the question of *social* conditions that tend to facilitate or impede the possibility of rational action. And, when he arrives at his sixth and final class of residues, it becomes even more evident than before that he is putting forth an instinctual psychology.

Class VI: The Sex Residue

"Mere sexual appetite," writes Pareto, "though powerfully active in the human race, is no concern of ours here. . . . " The sex "instinct" interests him "only so far as it influences theories, modes of thinking—as a residue" (Vol. II, 1324). This instinct is "often . . . `logicalized' and `dissembled' under the guise of asceticism; there are people who preach virtue as a way of lingering, in their thoughts, on sex matters." Here, Pareto clearly employs the concept of residue as a manifestation of an instinctual urge rooted in the biochemical bodily processes. If in the case of the other residues he appears never to have decided whether "instinct" is a biological force or a cultural factor, now it is unequivocally the former. The sex instinct "gives rise" to actions that are constant, that have persisted throughout history, and that are ubiquitous in the present. Such actions, the residues, are attempts to control, regulate, repress, pervert, and invert the natural instinct. That has resulted in the "religion of sex" and "as in many other religions, inflexibility in forms gives rise to perversion and hypocrisy . . ." (Vol. II, 852). The various sex taboos, forms of prudery, abstinence, and asceticism are just so many ways of hiding sexual desire—just so many forms of a "nonlogical" reaction to a powerful internal force.

Again, it is Pareto the psychologist talking: The "sex residue is active not only in mental states looking to unions of the sexes or lingering in recollections of such things, but also in mental states that evince censure, repugnance, or hatred towards matters of sex . . ." (Vol. II, 1331). One seeks in vain an attempt to explain certain taboos, proscriptions, ascetic practices, and so on, by relating them to other sociocultural conditions; the absence of such an attempt is all the more striking when one recalls that Pareto has been honored as one of the founders of functional analysis in sociology. Actually, one finds no analysis of any kind—only illustrations of "omnipresent" residues. Thus we learn that the residue is "active" in speech and writing; it "figures actively" in literature, and when moderns talk of "immoral" literature, for instance, that "oftentimes is a mere matter of hypocrisy, people shrinking at the word and not at the thing, and doing the thing but avoiding the word . . ." (Vol. II, 1334). Pareto is engaged here in an "unmasking" venture. Virtue, sexual morality, and so on are just rhetoric designed to hide one's lust.

The sex residue is a "constant" as are the others. That is evident, says Pareto, from the "constant" [?] types of reaction one witnesses throughout history to violations of taboos. Such violations of the dogmas of the "sex-religion" engender reactions not unlike the reactions to violations of other religious dogmas. The changes through time in sexual morality and the variations from one culture to another are viewed as mere changes in "form." Why do the "nonlogical" manifestations of the sex residue so annoy him? Because in the United States, for example, that "paradise of sex hypocrisy," the "mails refuse to carry an English novel because it is deemed `sensuous'; but they carry without the slightest scruple publications that preach slaughtering the moneyed class and robbing them of their property. But, really, can anyone keeping strictly to logic and experience consider such activities less harmful to individual and society than a little `sensuality' in print?" He continues: "In some cities in the United States the authorities send policewomen about the streets to provoke `mashers' and arrest them, but they never [?] hire detectives to provoke anarchists to crimes of violence and then arrest them" (Vol. II, 1345).

The sex residue, for Pareto, epitomizes the general character of residues: unchanging, invincible forces over which man has little or no control. Only the "derivations" change, but they do not significantly affect the nature of man's existence.

SENTIMENT IN THINKING: THE THEORY OF DERIVATIONS

People have a "need" to make their nonlogical conduct appear logical; they therefore provide pseudological explanations for their acts and mistakenly believe the "explanation" is the cause of their conduct. In actuality, however, says Pareto, they are impelled into action by sentiments. Derivations "derive the force they have, not, or at least not exclusively, from logico-experimental considerations but from sentiments" (Vol. III, 1397). The qualifying phrase, "or at least not exclusively," which Pareto sees fit to insert from time to time, would seem to indicate some reservation on his part. Yet, he does not deem it scientifically worthy of his attention to ask certain obvious sociological questions: (1) Which areas of social life seem to be dominated by sentiment and which by rational considerations? (2) Have there been any historical changes in that respect? (3) What appear to be the *social* correlates of greater rationality in certain contexts and periods and, conversely, of the greater role of sentiment in other contexts and periods? (4) What is the significance of a preponderance of rationality or nonrationality in given contexts?

Further, is it a fruitful way of viewing things to argue that all nonrational conduct is the same? That magic, nationalism, sex, idol worship, class solidarity, socialism, and so on are all different "forms" of the same psychic force? To pursue the problem of the relation of the rational to the nonrational, it may be worthwhile to contrast Pareto's procedure with that of another sociologist.

Pareto notes that in certain primitive societies men are confronted with the phenomenon of a storm and seek ways of dealing with it—all nonlogical. Another "functionalist," Bronislaw Malinowski, studied the same phenomenon among the Trobrianders. Malinowski observed the use of canoe magic and sought to understand it, not by inventing a series of residues, but by relating magic to the social context in which it was employed—deep-sea fishing. As he proceeded to study the phenomenon, he concluded that these people are both rational and nonrational; they employ both "scientific" and supernatural techniques and the degree to which one dominates, or supplements, the other depends on the circumstances in question.

These "primitives," Malinowski noted, understood very well indeed that, for instance, the outrigger canoe had to be constructed according to definite specifications if it was to be serviceable at sea; a minimum of "scientific" or technical knowledge was necessary. They knew what kind of equipment was most appropriate for deep-sea fishing; they had learned from experience that certain forms of social cooperation were most effective in that type of undertaking and they also had and used experiential knowledge about weather conditions at sea. They were not so foolish (in Pareto's terms, nonlogical) as to begin the expedition when the sky was overcast and a storm seemed likely. In all those terms, then, they were rational, and employed, in however rudimentary a way, naturalistic knowledge (logico-experimental norms, in Pareto's terms).

Yet, much to their chagrin, these stalwart fishermen had learned that their "scientific" knowledge was not enough to ensure their success and their safe return home. Why not? Because after they had carefully taken into account and controlled all the factors they could, unanticipated disasters befell them. Occasionally, they embarked on an expedition when the sea behaved as an inland lake on a summer day. Then, at sea, suddenly a bolt from the blue, an unexpected storm, and disaster. Here was an event they could neither foresee nor control. Hence, notes Malinowski, it was the task of the canoe magician to cope with that force to forestall unforeseen disasters. To be sure, from the standpoint of a modern Western observer, magic here as elsewhere is "nonlogical," or supernatural nonsense, but Malinowski provides insight into the conditions in which magic supplements "science." When magic is employed, some of its *latent functions*—for example, allaying anxiety—are now better understood than before. To strengthen his thesis that magical practices are resorted to only under certain circumstances, he investigated lagoon fishing and found that where knowledge and control are sufficient, magic is *not* employed.

Surely, this "functional" approach is a much more fruitful one than Pareto's, in which no insights are given into the conditions of social life under which men tend to be more or less rational. Pareto's treatment of residues as constants obscures the extent to which all conduct, and not least what he calls nonlogical conduct, varies with other conditions. If Marx's method made it possible to ask how social consciousness varied with the conditions of social existence, Pareto's method, in contrast, is designed to deny historical change. He always comes back to the "sentimental" determination of thinking and doing and insists that despite "apparent" changes, the sentimental force remains dominant.

Derivations are persuasive because they are, together with the residues, manifestations of the sentiments. They are persuasive not only because they are derived from an individual's own sentiments, but also because they appeal to the dominant sentiments: to the authority of maxims prevalent in the community, to the authority of outstanding individuals, to the authority of supernatural beings. But all such derivations are just so much "fatuous, inconclusive `talk' " covering up the ultimate cause—sentiment—where Pareto always stops his analysis. When, he writes, a student of human conduct "sets out to study social phenomena, he halts at manifestations of social activity, that is to say at derivations, and does not carry his inquiry into the causes of the activity, that is to say, into residues" (Vol. III, 1402). Did Pareto not see that he, too, has halted arbitrarily—with the sentiments? He was dogmatically committed to the proposition that in order to induce "people to act in a given way, one must necessarily resort to derivations, for they are the only language that reaches the human being in his sentiments . . ." (Vol. III, 1043).

Not surprisingly the residue is a force that transcends different cultures, or, in other words, it is one and the same determinant of action in all cultures: "A Chinese, a Moslem, a Calvinist, a Catholic, a Kantian, a Hegelian, a Materialist, all refrain from stealing; but each gives a different explanation of his conduct. In other words, it is a case of a number of derivations connecting one residue that is operative in all of them with one conclusion which they all accept" (Vol. III, 1416).

Two problems must be kept distinct, says Pareto: first, how residues and derivations function, and, second, their bearing on social utility. He wants to examine the problems in that order but as he proceeds, his definitions, one finds, are confused and even contradictory. Henceforth, we are told, it would be better to view a "derivation" (presumably itself a "manifestation") under two aspects: "derivation proper and the manifestation to which it leads." By "derivation proper" Pareto refers to "the need for logical developments which human beings feel." That "need" also has a "manifestation"—"reasonings of different kinds." So cryptic is Pareto's discussion here that the editor, A. Livingston, is brought to remark: "The `manifestation' would really be a `derivative' and why Pareto discards this term, which is quite his own, for an obscurer `manifestation' must remain a mystery" (Vol. III, 1688).

The impression is inescapable that Pareto himself is not sure how he wants to use his terms. He writes that "since sentiments are manifested by residues we shall often, for the sake of brevity, use the word `residues' as including the sentiments that they manifest." Therefore, when he says that residues are the elements which determine the social equilibrium, Pareto wants us to translate that to mean: "The sentiments manifested by residues are among the elements which stand toward the social equilibrium in a relationship of reciprocal determination." He is still not satisfied, however, for he notes that this remains too elliptical and might be taken to mean that he is ascribing objective existence to sentiments, something he assures us he does not want to do. "What we observe in reality," he writes, "is a group of human beings in a mental condition indicated by what we call sentiments." So, again we are requested to translate his proposition into the following terms: "The mental states that are indicated by the sentiments expressed in residues are among the elements that stand in a relation of reciprocal determination with the social equilibrium." Recognizing that he has gained nothing by that, he adds:

> But if we would express ourselves in a language altogether exact, that is still not enough. What in the world are those "mental states" or, if one will, those "psychic conditions"? They are abstractions. And what underlies the abstractions? So we are obliged to say: "The actions of human beings are among the elements that stand in a relationship of reciprocal determination with the social equilibrium. Among such actions are certain manifestations that we designate by the term `residues' and which are closely correlated with other acts so that once we know the residues we may, under certain circumstances, know the actions. Therefore, we shall say that residues are among the elements that stand in a relationship or reciprocal determination with the social equilibrium." (Vol. III, 1690)

So we are back to residues which are actions correlated with other actions. Acts now seem to be the key factor. Now that he has "clarified" matters for us, to avoid being pedantic, he will use the short form of the proposition: "residues are among the elements that determine the social equilibrium." But in a footnote to the same proposition, he reverts to the term "sentiment" which corresponds, he says, to the term "force" in the study of mechanics. Having sensed, perhaps, that speaking of acts and acts alone might undermine his entire thesis, he refuses to abandon the underlying nonlogical force and returns, in the next paragraph, to the older formulation: ". . . derivations also manifest sentiments. Directly they manifest the sentiments that correspond to the residues in which they originate. Indirectly they manifest sentiments through the residues that serve for purposes of derivation" (Vol. III, 1690).

The old causal chain is thus restored. It begins with "sentiment," or "instinct," which motivates nonlogical actions (residues), which in turn are "logicalized" (always with pseudologic) as "derivations." Pareto continues to view what he regards as the nonlogical acts of humans as *instinctive* in the same sense as is true of chicks: "The hen defends her chicks" expresses a uniformity, and "present in the hen is the sentiment that prompts her to defend her chicks," and "that defense is a consequence of a given psychic state." Likewise, says Pareto, uniformities in human conduct may be explained "by saying that human beings—or some human beings—sacrifice their lives for their countries, that present in them is a sentiment which prompts them to sacrifice their lives for their countries, that such sacrifice is the consequence of a given psychic state" (Vol. III, 1690). On the one hand, he traces acts to sentiments, and, on the other, he acknowledges that in speaking of sentiments, instincts, psychic states, and so on, he is adding something nonempirical to his proposition. "All that experimental observation shows is a set of simultaneous facts—men dying for their countries and using certain modes of speech." But he has closed himself off from a sociological analysis of that datum—Under what social circumstances do men act that way?—and never abandons "sentiment" and "instinct" as his chief explanatory principle.

Ultimately, his theory of the structure of society is *psychological*: The so-called social equilibrium is determined by the distribution of psychological attributes or, more precisely, by the distribution of individuals holding those attributes. All other conditions are virtually ignored. What emerges, then, is a conception in which societies change little or not at all. Pareto argues this by means of his distinction between "substance" and "form," which when used by others is metaphysical but used by him is "scientific." "Observable in . . . historical societies are phenomena that vary little in substance, but widely in forms. As the various religions succeed one another in history, their forms may be as different as one pleases, but after all they are all expressions of religious sentiments that vary but slightly. The same may be said of the various forms of government . . ." (Vol. III, 1695).

"There is nothing new under the sun," said Ecclesiastes; there are no substantial changes in history nor will there ever be, says Pareto. How does Pareto explain the absence of "substantial" change? By the substantial proportion of people who believed, and continue to believe, nonlogical nonsense. "We have no accurate statistics," he writes, "to show the exact number of such persons and therefore whether and to what extent their relative proportion to population has changed. Certain it is that the proportion has been and remains a very considerable one, that it has never been and is not now small." That proportion can never be reduced and the "people" will remain eternally incompetent and stupid. All religions are "varying forms of a single substance. . . . Socialism made room for itself by crowding back some of the prevailing faiths such as Catholicism and nationalism, and assimilating others . . . " (Vol. III, 1702). Pareto's social equilibrium thus rests on the unchanging sentiments. All religions stem from the same sentiment. In any single society, therefore, the decline of one form is accompanied by the rise of another. "Religion" in general will remain constant, since it is forever generated anew by the sentiments. Similarly, the "submissiveness" of the "people" has not changed; the sentiments of subordination which in the past led to the submission of the lower to the higher classes express themselves today in the submission of the lower classes to the leaders of the trade unions and political parties.

Pareto therefore sees "advantages" for "society" in "having a community divided into two parts, the one in which knowledge prevails, ruling and directing the other in which sentiments prevail so that, in the end, action is vigorous and wisely directed" (Vol. III, 1786). "The art of government lies in finding ways to take advantage of such sentiments, not in wasting one's energies in futile efforts to destroy them . . ." (Vol. III, 1843). As Pareto proceeds to apply his "utilitarian calculus," his ideological position occasionally becomes more explicit. He unabashedly tells us, for instance, that "it is advantageous to society that individuals not of the ruling classes should spontaneously accept, observe, respect, revere, love, the precepts current in their society . . ." (Vol. III, 1932). Pareto has determined what is best for "society" and how it is best maintained—by an élite that exploits the sentiments of the ignorant masses. In an earlier era, their ignorance could be explained by the "difficulties that lay in the way of teaching the ignorant. But that excuse is no longer valid," says Pareto, for now "it is evident even to the blind that if the ignorant do not learn, it is because they will not" (Vol. III, 2016).

SOCIETY, ÉLITES, AND FORCE

Social differentiation, for Pareto, refers primarily to the fact that individuals are "physically, morally, and intellectually different." More, some individuals are "superior" to others. Pareto uses the term *élite* to refer to "superiority"—in intelligence, character, skill, capacity, power, and so on. Although he allows for the possibility that some people are given the label of élite without in fact possessing those qualities, on balance he sticks to the proposition that those who possess élite qualities become élites. One can measure the degree of excellence in every human endeavor, in prostitution and theft as well as in law and medicine, and assign to the individuals in each an index ranging from 0 to 10. A grade of 10 may thus be assigned to the very best in each field, reserving 0 for the man who is a good-for-nothing or an "out-and-out idiot." Napoleon, he says, "was certainly not an idiot, nor a man of little account, as millions of others are. He had exceptional qualities . . ." (Vol. III, 2029). Thus the élite of a society consists of those with the highest indices in their branches of activity. This Pareto divided into two: a *governing élite,* that is, those "who directly or indirectly play some considerable part in government, and a *nongoverning élite,* comprising the rest" (Vol. III, 2032). Together they constitute the higher stratum, or class, of the society. The lower stratum or nonélite, in contrast, are those with whose political influence "we are not just here concerned"—and whose influence turns out to be practically nil from Pareto's standpoint. To the rulers and the ruled, Pareto relates his residues—but only the first two classes of residues, for he has nothing more to say about the remaining four.

There is, according to Pareto, a predominance of Class I residues in the higher stratum, and a predominance of Class II in the lower. More precisely, in the higher stratum "Class II residues gradually lose in strength, until now and again they are reinforced by tides upwelling from the lower stratum." Revolutions are in fact great religious tides, the upward thrusts of lower classes strong in class II residues. Residues are also invoked to explain why "history is the graveyard of aristocracies;" for the élite decays in quantity and quality—that is, in the requisite residues that "enabled them to win their power and hold it. The governing class is restored not only in numbers, but—and this is the more important thing—in quality, by families rising from the lower classes and bringing with them the vigor and the proportions of residues necessary for keeping themselves in power. It is also restored by the loss of its more degenerate members" (Vol. III, 2054). If the circulation ceases, the governing class collapses and "sweeps the whole of a nation along with it. Potent cause of disturbance in the equilibrium is the accumulation of superior elements in the lower classes and, conversely, of inferior elements in the higher classes" (Vol. III, 2055). Thus the rudiments of Pareto's theory of revolution. But the "theory" includes another important element, *force*, which, for Pareto, may be the more important one. "Superior elements" are not only those "fit to rule" but those willing to use force. Inferior and decadent elements are unfit and fear its use. The "decaying" élite, shying away from the use of force, tries to buy off its adversaries; it becomes less the lion and more the fox and, therefore, increasingly vulnerable to the new lions.

"Societies in general subsist," writes Pareto in one of his typical "explanations," "because alive and vigorous in the majority of their constituent members are sentiments corresponding to residues of sociality (class IV). "A gregarious instinct in men binds them together. "But," he adds, "there are also individuals in human societies in whom some at least of those sentiments are weak or indeed actually missing." Whether the society will subsist or dissolve depends on the relative proportion and strength of social sentiments within it. Corresponding to the distribution and intensity of such sentiments (that is, individuals holding them), one will find a society either more or less "uniform" or inclined to change: The greater the proportion and intensity of the residues of sociality, the greater the uniformity, and conversely, the weaker they are, the greater the tendency toward change. Societies are essentially "heterogeneous," says Pareto, in the distribution of residues; "the requirement of uniformity is very strong in some individuals, moderately strong in others, very feeble in still others, and almost entirely absent in a few." And "one may add as a datum of fact that the number of individuals in whom the requirement of uniformity is stronger than the average requisite of the intermediate state in which the society is situated is much greater than the number of individuals in whom the requirement is weaker than the average, and very, very much greater than the number in whom it is entirely missing" (Vol. IV, 2172). Why is that a "datum of fact" for Pareto? Because "if the requirement of uniformity [apparently his term for unity and solidarity] were to fail, society would not hold together, and each individual would go his own way, as lions and tigers, birds of prey, and other animals do." So societies hang together due to the predominance in them of individuals with strong social instincts; the "proof" lies in the fact that societies do not dissolve.

That is not all. What Pareto calls derivations, theologies, and so on, correspond to the "greater or lesser potency of the sentiments of uniformity."

Thus one theology "will glorify the immobility of one or another uniformity, real or imaginary, the other . . . will glorify movement, progress, in one direction or another" (Vol. IV, 2173). That is what actually happened in history. Men have sought merely to justify whatever sentiments they have held; moved by those blind forces, they "explain" and justify their practice post hoc by talk. The same is true with respect to force, which "is used by those who wish to preserve certain uniformities and by those who wish to overstep them. And when each says he abhors the use of force, he means by the other."

Pareto goes on to suggest that the question whether "the use of violence to enforce existing uniformities is beneficial to society, or whether it is beneficial to use force to overstep them," can be solved by a kind of utilitarian (functional) calculus. The

> . . . various uniformities have to be distinguished to see which of them are beneficial and which deleterious to society. Nor, indeed, is that enough; for it is further necessary to determine whether the utility of the uniformity is great enough to offset the harm that will be done by using violence to enforce it, or whether detriment from the uniformity is great enough to overbalance the damage that will be caused by the use of force in subverting it; in which detriment and damage we must not forget to reckon the very serious drawback involved in the anarchy that results from any frequent use of violence to abolish existing uniformities, just as among the benefits and utilities of maintaining frankly injurious uniformities must be counted the strength and stability they lend to the social order. So, to solve the problem as to the use of force, it is not enough to solve the other problem as to the utility in general, of certain types of social organization; it is essential also and chiefly to compute all the advantages and all the drawbacks, direct and indirect. (Vol. IV, 2175)

But this calculus, to determine what is "beneficial to society," we now learn, is best left to the scientific élite and to the ruling class, for "social utility is oftentimes best served if the members of the subject class, whose *function* it is not to lead but to act, accept one of the two theologies according to the case—either the theology that enjoins preservation of existing uniformities, or the theology that counsels change" (Vol. IV, 2175, italics added). In spite of the cautious wording, what we have here is a thinly veiled assumption of the incompetence of the "people" to decide for themselves what is or is not good for them; "social utility" is best served if they follow passively and accept the judgments of the various élites.

When the rule of the governing élite is threatened, and out of humanitarian (or other) sentiments it declines to meet force with force, even a small group can impose its will upon it. If the governing class shies away from the use of force for reasons of expediency, and resorts instead to fraud and deceit in order to outwit its adversaries, that eventually brings about a change in its composition—power passes "from the lions to the foxes." Foxiness, resting on the residues of the combinations instinct (class I), becomes preponderant and intensified in that class while class II residues decline. It is precisely the increase of class I residues supplying the "artistry and resourcefulness" now needed to outsmart one's opponents, that makes the governing class increasingly vulnerable to those willing and able to use force—the lions—either from within that class or from the subject one.

The leaders of the subject class, ready, willing, and able to employ force, topple the governing class; that is accomplished all the more easily if it is moved by humanitarian sentiments and if it has found few or no ways of assimilating into its midst the élite of the subject class. A closed aristocracy is most vulnerable and insecure. On the other hand, the more adept is the governing class in absorbing those subject elements who are skilled at "chicanery, fraud, and corruption," the more secure is its rule, for it undercuts the possibility that the "talented" elements will "become the leaders of such plebeians as are disposed to use violence. Thus left without leadership, without talent, disorganized, the subject class is almost always powerless to set up any lasting regime" (Vol. IV, 2179). There will always be a subject class. That is inevitable because it has no real leadership; its élite elements are consistently coopted by the governing élite.

Although the governing élite, being small, is greatly strengthened by the influx of class I residues (that is, individuals holding them who are inclined to rule), the subject class is enfeebled not only by the loss of those elements, but also by the fact that though it

> is still left with many individuals possessed of combinations-instincts, [they] are applied not to politics . . . but to arts and trades independent of politics. That circumstance lends stability to societies, for the governing class is required to absorb only a small number of new individuals in order to keep the subject class deprived of leadership. However, in the long run the differences in temperament between the governing class and the subject class become gradually accentuated, the combinations-instincts tending to predominate in the ruling class, and instincts of group-persistence in the subject class. When that difference becomes sufficiently great, revolution occurs. (Vol. IV, 2179)

That is Pareto's theory of revolution, based on residue, sentiments, and temperament. The general formula, he tells us, can be applied to nation-states. Those who have not lost "the habit of applying force" will win over those who have lost the "habit"; in the long run, the latter situation "leads a country to ruin" (Vol. IV, 2179).

As for the oppressed, or those who think they are, derivations, such as humanitarianism, are used to arouse them or to bring the neutrals over to their side, or to get them to condemn or otherwise weaken the governing powers. Pareto has nothing but contempt for "those whose spinal columns have utterly rotted from the bane of humanitarianism" (Vol. IV, 2186). The temptation is irresistible to present just a few examples of Pareto's "scientific-sociological" approach to "force." In a country where the ruling class, A, out of humanitarian or other considerations, "is becoming less and less capable of using force," it is "shirking the main duty of a ruling class. Such a country is on its way to utter ruin." But then the B's, the subject class, "apply force on a far-reaching scale, and not only overthrow the A's but kill large numbers of them—and, in so doing, to tell the truth, they are performing a useful public service, something like ridding the country of a baneful animal pest." Owing to that, "the social fabric is acquiring stability and strength. The country is saved from ruin and is reborn to a new life." Again, ". . . slaughter and rapine are external symptoms indicating the advent of strong and courageous people to places formerly held by weaklings and cowards." Commenting on the French Revolution of 1789, if the governing class "had had the faith that counsels use of force and the will to use force, it would never have been overthrown and, procuring its own advantage, would have procured the advantage of France." Failing in its function, however, it "was a good thing that power should pass into the hands of people who showed that they had the faith and the resolve requisite for the use of force" (Vol. IV, 2191). He has much to say about force, about the spineless and the courageous, but one finds nothing more than that in his functional calculus for determining what is good for "society."

Other phenomena which Pareto takes up further illustrate his dependence on the notion of instinct. There are, he notes, *rentiers* and speculators, or "savers" and entrepreneurs. How, ultimately, are we to understand "saving"? "All human conduct based on instinct may be more or less modified by reasoning, and it would be going too far to assert that that does not apply also to conduct based on the instinct for saving. But that does not prevent that instinct from being the primary element in saving, which remains none the less a nonlogical act" (Vol. IV, 2232). *Rentiers* and speculators are not sociological but psychological categories, for each rests on basically different instincts. In the category "speculator," Pareto tells us, "we are putting together all persons who directly or indirectly speculate and in one way or another manage to increase their incomes by ingeniously taking advantage of circumstances" (Vol. IV, 2233). That includes not only capitalistic entrepreneurs but "lawyers, engineers, politicians, working people, [and] clerks. . . . " Of course, they all share an "ingeniousness" which can be traced to the type I instinct, just as the behavior of the *rentier* can be traced to type II.

Pareto occasionally reminds us, contrary to his practice, that residues are not to be regarded as the only determining factor. However, Pareto can explain almost any problem in terms of the proportion of class I and class II residues. If, for instance, Alcibiades persuaded the Athenians "against the better judgment of the conservative Nicias, to undertake the Sicilian expedition," that was due to the preponderance among them of class I residues. And Pareto adds: "Had sentiments of group-persistence been at all strong in the Athenians, they would have followed the view of Nicias, or would at the most have been satisfied with sending a small expedition that would have been no great tax on their resources" (Vol. IV, 2421). That is typical of what Pareto considers to be "explanation." After recounting some of the historical events in very superficial terms, he concludes: "It is plain enough that what was lacking in Athens was such a balance between the combinations-instincts and the residues of group-persistence that while the combinations-instincts encouraged to adventure, the group-persistences would supplement them with the perseverance and firmness of resolve required for success in the schemes imagined" (Vol. IV, 2424). More, the fact that Alcibiades could be more effective leading the "slow-thinking" Spartans than the natives of his own city, "demonstrates how desirable it is that combination-instincts should predominate in the leaders and the instincts of group-persistence in subordinates." It is desirable, in other words, that the "masses," in any case predominantly nonrational, blindly follow and leave to the élite the work of making ingenious combinations. Both Sparta and Athens would have been easily defeated had they fought "with a people possessing ability to innovate combined with ability to make the proper use of novelties, a situation that arises in countries where our class I residues predominate in the leaders and Class II residues in the subject classes" (Vol. IV, 2429). Pareto's "proof": Thebes and Macedonia were equally endowed in a number of respects—both made improvements simultaneously in the arts of war, both had leaders with highly developed combination-instincts who commanded peoples with "the group-persistences required for steadfastness of purpose." Why then did the Macedonians fare better? This is Pareto's reply: "Through a greater intensity in their Class II residues, the Macedonians stood by their leaders more consistently than the Thebans did" (Vol. IV, 2429).

In effect, the combination-instinct, for Pareto, is the intelligence of the élite to take advantage of the superstitions of the masses but never to believe the absurdities themselves. He relates how Nicias, when commanding the Athenians, "was induced by his group persistences to place his trust in oracles and so led the army under him to complete ruin." He concludes

> that oracles are good things if they are used by rulers, who perhaps have no faith in them, as means of persuading their subordinates, but harmful if they are taken at face value by rulers and used as an end in themselves, not as means of persuasion. To make the proposition general, and so applicable to times that know no oracles, one need merely replace the term "oracles" with the term "group-persistences." (Vol. IV, 2440)

Pareto goes on to say that the élite will achieve its ends all the more efficiently, the more the masses are kept unaware of that doctrine, suggesting thereby that they are able to learn of their deliberate manipulation and, given such knowledge, could prevent it. He thus leaves himself open to the inference that the "stupidity" and acquiescence of the "people" need not be permanent. Explicitly, however, this is his formula for success: A people's prejudice (class II residues) should be strong enough to assure its obedience to the leader, but not so strong as to prevent certain innovations. It is this "scientific-sociological" proposition which explains victory in war and prosperity and progress in peace.

Forms of government do have some influence on social events and development, Pareto acknowledges, but such forms are themselves "products of the character traits of the peoples involved, the traits, therefore, being far more important as causes of the social phenomena . . ." (Vol. IV, 2445). He quotes Von der Goltz's remarks about conditions in Prussia before the battle of Jena to the effect that in France the civil authority always defers to the military "whereas in Germany the prevailing spirit in the civil government, as well as in the public at large, is always to block the military authority" (Vol. IV, 2447). Pareto notes parenthetically that in his time the situation has reversed itself. The "constant" character traits have *not only changed* but have also switched places—with no further light thrown on the phenomenon.

Having the right traits and using force will ensure the maintenance of the governing class. How might a governing class best defend itself and eliminate those who threaten it? "The infliction of death," replies Pareto, "is the surest means, but also the most harmful," since it could lead to a destruction of society's best individuals. Persecution is also not very practical since that tends to create martyrs, who are even more dangerous to the élite. In general, then, he leaves one effective formula for rulers: "One may say . . . that a governing class offers effective resistance only as it is disposed to go to the limit in resistance, without hesitation, using force and resorting to arms whenever necessary" (Vol. IV, 2480).

PARETO AND FASCISM

It is not known how much direct influence Pareto had upon Mussolini, or even whether there was any direct contact between the two men when the latter was a political refugee in Lausanne. Before the march on Rome, Pareto had a very reserved and occasionally even hostile attitude toward the fascist movement. It is indisputable, however, that once the Italian dictator had established himself in power, Pareto gave his wholehearted approval to what he apparently regarded as the "moderate form" fascism assumed in its early phase. Later, he maintained his support and approval of the regime but, according to his biographer, G. H. Bousquet, underscored "the necessity of safeguarding a number of liberties."[10]

Fascism, for Pareto, seemed not only to confirm his theories but also to hold out hope for a "new era." That he identified with the new order is borne out by the fact that on March 23, 1923, he accepted an appointment as senator—a position he had declined to accept in the prefascist government. In a letter to an acquaintance at the time of acceptance, he wrote: "I am happy to see that you are favorably disposed to the new regime, which, in my opinion, is the only one capable of saving Italy from innumerable evils."[11] And, in the same vein, "France will save herself only if she finds her own Mussolini."[12]

In general, Pareto's attitude seems to have been that because the pre-fascist regime did not, or could not, save the country from "anarchy" by legal means, fascism had to do it by force. Having accomplished that, however, the regime should have strived to establish a "new legality." Fascism would be good for Italy if it avoided wars and if it refrained from imposing "exaggerated" restrictions on freedom. In short, fascism would be good if it were not fascism! His call for "liberties," however, was typically Paretian: What is most essential is that the new élite govern "effectively"—and that requires that it concede a "certain dose of liberty" to the people. Reflecting on fascism a year or so before he died, Pareto wrote, "We have arrived today at a point where there appears, among . . . the clouds of the future, the beginning of the transformation of democracy, of parliamentarism, of the cycle of demagogic plutocracy; and Italy which formerly was the mother of so many forms of civilization, could very well have a grand role to play in bringing into the world another."[13]

In his attitude toward fascism, then, we have a clearer view of Pareto's own firmly held sentiments, whose manifestations may also be found throughout his work.

NOTES

1. For these and other biographical details, I rely on G. H. Bousquet, *Pareto: Le Savant et L'Homme* (Lausanne: Payot and Cie. S. A. Libraire de L'Université, 1960). Note: All translations from the French are the author's.
2. Vilfredo Pareto, *The Mind and Society*, 4 vols., ed. Arthur Livingstone (New York: Harcourt Brace Jovanovich, 1935), pp. iv, 1477 n.
3. Bousquet, *Pareto,* p. 41.
4. Ibid., p. 61.
5. Vilfredo Pareto, *Oeuvres Complètes*, Tome V, *Les Systémes Socialistes* (Geneva: Giovanni Busino, Librarie Droz, 1965), p. 25. (Hereafter all page references to this work will be indicated in parentheses immediately following the quoted passage.)
6. Pareto, *Oeuvres Complètes,* Vol. V.
7. I find it very difficult to understand how Talcott Parsons, in his *Structure of Social Action*, could interpret residues as values; this interpretation may suit his thesis that the works of Weber, Pareto, Durkheim, and others converged conceptually and theoretically, but it can be upheld only by means of a very selective reading of Pareto's work.
8. Pareto, *Oeuvres Complètes*, Vol. I, 88. (Hereafter all page references to this work will be indicated in parentheses immediately following the quoted passage.)
9. Pareto, *Oeuvres Complètes,* Vol. II, no. 850, p. 501. (Hereafter all references are to paragraphs or sections that Pareto numbers and not to pages.)
10. See Bousquet, *Pareto,* p. 89.

11. Ibid., p. 193.
12. Ibid., pp. 193–94 n.
13. Ibid., p. 197. See also H. Stuart Hughes, *Consciousness and Society*, rev. ed. (New York: Vintage Books, 1977), pp. 270–74.

19

Gaetano Mosca

(1858–1941)

Mosca, like Pareto, conceived of his life's work as an effective repudiation of the prevailing democratic and collectivistic theories, particularly Marxism. Those theories, elements of which could be traced to ancient Greece, were given a more explicit formulation by the representatives of the Enlightenment in the eighteenth century; in the nineteenth century, they were logically extended by Karl Marx and thus given a renewed impetus. Rousseau, in those terms, was the real parent of Marx, and Marx the true heir of the Enlightenment. Though Marx is regarded as the founder of modern socialism, writes Mosca, its "first intellectual and moral parent was undoubtedly Rousseau."[1] The various doctrines emanating from those sources are precisely the ones Mosca is "combating all along in these pages" (p. 152). Like Pareto, he wants once and for all to destroy the Rousseauian-Marxian fantasy "that once collectivism is established, it will be the beginning of an era of universal equality and justice, during which the state will no longer be the organ of a class and the exploiter and the exploited will be no more" (p. 447). Mosca's entire output, in particular *The Ruling Class*, is intended as a refutation of that "utopia" against which he advances his own theory: There will always be a ruling class!

To support his thesis, Mosca relies ultimately, as did Pareto, on the assumption of "constant psychological tendencies determining the behavior of the human masses" (p. 1). Yet, what emerges from this total work is a theory which is, on balance, less dogmatic and less rigid as well as more *sociological* than Pareto's—though he prefers to describe his work as political science rather than sociology. His sociological view is evident not only in his rejection of geographic, climatic, social Darwinian, and racial theories, but especially in his explicit use of concepts such as "social structure," "social types," and "social forces." It is, he writes, "social structure, upon which, after all, decision as to whether a people is to rule or to be ruled depends" (p. 61). Those concepts lead him to the view that it is not categories such as race, topography, climate, struggle for existence, and so on, which account for the relative cultural backwardness of certain groups, but definite social relationships: "We are obliged to agree . . . that European civilization has not only hindered but actually thwarted any effort toward progress that Negroes and Indians might have made of their own accord" (p. 23). Given identical social and cultural conditions, there is no reason to believe that blacks could not distinguish themselves as well as whites. When black children recognize their condition, that is, "realize that they belong to a race that is adjudged inferior, and that they can look forward to no better lot than that of cooks and porters, they lose interest in studying and lapse into apathy" (p. 24).

Mosca is also aware that "every individual is wont to adopt the ideas, the beliefs, the sentiments that are most current in the environment in which he has grown up" (p. 26). His more consistently sociological approach may be further illustrated in his insistence that it is not any alleged organic differences among peoples that determine "the differences in social type that they have adopted, but rather the differences in social contacts and in historical circumstances to which every nation . . . is fated to be subject" (p. 28). The doctrine which has mechanically transposed the Darwinian view from the natural to the social realm is also erroneous: It is not primarily a struggle for *existence* which prevails in society but a struggle for *preeminence*; that is "a constant phenomenon that arises in all human societies . . ." (p. 29).

Struggle for preeminence is Mosca's term for the social competition and conflict over wealth, power, and prestige, for "control of the means and instruments that enable a person to direct many human activities, many human wills, as he sees fit. The losers, who are of course the majority in that sort of struggle, are not devoured, destroyed, or even kept from reproducing their kind, as is basically characteristic of the struggle for life. They merely enjoy fewer material satisfactions and, especially, less freedom and independence" (p. 30). In opposition to the various nonsociological doctrines, Mosca emphasized that it is the accumulation of experience and positive knowledge which accounts for the advance of civilization, and that the rise and decline of societies must be viewed as the effects of "changes in their types of social structure" (p. 35). If Frenchmen, for example, are different today from what they were one hundred years ago, then that is due to the radical changes that have taken place in "the economic and political situation in France" and to the different intellectual atmosphere now prevailing there.

Mosca gives so much attention to social and cultural variables that his so-called "constant psychological laws" are relegated to a relatively subordinate position. In Pareto's system, as we have seen "sentiments" and the basic irrationality of man play so fundamental a role as to virtually exclude a consideration of sociocultural conditions. Mosca, on the other hand, keeps those conditions constantly in view. The "great psychological laws," he writes, "reveal their operation . . . in administrative and judicial institutions, in religions, in all the moral and political customs of the various nations; and it is therefore upon these last categories of facts that we must concentrate our attention" (p. 46). Although his general argument rests somewhat less than Pareto's on psychological laws, Mosca too, ultimately falls back upon such "laws" for his explanation of why the struggle for preeminence, as well as the ruling class, must be eternal phenomena.

THE RULING CLASS

The observation that rulers and ruled have existed throughout history obviously did not originate with Mosca, as he readily acknowledged. Plato, for example, had given considerable attention to the rulers and the ruled of his Ideal State. It was, however, only in the work of Saint-Simon, Mosca believed, that one could see a definite and clear-cut anticipation of his own doctrine: That once a society reaches a certain stage of development, "political control in the broadest sense of the term (administrative, military, religious, economic, and moral leadership) is exercised always by a special class, or by an organized minority . . ." (p. 239). Saint-Simon had not only asserted "the inherent necessity of a ruling class. He explicitly proclaimed that that class has to possess the requisites and aptitudes most necessary to social leadership at a given time and in a given type of civilization" (pp. 329–30).

In 1883, in his first work, *Teorica dei Governi e Governo Parlamentare,* Mosca elaborated on Saint-Simon's view and argued "that even in democracies the need for an organized minority persists, and that in spite of appearances to the contrary, and for all of the legal principles on which government rests, this minority still retains actual and effective control of the state" (p. 331). To emphasize that he was the *first* among his contemporaries to give that thesis explicit form, he adds: "In years following came the first edition of the present work, *Elementi di scienza politica,* and, among others, works by Ammon, Novikov, Rensi, Pareto and Michels" (p. 331).[2]

Mosca's thesis—that under all systems, including politically democratic ones, a ruling class prevails—was obviously one with which Marx or the Marxists would not have disagreed. They knew very well that the "history of all hitherto existing society is the history of class struggles." That was, after all, the first observation Marx and Engels made in the *Communist Manifesto.* Three paragraphs later, they also state quite clearly that modern bourgeois society "has not done away with class antagonisms. It has but established new classes, new conditions of oppression, new forms of struggle in place of the old ones." If Marx had stopped there, his thesis would have been identical with Mosca's. But, of course, Marx did not stop there and went on to argue that classes (including ruling classes) and class conflict rest on definite socioeconomic conditions and that the elimination of those conditions could lead to a society in which a ruling class would be superfluous and unthinkable. What was inevitable under some conditions was altogether avoidable under others. The point for Mosca, in contrast, was that history gives us no realistic basis for such a vision, since it is a fundamental and inexorable psychological law, and not primarily social conditions, which determines man's nature. What has been true "of all hitherto existing society" will continue to be true in all future societies. In that way Mosca reversed the implications of Marx's thesis and transformed it into a conservative one. The ruling class is a permanent attribute of society, as is the struggle for preeminence. In all societies there have been and will continue to be two classes: one that rules and the other that is ruled. In Mosca's scheme, however, the ruled are assigned a somewhat less passive role than in Pareto's.

The ruled masses, Mosca acknowledges, are able to bring pressures to bear upon the rulers. The "pressures arising from the discontent of the masses who are governed, from the passions by which they are swayed, exert a certain amount of influence on the policies of the ruling, the political class" (p. 51). Popular discontent may even result in the overthrow of a ruling class, but another such class would inevitably emerge from the "masses themselves to discharge the functions of a ruling class. Otherwise all organization, and the whole social structure, would be destroyed" (p. 51). The ruling or political class assumes "preponderant importance in determining the political type, and also the level of civilization, of the different peoples" (p. 51).

The power of the ruling class as well as the inevitability of its dominion rests on the fact that it is an *organized minority,* which is accompanied in Mosca's system by an *unorganized majority.* The unorganized state of the majority renders each of its individual members quite powerless before the organized might of the minority. Precisely because it is a minority, a relatively small group, it can achieve what the majority cannot: mutual understanding and concerted action. "It follows," writes Mosca, "that the larger the political community, the smaller will the proportion of the governing minority to the governed majority be, and the more difficult will it be for the majority to organize for reaction against the minority" (p. 53).

Not only difficult, perhaps even impossible. There is an inexorable social law rooted in the nature of man which makes it inevitable that the representatives of the people—whether elected or appointed—will transform themselves from servants into masters. Appointed to represent and defend the common interests of the group as a whole, they soon develop special interests of their own; in their zealous pursuit of those interests they become a well-organized, powerful, and dominant minority. The ruling minority is strengthened not only by its organization but by the superior qualities—material, intellectual, moral—which distinguish it from the mass. Members "of a ruling minority regularly have some attribute, real or apparent, which is highly esteemed and very influential in the society in which they live" (p. 53).

The basic psychological law which impels men to struggle for preeminence always results in the victory of the minority, which by virtue of its organization and other superior qualities gains decisive control over certain "social forces." Control of any one social force—for example, military, economic, political, administrative, religious, moral, and so on—may lead to control of others. The military power of warrior lords, for instance, enabled them to demand and receive "the community's whole produce minus what was absolutely necessary for subsistence on the part of the cultivators; and when the latter tried to escape such abuses they were constrained by force to stay bound to the soil, their situation taking on all the characteristics of serfdom pure and simple" (p. 55). That has been true generally of societies in which land was the chief source of wealth: Military power led to wealth just as later wealth in the form of money led to political and military power. When "fighting with the mailed fist is prohibited whereas fighting with pounds and pence is sanctioned, the better posts are inevitably won by those who are better supplied with pounds and pence" (p. 57). In all societies, including, of course, representative democracies, the rich have readier access to agencies of social influence than the poor. In some societies during specific periods, control of "religious forces," as might be the case with priests, leads to wealth and political power; in other societies, specialized scientific knowledge becomes an important political force.

The various advantages of the ruling minority—organization, superior qualities, and control of social forces—conduce to the situation in which "all ruling classes tend to become hereditary in fact if not in law." There "is no eliminating that special advantage in favor of certain individuals which the French call the advantage of *positions déjà prises*." Among others, those advantages are the "connections and kinships that set an individual promptly on the right road, enabling him to avoid the gropings and blunders that are inevitable when one enters an unfamiliar environment without any guidance or support" (p. 61).

Arguing against social Darwinism and against the racial theories of Gumplowicz, Mosca adamantly insists on the social and cultural basis of the "superiority" of the various aristocracies and ruling classes in history. They "owe their special qualities not so much to the blood that flows in their veins as to their particular upbringing, which has brought out certain intellectual and moral tendencies in them in preference to others." And again, "the truth is that social position, family tradition, the habits of the class in which we live, contribute more than is commonly supposed to the greater or lesser development of the qualities mentioned" (p. 63).

Thus Mosca rejects any attribution of organic superiority to the members of the ruling class, but he rejects equally the sociological implications of his statement that "social position, family tradition, and habits of class" determine the character of men. He is unwilling seriously to entertain the possibility that the psychology of men could be changed by changing social conditions and institutions. For Mosca, the existing institutions, notably the ruling class, though owing their existence in part to other sociocultural conditions, are ultimately the result of a basic, unchanging psychological nature in man. Only by clinging to that assumption can he support his theory: Men under all conditions will struggle for preeminence, and this must result in the basic dichotomy of rulers and ruled.

Although the organized minority has superior might and can therefore repel challenges to its rule by force, it does so only as a last resort. Generally, it succeeds in stabilizing its rule by making it acceptable to the masses. That is done by means of a "political formula," a term roughly equivalent to Marx's ruling-class ideology, Weber's "legitimation" of power, Sorel's "myths," and Pareto's "derivations." Every governing class, writes Mosca, "tends to justify its actual exercise of power by resting it on some universal moral principle" (p. 62).

The "political formula" is not invented and employed "to trick the masses into obedience" (p. 71). It is a "great superstition" or illusion that, at the same time, is a great social force; without it, Mosca maintains, it is doubtful that societies could persist. "Political formula," then, is a broader concept than the term suggests; it includes the common values, beliefs, sentiments, and habits that result from a people's community of history, making that people receptive to the fictions employed by the governing class to legitimize its rule.

Nationalism is an obvious example in the modern era of such a formula: ". . . a man feels, believes, loves, hates, according to the environment in which he lives" (p. 73). In previous eras, rule by "divine right" was the prevalent formula. Formulas change with the sociohistorical circumstances, but under all circumstances the consent of the governed is based on a formula of some kind:

> The majority of a people consents to a given governmental system solely because the system is based upon religious or philosophical beliefs that are universally accepted by them. To use a language that we prefer, the amount of consent depends upon the extent to which, and the ardor with which, the class that is ruled believes in the political formula by which the ruling class justifies its rule. (p. 97)

Every successful regime rests on the careful cultivation of the beliefs of the lower classes in the ruling political formula. Failure to develop such all-embracing, general beliefs means that the rulers have failed to unify the different social groups and classes of the society.

Ruling ideas cannot depart too far from the culture of the governed without resulting in conflict and antagonism that threaten the very survival of the society. The principles underlying the formula must be rooted in the "consciousness of the more populous and less well educated strata of society" (p. 107). When such principles have sunk deeply enough into the consciousness of the poorly educated, the governing class, however corrupt and oppressive, gets remarkable results: the unswerving devotion of the poor, exploited, and oppressed masses. Nationalistic political formulas, properly cultivated, can effectively counter the internationalist doctrine of social democracy; Mosca saw a vivid demonstration of that thesis during World War I. It is of interest to note in this connection that nationalism was a greater social force than even he had believed. Before the war he wrote,

> These theories [proletarian internationalism] might have a certain practical efficacy in the event of a war between the Germans and the French, or between the Italians and the English, since all these nations belong to approximately the same social type. But if it were a question of repelling a serious Tatar or Chinese invasion, or merely a Turkish or Russian invasion, we believe that the great majority of proletarians even in countries where they are most strongly imbued with doctrines of worldwide collectivism would eagerly cooperate with the ruling class. (p. 115)

Thus even Mosca was probably astonished to see that it took less than a Tatar invasion to mobilize and unite the workers behind their respective governments. In that instance, narrow-minded nationalistic sentiments had overwhelmed the peoples of Europe and had brought upon them a terrible carnage. Must, however, the ruling "political formula"—for example, nationalism leading to war—always win out? Mosca grants that such formulae gain acceptance among the masses primarily because they have so little education and so little understanding of their condition. But he does not envisage the possibility of raising the general level of their consciousness to the point where they might reject political formulas obviously not to their interest.

Another major social process to which Mosca calls attention is the emergence within the lower classes of a "directing minority," a kind of plebeian ruling class, which is often "antagonistic to the class that holds possession of the legal government" (p. 116). The directing minority becomes a state within the state, wielding more influence over the masses than the legal government. The greater the isolation of the classes from one another, and the greater the discontent of the lower classes, the greater, too, is the likelihood that they will support the overthrow of the existing legal government. One ruling class then replaces the other, but that avails the masses little or nothing. The really great danger in the growing cultural differences among classes, and in their mutual cultural isolation, "is a decline in energy in the upper classes, which grow poorer and poorer in bold and aggressive characters and richer and richer in 'soft,' remissive individuals" (p. 117). The more closed the upper classes are to aspiring individuals from the lower classes, the greater their vulnerability and degeneracy, for it is only from the lower classes that the vigorous and strong elements may be recruited. In those classes, "the hard necessities of life, the unending and carking scramble for bread, the lack of literary culture, keep the primordial instincts of struggle and the unfailing ruggedness of human nature, alive" (p. 119). Here we recognize an idea Pareto formulated in a much less simple and straightforward fashion.

For Mosca, the fate of a ruling class depends on its energy, wisdom, and political sophistication. It has considerable control of its destiny. A ruling class of some sort is a permanent institution, and efforts to abolish it will always remain quixotic. The point, therefore, is to devise the best political system possible in the light of that fact; one could learn much in that regard from the great political thinkers of the past.

ARISTOTLE AND MONTESQUIEU

In 1908, Mosca became a Liberal-Conservative member of the Italian Chamber of Deputies. Thus, unlike Pareto, who had isolated himself from political life and had produced a correspondingly rigid system, Mosca was actively engaged in Italian politics. That, perhaps, contributed in his case to the formation of a more flexible political theory, which was reflected in his official party affiliation. Though he was indeed an élitist in some sense, he advanced what may be more precisely termed a liberal-aristocratic theory of politics.

He was a liberal in the sense that he had great respect and admiration for liberal principles, traditions, and institutions. The liberal principle, he believed "has had a more brilliant record than the autocratic principle . . ." (p. 409). Political systems based on liberal principles have been more successful than others precisely because they have rested "upon the consent of the majority of citizens," but, he is quick to add, "though only a small fraction of the inhabitants may be citizens" (p. 409). The models for his "good polity," therefore, were the ancient city-state of Greece, about which Aristotle had written, and the English system before the institution of universal suffrage—the system Montesquieu had so much admired.

Liberalism is the proper mediation between two fundamental principles forever at work in all political systems, vying with each other for hegemony: aristocracy and democracy. Liberalism is best in the sense that it allows both principles to work side by side with neither overpowering the other. Officials are appointed or elected from "below"—that is, directly or indirectly by their subordinates; they are drawn, however, from a limited pool of wise, experienced, responsible, and devoted men who are best fit to rule—the aristocratic minority. They have authority but not unlimited power, since definite limits are imposed upon their powers in relation to "individual citizens and to associations of citizens." Those limits—checks and balances—are the essence of liberalism; they are the fundamental elements of what Mosca calls "juridical defense," which in turn is the real criterion of the advance of civilization.

> Such limits [writes Mosca] were not entirely unknown to classical Greece and ancient Rome. They are almost always recognized in modern constitutions. They relate to such things as freedom of worship, of the press, of education, of assembly, and of speech. They guarantee personal liberty, private property, and inviolability of domicile. (pp. 409–10)

The liberal principle does not preclude the existence of an aristocratic minority or even closed cliques within it. In fact, a certain degree of closure is essential and good. On the other hand, too much closure results in *autocracy*, something to be eschewed since it leads to the isolation of rulers and eventually to their downfall. The proper balance may be found in liberal systems which "steer the inclinations of at least the whole second stratum of the ruling class, which, if it does not in itself constitute the electorate, at least supplies the general staffs of leaders who form the opinions and determine the conduct of the electing body" (p. 410). The "second stratum" to which Mosca alludes here, though varying with the society, corresponds to Aristotle's great middle class, the basis of political moderation. For Mosca, too, it "forms the backbone of all great political organization" (p. 413). The existence of a large and stable second stratum makes it possible for a government to succeed without "paying homage to the beliefs and sentiments of the more ignorant classes. Only under such circumstances can one of the chief assumptions of the liberal system be made, we do not say complete, but not wholly illusory—namely, that those who represent shall be responsible to the represented" (p. 413).

In those terms, Mosca regards it as essential to preserve and properly balance the aristocratic and democratic tendencies present in varying degrees of strength in all political organizations. "If it is confined within moderate limits," he writes, "the democratic tendency is in a sense indispensable to what is called 'progress' in human societies" (p. 415). Excessive suppression of that tendency results in social stagnation: If the aristocracies of Homeric times, for example, had remained closed and stationary, then civilization never would have advanced beyond that stage.

Class conflict, Mosca acknowledges to the Marxists, has been a major force in the development of civilization. "The struggle between those who are at the top and those who are born at the bottom but aspire to climb has been, is, and will ever be the ferment that forces individuals and classes to widen their horizons and seek the new roads that have brought the world to the degree of civilization that it attained in the nineteenth century" (p. 416). Now, however, the democratic tendency has gotten out of hand; if it could be brought under control, then it would again become the conservative force that it ought properly to be.

> When the democratic tendency does not exert too great an influence, to the exclusion of other tendencies, it represents a conservative force. It enables ruling classes to be continually replenished through the admission of new elements who have inborn talents for leadership and a will to lead, and so prevents that exhaustion of aristocracies of birth which usually paves the way for great social cataclysms. (p. 416)

The best system, then, is one in which the democratic tendency is appropriately bridled and curbed. But the principle of balance and moderation is constantly being threatened and undermined in practice by the Rousseauian-Marxian dogma of equality—a fantastic utopia; "every time the democratic movement has triumphed, in part or in full, we have invariably seen the aristocratic tendency come to life again through efforts of the very men who had fought it . . ." (p. 417).

If, therefore, Mosca was combating the ideas of the Enlightenment, it was specific aspects of that intellectual movement that he opposed. He admired Montesquieu but rejected Rousseau. The former had asserted the need for checks and balances, in short—moderation. A system based on a balance of powers was more realistic and hence superior to the unbridled democratic theory of Rousseau. Although the latter had called for popular sovereignty and absolute equality, he had also recognized, Mosca alleges, the need for a ruling class. In Rousseau's *Social Contract*, Mosca found the following statement: "Taking the term in its strictest sense there has never been a real democracy and there never will be. It is against the natural order that the great number should rule and the small number be ruled" (p. 391). But as Meisel has shown, that passage was quoted out of context, and it was only by so doing that Mosca could have used it for his purposes. Rousseau goes on to say: "It is inconceivable that the People should be in permanent session for the administration of public affairs. . . ."[3] The real point Rousseau was making in that context was, in Meisel's words, "that *government* by all would be as much against 'the natural order' (since the result would be anarchy) as would be *sovereignty* (which is and remains inalienable) if possessed by less than all the people."[4] What Mosca feared most was "a demagogic dictatorship by a few experts in mob leadership" and he used the passage from Rousseau just quoted to show that he had also recognized the dangers of that kind of "democracy."

From Mosca's standpoint, then, Montesquieu and *even* Rousseau had admitted the necessity of a ruling class. Greatly impressed by the English system of restraining the ruling class, Montesquieu had extolled that system and suggested it be adopted as a model. But, after all, long before him, the basis of political balance and moderation, and their virtues, had been explored by Aristotle, that great thinker of antiquity whose ideas on the subject were still viable.

Aristotle's "classification of governments," writes Mosca, "into monarchies, aristocracies, and democracies (a classification that might now be judged superficial and incomplete) was certainly the very best that the human mind could contrive in his day."[5] It was an "extraordinary intellectual feat." The genius of Aristotle, in Mosca's view, was to anticipate what modern scholarship has increasingly established as fact—namely, "that democratic, monarchical, and aristocratic principles function side by side in every political organism" (p. 52). The philosopher had recognized that good government is "mixed" government—that is, one in which the monarchy, the landed aristocracy, and the monied classes were properly balanced. In Mosca's terms, there "were so many political forces, the interplay of which, so long as any one of them did not prevail to the exclusion of others, was such as to provide a type of political organization in which due process of law was, in ordinary times, relatively secure" (p. 137).

Aristotle had maintained, moreover, that the stability and efficacy of a political organization depend on the existence of intermediate strata sufficiently large, prosperous, and independent to mediate between the extremes at the top and the bottom. To assure that, and thus the proper functioning of the Greek city-state, moderate property ownership was essential. Artistotle had thus intuited a principle which held true not only in his own time but in Mosca's as well. For Mosca had observed that wherever and whenever the middle strata have declined economically, and thus politically, "the modern representative system has yielded its worst results" (p. 391).

What Mosca liked particularly about Aristotle's system was that in it "not even the working classes, let alone slaves and metics, would be admitted to public office" (p. 427). Furthermore, he had already perceived clearly in his time what certainly could not be doubted in the twentieth century: that it is human selfishness, that basic psychological trait, which makes private property inevitable. That is something which extreme democrats and collectivists deny, asserting instead the precise opposite: Man is not inherently selfish; it is the institution of private property which has engendered selfish conduct in him.

One must follow Aristotle and adapt his teachings to present conditions: Make whatever economic concessions to the lower and more populous classes that are absolutely necessary without, however, "impairing the inviolability of private property too seriously and without laying unbearable burdens upon large and moderate fortunes. Among these concessions one might mention shorter working hours, insurance against old age, illness, unemployment and accidents, and restrictions on labor by women and children" (p. 472). Concessions may be made but they must not be carried "too far." They must be sufficient to assure political stability; toward that end it has become evident that "improved economic conditions have on the whole made the laboring classes less prone to resort to desperate and violent acts" (p. 472).

Mosca was thus reviving the "old doctrine of the golden mean" first found in Aristotle and later elaborated by others, notably Montesquieu.

Although the latter had replaced Aristotle's classification with his own—despotic, monarchical, and republican governments—he retained the theory of balance. Looking to England, he advocated a modified monarchy in which the executive, legislative, and judicial powers were separate, independent, and reciprocally checked and balanced. Those principles could be found in their classic form in the English constitution whose advantages he described enthusiastically. Montesquieu had thus placed less emphasis than Aristotle on the role of social strata and forces and more on political, constitutional safeguards. Mosca therefore criticized Montesquieu and especially his followers who stressed the formal or legalistic aspect of the problem "rather than [its] substantial or social aspect. They have often forgotten that if one political institution is to be an effective curb upon the activity of another it must represent a political force—it must, that is, be the organized expression of a social influence and a social authority that has some standing in the community, as against the forces that are expressed in the political institution that is to be controlled" (p. 138).

It is the "social forces" and the relationship among them that are of primary importance in maintaining a social equilibrium, but the formal and legal political devices, though only secondary, are nonetheless essential. Montesquieu's theory was perhaps incomplete but not "mistaken in any substantial respect." "To make his doctrine complete," writes Mosca, "one need add that a controlling and limiting political institution can be effective only when it represents a section of the political class that is different from the section represented by the institution to be limited and controlled" (p. 475). Building in that way on the work of two great predecessors, Mosca develops the view that a ruling class is inevitable and the most one can hope for is a system of properly balanced social forces. Such balances have yielded the best political systems characterized by what he calls "juridical defense." The extension of juridical defense is the real meaning of progress.

JURIDICIAL DEFENSE

The level of moral conscience of a people, as expressed in public opinion, religion, and law, is an indication of how far it has advanced from, say, barbarism to the various stages of civilization. In common with other nineteenth-century thinkers, Mosca accepted the evolutionary hypothesis—human history is an account of man's development from lower to higher cultural stages. A study of history shows that morality, justice, social order, and the like cannot be assured without instituting definite mechanisms to discipline the individuals and groups of society and to regulate the relations among them. The extent to which those mechanisms to assure respect for law have been developed determines the level of *juridical defense* and therefore the level of civilization a given society has achieved.

Men have instincts which are refractory to social order and discipline, and the control of those instincts cannot be entrusted to morality and religion alone. Adequate control requires a whole legislative system. The more a society succeeds in developing such effective systems, the better it is. In opposition to Rousseau (and Marx), then, who believed "that man is good by nature but that society makes him wicked and perverse," Mosca believed "that social organization provides for the reciprocal restraint of human individuals by one another and so makes them better, not by destroying their wicked instincts, but by accustoming them to controlling their wicked instincts" (p. 127).

That religion alone is insufficient for the control of those instincts is proved by the fact that "if we place side by side two peoples of the same degree of barbarism, one of which has embraced Christianity and the other not, it will be found that in practice their behaviors are very much the same, or at least there is no appreciable difference between them" (p. 218). Religious and moral sentiments are in themselves inadequate to afford the weak the protection they need. One sees, for example, that in "very religious countries, where the lower classes are completely at the mercy of the higher, it is no unusual thing to see masters beating their servants or other subordinates" (p. 129). The conclusion is inescapable, therefore, that institutionalized juridical and legal means of defense are required if a society is to achieve some semblance of justice. The class structure of society and the consequent social inequalities and injustices will always be with us; such injustices can only be mitigated under an adequate political, legal, and juridical system. In Mosca's words,

> The political organization proper, the organization that establishes the character of the relations between the governing class and the governed and between the various levels and various sections of the ruling class, is the factor that contributes more than any other to determining the degree of perfection that juridical defense, or government by law, can attain in a given people. (p. 130)

Ultimately, such a system can prevail only where several "social forces" mutually balance one another and where no single one of them is omnipotent or almost so. The absence or presence of such a balance explains, respectively, the difference between the system under the Czars, for instance, and the system in "England, where every arrest of an individual has to be legalized in earnest and very promptly" (p. 132). For Mosca, as for Montesquieu, England was the model. There, juridical defense was more highly developed than elsewhere; classes and other social forces were reciprocally balanced, and government by law, civil liberties, and due process were firmly established principles. Moreover, the honesty and integrity of English governmental officials were beyond question. The more a political system departed from that model, the less just and moral it was.

Whatever the "political formula," whether it is divine right or popular sovereignty, "when no other organized social forces exist apart from those which represent the principle on which sovereignty over the nation is based, then there can be no resistance, no effective control, to restrain a natural tendency in those who stand at the head of the social order to abuse their powers." In the absence of resistance, the ruling class "undergoes a real moral degeneration, the degeneration that is common to all men whose acts are exempt from the restraint that the opinion and the conscience of their fellows ordinarily impose" (p. 134). The absence of resistance leads to despotism or to what one might today call totalitarianism.

Juridical defense depends on the ability of social forces to check and balance one another and on the separation of powers in the political system. Equally important is the separation of the ecclesiastical and temporal authorities and that the "political formula" should "have nothing sacred and immutable about it." If the rulers rule in the name of a formula which has a monopoly on truth and justice, then "it is almost impossible that its acts should be debated and moderated in practice" (p. 139).

But there are still additional conditions on which juridical defense depends: (1) the distribution of wealth in a society and (2) the organization of its military forces. From his discussion of the first point, it becomes clear that Mosca felt that the issues raised by the socialists could not be ignored. The distribution of wealth had much to do not only with the social stability he desired, but with justice as well. Here important differences between his approach and Pareto's emerge even clearer than before.

Whereas Pareto's élites seem to be floating above society, without roots in its class structure, Mosca gives explicit attention to the phenomenon of class. Political power is always rooted in definite "social forces," and the economic is among the most important of such forces. Although he does not arrange them in any permanent hierarchy of importance, since that would vary according to time and place, he does regard the economic, political, legal, and military as the major social forces. In those terms, he generalized Marx's theory, much as did Weber, and argued that the control of the means of production, of political administration, of violence, and so on are all important in determining the structure of a society and its processes of change. Mosca also seems to have a greater concern with the issue of justice than Pareto, whose sociology often reads like a handbook for rulers. In the following passage, Mosca's treatment of the issue was not unlike that of the socialists in general and of the Marxists in particular:

> Laws and institutions that guarantee justice and protect the rights of the weak cannot possibly be effective when wealth is so distributed that we get, on the one hand, a small number of persons possessing land and mobile capital and, on the other, a multitude of proletarians who have no resource but the labor of their hands and owe it to the rich if they do not die of hunger from one day to the next. In that state of affairs to proclaim universal suffrage, or the rights of man, or the maxim that all are equal before the law, is merely ironical; and just

> as ironical is it to say that every man carries a marshal's baton in his knapsack, or that he is free some day to become a capitalist himself. (p. 143)

Clearly, then, *real* juridical defense and just relationships require more than formal, legal mechanisms; to the degree that liberal democracy ignores that fact, it connives in the perpetuation of sham liberalism and injustice. On the other hand, public ownership of the means of production is also no solution, for it may result in something worse than the present system. Raising an objection to socialism not unlike Weber's, Mosca writes: "Insofar as the state absorbs and distributes a larger and larger portion of the public wealth, the leaders of the ruling class come to possess greater and greater facilities for influencing and commanding their subordinates, and more and more easily evade control by anybody" (p. 143). Neither socialism nor sham liberalism is the answer; the only real solution is to follow the leads of Aristotle and to work out a system based on the proper balance of liberal-democratic and aristocratic principles.

That means, first of all, that the distribution of wealth should be such as to eliminate the great extremes resulting in haves and have-nots. The good polity, or what Mosca calls "a relatively perfect political organization," is one that "contains a large class of people whose economic position is virtually independent of those who hold supreme power." At least some of the members of that class must

> have sufficient means to be able to devote a portion of their time to perfecting their culture and acquiring that interest in the public weal—that aristocratic spirit, we are almost tempted to say—which alone can induce people to serve their country with no other satisfactions than those that come from individual pride and self-respect. In all countries that ever have been, or now are, in the lead as regards juridical defense—or liberty, as it is sometimes called—such a class has been prominent. (p. 144)

Thus a large middle class and an aristocratic spirit are among the essential preconditions of the good society; when they are lacking, "parliamentary government bears its worst fruits, as would any other political system" (p. 144).

There are social forces that militate against the establishment of a juridical equilibrium, chief among them being nationalism, the Church, large monied interests, and finally, social democracy. Any political system organized primarily on the basis of any single one of those forces, and its corresponding principles, makes it "difficult for all social forces to participate in public life, and more difficult still for any one force to counterbalance another. That is as true when power is in the hands of elected officials who are said to be chosen by the people as it is when power is entrusted exclusively to employees who are assumed to be appointed by a prince" (p. 147). For Mosca, then, government in the name of the "people" may become as autocratic as any other.

UNIVERSAL SUFFRAGE

"Popular sovereignty" as a result of universal suffrage is a myth—a very dangerous myth, moreover, because through it the people are led to believe that they rule and that the elected officials are mere servants. In reality, however, the officials are just as much masters under that system as they are in all others. That, in essence, is Mosca's view of representative democracy; of course, it did not originate with him. The entire thesis was anticipated almost verbatim by Marx and Engels, as Mosca knew very well. On the twentieth anniversary of the Paris Commune, Engels wrote,

> Society had created its own organs to look after its common interests, originally through simple division of labor. But these organs, at whose head was the state power, had in the course of time, in pursuance of their own special interests, transformed themselves from the servants of society into the masters of society. This can be seen, for example, not only in the hereditary monarchy, but equally so in the democratic republic. Nowhere do "politicians" form a more separate and powerful section of the nation than precisely in North America.[6]

But for Engels the process by which servants are transformed into masters was inevitable only under certain social conditions. The point of the Marxian analysis was to specify what those conditions were and, by abolishing them, to create new conditions of freedom. In Mosca's hands, however, Marx's *historically specific* thesis becomes a universal law: The transformation of servants into masters is inevitable in all systems, past, present, and future. Moreover, the so-called "servants" of the people under the representative system were never servants to begin with.

In actuality, the "representative" "has himself elected"; if that sounds "too inflexible and too harsh to fit some cases, we might qualify it by saying that *his friends have him elected*."[7] Elections do not change the fact that "those who have the will and, especially, the moral, intellectual, and material means to force their will upon others take the lead over the others and command them" (p. 154). It is unavoidable in all social organizations that a minority will gain control of those *means* and thus over the lives and fate of the majority of men. Elections give the people no real freedom of choice "and the only ones who have any chance of succeeding are those whose candidates are championed by groups, by committees, by *organized minorities*" (p. 154). What are the criteria by which such minorities choose and support certain candidates? Mosca's reply, not unlike one Marx and Engels would have given, is that "as a rule they are based on considerations of property and taxation, on common material interests, on ties of family, class, religion, sect, or political party" (p. 155).

But would Mosca go so far as to deny any and all influence on the part of the people? No! As was indicated in a previous comparison with Pareto's work, Mosca allows for some measure of influence on their part. The representative system, writes Mosca, "results in the participation of a certain number of social values in the guidance of the state, in the fact that many political forces which in an absolute state, a state ruled by a bureaucracy alone, would remain inert and without influence upon government become organized and so exert an influence on government" (p. 155). After all, the candidates and other representatives of the ruling minorities cannot altogether ignore the various organized publics nor even the unorganized voters. They must win over their goodwill. The "sentiments and passions of the 'common herd' come to have their influence on the mental attitudes of the representatives themselves, and echoes of a widely disseminated opinion, or of any serious discontent, easily come to be heard in the highest spheres of government" (p. 155).

Even the most despotic of regimes cannot ignore the sentiments of the masses or offend them with impunity. The representative system, however, allows for greater sensitivity to their discontent, since each incumbent knows that the grumblings and dissatisfaction of all the people could easily lead to his ouster and to the victory of another organized minority.

In Mosca's various discussions, the "people" is occasionally portrayed as a "common herd" whose behavior is governed by "sentiments" and "passions"—by irrational forces. There is some resemblance here between his conception and Pareto's, but Mosca remains, by and large, more consistently sociological. If the people generally have little or no rational understanding of their existential conditions and interests, it is because they are "poor and ignorant." They are uneducated, culturally impoverished, unorganized, and powerless. Normally, they have no means of control over the powerful. "In these circumstances," Mosca writes, "of the various organized minorities that are disputing the field, that one infallibly wins which spends most money or lies most persuasively" (p. 156). The recurring emphasis on social conditions leaves the door open to the *possibility* of changing them—a point to which we shall later return.

Disposition over social forces is what gives the various organized minorities their political significance. One of them will always win out, become the *political class*, and fulfill the political function. The point, then, is not to dream of a day when classes and ruling classes will be no more, but to devise, under the given circumstances, the best political system possible. Returning once more to Aristotle, Montesquieu, and the English political system, Mosca writes that such a system "enables all the elements that have a political significance in a given society to be best utilized and specialized, best subjected to reciprocal control and to the principle of individual responsibility for the things that are done in the respective domains" (p. 159). In England, though it is true that officials are elected or appointed, it is nonetheless true that it is the "prominent people" who fulfill the main political functions, and without pay. Such persons have that aristocratic spirit expressed so well in the French saying, *noblesse oblige*, which is so essential for the good polity.

PARLIAMENTARISM

In Mosca's discussion of parliaments, one sees some similarities to Pareto's treatment of representative government, but the similarities are superficial, because despite Mosca's criticisms, he regards parliamentary institutions as an essential aspect of liberal government—an opinion Pareto, judging from his later writings, did not share. It is true, Mosca acknowledges, that particularly the elective, lower houses of parliaments are often characterized by "prattlings," "long-winded speeches," and "futile bickerings." It is also true, as the socialists and anarchists allege, that it is not the majority's interests, opinions, and aspirations that are there represented, "but the interests of the wealthy ruling classes" (p. 255). Finally, there is no denying the excessive interference on the part of individual members in the workings of the administration generally and in the distribution of wealth through taxation and other devices. These main defects of parliament as an institution had become so conspicuous by Mosca's time that they came to be designated by the pejorative term "parliamentarism."

Yet, those defects are as nothing in their evil consequences compared with the situation that would result from the abolition of parliament and other representative institutions. Under prevailing conditions, Mosca insists, "the suppression of representative assemblies would inevitably be followed by a type of regime that is commonly called 'absolute.'" Suppression would result in a totalitarian system in which all social forces and values were subordinated to the ruling group and its bureaucracy. A disgust with "parliamentarism" and a fear of the revolutionary fervor of social democracy could lead, Mosca prophetically observes, to an "absolutely bureaucratic" order. "What we cannot admit is that such a step would be a wise one. We need give no long demonstration of that thesis in view of all that we have been saying as to the dangers and drawbacks involved in giving absolute predominance to a single political force that is not subject to any limitation or discussion whatever" (p. 256).

Thus Mosca is unequivocally opposed to the weakening of the representative system. The repeatedly pronounced emphasis he places on the vital importance of liberal institutions is altogether absent from Pareto's later works. The collapse of those institutions, Mosca maintains, would lead to "moral ruin," to the violations of "juridical defense, of justice, of everything that we commonly call 'liberty'; and those violations would be far more pernicious than any that can be laid to the charge of even the most dishonest of parliamentary governments, let alone of representative governments" (p. 257).

Mosca is thus directing his argument in two opposing directions. Against the more zealous opponents of democracy and socialism he is arguing that the destruction of representative and liberal government would result in something far worse. And to the socialists, Marxian and others, he is saying that they ought to abandon their utopian dogmas about the abolition of classes—including the ruling class. The best system (and best, too, because capable of realization) is not the classless society but the one advocated by Aristotle, Montesquieu, and himself—namely, a system permitting the various organized social forces to moderate and balance one another. The socialists would resign themselves to that if they were to realize that even under the most equalitarian of systems a ruling class would inevitably arise, since the people would still have to choose their representatives "from among candidates who would be put forward by groups, or committees, and these groups would be made up of persons who by taste and by interest would be actively devoted to political life" (p. 259).

The primary evil of the parliamentary form of government is that more often than not it is the members of the lower, elected chamber who control the bureaucracy; it is precisely those men who have only one eye on their professional responsibilities, the other being on the electorate. That makes for a situation in which their desire to govern well is "effectively thwarted by their no less natural desire to serve their own personal interests, and the sense of professional duty in ministers and representatives is always balanced by all sorts of ambitions and vanities, justified and unjustified" (p. 259). What Mosca is suggesting here, once more, is that the "evil" results from the inadequate assertion of the aristocratic tendency, so necessary for sound and healthy government. If ministers were sufficiently independent of the electorate, they would be less subject to pressures of personal ambitions and party interests and hence more concerned with their professional responsibilities. What is required is that the "governors" be drawn from that stratum of citizens who are both wealthy enough to be incorruptible and educated enough to govern wisely.

Mosca was calling for the development of a public-spirited, nonbureaucratic civil service, "a special class of volunteer unsalaried officials," as it once prevailed in England. Eventually, the "democratic current" swept away that institution, revealing pointedly, again, the main dangers and evils of the democratic philosophy: It "recognizes no political act, no political prerogative, as legitimate unless it emanates directly or indirectly from popular suffrage" (p. 270). The democratic principle has successfully suppressed the aristocratic, and with very undesirable results. Historically, it was a mistake to grant universal suffrage, but now it is too late to "go back on it without committing a second mistake which might have unforeseeable consequences of a very serious nature" (p. 492). One must therefore make the best of the existing situation by strengthening the aristocratic principle. That, together with a large middle class, a system of balanced forces, and institutions of juridical defense, makes for the best system possible. But the good system requires still another condition which, strange as it may sound, is a standing army.

STANDING ARMIES

History teaches, writes Mosca, "that the class that bears the lance or holds the musket regularly forces its rule upon the class that handles the spade or pushes the shuttle" (p. 228). This was also true of premodern Europe, where the class that controlled the means of violence acquired economic and political power as well. What Mosca found altogether intriguing, then, was the contemporary situation where the military was successfully subordinated to the civil authority. That became possible "only through an intense and widespread development of the sentiments on which juridical defense is based, and especially through an exceptionally favorable sequence of historical circumstances" (p. 229). Ironic as it may appear, Mosca asserts, the control by the civil authority of the military and other groups with access to means of violence was facilitated by the institution called the *standing army*.

Mosca's reasoning rests on the assumption that in every society there are those who have a greater inclination than others toward adventure, belligerence, aggression, and violence. They make up the bands of armed men who in some societies, the "loosely organized," rule and terrorize every village and town. In other societies, the "better organized," they become a ruling class, "lords and masters of all wealth and political influence," as they did in medieval Europe. In bureaucratic states, finally, the standing army, being unrestrained and unchecked, has "no difficulty in dictating to the rest of society" (p. 228). In none of those types of society is the military controlled by a civil authority. Only in those societies, therefore, in which (1) *the standing army is combined with (2) institutions of social balance and juridical defens*e does one find the hegemony of the civil authority. One without the other would not have produced that result.

Before the standing army was institutionalized, it was the adventurers and criminals who were recruited as needed. But by the beginning of the eighteenth century, the "necessity of keeping many men in arms and the difficulty of paying wages large enough to attract volunteers brought on conscription in most countries on the European continent. That system meant that common soldiers no longer came from the adventurous and criminal classes but were recruited from among peasants and workingmen . . ." (p. 232). It meant, too, that now the class structure of the society as a whole became the basis of the military structure—that is, that the authority of the upper classes as well as the submissiveness of the lower were transferred to the military sphere. Officers were recruited almost exclusively from the upper strata and common soldiers from the lower. The men at the top of the military hierarchy retained "close ties with the minority which by birth, culture, and wealth [stood] at the peak of the social pyramid" (p. 233). That, together with the deeply rooted institutions of juridical defense, explains, according to Mosca, why in England and the United States, for example, the army did not become "a tool for coups d'état." In those countries and others with similar conditions, "the standing army has so far stripped the class of persons who have natural tastes and capacities for violence of their monopoly of the military function." It follows, Mosca reasons, that enduring peace would bring with it the dissolution of the standing army and, hence, a regression to the state in which the bold and violent oppressed "the weak and peaceful." Therefore, he concludes, "war itself—in its present forms the root of so many evils, the parent of so many barbarities—becomes necessary every now and again if what is best in the functioning of our Western societies today is not to decline and retrogress to lower types of juridical defense" (p. 243). Ultimately, Mosca was led to that pessimistic conclusion, which he himself called "grave and terrible," by his view of human nature as essentially *base, selfish,* and *brutish.*

We see, then, that although Mosca argued the necessity of a ruling class, he nevertheless qualified his thesis rather severely. He recognized that a good society requires (1) the elimination of extreme inequalities and (2) the creation of a balance of social forces in which none could aggrandize to itself sufficient power to tyrannize over all the rest. It is precisely such qualifications, however, that tend to undermine Mosca's central thesis. What really emerges from his brilliant analysis is not the necessity of a ruling élite or even the necessity of a plurality of competing élites. Rather, it is that a good polity presupposes the existence of many different social groups (not élites) capable of checking and limiting one another's powers and especially the power of the state. Mosca understood very well that democracy requires the diffusion of power in a wide range of social and political organizations which can set limits on the powers of the leadership. A society that fails to institutionalize a division of powers along those lines will unavoidably become totalitarian.

Thus interpreted, Mosca's theory appears in a new light, and his work may be read quite differently from the way it has been in the past. For his analysis, far from proving the necessity of a ruling class, effectively shows how the traditional gap between rulers and ruled can be significantly reduced.

NOTES

1. Gaetano Mosca, *The Ruling Class*, trans. (from *Elementi di Scienza Politica*) Hannah D. Kahn, ed. and rev. Arthur Livingstone (New York: McGraw-Hill Book Company, 1965), p. 170. (Hereafter all page references to this work will be indicated in parentheses immediately following the quoted passage.)
2. For an account of the dispute over who had priority in this regard, see James H. Meisel's *The Myth of the Ruling Class* (Ann Arbor: University of Michigan Press, 1962), pp. 170–89.
3. Quoted in Meisel, *Myth of the Ruling Class*, p. 254.
4. Ibid., p. 255.

5. Mosca, *Ruling Class,* p. 43. (Hereafter all page references to this work will be indicated in parentheses immediately following the quoted passage.)
6. Karl Marx and Frederick Engels, *Selected Works* (Moscow: Foreign Languages Publishing House, 1950), Vol. I, p. 438.
7. Mosca, *Ruling Class,* p. 154. (Hereafter all page references to this work will be indicated by parentheses immediately following quoted passage.)

20

Robert Michels (1876–1936)

In common with Weber, Pareto, and Mosca, Robert Michels devoted a large part of his intellectual labors to the challenge of Marxism. It was primarily the ideas of those antecedent thinkers that Michels employed and elaborated in the development of his own critique. Yet, despite certain criticisms of Marx's social thought, he remained something of a reconstructed Marxist himself; rejecting what he regarded as the utopian aspects of the Marxian vision, he retained elements of the Marxian method of analysis.

In 1927, sixteen years after *Political Parties* first appeared, Michels delivered at the University of Rome a series of lectures on political sociology. In those lectures, published under the title *Corso di Sociologia Politica*, he concerned himself with what he considered to be a major theoretical issue: the relative validity of Marx's conception of society and history. Noting a fact Marx himself was the first to acknowledge—that aspects of his economic interpretation of history had been anticipated by many thinkers before him—Michels writes: "The Arab philosopher, Ibn Kaldun, who lived in the fourteenth century, may have been the earliest scientific exponent of the economic conception of history."[1]

As for classes and class conflicts, those phenomena were also observed before Marx placed them at the center of his investigation. Michels cites Benjamin Disraeli, who had portrayed in his novel entitled *Sybil* the great cultural chasm that lay between the upper and lower classes. So great was the chasm, in fact, that English society could be viewed as *two nations*. In his novel, Disraeli "repeated the idea that had caused him in his parliamentary discourse of 1840 to declare that the recognition of the proletariat's rights to its political emancipation and the betterment of its economic conditions was the only way to close the abyss that already separated the 'two nations.'"[2] Other thinkers—English, French, and German—had also anticipated elements of Marx's general conception, but that is not to deny, Michels emphasizes, the originality of the Marxian synthesis. It "is an indisputable merit of Marx and Engels to have been the first not only to erect as a system the particular part that the productive forces play in the historic process, but also to have assigned to them, with the creation of a new philosophy, their place in science."[3]

To underscore this point, Michels shows that even Pareto, a major opponent of Marxism, appreciated the scientific aspects of Marx's system. "Historical materialism," wrote Pareto in his *Trattato di Sociologia Generale,*

> has been a notable scientific advance because it has helped to clarify the contingent character of certain phenomena, such as moral phenomena and religious phenomena, to which was given, and is given yet by many, an absolute character. Besides it certainly has an element of truth in insisting on the interdependence of economic phenomena and other social phenomena; the error stands in having changed this interdependence to a relationship of cause and effect.[4]

Pareto also acknowledged the value of Marx's sociological principles which "discredited the unreal notion of those who want to explain facts with the ideas that men hold."[5]

This general attitude toward Marxism, shared in varying degrees by Pareto, Weber, and Benedetto Croce, was Michels's as well. There are invaluable principles and insights to be found in Marx's "materialist conception" which can be incorporated into a scientific sociology minus the "subversive flavor" of Marxism. Michels thus agreed with Croce who observed that

> historical materialism, deprived of the elements of finality or inevitable utopia which Marxist socialism wanted to confer upon it, cannot give any support to socialism or to any other practical way of life. The economic conception of history is a doctrine that explains the reasons, the genesis, but does not help to illuminate socialism, which is a wishful vision of the future. It is silent on the outcome of the struggle it has traced through history.[6]

In the remainder of his lectures, Michels seeks "to mark the boundaries within which historical materialism conforms to historical truth, and above all to examine its place in political science."[7]

Following Weber, Pareto, and Mosca, Michels reconstructs Marx's method and calls for a more pluralistic approach: "The complete view of things results from the action of several forces of dissimilar nature."[8] He fully acknowledges the fundamental importance of economic developments for social change; in that Marx was right. But what Marx had overlooked was that there were other forces or tendencies at work sufficiently strong to preclude the realization of democracy and socialism as he had envisioned it. For Michels, these tendencies were "dependent: (1) upon the nature of the human individual; (2) upon the nature of the political struggle; and (3) upon the nature of organization."[9] What Marx had not seen, according to Michels, was that as a result of those tendencies, "democracy leads to oligarchy, and necessarily contains an oligarchical nucleus." That is the central thesis which Michels develops in his classic study, *Political Parties.*

The most effective documentation of this thesis could be made, Michels reasoned, by describing the structure and tendencies of the various social-democratic parties in Europe. The aristocratic and oligarchical character of the various *conservative* parties was indisputable. But that, after all, was to be expected and proved nothing since they had no commitment to democracy and based themselves quite frankly on conservative principles. If, on the other hand, oligarchical phenomena could be found "in the very bosom of the revolutionary parties," which professed to represent or to be working toward the negation of those phenomena, then that would constitute "conclusive proof of the existence of immanent oligarchical tendencies in every kind of human organization which strives for the attainment of definite ends" (p. 11).

Ultimately, the "immanence" of those tendencies rests, for Michels, on certain innate human tendencies which urge man to transmit his material possessions to his legitimate heir or other kin. The same applies to "political power [which] comes also to be considered as an object of private hereditary ownership" (p. 12). Those tendencies prevail due to "the peculiar and inherent instincts of mankind," but they are also "vigorously nourished by the economic order based upon private property in the means of production . . ." (p. 12). Herein lies the theoretical dilemma Michels never managed to resolve: Is the quest for power and material goods to be regarded as a function of the socioeconomic order in which men live, or is it a result of an immutable human psychology? By his own admission, an ideal democracy is impossible under "the existing economic and social conditions." But if he followed that logic to the end, there could be no "iron law," since oligarchic and other social tendencies are contingent upon the existing social system. Michels therefore places great emphasis on so-called innate psychological laws.

Like Pareto and Mosca before him, Michels rested his general argument as to the inevitability of oligarchy on a conception of human nature precisely the opposite of that held by Marx. It is man's *inherent* nature to crave power and, once having attained it, to seek to perpetuate it. On the basis of that psychological assumption, Michels generates his theory that democracy requires organization which in turn leads necessarily to oligarchy. His "iron law of oligarchy" is, he says, "like every other sociological law, beyond good and evil;"

this so-called "sociological law" rests on what he took to be a constant, his conception of human nature.

In Marx's view social conditions typically elicit a subjective response from men; how they define those conditions, whether good or evil, can make a difference for the perpetuation or abolition of those conditions. There are, to be sure, certain periods when social conditions appear to impose insuperable limits on the actions of men, but there are other periods when opportunities for change emerge. Given the consciousness of such opportunities on the part of a sufficient number of individuals who are willing to act in concert, the opportunities may be seized. Michels himself acknowledged that the "democratic currents of history," though they "break ever on the same shoal" are "ever renewed." It would seem undeniable that at least part of the reason for the renewal is that the oligarchies are felt by the people to be oppressive and are thus overthrown. What Michels insists upon, however, is that the democratic currents will inevitably break again and again upon the same shoal. That is his "universally applicable iron law."

There can be no doubt that the facts *qua* facts that Michels described were true. His study is a sound sociological description of what is—which is not to say that the pessimistic conclusions often drawn from his analysis are valid. Moreover, a brief review of that analysis will show that he himself had his more optimistic moments and that in the end he allowed for the interpretation that his "iron law" must not be regarded as anything more than a metaphor—a metaphor that he employed to dramatize certain conspicuous tendencies of men in organizations under specific sociohistorical circumstances.

The people are incapable of governing themselves! Michels's support of that assertion is based first on the theory of crowds and crowd psychology: "It is easier to dominate a large crowd than a small audience." A crowd is easily given to suggestion and irrational outbursts; both serious discussion and thoughtful deliberation are impossible in its midst. Second, and more important, however, is the technical and practical problem of involving the huge multitudes in democratic decision making. If democratic is taken to mean that the multitude adopts resolutions and makes decisions *directly*, then democracy is indeed impossible. Rousseau understood that and so did most of the other, later democratic theorists. Michels quotes Louis Blanc who in his polemic against Proudhon asked "whether it is possible for thirty-four millions of human beings (the population of France at the time) to carry on their affairs without . . . the intermediation of representatives" (p. 25). What is true of nation-states is also true of modern organizations. The staggering demographic proportions of the socialist parties Michels studied made both direct discussion and direct action impossible. The party in Berlin alone, for example, had a membership "of more than ninety thousand."

The enormity of the populations in modern party organizations renders it technically impossible for all members to govern or administer directly their common affairs. Unavoidably, then, once a collectivity is formed for any specific purpose and attains a certain demographic size, a division of labor becomes necessary. As the organization grows larger, its growth is accompanied by an increasing complexity. New functions emerge and are distributed, and along with the differentiation of functions comes the delegation of authority. Men are chosen to "represent the mass and carry out its will."

In the early stages of this development—speaking more particularly about organizations based upon democratic and socialistic ideals—the various functions stand in a *coordinate* relationship to one another: No hierarchy is implied in the various functions and positions. They are all equal in the sense that differential amounts of wealth or power are not associated with the various positions. The social honor accorded the "chief" does not enable him to transform that honor into special perquisites and privileges. In Michels words: "Originally the chief is merely the servant of the mass" (p. 27).

At first the democratic and equalitarian character of the organization is assured by the strong commitment on the part of its members to the principles of democracy and equality. Functions are rotated, delegates and representatives are totally subject to the will of the collectivity, and in general a high degree of camaraderie prevails. That was true of the early English labor movement, for example. But that state of affairs is possible only when the organization in question is relatively small in scale. The growing scale of the organization makes this form of democracy increasingly inapplicable. In addition to size, however, there is still another important variable involved, which is at least in part a function of the organization's growth. Within the division of labor, certain tasks and duties become more complicated and require ability, training, and "a considerable amount of objective knowledge" (p. 28). Differentiation of functions now implies specialization and specialization, in turn, expertise. Party schools are established to train functionaries and officials, and what results is "a class of professional politicians, of approved and registered experts in political life." Michels notes that "Ferdinand Tönnies advocates that the party should institute regular examinations for the nomination of socialist parliamentary candidates, and for the appointment of party secretaries" (p. 29).

Expertise becomes a "foot in the door." The experts increasingly resemble not servants but masters, and the organization becomes increasingly hierarchical and bureaucratic. Acquiring to an ever greater degree the attributes of leaders, the experts withdraw from the masses and concentrate in their hands a variety of prerogatives. In Michels's words,

> It is undeniable that all these educational institutions for the officials of the party and of the labor organizations tend, above all, toward the artificial creation of an élite of the working class, of a caste of cadets composed of persons who aspire to the command of the proletarian rank and file. Without wishing it, there is thus effected a continuous enlargement of the gulf which divides the leaders from the masses. (p. 31)

Thus results the familiar process by which men originally appointed to serve the interests of the collectivity soon develop interests of their own often opposed to that collectivity. What began as a democratic and equalitarian situation culminated in leaders and led, in rulers and ruled. It is organization *qua* organization which is the efficient cause of that transformation. Democracy implies organization, and organization, in turn, "implies the tendency to oligarchy. . . . As a result of organization, every party or professional union becomes divided into a minority of directors and a majority of directed" (p. 32). Michels expresses that general proposition in a variety of ways: "With the advance of organization, democracy tends to decline. Democratic evolution has a parabolic course. . . . It may be enunciated as a general rule that the increase in the power of the leaders is directly proportional with the extension of the organization" (p. 33).

According to Michels, then, every organization, however democratic in its inception, given a growth in its membership and complexity, increasingly exhibits oligarchic and bureaucratic tendencies. What began as a technical and practical necessity is transformed into a virtue: Democracy and equality within the party are now no longer regarded as essential and a new ideology emerges to justify the changes wrought by the "inexorable" processes of organization.

> Not even the most radical wing of the various socialist parties [writes Michels] raises any objection to this retrogressive evolution, the contention being that democracy is only a form of organization and that where it ceases to be possible to harmonize democracy with organization, it is better to abandon the former than the latter. Organization, since it is only the means of attaining the ends of socialism, is considered to comprise within itself the revolutionary content of the party, and this essential content must never be sacrificed for the sake of form. (p. 35)

In that way, and by insisting in addition, "that true democracy cannot be installed until the fight is over," the members are persuaded that it is the highest revolutionary virtue to be disciplined and to follow faithfully a few individuals at the top. The organization as an instrument of class struggle now adopts rather easily the vocabulary of military science: "There is hardly one expression of military tactics and strategy, hardly even a phrase of barrack slang, which does not recur again and again in the leading articles of the socialist press" (p. 43).

"Experience" and "expertise" are among the main words the leaders use to legitimize their positions of power. The impression is created among the rank and file that their leaders are indeed indispensable. Indispensability, whether apparent or real, becomes an efficient tool in the leader's hands. Whenever his decisions or judgment are challenged, he threatens to resign—which appears as a fine democratic gesture, but which in reality is intended to remind his followers of his indispensability and hence to force their submission to his will.

Generally, it is Michels's view that the masses have a need for leadership and are actually quite content to have others attend to their affairs. Of course, that serves to strengthen the aristocratic and bureaucratic character of the party or union.

The masses are apathetic. None of the reasons, however, which Michels adduces need lead to the conclusion that that must be their permanent attribute—what he later calls the "perennial incompetence of the masses." That they are indifferent is evident, Michels writes, from the "slackness of attendance at ordinary meetings." And, since the various political and ideological issues "are not merely beyond the understanding of the rank and file, but leave them altogether cold," they are incompetent. Some of the reasons for slackness of attendance, Michels himself notes, are really quite simple and prosaic: "When his work is finished, the proletarian can think only of rest and getting to bed in good time" (p. 52). There is, then, "an immense need for direction and guidance [which] is accompanied by a genuine cult for the leaders, who are regarded as heroes" (p. 53). Add to that the great differences in culture and education between the leaders and the rank and file (the former more often than not being of bourgeois origin, as we shall see), and one understands the submissiveness of the ordinary members.

Although such tendencies are "manifest in the political parties of all countries," Michels notes that Germany is a special case. His observations in this connection must be considered important, because his own earliest experiences and impressions were in the German movement—where the submission of the masses and adulation of the leaders were greater than elsewhere. Michels writes,

> The German people in especial exhibits to an extreme degree the need for someone to point out the way and to issue orders. This peculiarity, common to all classes not excepting the proletariat, furnishes a psychological soil upon which a powerful directive hegemony can flourish luxuriantly. There exist among the Germans all the preconditions necessary for such a development: a psychical predisposition to subordination, a profound instinct for discipline, in a word, the whole still persistent inheritance of the influence of the Prussian drill sergeant, with all its advantages and disadvantages; in addition, a trust in authority which verges on the complete absence of a critical faculty. (p. 53)

Michels notes further that Marx was quite aware of the "risks to the democratic spirit" of this national character and that "he thought it necessary to warn the German workers against entertaining too rigid a conception of organization." Marx insisted that in Germany, "where the workers are bureaucratically controlled from birth upward, and for this reason have a blind faith in constituted authority, it is above all necessary to teach them to walk by themselves" (p. 55).

As for the German leaders, on the other hand, "Engels," writes Michels, "regarded it as deplorable that [they] could not accustom themselves to the idea that the mere fact of being installed in office did not give them the right to be treated with more respect than any other comrade" (p. 222). The leaders of the German socialist party thought and acted in a manner reminiscent of the Sun King; each was inclined to think of himself, in Michels's phrase, *"Le Parti c'est moi."*

Michels cites the remarkable stability of both the German and the Italian socialist parties. The latter, he says, "for the same reasons as in Germany, has exhibited a similar stability" (p. 93). It is interesting that those were the parties with which he had firsthand experience and the two main cases on which he based his generalizations.

The masses, then, are politically indifferent and incompetent (in need of guidance), and those factors together with the gratitude and veneration they show toward those "who speak and write in their behalf" strengthen the position of the leaders. Their need for a religion is evident from the idolatrous manner in which they venerate the party's secular books, symbols, and leaders; that "is not peculiar to backward countries or remote periods; it is an atavistic survival of primitive psychology" (p. 66). Moreover, they are easily hoodwinked and deceived, more inclined to follow mediocre men with a flair for showmanship than men of talent and cultivation. That explains why Eduard Bernstein and Paul Lafargue, for instance, remained relatively unknown to the rank and file of their respective parties: Both were men of outstanding intelligence and scientific sophistication, but they were also lacking in oratorical talent.

There are still other "peculiarities of the masses" that contribute to both their incompetence and indifference and to the superiority of the leaders. Those peculiarities are reflected in the age composition of the general membership of the socialist parties and unions. "The great majority of the membership ranges in age from 25 to 39 years." The young have other things to do with their leisure; "they are heedless, their thoughts run in erotic channels, they are always hoping that some miracle will deliver them from the need of passing their whole lives as simple wage earners, and for these reasons they are slow to join a trade union" (p. 78). The older men, on the other hand, who have become "weary and disillusioned, commonly resign their membership .... In other words, the leaders have to do with a mass of members to whom they are superior in respect of age and experience of life, whilst they have nothing to fear from the relentless criticism which is so peculiarly characteristic of men who have just attained to virility" (p. 78).

Many factors contribute to the widening distance between masses and leaders. In many countries, party leaders are of a predominantly middle-class origin and therefore possess from the beginning a cultural or intellectual superiority. But even in those countries where there are few intellectuals in the leadership, as was the case in Germany in Michels's time, a similar *distance* develops between leaders of working-class origin and the general membership. That Michels explains in the following ways:

> Whilst their occupation with the needs of daily life renders it impossible for the masses to attain to a profound knowledge of the social machinery, and above all of the working of the political machine, the leader of working-class origin is enabled, thanks to his new situation, to make himself intimately familiar with all the technical details of public life, and thus to increase his superiority over the rank and file. (pp. 81–82)

And, again,

> The questions which they [leaders of working-class origin] have to decide, and whose effective decision demands on their part a serious work of preparation, involve an increase in their own technical competence, and a consequent increase in the distance between themselves and their comrades of the rank and file. Thus the leaders, if they are not "cultured" already, soon become so. But culture exercises a suggestive influence over the masses. (p. 83)

Finally,

> This special competence, this expert knowledge, which the leader acquires in matters inaccessible, or almost inaccessible, to the mass, gives him a security of tenure which conflicts with the essential principles of democracy. (p. 84)

Again and again we are told that "the incompetence of the masses is almost universal throughout the domains of political life, and this constitutes the most solid foundation of the power of the leaders" (p. 86). The expertise of the leaders also leads to oligarchy, since the incompetent masses submit to them and give them "an authority which is in the long run destructive of democracy" (p. 86). However, a careful reading of Michels's work shows that his analysis is "one-sided," as he himself admits in the end.

If he was asserting something more than the thesis that there will always be a need for some kind of leadership—in the sense that a symphony orchestra will always require a conductor—then he did not distinquish carefully the difference between leaders and oligarchs. As an objective scientific proposition, one could perhaps "demonstrate" the *technical* impossibility on the part of the masses of governing themselves *directly*. In that case one would be demonstrating the need for leadership, not for oligarchy.

To pursue the example of the symphony orchestra, many orchestras have tried, but have failed, *to conduct themselves*. It is generally agreed among musicians that a conductor is a technical necessity for the functioning of a symphony orchestra. If that is the case, one can say that so-and-so is a good or bad conductor, depending on the aesthetic results achieved, but it makes no sense to say that the conductor is an autocrat because he or she has remained in "office" for a long time.

Insofar as there may be objective criteria of oligarchy, Michels does not define them precisely—that is, he does not indicate at what point the elected representatives cease to be mere leaders and become oligarchs. At times Michels uses the term "oligarchy" simply to describe remarkable stability or longevity of leadership, for example, for more than thirty years. At other times, however, he uses the term to refer to the "aristocracy" of talent and expertise that inevitably emerges and separates itself from the mass. Specialization creates authority: "Just as the patient obeys the doctor," writes Michels, "because the doctor knows better than the patient, having made a special study of the human body in health and disease, so must the political patient submit to the guidance of his party leaders, who possess a political competence impossible of attainment by the rank and file" (p. 89).

But the analogy does not seem really appropriate for Michels's purposes. Was the purpose of his study merely to demonstrate that specialization leads to authority, in the sense conveyed by the just-quoted passage? Surely he was after something more than that. Otherwise why call it oligarchy? What he really wanted to demonstrate was the inevitability of the abuse of power and authority—to the extent of undermining democracy: That those who are placed in positions of authority to serve the interests of the collectivity soon develop interests of their own which are antagonistic to those of the collectivity. It would seem that whether or not that in fact occurs is the best criterion by which to determine whether those in authority have become oligarchs. Yet, that is not the way Michels proceeds: Too often he employs the concepts of leadership and oligarchy as if they were necessarily synonymous and interchangeable.

As compared with the leaders of other political parties, Michels acknowledges, the abuse of power was drastically reduced among the leaders of the social-democratic parties; party work was more often based on idealism and the leaders were enthusiastic volunteers. A few individuals carried on the party's work, for which they were "unpaid or almost wholly unpaid." In Germany, on the other hand, although many party functionaries were unpaid volunteers, certain positions, party journals and newspapers, had "a paid editorial staff and paid contributors." But paying the leaders does not necessarily lessen either their idealism or their relative immunity to "temptations." Michels pays a high tribute to the socialist leaders: "It would . . . be quite wrong," he insists, "to suppose that socialist propagandists and socialist officials are paid on a scale which enables them with the hard-earned pence of the workers to lead that luxurious existence which, with an ignorance bordering on impudence, is often ascribed to them by the 'respectable' press and the loungers of the clubs." A leader's labors "demand an abundance of self-denial and sacrifice and are nervously exhausting; whilst the remuneration he receives is a modest one when compared with the gravity of his task." Finally, Michels notes, "Men of the ability and education of Karl Kautsky, Max Quarck, Adam Müller, and a hundred others, would have been able, had they chosen to devote themselves to some other service than that of the workers, to obtain a material reward much greater than that which they secure in their present positions" (p. 115).

Nevertheless, idealism alone, at a number of levels at least, does not suffice to sustain the party, and paying for services does bring with it some negative results. It impairs somewhat the initiative of members and their socialist values and at the same time contributes both to the growing bureaucratization of the party and to the centralization of power. Ironically, however, paying and not paying, or paying poorly, all tend to lead, Michels observes, to the same result—that is, they conduce to oligarchy. For example, "In France, where it is still the rule to pay the trade union leaders very small salaries, there is lacking a new generation of leaders ready to take the place of the old, and for this reason at the trade union congresses the same members continually appear as delegates" (p. 127). That results in a concentration of power that inevitably perverts the original aims of the party. The men at the top abuse their power by gaining control of the party press so as to diffuse their fame and popularize their names, and the parliamentary leaders often become "a closed corporation, cut off from the rest of the party."

The controls the masses have over that process are merely theoretical. In the constant struggle between the leaders and the masses, the former are destined always to win out. "It cannot be denied," Michels writes, "that the masses revolt from time to time, but their revolts are always suppressed" (p. 162).

The so-called masses never revolt spontaneously—that is, without leadership. The process of revolt presupposes that the masses are being led by certain leading elements of their own who, once having achieved power in the name of the people, transform themselves into a relatively closed caste apart from and opposed to the people. Moreover, in "normal," nonrevolutionary situations, the most "talented elements," the potential revolutionary leaders, are always subject to a variety of seductive influences; they are smitten by the ambition to enter the privileged positions of the labor movement. That is a particular manifestation of the general process of cooptation described by Pareto whom Michels quotes: "*Si les B [nouvelle élite] prennent peu à peu la place des A [ancienne élite] par une lente infiltration, et si le mouvement de circulation sociale n'est pas interrompu, les C [la masse] sont privés des chefs quie pourraient les pousser à la révolt*" (pp. 161–62 n).

Thus it would appear unavoidable that "the rank and file becomes continually more impotent to provide new and intelligent forces capable of leading the opposition which may be latent among the masses" (p. 161). The *real* struggle is not between masses and leaders but between the existing leaders and the new, challenging, ascending ones. Even when appearances are to the contrary and the existing leaders seem to be guided by the good will and pleasure of the mass, that is not actually the case: "The submission of the old leaders is ostensibly an act of homage to the crowd, but in intention it is a means of prophylaxis against the peril by which they are threatened—the formation of a new élite" (p. 165). The struggle between the old and the new élites very rarely culminates "in the complete defeat of the former." Slightly modifying Pareto's doctrine, Michels states that "The result of the process is not so much a *circulation des élites* as a *réunion des élites*, an amalgam, that is to say, of the two elements" (p. 177).

For Michels, the benefits which accrue to the majority of the party members as a result of that process are "practically nil." His description, in a brilliant passage, of the impact of bureaucracy on socialist values probably is as valid today as it was in his time:

> As the party bureaucracy increases, two elements which constitute the essential pillars of every socialist conception undergo an inevitable weakening: an understanding of the wider and more ideal cultural aims of socialism, and an understanding of the international multiplicity of its manifestations. Mechanism becomes an end in itself. (p. 187)

Furthermore, *decentralization* in itself cannot prevent such a development from taking place. It does not lead to greater individual liberty nor does it enhance the power of the rank and file. More often than not, it is a mechanism by which the weaker leaders seek to escape the dominion of the stronger, but that, of course, does not prevent the weaker from establishing a centralized authority within their own domains. The party is "saved" from one gigantic oligarchy only to fall into the hands "of a number of smaller oligarchies, each of which is no less powerful within its own sphere. The dominance of oligarchy in party life remains unchallenged" (p. 201). And the causes of that, for Michels, are not only sociological—need for organization, mass apathy, and so on—but psychological, that is, due to the leaders' "natural greed for power" and "the general characteristics of human nature" (p. 205).

Earlier it was asserted that Michels, despite his criticism of Marxism, retained certain elements of the Marxian method of analysis. That is true, but he employed the reconstructed method to expose the apparent errors—primarily of omission—of the "master."

Classes, class conflict, and class consciousness are all essential categories in Michels's thinking. He agrees, for instance, that it is not oppressive conditions in themselves but the *recognition* of those conditions that has been "the prime factor of class struggles" (p. 236). Historically, it has been the bourgeoisie that has played a central role in generating proletarian class consciousness. The bourgeoisie, having to defend its existence on a number of fronts at once—against the aristocracy and against those sections of its own class whose interests are opposed to industrial development—and unable to carry on the struggle alone, is compelled to mobilize the proletariat and thus places in its hands a weapon (political consciousness and experience) which it can employ against the bourgeoisie itself. In addition, there have always been those bourgeois intellectuals who for a variety of reasons have detached themselves from their original class and have joined the ranks of the workers to give them direction. As a matter of fact, Michels regards it as a

> psychologico-historical law that any class which has been enervated and led to despair in itself through prolonged lack of education and through deprivation of political rights, cannot attain to the possibility of energetic action until it has received instruction concerning its ethical rights and politico-economical powers, not alone from members of its own class, but also from those who belong to what in vulgar parlance are termed a "higher" class. (p. 237)

What better example of that is needed than the founders of modern socialism themselves? They "were with a few exceptions men of science primarily, and in the second place only were they politicians in the strict sense of the term" (p. 238). Moreover, Michels continues, it "was only when science placed itself at the service of the working class that the proletarian movement became transformed into a socialist movement, and that instinctive, unconscious, and aimless rebelling was replaced by conscious aspiration, comparatively clear, and strictly directed towards a well-defined end" (p. 238). Finally, Michels concurs that "The proletariat is . . . perfectly logical in constituting itself into a class party, and in considering that the struggle against the bourgeoisie in all its gradations, viewed as a single class, is the only possible means of realizing a social order in which knowledge, health, and property shall not be, as they are today, the monopolies of a minority" (p. 247).

But Marx had not anticipated the extent to which the entry of the bourgeois intellectuals into the socialist movement, and their occupation of leadership positions, would bring about basic changes in that movement that "may be summed up in the comprehensive customary term of the *embourgeoisement* of working-class parties." Also, although Marx had been quite aware of strata within the working class, on balance he tended to underestimate the conflicts that could arise among them; instead he viewed it as a much more unitary category than it turned out to be in practice. Ironically, moreover, the socialist movement itself, Michels argues, has created new petty-bourgeois strata. A variety of leadership and other functions are given over to workers—or more precisely to *former* workers—who now inevitably undergo a profound psychological transformation that creates as great a social distance between them and the rank and file as between the bourgeois and proletarian. In that way, "Certain groups of individuals, numerically insignificant but qualitatively of great importance, are withdrawn from the proletarian class and raised to bourgeois dignity" (p. 271). The socialist party and other organizations, in providing opportunities for social ascent to former manual laborers, generate the very same tendencies one sees in originally bourgeois leadership.[10]

None of the traditional democratic mechanisms, either within socialist parties and other working-class organizations or in larger national political systems, has been effective in countering the oligarchic abuse of power. The *referendum,* for instance, has not only proved to be for the most part impracticable due to the incompetence of the masses and the lack of time to submit every question to popular vote; it has also yielded *less*, not more, democracy—for example, the well-known phenomenon of plebiscitarian "democracy," in reality, a dictatorship. Michels notes that George Sand had regarded "the plebiscite, if not counterpoised by the intelligence of the masses, as an attack upon the liberty of the people." He himself cites Bonapartism whose power was "based on the referendum" (p. 337).

As for the syndicalists and anarchists, they are merely deluding themselves when they "reason as if they were immunized against the action of sociological laws of universal validity" (p. 347). They have not avoided the situation in which "the masses do not represent themselves but are represented by others" (p. 348). Often their "direct action," for example, "the strike, instead of being a field of activity for the uniform and compact masses, tends rather to facilitate the process of differentiation and to favor the formation of an *élite* of leaders" (pp. 349–50).

None of the various proposed "prophylaxes," then, has proved effective in preventing what élite theorists have deemed an inexorable process. Those prophylaxes include Marxism, too—Michels' primary target, of course; at first Marxism seems the "only scientific doctrine which can boast of ability to make an effective reply to all theories, old or new, affirming the immanent necessity for the perennial existence of the 'political class'" (pp. 381–82). But Marxism also fails because the members of the new society in their very efforts to abolish class distinctions will create new ones. That is inevitable because the delegation of authority will be necessary to administer and to allocate material resources. The administrators would thus acquire enormous "influence at least equal to that possessed by the private owner of capital" (p. 383). And, Michels continues, there is no basis for assuming that administrators "will not utilize their immense influence in order to secure for their children the succession to the offices which they themselves hold" (p. 383). Once a group of men, elected or not, gains control of the existing instruments of power, they will do everything they can to retain it.

Thus the weakest link in the Marxian view of the new society is the whole gamut of problems relating to administration—that is, the concentration of power in the hands of administrators and the means those individuals might utilize to retain their privileges. It seems inescapable, concludes Michels, that conflicts of interest will emerge between leaders and led, not unlike the class conflicts of the old society. That process appears to be subsumed under an absolute social law.

> By a universally applicable social law, every organ of the collectivity, brought into existence through the need for the division of labor, creates for itself, as soon as it becomes consolidated, interests peculiar to itself. The existence of these special interests involves a necessary conflict with the interests of the collectivity. Nay, more, social strata fulfilling peculiar functions tend to become isolated, to produce organs fitted for the defense of their own peculiar interests. In the long run they tend to undergo transformation into distinct classes. (p. 389)

This Michels intends not as a refutation of Marx's theory of class struggle but of his utopia, the classless society (pp. 390–91). "The socialists might conquer," he writes, "but not socialism, which would perish in the moment of its adherents' triumph" (p. 391).

Michels had written those lines before a single socialist regime had taken power anywhere. However, the victory of the bureaucratic organization over the socialist soul had already become evident in the violation of a fundamental socialist principle: international solidarity. The working-class masses were fated to suffer most from the violation of that principle. Yet, as Michels notes of the German workers during World War I, "throughout the proletarian mass there has not been reported a single instance of moral rebellion against the struggle which enlists socialists to fight on behalf of German imperialism and to contend with the comrades of other lands." Ultimately, that must be viewed as a consequence of *organization* itself "which gives birth to the domination of the elected over the electors, of the mandatories over the mandators, of the delegates over the delegators. Who *says organization, says oligarchy*." That is predicated, for Michels, on the inherent nature of the masses, which, however much they may advance educationally, culturally, or morally, will remain *perennially* incompetent. The mass "per se is amorphous, and therefore needs division of labor, specialization, and guidance"—the very processes that lead inevitably to its manipulation and subordination.

However, nothing could be farther from Michels's intention than to provide a rationale for resignation to those processes. He emphatically states that in this work he "desired to throw light upon certain sociological tendencies which oppose the reign of democracy, and to a still greater extent oppose the reign of socialism." He quite deliberately adopted a one-sided view and laid "considerable stress upon the pessimistic aspect of democracy which is forced upon us by historical study" (p. 405). He employed the term "iron law" to dramatize the difficult and formidable obstacles that lay before the realization of democracy, but not in order to deny altogether the possibility of its realization. From his analysis, "it would be erroneous to conclude," Michels maintains, "that we should renounce all endeavors to ascertain the limits which may be imposed upon the power exercised over the individual by oligarchies (state, dominant class, party, etc.). It would be an error to abandon the desperate enterprise of endeavoring to discover the social order which will render possible the complete realization of the idea of popular sovereignty" (pp. 404–5). Moreover,

> the writer does not wish to deny that every revolutionary working-class movement, and every movement sincerely inspired by the democratic spirit, may have a certain value as contributing to the enfeeblement of oligarchic tendencies. (p. 405)

In the end, furthermore, he emphasized that free inquiry, and criticism and control of the leaders, so essential for the strengthening of democracy, can be developed increasingly among the masses themselves: "A wider education involves an increasing capacity for exercising control." As Michels develops that point it becomes clear that although there are in his view at any given time certain limits on the degree of perfection democracy can attain (here as elsewhere, the actual falls short of the ideal), still, the ideal can more and more be approximated. "It is," he insists, ". . . the great task of social education to raise the intellectual level of the masses, so that they may be enabled, within the limits of what is possible, to counteract the oligarchical tendencies of the working-class movement" (p. 407).

In the concluding paragraphs of his work, Michels goes on record, unequivocally, in favor of democracy: "The defects inherent in democracy are obvious. It is none the less true that as a form of social life we must choose democracy as the least of evils" (p. 407). Finally he writes: "It may be said, therefore, that the more humanity comes to recognize the advantages which democracy, however imperfect, presents over aristocracy, even at its best, the less likely it is that a recognition of the defects of democracy will provoke a return to aristocracy" (p. 407).

It is in that spirit, therefore, that Michels's classic study should be read—namely, as "a serene and frank examination of the oligarchical dangers of democracy [which] will enable us to minimize these dangers, even though they can never be entirely avoided" (p. 408).

NOTES

1. Roberto Michels, *First Lectures in Political Sociology*, trans. Alfred de Grazia (New York: Harper & Row, 1965), p. 10.
2. Ibid., p. 16.
3. Ibid., p. 18.
4. Quoted by Michels in ibid., p. 19.
5. Ibid., p. 21.
6. Ibid.
7. Ibid.
8. Ibid., p. 54.
9. Robert Michels, *Political Parties* (New York: Dover Publications, 1959), p. viii. (Hereafter all page references to this work will be indicated in parentheses immediately following the quoted passage.)
10. In some cases, Michels argues, former proletarians as leaders may be worse. See Ibid., p. 302.

21

Émile Durkheim (1858–1917)

To understand the sociology of Émile Durkheim, one must, in his case as in the case of so many of his contemporaries, examine his relation to socialist thought and to the socialist movement of his time. Apparently Durkheim had begun to concern himself with the problems of socialism as early as 1883, about the same time that he had drawn up the first plan of his *Division of Labor.* As he progressed in his work on the *Division of Labor, Suicide, The Family,* and *Religion,* all eventually to become full-scale studies, his interests shifted from socialism to sociology and then mainly to social problems. As Marcel Mauss observed, however, Durkheim never lost sight of his point of departure.[1] When, in 1895, he again took up the study of socialism and delivered a series of lectures on the subject at the University of Bordeaux, he sought to treat it both objectively and sociologically: How does one explain the various forms of socialist ideology? What were the social conditions and pressures that prompted Saint-Simon, Fourier, Owen, and Marx to advance their respective theories? Thus Durkheim's studies of socialism were to be an "analysis of the causes of an idea."[2]

Durkheim had an intimate knowledge of socialist literature, including the works of Karl Marx, "whom a Finnish friend, Neiglick, had advised him to study during his stay in Leipzig" (p. 3). Nevertheless, throughout his life, he remained opposed to socialism though his closest friends and students were committed to it in its Marxian, Guesdist, and other forms. The features of socialism which, according to Mauss, he disliked were "its violent nature, its class character—more or less purely workingmen's—and therefore its political and even politician-like tone" (p. 3). Thus in opposition to a conception of society and social change based on classes and class conflict, Durkheim put forward a theory based on "organic solidarity."

Durkheim's concern with "solidarity" was related to his fear of the social and political conflicts of his time. The strength and prominence of the socialist movement, as well as the analyses and solutions it proposed, pressed him to seek some kind of intellectual mediation between two prominent theoretical systems: the Comtean and the Marxian. That he attempted to do by exploring the work of their common intellectual ancestor, Saint-Simon; it is in Durkheim's study, *Socialism and Saint-Simon,* that much of his later thinking is anticipated.

DURKHEIM AND SAINT-SIMON

Although class conflict, for Saint-Simon, played an important role in the transition from the feudal to the bourgeois order, it lost virtually all significance once the new scientific-industrial order was established. Though he clearly recognized the existence of classes and strata in the new society, he believed that the new conditions could lead to a hierarchical but nonetheless organic order of social peace and stability. Integration was to be achieved primarily by instituting the appropriate moral ideas. That becomes the leading idea of Durkheim's system as well. The new division of labor—that is, science and industry—need not lead, as Comte had feared it would, to "disorganization" and "anarchy." Everything depended, for Saint-Simon as for Durkheim, on whether the *appropriate* moral order could be developed to suit the new social and technical conditions.

By reviewing the basic principles of Saint-Simon's philosophy, the degree to which Durkheim was indebted to him will become clearer, for it is quite evident that it was Saint-Simon and *not* Comte whom Durkheim regarded as his intellectual master. The "idea, the word, and even the outline of positivist philosophy," wrote Durkheim, "are all found in Saint-Simon. . . . Therefore, it is to him that one must, in full justice, award the honor currently given Comte" (p. 104). In these essays, Durkheim vehemently defends and proves that proposition. It was important for him to establish that fact, since the Saint-Simonian principles (which Durkheim summarizes rather well) all reappear in his own works; in fact, those principles form the basis of his own sociology.

Moral ideas for Saint-Simon as for Durkheim are the real cement of a society. For both thinkers a society is above all a community of ideas: "The similarity of positive moral ideas is the single bond which can unite men into society" (p. 91). If Saint-Simon saw as his major task to determine what kind of moral system post-Revolutionary European society required, Durkheim viewed his own work in a similar light: to provide a secular, moral system that would bind together into a unified social order the classes, strata, and occupational groups of contemporary France. Like Saint-Simon, he viewed the role of theory as essentially positive and constructive and shared with the founder of positive philosophy a certain disdain for the negative-critical outlook of the *Philosophes* and the Revolutionaries. Durkheim wholeheartedly agreed that contemporary philosophy must be constructive and organizational, not critical and revolutionary. His emphasis on the constructive and organizational, however, was to serve as an antidote to the critical and revolutionary ideas of the socialists.

It was Saint-Simon's conception of society as enunciated in his *Physiologie Sociale* and elsewhere that led Durkheim to his own positivistic and functional view and that inspired the organismic analogies and metaphors we find throughout his work. Durkheim's fundamental premise, that "society" is not a simple aggregate of individuals but a reality sui generis, had already been explicitly defined by Saint-Simon:

> Society is not at all a simple conglomeration of living beings whose actions have no other cause but the arbitrariness of individual wills, nor other result than ephemeral or unimportant accidents. On the contrary, society is above all a veritable organized machine, all of whose parts contribute in a different way to the movement of the whole. The gathering of men constitutes a veritable being whose existence is more or less certain or precarious according to whether its organs acquit themselves more or less regularly of the functions entrusted to them. (p. 99)

Likewise, Durkheim's evolutionary conception of society is anticipated in Saint-Simon's "law of progress." The Saint-Simonian emphasis—that men are the instruments rather than the authors of that law—remains a dominant theme in Durkheim's treatment of the individual and in his reification (and sometimes even deification) of society and social processes. For both thinkers, social laws dominated men; the best they could hope for was to discover the direction of those laws—the task of positive science—so as to adjust to them with the least pain.

Saint-Simon had described, in essentially a dialectical way, the origins of the scientific-industrial order within the womb of the feudal-theological system. The two contradictory systems could not coexist indefinitely, and the tensions and conflicts ultimately resulted in the French Revolution. The conflict and anarchy of the post-Revolutionary epoch could be eliminated by imposing a religious-moral order *appropriate* to the new scientific-industrial conditions. Eventually, that led to his call for a "new Christianity."

That Durkheim took over Saint-Simon's view in its essentials is quite clear, notably in his *Division of Labor* in which *mechanical* solidarity was giving way to a "higher" solidarity he called *organic*. Although both thinkers viewed the older social order as based on conflicting principles, classes, and class interests, they both read conflict out of their respective higher, organic societies. There was nothing normal about conflict in the new society; the existence of classes did not preclude the moral unity and solidarity of the society as a whole. Durkheim believed that the mission Saint-Simon had set himself—to elaborate a new and appropriate body of universally acceptable moral and rational beliefs—still remained unaccomplished in his time. He agreed that the old order could not be restored; therefore the new one had to be "integrated." That was essential to avoid the recurring economic and political crises, the chronic mood of exasperation and discontent, and, finally, the "disintegration" of society. The "revolution" Saint-Simon had envisioned was still incomplete in his own time, Durkheim believed, because the new integrative institutions appropriate to the modern division of labor had yet to be established. A new law and morality had to be developed to mediate among the diverse interest groups of industrial society and thus serve to integrate all its parts and functions.

That appeared feasible to Durkheim because he accepted the Saint-Simonian view of industry as a unifying and pacific force. Describing Saint-Simon's view, Durkheim writes: "From military—which it was formerly—the human spirit became pacific. Industry was offering nations a means—as fruitful as war—of becoming rich and powerful" (pp. 130–31). Once the old feudal, military, and theological functions had lost their significance, there was no apparent reason for social conflict in the new "organic" society. The main source of conflict in the older system had been the conflicting interests and principles of the feudal and industrial classes—ergo, to achieve an "organic" quality, the new society had to be based on only *one* of those principles. Modern societies, writes Durkheim, following Saint-Simon's formula, "will be definitely in equilibrium only when organized on a purely industrial basis" (p. 131). Like his master, Durkheim saw a harmony of interests not only among the many and varied occupational groups ("functions") but between the industrial capitalists and workers as well. He adopts Saint-Simon's formula that "the producers of useful things—being the only useful people in society—are the only ones who should cooperate to regulate" the course of the new industrial society (p. 134). That formed the basis for the role Durkheim assigned to "occupational guilds." Only those who live on unearned income, Saint-Simon argued, should be placed beyond the pale of regular society. "As for those who themselves make their wealth productive, who enrich it with their toil—they are industrials. Consequently, industrial society comprises all those who actively participate in the economic life, whether they are owners or not."

Durkheim's theory of the integrative consequences of the growing division of labor is likewise derived from Saint-Simon. That Durkheim elaborated in his *Division of Labor* ideas that had already appeared in all their essentials in Saint-Simon's scheme may be seen from the following excerpts from

Système Industriel. In that work and others, Saint-Simon held that the growing division of labor would lead to greater interdependence and mutual responsibility among individuals, and to a greater dependence upon society as a whole.

> In the measure that civilization makes progress, the division of labor—considered from the spiritual as from the secular side, grows in the same proportion. Thus men depend less on others as individuals, but more on the mass. . . . [The] organization of a well-ordered system requires that the parts be strongly tied to the whole and subordinated. (p. 138)

Even Durkheim's frequently reiterated idea of the integrative role of occupational guilds and corporations was first expressed by Saint-Simon. In order that the division of labor should result in a solidary industrial society, it was necessary "that in the large majority of the nation, individuals be joined in industrial associations, more or less numerous and connected . . . to permit their formation into a generalized system by being directed toward a great common industrial goal" (p. 139). Like Saint-Simon, Durkheim sees the industrial system as possessing an inherent unity. His summary of Saint-Simon's conception describes his own equally well. The growing division of labor was, in his view, leading to a solidarity of interests among all classes ("parts") of society. Classes are termed "functions" and are regarded as coordinative, cooperative, and unifying—never as conflictive. "Each people today," he writes, "forms a homogeneous whole, not because it acquired the habit of identifying itself with such and such a function or class, but because it is a system of functions inseparable from one another and mutually complementing each other" (p. 148).

If the industrial system was only a system of "functions," all that was necessary to assure their harmonious operation was proper regulation. Here, too, the rudiments of his theory appear first in Saint-Simon. In the new society, ". . . it is not the strongest who control but those most capable in science or industry. They are not summoned to office because they have the power to exercise their will but because they know more than others, and consequently their functions do not consist in saying what they want, but what they know. They do not dictate orders, they only declare what conforms to the nature of things" (p. 150). And again, "Those who direct are not above those who are directed; they are not their superiors. They fulfill a different function—that is all" (p. 151).

Throughout Durkheim's work, one encounters the injunction, "Fight egoism!" for egoism left unbridled "would of necessity finally result in the dissolution of society." But those words are Saint-Simon's and first appear in his *Système Industriel.* What Durkheim regarded as the best antidote for egoism—namely, an altruistic moral commitment to "Society"—was derived from Saint-Simon's *New Christianity.* "Love one another" was Saint-Simon's motto. "The fundamental principle established by the divine author of

Christianity commands all men to regard themselves as brothers and to cooperate as completely as possible for their well-being. This principle is the most general of all social principles" (p. 165). The real task was to organize "temporal power in conformity with this divine axiom." A new charity and a new philanthropy were required, Saint-Simon emphasized, "to improve as much as possible the fate of the class which has no other means of existence but the labor of its hands" (p. 166). That is important not only for its own sake but for the sake of social peace. Durkheim correctly observed about that aspect of Saint-Simon's doctrine (and his own as well) that it was inspired by "compassion for the unfortunate, along with a fear of their dangers to the social order" (p. 168).

Durkheim follows Saint-Simon in still another point: the integrative role of moral sentiments. When he argues that the division of labor conduces to a higher solidarity, he does so only in the sense that men are increasingly dependent on one another; but he recognizes at the same time that interdependence is not sufficient to bring about real solidarity—which can only be effected through a moral education and commitment to "society as a whole."

In his discussion of Saint-Simon, Durkheim's moral values clearly emerge. He despised and feared restlessness, social conflict, and "anarchy"; the insatiable appetites of modern man were a sign of his morbidity. Along with Bonald, Maistre, and Saint-Simon, Durkheim believed that the decline of religious forces had left a moral vacuum. A morality of contentment was required because social peace could never be achieved so long as men were not content with their lot. "What is needed if social order is to reign," writes Durkheim, "is that the mass of men be content with their lot. But what is needed for them to be content, is not that they have more or less but that they be convinced they have no right to more. And for this, it is absolutely essential that there be an authority whose superiority they acknowledge and which tells them what is right" (p. 200). What is necessary above all is a strong moral force capable of moderating and regulating the various "functions" and of curbing "egoism" and special interests.

Durkheim thus wanted to pose the social question in a manner entirely different from the way the socialists did. His way of posing the question, he believed,

> no longer stirs questions of classes; it no longer opposes rich to poor, employers to workers—as if the only possible solution consisted of diminishing the portion of one in order to augment that of the other. But it declares, in the interest of both, the necessity of a curb from above which checks appetites and so sets a limit on the state of disarrangement, excitement, frenzied agitation, which do not spring from social activity and which even make it suffer. Put differently, the social question, posed this way, is not a question of money or force; it is a question of moral agents. What dominates it is not the state of our economy but, much more, the state of our morality. (p. 204)

THE PROBLEM OF ORDER

Durkheim's central concern, therefore, was with the "problem of order"—that is, with the question of how the society of his time might establish and maintain social stability and cohesiveness. Thomas Hobbes, we shall recall, explained social order as a result of the fear of a Leviathan, a central power. For Hobbes, that was the single most important condition which made society possible. In France of Durkheim's time, it was the Saint-Simonians and Comteans who advocated a Hobbesian solution to the problem of order. They recognized that industrial developments and the conflicts of interest accompanying them were tearing the fabric of existing society and undermining the social peace. Their solution was a state-imposed social peace.

At the other extreme were the *utilitarians.* If Hobbes rested his theory of order on the fear of a central authority, the utilitarians dispensed with a central authority altogether. For the utilitarians, social order and harmony resulted from the division of labor. Order was viewed as an *automatic* consequence of an economic system in which every individual pursued his own interests. That theory expressed itself in laissez faire—the doctrine that the economy works best when left alone. No central regulatory agency is required for the smooth operation of the economy. Indeed, the intrusion of such an agency can only serve to disrupt what is essentially a self-regulating system. All economic affairs take place through the medium of free exchange, and if each individual dedicates himself to the pursuit of his own interests, that will lead to the "greatest good of the greatest number."

It is doubtful whether the market system ever worked in the automatic, self-regulating way in which the classical economists and other utilitarians conceived of it. It is even more doubtful that it worked for the general good. As early as the second decade of the nineteenth century, the economist Sismondi in his *Nouveaux Principes d'Economie Politique* (1819) demonstrated that the poor suffer most from economic crises, and that the utilitarians were therefore simply wrong. Those matters aside, however, the important sociological question is whether free exchange and other contractual relationships must lead to social order.

In a most telling critique, Durkheim observed that if we look carefully into the so-called total harmony of interests of the utilitarians, we can see that it conceals a latent conflict. It is clear that if an individual's own interests are the sole regulator of his conduct, there is nothing to prevent everyone's relentless pursuit of self-interest from degenerating into a Hobbesian war of all against all. "There is nothing less constant than interest," writes Durkheim in his *Division of Labor in Society*. "Today it unites me to you; tomorrow it will make me your enemy."[3] It is true, argues Durkheim, that interests can bind people together, but they can do so only temporarily and partially. When the mutual interest in exchange of two or more parties ceases, they will either turn away from each other or even turn against each other. It follows that *con-*

tractual interests alone no more than *fear of the Leviathan* alone, can account for social order. Each of those may constitute one element of order, but neither element in and of itself can serve as a sufficient condition of order. In developing his critique, Durkheim provides the third element that any adequate theory of order must include.

What the utilitarians have overlooked, Durkheim notes, is that not everything in a contract is contractual. Every contract contains *noncontractual* or *sociomoral* elements that exercise some regulative control over the parties concerned. In fact, a contract has no validity if it fails to fulfill the conditions required by law. The contracting parties acquire obligations of a moral or legal kind that are not specified in the terms of the contract. Thus contract law, rooted in custom, tradition, and precedent, provides the sociomoral context of every exchange relationship. We may exchange and cooperate because it is in our mutual interest, but the relationship we thereby form is necessarily hedged in by duties and obligations not of our own making. "The agreement of parties," writes Durkheim, "cannot render a clause just which by itself is unjust, and there are rules of justice whose violation social justice prevents, even if it has been consented to by the interested parties" (p. 216).

But Durkheim also rejected a third approach to the problem of order, that of the socialists. In his first major work Durkheim set himself the task of demonstrating that the expanding industrial division of labor brings with it a higher form of solidarity than existed before. That idea, borrowed from Saint-Simon, was not only a positive thesis but a polemical one as well. Contemporary socialists, and particularly the Marxists, had also regarded the growth of science and industry as inevitable, but for them, in order that humanity in general should reap the benefits of modern technical developments, a fundamental restructuring of social relations was necessary. In the Marxian view the modern industrial division of labor was not merely a system of coordinate functions; quite to the contrary, it was a system of structural inequalities based on socioeconomic classes with antagonistic interests.

What Durkheim sought to provide, then, was a cogent rebuttal to both the Comtean and Marxian positions, while exposing at the same time the erroneousness of the utilitarian view. In the main, however, Durkheim's theory is a form of mediation between Comte and Marx. To Comte, Durkheim conceded that moral consensus was a precondition of social order, but against him, he argued that the division of labor need not lead to a dispersion and conflict of interests. There were other, *nonmoral* conditions that were at least equally important for the establishment of social solidarity. The development of science and industry, promoting an increasing interdependence among individuals and groups within society as a whole, could serve as the objective basis of a new and higher solidarity.

To the Marxian and other socialists, Durkheim conceded the need for significant socioeconomic reforms, without which there could be neither true solidarity nor true justice. But against them he argued that no fundamental restructuring of socioeconomic relations was necessary. Thus Durkheim proceeded to mediate between the Comteans and the socialists; he did so by adapting the ideas of their common ancestor, Saint-Simon, to the society of his time.

Durkheim begins by proposing that the modern, industrial division of labor be viewed in a new light. The ". . . economic services that it can render are picayune compared to the moral effect that it produces, and its true function is to create in two or more persons a feeling of solidarity. In whatever manner the result is obtained, its aim is to cause coherence among friends and to stamp them with its seal" (p. 56). Once upon a time, society was unified because it was homogeneous; everyone was alike. With the growing differentiation of occupations, however, and the increasing complexity of society, the original solidarity was undermined and lost. But that does not mean that solidarity is forever destroyed. A new and higher type of social solidarity is being generated by the industrial division of labor. That is the central thesis which Durkheim developed in his first major work.

Constructing his model on the basis of what was known about primitive societies, Durkheim posits an original unity which he calls "mechanical solidarity." Such solidarity rested on common collective sentiments, on a *conscience collective*, which in French carries the connotation of both a common consciousness and a common conscience. The collective sentiments are engraved, rather strongly, on all the individual consciences. The best empirical indication of the existence of a "totality of social similitudes" is the social reaction to crime. In fact, an act is "criminal," for Durkheim, precisely because it is carried out in opposition to the collective sentiments. We "must not say," he writes, "that an action shocks the common conscience because it is criminal, but rather that it is criminal because it shocks the common conscience" (p. 81). Crime is "an offense against an authority in some way transcendent" (p. 85). Anything that offends or violates the common conscience threatens the solidarity—the very existence—of society. An offense left unpunished weakens to that same degree the social unity. Punishment therefore serves the important function of restoring and reconstituting social unity. In the primitive context, it is expiatory and retaliatory; it is a passionate reaction by society against those who dared violate its basic rules. Restitution is not enough; the social body "must have a more violent satisfaction. The force against which the crime comes is too intense to react with very much moderation. Moreover, it cannot do so without enfeebling itself; for it is thanks to the intensity of the reaction that it keeps alive and maintains itself with the same degree of energy." Thus Durkheim describes a social state based on a uniform conscience present in all members of society.

If repressive and expiatory law is characteristic of mechanical solidarity, it is *restitutive* law which is most typical of organic solidarity. Here the point is not punishment, but restoring damaged interests; law becomes "a means of reviewing the past in order to reinstate it, as far as possible, to its normal form." And now, since society is a complex of many and diverse groups and interests, law acts through specialized organs. Nevertheless, it is society that empowers those organs and acts through them. Even contractual relations, which are ostensibly private and individual, are binding precisely because society gives power to such relations; society sanctions "the obligations contracted for. . . . Every contract thus supposes that behind the parties implicated in it there is society very ready to intervene in order to gain respect for the engagements which have been made" (p. 114).

Not all the relationships in the complex society, Durkheim acknowledges, conduce to solidarity. Some are negative. For instance, the rights of some persons are different from those of others. ". . . I cannot enjoy my right without harming someone else; such is the case with certain servitudes" (p. 118). Law is then necessary to repair wrong and to prevent it. But such rules do not demand real cooperation; "they simply restore or maintain, in the new conditions which are produced, this negative solidarity whose circumstances have troubled its functioning" (p. 118). Rules governing those relationships do not lead to "positive social links"; they lead to the separation of spheres but not to cooperation. The other rules of restitutive law, the residue, Durkheim writes, "express a positive union, a cooperation which derives, in essentials, from the division of labor" (p. 122).

Durkheim begins now to develop his thesis on the positive consequences of the division of labor: It leads to exchange of services, reciprocity of obligations, interdependence, and so on. Contracts and other formal-legal relationships governing exchange lead to what he defined as *organic solidarity:* ". . . Spencer has not without justice qualified as a physiological contract the exchange of materials which is made at every instant between the different organs of the living body" (p. 125). In that way Durkheim conceives of the complex social system as a multiplicity of distinct functions which need to be coordinated.

Durkheim thus maintains that the division of labor, in its *normal* condition, engenders cooperation and solidarity. In opposition to those who thought otherwise, Durkheim held that modern economic developments need not lead to social conflict and disorder. A higher, organic solidarity could be achieved, for it ". . . is the division of labor which, more and more, fills the role that was formerly filled by the Common Conscience. It [the division of labor] is the principal bond of social aggregates of higher types" (p. 173). Yet, Durkheim felt a certain uneasiness with that proposition, because, after all, it was quite evident that the division of labor had so far failed to bring forth the results he was predicting. How did he deal with that fact?

If the increasingly complex division of labor had yet to produce social solidarity, that was a result of the *abnormal* or pathological forms that the division of labor presently assumed. "Though *normally,*" writes Durkheim, "the division of labor produces social solidarity, it sometimes happens that it has different, and even contrary results. Now, it is important to find out what makes it deviate from its natural course, for if we do not prove that these cases are exceptional, the division of labor might be accused of logically implying them" (p. 353).

In Durkheim's treatment of the so-called pathological forms of the division of labor, one sees clearly an attempt on his part to deal with the issues raised by the socialists. There were, for example, the recurrent industrial and commercial crises which Marx had regarded as inherent in capitalist relations of production. For Durkheim, such crises were explained by the lack of adjustment among the various "functions" of the social organism. He acknowledges that ". . . insofar as labor is divided more, these phenomena [crises] seem to be more frequent, at least in certain cases. From 1845 to 1869, failures increased 70%" (p. 354). "The conflict between capital and labor," he continues, "is another example, more striking, of the same phenomenon. Insofar as industrial functions become more specialized, the conflict becomes more lively, instead of solidarity increasing" (p. 354). So, Durkheim observed those salient facts and even agreed that class conflicts assume the greatest intensity with ". . . the birth of large-scale industry" (p. 355). With the growth in the division of labor, class warfare has become more violent. For Durkheim, however, all that is a consequence of the division of labor not in its normal form, but in its *abnormal* forms.

The first of the abnormal or pathological forms he calls the *anomic* division of labor. That word comes from the Greek *anomia*, referring to a state of society in which normative standards of conduct are weak or absent. Durkheim employed that term to convey that what was lacking or poorly developed in modern industrial society was a moral-legal code appropriate to the new conditions. Such a code was essential in order to mediate among the many and diverse interest groups in society and thus to regulate and moderate social conflicts.

But Durkheim realized that rules and regulations cannot be the whole solution and that often the rules themselves serve to perpetuate certain social ills. That is particularly evident in class conflicts. Socioeconomic classes, an integral aspect of the industrial division of labor, are a source of dissension and conflict. The "lower classes not being . . . satisfied with the role which has devolved upon them from custom or law aspire to functions which are closed to them and seek to dispossess those who are exercising these functions. Thus civil conflicts arise which are due to the manner in which labor is distributed" (p. 394). Thus Durkheim introduces a second major pathological form—the *forced division of labor.*

Under the heading "forced division of labor," Durkheim examines the relationship between order and justice. The higher organic solidarity requires new rules, but if those rules are inherently unjust, the solidarity will never materialize. Justice, for Durkheim, implied a basic social equality:

> If one class of society is obliged in order to live, to take any price for its services, while another can abstain from such action thanks to resources at its disposal . . . , the second has an unjust advantage over the first at law. In other words, there cannot be rich and poor at birth without there being unjust contracts. (p. 384)

Durkheim therefore considers the task of modern society as a "work of justice."

At the same time, another theme emerged and became a leading idea in Durkheim's proposal for reform. If the prevailing anarchy and anomy are to decline and ultimately to disappear, what is required is the resurrection of an old social institution and its reintroduction, in a modified and appropriate form, into modern social life. Comte was wrong in assigning the regulative function exclusively to the State; modern economic life is much too complex for its regulation to be given over to that institution. Instead, that tried and tested institution, the *occupational corporation or guild*, which was already known in antiquity and which flourished during the Middle Ages, can be readapted to modern conditions and can again serve the regulatory function it had served so well in the past. The men of the French Revolution acted rashly when they destroyed that institution instead of only modifying it. The occupational group should become the basis of an occupational ethic, for "[a]n occupational activity can be efficaciously regulated only by a group intimate enough with it to know its functioning, feel all its needs, and able to follow all their variations."

The occupational guilds must again become a public institution. They are to be based on the existing class structure and their function would be to lay down general moral and legal principles according to which relations among the various occupations and classes would be regulated. Representatives of both the employers and employees would be elected to the corporation assembly "in proportions corresponding to the respective importance attributed by opinion to these factors in production" (p. 25 n.). And Durkheim adds,

> But if it is necessary that both meet in the directing councils of the corporations, it is no less important that at the base of the corporative organization they form distinct and independent groups, for their interests are too often rival and antagonistic. To be able to go about their ways freely, they must go about their ways separately. The two groups thus constituted would then be able to appoint their representatives to the common assemblies. (p. 25 n.)

ORDER AND JUSTICE

Just as Saint-Simon had called for a new secular religion, Durkheim now called for a new secular morality. A theme that would become stronger as he grew older—the need for altruism, and the individual as well as social hazards of egoism—already finds expression here.

> We are not naturally inclined [he writes] to put ourselves out or to use self-restraint; if we are not encouraged at every step to exercise the restraint upon which all morals depend, how should we get the habit of it? If we follow no rule except that of a clear self-interest, in the occupations that take up nearly the whole of our time, how should we acquire a taste for any disinterestedness, or selflessness, or sacrifice?[4]

The employer as well as the worker "is aware of no influence set above him to check his egotism; he is subject to no moral discipline whatever and so he scouts any discipline at all of this kind." Moral standards have to be raised "so that the conflicts which disturb [economic life] have an end. . . . There should be rules telling each of the workers his rights and his duties, not vaguely in general terms but in precise detail, having in view the most ordinary day-to-day occurrences." Employers and workers must, in their respective groups, impose restraint upon their special and selfish interests; they must see the interests of the whole, and then conflict will diminish and become moderate while the solidarity of society is correspondingly enhanced.

In his concluding discussion of property, property rights, and contracts, Durkheim returns to the problem of justice. Inheritance and exchange by contracts are the two main ways of acquiring property; he tries to show by means of historical analysis that the former is "bound up with archaic concepts and practices that have no part in our present-day ethics" (p. 174). Of "the two main processes by which property is acquired, inheritance is the one that is going to lose its importance more and more" (p. 175). What remains then is the contract, and whether the conditions under which it is made can be just.

The contract is a juridical-moral bond between two subjects that specifies their mutual rights and obligations. Generally, says Durkheim, "a right exists on both sides" (p. 176). He is quick to add, however, that "these mutual rights are not inevitable. The slave is bound in law to his master and yet has no right over him" (p. 176). Thus Durkheim returns to a fundamental issue: Some contracts are made between social unequals where one dominates and the other serves and where the latter has no choice but to serve or to suffer worse consequences. Can such a contract, though sanctioned by "a moral authority that stands higher," be just? To that question Durkheim replies with an unequivocal no.

In tracing its development as an institution, Durkheim shows that a bona fide consensual contract "could not be one of good faith except on condition of its being one by mutual consent" (p. 203). But consent "binds truly and absolutely the one who consents only on the condition that it has been *freely* given. Anything that lessens the liberty of the contracting party, lessens the binding force of the contract." As Durkheim proceeds to develop his argument, one sees just how close he moved in that instance to the socialist point of view:

> This rule should not be confused with the one that requires the contract to be made with deliberate intent. For I may very well have had the will to contract as I have done, and yet have contracted only under coercion. In this case, I will the obligations I subscribe to, but I will them by reason of pressure being put upon me. The consent in such instances is said to be invalidated and thus the contract is null and void. (p. 204)

Thus a contract cannot be viewed as just simply because a person has subjectively willed it. What is crucial is how much freedom and power one has to resist entering into certain contractual relationships. Whether a contract is binding or not depends, therefore, not merely on subjective will but on the *objective* conditions under which it is made. If

> contracts imposed by constraint, direct or indirect, are not binding, this does not arise from the state of the will when it gave consent. It arises from the consequences that an obligation thus formed inevitably brings upon the contracting party. It may be, in fact, that he took the step that has bound him only under external pressure, that his consent has been extracted from him. If this is so, it means that the consent was against his own interests and the justifiable needs he might have under the general principles of equity. The use of coercion could have had no other aim or consequence but that of forcing him to yield up something which he did not wish to, to do something he did not wish to do, or indeed of forcing him to the one action or the other on conditions he did not will. Penalty and distress have thus been undeservedly laid on him. (p. 206).

Such a contract, Durkheim observes, is increasingly regarded as invalid and that is not merely because "the determining cause of the obligation is exterior to the individual who binds himself. It is because he has suffered some unjustified injury, because, in a word, such a contract is unjust." Increasingly, a contract is regarded as moral and just only if it is not a "means of exploiting one of the contracting parties." The *objective consequences* for the parties concerned, and not their formal, subjective consent, must constitute the real criterion of a just contract.

Here, in the final pages of *Professional Ethics and Civic Morals*, Durkheim draws certain far-reaching conclusions from the class structure of society. The institution of inheritance is again singled out by Durkheim as a "supreme obstacle" to just relations in society:

> Now inheritance as an institution [writes Durkheim] results in men being born either rich or poor; that is to say, there are two main classes in society, linked by all sorts of intermediate classes: the one which in order to live has to make its services acceptable to the other at whatever the cost; the other class which can do without these services, because it can call on certain resources. . . . Therefore as long as such sharp class differences exist in society, fairly effective palliatives may lessen the injustice of contracts; but in principle, the system operates in conditions which do not allow of justice. (p. 213)

Durkheim conceived of social change not as a function of class and other social conflicts, but as a result of the slow evolution of the collective moral conscience. One important change, however, was immediately possible, which would at one stroke eradicate a fundamental source of inequality and thus make for a qualitatively new stage of justice: "One primary reform is possible at once and almost without any transition. This is the discontinuance of inheritance *ab intestat* or by next of kin . . ." (p. 216). Who, then, will inherit the wealth? Durkheim regarded the occupational corporations as best suited to fulfill that function. Like the socialists, he thus saw the need to socialize property and wealth, but it is the professional groups that, in his opinion, "would satisfy all the conditions for becoming in a sense, in the economic sphere, the heirs of the family" (p. 218).

But Durkheim is prepared to go even farther. Even after the abolition of inheritance, inequalities will remain—differences of talents and intelligence. Can it not be said that such inequalities of merit are also fortuitous?

> To us it does not seem equitable that a man should be better treated as a social being because he was born of parentage that is rich or of high rank. But is it any more equitable that he should be better treated because he was born of a father of higher intelligence or in a more favorable moral milieu? It is here that the domain of charity begins. Charity is the feeling of human sympathy that we see becoming clear even of these last remaining traces of inequality. It ignores and denies any special merit in gifts or mental capacity acquired by heredity. This, then, is the very acme of justice. (p. 220)

That is the note on which Durkheim concludes *Professional Ethics and Civic Morals.*

DURKHEIM'S SOCIOLOGY OF DEVIANT BEHAVIOR

Durkheim was a pioneer in the sociological analysis of deviant behavior. He was the first to set forth the proposition that deviance is no less firmly rooted in social conditions than conformity. Deviance, he maintained, is neither morbid nor pathological but rather normal. In any society there exists an inevitable diversity of human conduct as well as a variation in moral values. How, then, does one distinguish "normal" from "deviant" behavior?

For Durkheim, a scientific reply to that question rests on a statistical criterion. The "normal," he writes, refers to ". . . those social conditions that are most generally distributed. . . ."[5] The social norm consists of the most frequent forms of behavior. Other, less frequent forms which depart from the norm are deviant. Yet, paradoxically perhaps, although crime is a form of deviance, it is nonetheless normal.

Most criminologists in Durkheim's time looked upon crime as a pathology rooted in an individual's physiological or psychological makeup. Durkheim, in contrast, insisted that crime is a normal phenomenon. It is normal because it is present

> in all societies of all types. There is no society that is not confronted with the problem of criminality. Its form changes; the acts thus characterized are not the

> same everywhere; but, everywhere and always there have been men who have behaved in such a way as to draw upon themselves penal repression.[6]

If a society utterly devoid of crime is unknown, then crime must be a normal and integral facet of every social order.

That conception of things should not be misunderstood. When Durkheim asserts that crime is necessary, he does not mean that *specific types* of crime are inevitable or that crime *rates* cannot be decreased by appropriate social measures. No, what Durkheim intends to argue instead is, first, that wherever human beings congregate, they display diverse forms of behavior; and, second, that some of those forms will be seen as departing from established norms, and will be punished accordingly. "Crime" thus ranges all the way from minor infractions of decorum at one end of the scale to major felonies on the other.

> Imagine a society of saints [writes Durkheim], a perfect cloister of exemplary individuals. Crimes, properly so called, will there be unknown; but faults which appear venial to the layman will create there the same scandal that the ordinary offense does in ordinary consciousness. If, then, this society has the power to judge and punish, it will define these acts as criminal and will treat them as such. For the same reason, the perfect and upright man judges his smallest failings with a severity that the majority reserves for acts more truly in the nature of an offense.[7]

Individuals in every society differ in respect to the social and cultural milieux in which they find themselves. No society, therefore, is capable of achieving perfect moral uniformity. The diversification of behavior is a social process which results in both extraordinary and ordinary deviants. It produces individuals who may be geniuses and "criminals" at one and the same time. Thus Durkheim observes,

> according to Athenian law, Socrates was a criminal, and his condemnation was no more than just. However, his crime, namely, the independence of his thought, rendered a service not only to humanity but to his country. It served to prepare a new morality and faith which the Athenians needed, since the traditions by which they had lived until then were no longer in harmony with the current conditions of life. Nor is the case of Socrates unique; it is reproduced periodically in history. It would never have been possible to establish the freedom of thought we now enjoy if the regulations prohibiting it had not been violated before being solemnly abrogated. At that time, however, the violation was a crime, since it was an offense against sentiments still very keen in the average conscience.[8]

It is the process of social diversification that yields the higher order of deviant such as Socrates; it is the same process that brings forth ordinary deviants and common criminals. Among all the divergent actions that one finds in any given society, some will inevitably acquire a criminal character. It is not the intrinsic quality of the actions themselves that confers a criminal character upon them. It is rather the definition that is placed on those acts by the dominant consensus.

For Durkheim, then, crime is fundamentally bound up with the conditions of social life. Crime, far from being a pathology, is a normal phenomenon. Indeed, crime is not an unmitigated evil since it is indispensable for the development of morality and law.

CRIME AND PUNISHMENT

If the criminal character of an act does not reside in the act itself, where, then, does it reside? What makes an act criminal? Durkheim believed that the small, primitive society, characterized by "mechanical solidarity," presents the clearest and most direct reply to that question. In such a society, he noted, there are numerous acts which are considered crimes—for example, touching a tabooed object, failing to make a traditional sacrifice, departing from a precise ritual-formula, and so forth. Upon reflection it is clear that such diverse acts have only one thing in common: They are universally disapproved of by the members of the society in question. Those acts are crimes because they shock the collective conscience. In order for an act to qualify as a crime, it must offend strong and intense sentiments and break precise rules. A crime, therefore, is an act which antagonizes the powerful and well-defined sentiments of a collectivity. In Durkheim's words, "we must not say that an action shocks the common conscience because it is criminal, but rather that it is criminal because it shocks the common conscience. We do not reprove it because it is a crime, but it is a crime because we reprove it."[9] An act is a crime because it offends the transcendent authority of society.

If that conception of crime is sound, Durkheim reasoned, it ought to account for the nature of punishment. Punishment is first and foremost a passionate social reaction against the offender. That is especially evident in a primitive setting. Punishment is a form of vengeance, which may appear socially useless and unnecessarily cruel. But, actually, it enables the community to do something vital for itself. By means of punishment society heals the wounds inflicted upon it by the offender; through punishment, society restores its moral integrity and reaffirms its most fundamental values.

In modern society the essence of punishment remains much the same. It is still "at least in part, a work of vengeance." We may attempt to rationalize our treatment of the offender in terms of rehabilitation and the like, but we find it just that he should expiate his outrage through suffering. For us as for our ancestors, Durkheim convincingly argues, punishment remains a passionate reaction by means of which we reaffirm the validity of our rules and laws. That the reaction is passionate is evident from the conduct of both the prosecutor and the defense attorney in the modern courtroom. The former strives to awaken in the jury the sentiments that have been violated by the defendant, while the latter tries to rouse sympathy for him. Today punishment is carried out not by the collectivity as a whole but by the institutions of the State. But the essence of punishment continues to be a more or less zealous reaction against those who have violated our basic rules of conduct.

Crime therefore wounds the common conscience while punishment heals and restores it. Crime furnishes the community with an opportunity to revitalize itself by reacting intensely against the criminal offender. "Crime," writes Durkheim,

> brings together upright consciences and concentrates them. We have only to notice what happens, particularly in a small town, when some moral scandal has just been committed. They stop each other on the street, they visit each other, they seem to come together to talk of the event and to wax indignant in common. From all the similar impressions which are exchanged, from all the temper that gets itself expressed, there emerges a unique temper . . . which is everybody's without being anybody's in particular.[10]

The offended sentiments derive their peculiar force from the fact that they are common to everybody. They are unanimous, uncontested, and commonly respected. An act is a crime precisely because it damages the unanimity. To do nothing in the face of a crime, to let it go unpunished, would therefore result in the enfeeblement of the collective sentiments. It is only by acting in common against the offender that the community can reinforce itself and its basic values.

Hence, the main object of punishment, for Durkheim, is certainly not to chasten or correct the offender, nor even to deter others from following in his path. Its true object is to maintain the vitality of the community's fundamental values and to safeguard its social cohesion. Punishment enables society to repair the "evil" which the crime has inflicted upon it. There is thus a continuity between crime and punishment. The criminal violates the cherished standards of the community and the upright retaliate ". . . to heal the wounds made upon collective sentiments. . . ."[11] In that way Durkheim laid the foundation for a sociological understanding of crime and punishment.

Durkheim's sociological theory was an implicit repudiation of the theories of crime that were rampant in his day. Crime, it was widely believed, is the result of original sin or of innate depravity. It is caused by certain instinctual or racial predispositions; it is rooted in one's personality makeup or physiological structure. Clearly, Durkheim's conception of the *normality* of crime not only has nothing in common with such theories but is also a repudiation of them. One example will suffice to show just how far apart he was from some of his contemporaries.

One of the most famous nineteenth-century criminologists was a physician and psychiatrist named Cesare Lombroso (1836–1909). While serving as an army doctor, Lombroso thought he noticed that recalcitrant offender-soldiers differed from the disciplined troops by the greater prevalence and indecency of their tattoos. Later he employed experimental methods in studying insane patients. Comparing the insane patients with convicted criminals and those two in turn with normal persons, he measured their skulls and their sensitivity to touch. Once, while performing a postmortem examination of a notorious bandit, Lombroso found a distinct depression at the rear of the skull, in the opening in which the spine and the skull are connected. Earlier he had found a similar depression in animals. From that, Lombroso concluded that a criminal is an atavistic being, a kind of throwback to an earlier evolutionary stage, possessing the ferocious instincts of primitive humans. The physical stigmata of atavism, Lombroso believed, were a low forehead, a receding chin, ears standing out from the head, too many fingers, unusual wrinkling of the skin, atypical head size or shape, and eye peculiarities.

In response to criticism Lombroso eventually revised his "atavistic" theory. In his last book he conceded that there were environmental factors at work and listed a host of them from climate to religion. Retaining his original view that the "born criminal" and "insane criminal" are major types, he added a third category, the "criminaloid," who engages in vicious criminal behavior though he is born with neither physical stigmata nor mental aberrations. The "born criminal," he believed, comprised about a third of all criminals. Those he explained as a reversion to an earlier evolutionary stage. As for the "insane criminal," that was a mixed category of offenders suffering from paralysis, dementia, pellagra, alcoholism, epilepsy, idiocy, and hysteria—all of which Lombroso regarded as causes of crime.[12]

Today there is scarcely a criminologist who continues to subscribe to Lombrosian views. Indeed, few criminologists take seriously any theory that attempts to explain crime in terms of the alleged "organic inferiority" or "degeneracy" of criminals. Even the most sophisticated studies purporting to demonstrate the physiological basis of criminality are methodologically defective and lacking in scientific validity.[13] It is now increasingly recognized that early criminologists were deceived. They took the unattractive appearance of prisoners as a sign of their mental deficiency. "Abnormality" was reflected in their shaved heads, ungainly uniforms, and bitter facial expressions in reaction to harsh discipline. Durkheim, however, was not fooled by appearances. He recognized the normality of criminals. He rested his theory solidly upon *social*, and not upon physiological or psychological, foundations.

DURKHEIM'S SOCIOLOGY OF RELIGION

Durkheim's major study of religion is called *The Elementary Forms of Religious Life*. The main aim of that work was to lay bare the fundamental elements of religion. Such elements, Durkheim assumed, could not be easily discovered in the religions of advanced civilizations. Those religions are the product of long, complex historical developments in which the fundamental elements have been obscured. If, however, one may assume that small, simple, and economically primitive societies possess correspondingly simple religious forms, then perhaps the basic elements of religious life will be more readily accessible. That was in fact Durkheim's assumption. He attacked the problem by employing data on the most primitive contemporary societies known to anthropologists: the Australian aborigines.

The first task was to define the subject matter. What do we mean by religion and what does it comprise? The definitions prevalent at the time all stressed a belief in supernatural and spiritual beings. That was the view, for example, of the great British anthropologist E. B. Tylor. He suggested that the best minimal definition of religion is ". . . the belief in Spiritual Beings."[14] That definition is inadequate, Durkheim argues, since it fails to embrace those religions in which the idea of spirits or gods is absent. Buddhism is a case in point. In none of its basic principles does it concern itself with the notion of divinity.

After reviewing several other definitions and finding them deficient, Durkheim offers his own. All known religious beliefs divide the world into two domains: the *sacred* and the *profane*. For Durkheim, it is the totality of beliefs and practices concerned with the sacred that constitutes what we call "religion." When members of a society think and act in the same way with respect to the sacred, they share a common religion. They are members of a common "Church"—a moral community formed by all the believers in a single faith. Thus "a religion," writes Durkheim, "is a unified system of beliefs and practices relative to sacred things, that is to say, things set apart and forbidden—beliefs and practices which unite into one single moral community called a Church, all those who adhere to them."[15]

Armed with that definition, Durkheim confronted the leading theories of his day, which could be divided into two schools. The first put forth the theory of *animism*. Tylor, a leading representative of that school, held that primitive religion is a form of animism, a belief in souls, spirits, and a future state. Where did primitive man get the idea of a soul or spirit? He got it, wrote Tylor, by reflecting on two questions: ". . . what is it that makes the difference between a living body and a dead one . . .? [And] what are those human shapes which appear in dreams and visions?"

> Looking at these two groups of phenomena [Tylor continues], the ancient savage philosophers probably made their first step by the obvious inference that early man has two things belonging to him, namely, a life and a phantom. . . . As both belong to the body, why should they not also belong to one another, and be manifestations of one and the same soul? Let them then be considered as united, and the result is that well-known conception which may be described as an apparition-soul, a ghost-soul.[16]

For Tylor, then, the idea of the soul originated in the experience of dreams and fantasies.

But for Durkheim, that theory was quite unsatisfactory, for even if one admitted the plausibility of the dream origin of the soul-idea, the theory had one crucial defect: It failed to explain why a phantom—"a simple reproduction of the individual"—should have been elevated to the rank of a *sacred* being, as in the ancestor cult, for instance. Animistic theory, Durkheim argues, fails to provide a convincing answer to this all-important question: "If it [the phantom-soul] was only a profane thing, a wandering vital principle, during life, how does it become a sacred thing all at once, and the object of religious sentiments?" (p. 61).

The other school with which Durkheim quarrels may be called naturism. Animistic theories had claimed that the divine was derived from internal, mental experiences. Naturistic theories, in contrast, held that the first objects of religious sentiment were external natural phenomena. The things and forces of nature were the first to be deified. Nature presumably presents to primitive man numerous awesome spectacles which suffice to inspire religious ideas in him. He personifies and spiritualizes those spectacles by means of metaphors and images.

For Durkheim, however, that theory suffers from the same defect as the first. Natural forces are, after all, natural forces, however intense and spectacular they might be. Missing from the theory, therefore, is an explanation of how they acquired a sacred character. It is doubtful, argues Durkheim, that the sense of sacredness can be directly derived from natural phenomena. Thus rejecting the conclusions of both schools, Durkheim has prepared the way for his own distinctive sociological theory.

Totemism: An Elementary Religion

The small, simple, aboriginal societies of Australia afforded the best opportunity for the study of totemic beliefs. Such beliefs, it was widely agreed, formed an elementary religion, the most elementary known to scholars. Totemism was first discovered among the natives of North America. Evidence for totemic beliefs also existed for ancient Egypt, Arabia, Greece, and the southern Slavs. But none of those societies was as primitive as the aborigines and in none did totemism appear in as pure a form as it did among the Australian groups. That is why Durkheim largely limits his attention to the Australian data.

The typical Australian grouping was a clan, an exogamous unit, the members of which presumed themselves to be descended from a common ancestor. Each clan had its "totem"—that is, an *emblem* designating a particular species of animal or plant, which, in turn, represented the clan. The emblems of the Kangaroo and Crow, for instance, represented two distinct clan groups, and every clan member identified himself by the name of the respective species. The totem, it should be stressed, was not a pictorial representation of a species but rather a sign or "coat-of-arms." Totemic images were placed on the walls of huts, on the sides of canoes, and on the bodies of men. In fact, one of the principal initiation rites by which a young man entered into the religious life of the group consisted of painting the totemic sign on his body.

That suggests that the totem is more than just a name and emblem. It is employed in religious ceremonies and is a part of the liturgy. It has a religious character. "It is the very type of sacred thing," says Durkheim. That becomes evident from the role of the *churinga*, a ritual instrument that anthropologists have called a "bull-roarer." Oblong pieces of wood or polished stone, suspended by a string, are rapidly whirled in the air so as to produce a loud humming sound. The churinga is employed in all important rituals. However, ritually profane persons, such as women and boys yet to be initiated into religious life, are prohibited from touching the instrument. The churinga is also believed to possess extraordinary properties. By contact it heals wounds and sickness; it gives clan members strength and courage, and it ensures an adequate reproduction of the totemic species.

The churinga is distinguished not only by its use in a ritual context, but also by the totemic mark engraved upon it. Typically such instruments are constructed each time anew, and then, once the rite is over, stripped of the sign, dismantled, and scattered. It is the totemic emblem which imparts a religious character to those instruments. It is the emblem that is sacred.

The next step in Durkheim's inquiry was to examine the clan's attitude toward the totemic species. As an animal or plant, its profane use would have been to serve as food. But its sacredness was demonstrated by the fact that all clan members were forbidden to eat it. And yet, surprisingly, although the churinga and other objects bearing the clan emblem were never to be touched or seen by ritually profane persons, the totemic animal or plant could be touched or seen. If, therefore, the degree of sacredness of an object may be measured by the pains taken to isolate it from the profane, ". . . we arrive at the remarkable conclusion that the *images of totemic beings are more sacred than the beings themselves*" (p. 133).

To Durkheim, that was a highly significant fact. If the totemic sign is more sacred than the totemic species, that suggests that the sign is so highly sacred not because it represents a species of plant or animal, but because it represents something else. Furthermore, since the totemic species and the clan members are also regarded as sacred, that must mean that the sign, the species, and the clan all share some common "principle." It is the common partaking of that principle that makes them all sacred. What is that principle? *It is an anonymous impersonal force*. It is independent of all subjects in whom it incarnates itself; it precedes them and survives them. That force is the *divine*. In a sense, says Durkheim, ". . . it is the god adored by each totemic cult. Yet it is an impersonal god, without name or history, immanent in the world and diffused in an innumerable multitude of things" (p. 189).

The divine principle is a "force" in both the physical and the moral sense. An individual failing to take proper ritual precautions receives a shock comparable to the effect of an electric charge. On the other hand, an individual observes his rites not merely out of fear of such physical effects. Rather, he observes them because his ancestors have always done so and because he feels a strong moral obligation to behave likewise. Thus the totemic cult, though it may appear to be addressed to plants, animals, or other objects, is actually directed to the "power" that permeates them. If a species of plant or animal, or even the sun, moon, or stars, are adored, it is not due to their intrinsic nature, but to the fact that they partake of that sacred power. The believers themselves have only a vague notion of the force. But an awareness of its existence is evident in more advanced polytheistic cultures. The Greeks, for example, called it *Moira* or Fate, and even the most powerful gods were powerless before it. Yet the gods partake of that force when they produce rain or wind or crops. Zeus, Poseidon, Hades, and the other Greek gods all retain marks of their original impersonality.

Moreover, the impersonal power lying behind the later personified gods is the chief cause of all the movements occurring in the universe. Hence, what we find in Australian religion is the first form of the idea of "force" as it was later conceived in Western philosophy and science. Students of ancient Greek culture have shown that Greek philosophical ideas such as Necessity, Cause, Substance, Nature, Matter, and so on, are all rooted in the much more ancient religious conceptions of a sacred, all-powerful, impersonal, cosmic Force.

But the most important question remains: What is the ultimate origin of the idea of a divine cosmic force or god?

We have said that the totemic emblem was so highly sacred because it was, above all, a symbol of something else. If we can discover what that "something else" actually is, reasoned Durkheim, then we will have found the real basis for the idea of the Divine.

If we have followed Durkheim's analysis thus far, we can see that the totem symbolized two things: (1) the impersonal divine force, or "god," and (2) a specific society called the clan. The totem is the clan's "flag," it is the sign by which one clan distinguishes itself from another. "So," writes Durkheim,

> if it is at once the symbol of the god and of the society, is that not because the god and the society are only one? How could the emblem of the group have been able to become the figure of this quasi-divinity, if the group and the divinity were two distinct realities? The god of the clan, the totemic principle, can therefore be nothing else than the clan itself, personified and represented to the imagination under the visible form of the animal or vegetable which serves as totem. (p. 206)

Upon reflection, argues Durkheim, it seems quite evident that Society has all the attributes necessary to inspire a sense of the divine. Society is, after all, experienced as a superior force on which everyone depends. Members submit to its authority even when it is felt to be repressive. They yield to its rules not only because it is strong enough to overcome them, but also because it is an object of respect. The social pressure brought to bear on individuals by "Society" is largely of a spiritual kind. Ultimately it is social reality that gives men the idea that there exists a superhuman principle, all-powerful and moral, on which they all depend. It is the experience of Society, therefore, that gives rise to what Durkheim calls a "collective representation"—a collective intuiting of the Divine.

But it is not the profane, everyday experiences that achieve that effect. It is rather those special, sacred ritual occasions in which men find themselves dominated and carried away by an external power. Often lasting days on end, such ceremonial occasions transport the participants from the gray world of everyday life into the extraordinary and effervescent world of the sacred. It "is out of this effervescence itself," writes Durkheim, "that the religious idea seems to be born. The theory that this is really its origin is confirmed by the fact that in Australia the really religious activity is almost entirely confined to the moments when these assemblies are held." Durkheim continues: "Since religious force is nothing other than the collective and anonymous force of the clan, and since this can be represented in the mind only in the form of the totem, the totemic emblem is like the visible body of the god" (pp. 218–19, 221).

Hence when men believe in a moral power on which they depend, that is no illusion. For that power exists; it is Society. Sacred assemblies serve the apparent function of strengthening men's bonds with the Divine, but at the same time they serve the real function of strengthening the bonds of an ". . . individual to the society of which he is a member, since the god is only a figurative expression of the society." "Religious force," concludes Durkheim, "is only the sentiment inspired by the group in its members, but projected outside of the consciousnesses that experience them, and objectified" (pp. 226, 229).

From that perspective the nature and origin of the soul are also illuminated. It follows from Durkheim's analysis that the "soul" is no mere phantom, dream-image, or mental reproduction of the individual. Rather it is the experience each clan member has of the totemic principle incarnate in him. Or, in sociological terms, the soul is what Society implants in every individual. The individual soul is a particle of the great collective soul of the group.

Similarly, the idea of immortality also originates in the reality of the group or society. Though individuals die, primitive man observed, the clan survives. There must therefore exist some principle or force that enables the clan-group to possess eternal life. Finally, the idea of spirits and deities, far from being directly aroused by natural spectacles, is awakened in us by the sociomoral processes of the social world.

In sum, the ultimate source of the religious experience, for Durkheim, is Society. Religion accordingly reflects both the good and bad sides of society, its just ideals and practices as well as its moral ugliness.

> There are gods of theft and trickery, of lust and war, of sickness and death. Christianity itself, howsoever high the idea which it has made of the divinity

may be, has been obliged to give the spirit of evil a place in its mythology. Satan is an essential piece of the Christian system; even if he is an impure being, he is not a profane one. . . . Thus religion, far from ignoring the real society and making abstraction of it, is in its image; it reflects all its aspects, even the most vulgar and the most repulsive. (p. 421)

Criticisms of Durkheim's Theory

For Durkheim and his followers, Society and God are therefore one. Society, unconsciously divinized, is the Stuff all religions are made of. Since Durkheim rested his theory on evidence from primitive cultures, it will be instructive to hear the critical comments of Bronislaw Malinowski, one of the outstanding anthropologists of all time.

It is evident, Malinowski observes, that Durkheim rests his entire case on the behavior of the collectivity, not the individual. Yet anyone who has experienced religion profoundly will agree that some of the strongest and most meaningful religious moments come in solitude, not in the group or crowd. That is no less true of primitive than of modern man.

Among primitives, the novice is often secluded at initiation, and he undergoes a personal ordeal including a communion with spirits and deities. It is hard to see the social basis of those sacred powers in such lonely spots. It is equally difficult to see how the belief in immortality can be explained without considering the state of mind of the *individual* facing his inevitable death in fear and sorrow. That is not all. Though Durkheim's theory virtually ignores the role of the individual, evidence is plentiful that in primitive religion prophets, seers, interpreters, and other practitioners play a key role. Those facts strongly indicate that the stuff of religion cannot be regarded as purely social.

Also questionable is Durkheim's central argument that the idea of the Divine is somehow derived from primitive ceremonies and festivities. The religious idea, he maintains, "is born out of their effervescence." Durkheim thus tends to place the entire weight of his argument on the emotional excitement one feels while participating in such gatherings. To that Malinowski replies that just

> . . . a little reflection is sufficient to show that even in primitive societies the heightening of emotions and the lifting of the individual outside of himself are by no means restricted to gatherings and to crowd phenomena. The lover near his sweetheart, the daring adventurer conquering his fears in the face of real danger, the hunter at grips with a wild animal, the craftsman achieving a masterpiece, whether he be savage or civilized, will under such conditions feel altered, uplifted, endowed with higher forces. And there can be no doubt that from many of these solitary experiences where man feels the forebodings of death, the pangs of anxiety, the exaltation of bliss, there flows a great deal of religious inspiration. Though most ceremonies are carried out in public, much of religious revelation takes place in solitude.[17]

As for the presumed connection between the religious idea and collective *effervescent* festivities, that too seems dubious. There are numerous exciting and effervescent occasions of a collective sort in primitive societies, which are nevertheless lacking in the faintest religious coloring. Malinowski cites the collective work in the gardens of Melanesia:

> . . . when men become carried away with emulation and zest for work, singing rhythmic songs, uttering shouts of joy and slogans of competitive challenge, [and which] is full of this "collective effervescence." But it is entirely profane, and society which "reveals itself" in this as in any other public performance assumes no divine grandeur or godlike appearance.[18]

Collective effervescence is also evident in battle, in sailing expeditions, in tribal gatherings for trading purposes, and in numerous other occasions, all of which generate no religious experience. It seems clear, then, that religious inspiration must take account of the solitary experiences of an individual, and that social effervescence may have no religious meaning at all.

There is still another objection raised by Malinowski. How can Society be the prototype of the Divine when so large a portion of what we inherit socially—traditions, knowledge, customs, norms, skills, and so on—are profane, not sacred? Society as keeper of both the sacred and profane traditions cannot be the basis of Divinity, for it is in the sacred domain only.

In sum, though there may be an element of truth in Durkheim's view, it is going too far to say, as he does, that society is the author of religious truths and that at bottom, the concepts of society and divinity are different aspects of the same notion. In expanding the role of the group to an extreme, as Durkheim does, he effectively eliminates the role of the individual. As Malinowski rightly insists, ". . . without the analysis of the individual mind, we cannot take one step in the understanding of religion."[19]

For Durkheim, God and society are one because what people call "God" is actually the symbolic manifestation of the powers of Society. Each man is right, says Durkheim, in believing that there exists a power greater than himself, for that is the "moral power upon which he depends and from which he receives all that is best in himself: this power exists, it is society" (p. 225). The divine and the sacred are thus reduced to the social. Implying that there is no essential difference between one religion and another, and between religious and national assemblies, Durkheim asks,

> What essential difference is there between an assembly of Christians celebrating the principal dates of the life of Christ, or of Jews remembering the exodus from Egypt or the promulgation of the decalogue, and a reunion of citizens commemorating the promulgation of a new moral or legal system or some great event in the national life? (p. 427)

The answer is, of course, that there exists a world of difference in the minds of the participants.

Hence, the inevitable result of Durkheim's approach is that it entirely ignores the *subjective meaning* that religious beliefs and acts have for the actors concerned. But one cannot grasp the authentic meaning of religious acts without recognizing that they are directed to the divine, not society. Grasped authentically, religious acts must be understood in their own right, and not reduced to the social. Thus Durkheim's approach was quite antithetical to that of Max Weber, for whom the meaning and motives of actions were of paramount importance.

Durkheim's sociology of religion is therefore defective in that it effectively ignores the role of the individual. It also overlooks the fact that "personal religion" is

> more fundamental than either theology or ecclesiasticism. Churches, when once established, live at second-hand upon tradition; but the founders of every church owed their power originally to the fact of their direct personal communion with the divine. Not only the superhuman founders, the Christ, the Buddha, Mahomet, but all the originators of Christian sects have been in this case;—so personal religion should still seem the primordial thing, even to those who continue to esteem it incomplete.[20]

Durkheim's expansion of the determining power of "Society" to an extreme, and his corresponding neglect of the individual, are not uncharacteristic of his other writings. Throughout his work he exhibits a conspicuous tendency toward the reification of society, a tendency that appears to be rooted in his social values and methodological principles.

DURKHEIM'S SOCIOLOGY AND ITS UNDERLYING SOCIAL VALUES

The truth in the sociological proposition that an individual becomes human in the process of social interaction, Durkheim formulated this way: "Society" implants in each individual a particle of itself so that society in effect creates the individual. Insofar as individuals may be discerned at all in Durkheim's sociology, they are predominantly "me's," or objects, whereas the "I," or active subject in George Herbert Mead's sense, is practically nonexistent. Hence, as we shall see, there is rarely any real tension between the individual and society in Durkheim's scheme, and, insofar as any such tension exists, it is resolved in favor of society.

An examination of a representative sample of Durkheim's writings on education, for instance, shows clearly that his central and abiding concern was how best to adapt the individual to "Society" and how best to prepare him to fulfill his specific "function" in a morally dutiful manner. "Education," writes Durkheim,

> *is the influence exercised by adult generations on those . . . not yet ready for social life. Its object is to arouse and to develop in each child a certain number of physical, intel-*

> *lectual, and moral states which are demanded of him by both the political society as a whole and the specific milieu for which he is specifically destined.* [italics in original][21]

The individual is "specifically destined" to fill a certain occupational role, and the function of education is to facilitate the individual's adjustment to his destiny. Durkheim avers, however, that by nature the human being is not inclined to submit to political authority; self-discipline and self-sacrifice are not modes of conduct to which the human being is congenitally disposed. Does that mean that when society fashions "individuals according to its needs," that it subjects them "to an insupportable tyranny?" No, replies Durkheim. For in reality individuals ". . . are themselves interested in this submission; for the new being that collective influence, through education, thus builds up in each of us, represents what is best in us" (p. 76).

If we reflect on some of the earlier thinkers considered in this book, notably the *Philosophes*, we can see striking contrasts between their conception of the individual and society, and that of Durkheim. For the *Philosophes*, the best in humanity was yet to be realized; it was precisely the existing social order that thwarted the realization of human perfectibility. In Marx's concept of alienation one finds a similar view. If the human being suffers more than he must and is less than he can become, that is the result of the prevailing form of society, which is unnecessarily oppressive and alienating. Clearly, both the *Philosophes* and Marx valued human needs and gifts and wished to remove the social obstacles to individual self-realization. Durkheim, in contrast, acknowledges no individual needs in his theory of education. In his desire to counter the Utilitarians, and their pursuit-of-self-interest doctrine, Durkheim transforms all individual values into egoism, pure and simple. Whatever the individual forfeits to Society is for the best. In his words: "It is society . . . that draws us out of ourselves, that obliges us to reckon with other interests than our own, it is society that has taught us to control our passions, our instincts, to sacrifice ourselves, to subordinate our personal ends to higher ends" (p. 76). In that way, restraint, deprivation, self-sacrifice, and subordination all become the cardinal values education must inculcate to serve the ends of "Society"; the more we have placed our selves and our inclinations under social control, the more fully human we are.

"Society" thus becomes a purely positive entity, for Durkheim; all social relations are humanizing, by definition, while dehumanization and alienation are excluded, also by definition, from social life. More than anything, Durkheim craved for social order and solidarity. Therefore, an antagonism of any kind between the individual and society had to be denied. The ". . . antagonism that has too often been admitted," he writes, "between the individual and society corresponds to nothing in the facts" (p. 78). Earlier, as we have seen, Durkheim himself eloquently called attention to the forced division of labor, the basic inequalities and injustices that stood in the way of genuine community. Yet now he describes "Society" as if it were free of inequalities and coercion. The State must ". . . remind the teacher constantly of the ideas, [and] the sentiments that must be impressed upon the child to adjust him to the milieu in which he must live" (p. 79).

Clearly there is nothing in the proposition "man is a social being" that is inherently either conservative or revolutionary. In Durkheim's hands, however, it becomes essentially conservative, for his emphasis throughout is on the adaptation of humans to circumstances but never on the adaptation of circumstances to human ends. Even his assertion of the absence of instincts in humans is applied to a conservative end. If, again, we use Marx as a foil, we can see more clearly the values underlying Durkheim's conception of society. Both Marx and Durkheim recognized that humans are what they are largely as a result of their modes of interaction with others. But each thinker drew diametrically opposite conclusions from that proposition. Since humanity, for Marx, was infinitely perfectible, the social forms which were unnecessarily oppressive had to be transformed to allow for the development of human creative faculties in freedom; the elimination of certain social relations and institutions would facilitate individual self-realization and widen the boundaries of freedom. For Durkheim, in contrast, because the human dispositions at birth are "very general and very vague," and because, as a consequence, the human child is malleable, the task of education was to render those dispositions more specific so that he could eventually "play a useful role in society." Here, "useful role" must be translated as the particular function one is destined to fulfill in the division of labor and in whatever "milieu" (Durkheim's euphemism for socioeconomic class) one happens to be born in. Education is a matter of getting the child to accept social authority and to learn his duty. Duty ". . . is, indeed, for the child and even for the adult, the stimulus *par excellence* of effort" (p. 88). "For to be free," Durkheim continues, "is not to do what one pleases; it is to be master of oneself, it is to know how to act with reason and to do one's duty" (pp. 89–90). That is the main burden of Durkheim's educational theory.

Can social control and discipline be regarded as a repressive, restrictive, constraining, authoritarian force, which might impede an individual's development? No, says Durkheim, for ". . . an inability to restrict oneself within determinate limits is a sign of disease—with respect to all forms of human conduct, and, even more generally, for all kinds of biological behavior."[22] Here, Durkheim is advancing a sociology *and* a psychological philosophy. In his sociology he insists that a society, like a living organism, is a ". . . complex equilibrium whose various elements limit one another; this balance cannot be disrupted without producing unhappiness or illness" (p. 39). For Durkheim, it is always the disruption, but never the maintenance of the "equilibrium" (status quo) which causes suffering and pain. As psychologist-philosopher, Durkheim advances a theory of the source of modern man's malaise—his unlimited appetites. In *Moral Education* he summarizes the main points he will make again in *Suicide*, where one finds an entire treatise on the need for moderation and restraint. He writes,

> A need, a desire freed of all restraints, and all rules, no longer geared to some determinate objective, . . . can be nothing but a source of constant anguish for the person experiencing it . . . . That is why historical periods like ours, which have known the malady of infinite aspiration, are necessarily touched with pessimism. (p. 40)

Durkheim is preaching the same moral message to all members of society regardless of the social position in which they find themselves. All members must set themselves finite goals and learn to be sated. The social changes Durkheim had earlier regarded as the precondition for a more just society were yet to be realized; nevertheless, those subject to unjust relations should curb their appetites and aspirations. Social constraint is transformed by Durkheim into an unqualifiedly *positive* phenomenon for it keeps "our vital forces within appropriate limits" (p. 41). Moral regulations form ". . . about each person an imaginary wall, at the foot of which a multitude of human passions simply die without being able to go further. For the same reason—that they are contained—it becomes possible to satisfy them" (p. 42). Thus constraint, containment, and limitation are the positive values. Discipline, the essence of moral education, is essential for individual health and social order. "Through it [discipline] and by means of it alone are we able to teach the child to rein in his desires, to set limits to his appetites of all kinds, to limit and, through limitation, to define the goals of his activity" (p. 43).

Whatever the element of truth in this general philosophico-psychological theory, it had necessarily to resolve itself into a morality of submission and resignation for the disadvantaged. Durkheim, however, seems not to have grasped that implication. It is an illusion, he insists, that the imposition of limits on our desires and faculties results in subordination. True power is a subjective quality. Imagine, he writes, the most absolute despot in history "liberated from all external constraint" and whose desires are irresistible. "Shall we say, then, that he is all-powerful? Certainly not, since he himself cannot resist his desires. They are masters of him as of everything else. He submits to them; he does not dominate them. . . . A despot is like a child; he has a child's weakness because he is not master of himself. Self-mastery is the first condition of all true power, of all liberty worthy of the name" (p. 45). It is as if Durkheim, having abandoned all hope of changing external social conditions, and fearing the "disruptive" consequences of unbridled appetites, had no choice but to counsel "self-mastery." Self-control as a moral injunction should be implanted in the child to dispense with the need for constant external controls. The internalization of controls is useful, desirable, and good for both the individual and society.

Durkheim was not altogether blind to the uncritical view of Society that emerged from his educational theory. He recognized the possibility that it might be interpreted as *authoritarian.* In defending his view, however, he resorts to the doctrine of "natural abilities." The limits he wants to impose are ". . . based on the nature of things, that is to say, in the nature of each of us. This has nothing to do with insidiously inculcating a spirit of resignation in the child, or curbing his legitimate ambitions, or preventing him from seeing the conditions existing around him." Nonetheless, the child simply must be made to understand that to be happy is to set himself goals that correspond to his "nature"; he must not strain ". . . neurotically and unhappily toward infinitely distant and consequently inaccessible goals." One must select a goal compatible with one's abilities, and not seek to surpass "artificially" one's "natural limits." Discipline is useful and necessary "because it seems to us demanded by nature itself" (p. 50).

Durkheim thus evidently believed that it was somehow possible to discover one's "natural" capacities and limits even while vast social inequalities, including inequalities of opportunity, persisted. He did not see that so long as such inequalities prevailed, it was in fact insidious to encourage children to recognize their so-called "natural" limitations. There can be no doubt that the educational system in Durkheim's time—and this is equally true today—did not even begin to realize the potential of most children, even supposing for a moment that such potentials have "natural" limits.

In fairness to Durkheim, we should note that he acknowledged certain dangers in a morality which was ". . . beyond criticism or reflection, the agents par excellence of all change" (p. 52). But he insists that the exercise of criticism, which leads to a weakening of the existing order of discipline and authority, is not required in normal circumstances. If ". . . in critical and abnormal circumstances," he writes, "the feeling for the rule and for discipline must be weakened, it does not follow that such impairment is normal" (p. 53). But there is a real problem with the distinction Durkheim attempted to make between normal and pathological conditions. In *The Division of Labor in Society* and in *Professional Ethics and Civic Morals* he himself criticized the great social inequalities which led to unjust relations. Those conditions were still in effect when he wrote *Moral Education.* For most of his contemporaries, those unjust disadvantages were in fact the normal conditions of their lives. Should it not then also be regarded as normal when humans who are subjected to injustice criticize and even resist the prevailing order? Moreover, should it not then be regarded as an essential part of the child's education that he be alerted to the existing injustices and encouraged to reflect on their causes critically? Finally, is it anything more than a definitional trick to define pervasive inequalities as "abnormal"?

It would be inaccurate and unfair to accuse Durkheim of abhorring all social change, but change had to be orderly, gradual, and organic. Injustices which precluded the free development of the majority of individuals were prevalent; that was bad. But if he found those injustices morally offensive, he found social disorder and conflict even more offensive. ". . . [W]e are living precisely in one of those critical, revolutionary periods when authority is usually weakened through the loss of traditional discipline—a time that may easily give rise to a spirit of anarchy" (p. 54). Therefore, the most immediate task was to develop as rapidly as possible a new discipline. Although Durkheim recognized that there can be no genuine social solidarity without social justice, the impression is unavoidable that it was order that he cherished above all. His overriding commitment was to "Society," that something which is above ". . . those sentient beings who are other individual human beings . . ." (p. 59).

Durkheim's attitude toward the individual becomes equally evident in his denigration of art and creativity. Leisure is dangerous, he tells us, and art frivolous: "In serious life, man is sustained against temptation by the obligation of work." Art is a game whereas morality is "life in earnest." The distance separating art from morality is that separating "play from work. Not therefore by learning to play that special game, art, will we learn to do our duty" (p. 273). To teach children to do their duty and to take society seriously, "Society" must become a divine and sacred entity in their minds. Hence, Durkheim's "methodological realism"—that is, the view that society is a living reality distinct from and greater than the individuals comprising it. We must never say, as the "methodological nominalists" do, that society is a mental construct. Why not? Because one ". . . doesn't [sic] cherish a mental construct" (p. 257).

METHODOLOGICAL RULES AND VALUES

Earlier we saw that in his sociology of deviance Durkheim used a statistical criterion to distinguish the "normal" from the "deviant." "We shall call 'normal' those social conditions that are most generally distributed, and the others 'morbid' or 'pathological.'"[23] That definition may be useful, as we have seen, for the study of socially deviant behavior. But Durkheim goes beyond the statistical criterion. His analogy between "society" and a living organism led him to conclude that what is most widespread is also best: "It would be incomprehensible," he asserts, "if the most widespread forms of organization would not at the same time be, at least in their aggregate, the most advantageous" (p. 58). Advantageous for whom? For the "social organism" as a whole, of course. But how does one determine what is advantageous for the society as a whole? Cannot widespread forms of organization be advantageous for some individuals and groups and not for others? Is it not true that certain widespread social forms prevail because some individuals and groups have the power to perpetuate them? Are there not in every society social relations and social forms that are positively disadvantageous to some groups and individuals? Such questions are never brought to the fore by

Durkheim, and the issues of power and domination are virtually ignored. Though he understands, of course, that every real society consists of a plurality of groups with different, competing and conflicting interests, and though he understands, too, that the power and advantages of some groups work to the detriment of others, he continues to speak of the good of the social organism as a whole.

If Durkheim is not saying that existing society is the best of all possible worlds, he is saying that at the present stage of evolution the prevailing conditions are necessary for the survival and adaptation of the social organism and are therefore useful and good. He is not, however, altogether happy with that conception of things. There are transition periods, he writes, when a

> . . . phenomenon can . . . persist throughout the entire range of a species although no longer adapted to the requirements of the situation. It is then normal only in appearance. Its universality is now an illusion, since its persistence, due only to the blind force of habit, can no longer be accepted as an index of a close connection with the general conditions of its collective existence. This difficulty is especially peculiar to sociology. (p. 61)

How shall sociology determine whether a given condition is "normal"? In "order to determine," he writes, "whether the present economic state of Europe . . . is normal or not, we shall investigate the causes that brought it about. If these conditions still exist in our present-day society, this situation is normal in spite of the dissent it arouses" (p. 62). The system under those conditions still has "utility." Here we must observe that Durkheim's method for determining whether the "normal" is real or illusory is not unambiguous; we must also observe that his not-unambiguous method is directed against socialists and other critics of the economic system. It is as if Durkheim is trying to persuade them that since the conditions that brought about the present economic system still exist, their dissent is pointless.

Durkheim apparently believed that by means of positivist-scientific methods one could determine whether a particular stage in a society's evolution is in fact "adaptive," whether it has "utility," whether it is "advantageous." When practices not adapted to any vital end persist, they are treated by Durkheim as "survivals"; they continue "to exist by the inertia of habit alone." On the other hand, "if the usefulness of a fact is not the cause of its existence, it is generally necessary that it be useful in order that it may maintain itself" (p. 97). Thus Durkheim insists upon talking about whether social facts are "useful," "harmful," "advantageous," and so on, without asking for whom. In effect, he solves deductively and tautologically the problem of "society's" survival: "If . . . the majority of social phenomena had a parasitic character, the budget of the organism would have a deficit and social life would be impossible" (p. 97). The fact that a given society does survive shows that somehow ". . . the phenomena comprising it combine in such a way to put society in harmony with itself and with the environment external to it" (p. 97).

In his *The Rules of the Sociological Method* Durkheim is supposed to be setting forth the principles of a scientific, sociological method based on logic and facts. Yet, we see that Durkheim provides no facts to substantiate his claim that certain conditions are adaptive, useful, and advantageous for the society as a whole. Instead, his "proof" is strictly deductive. That problem aside, however, it is not difficult to discern Durkheim's apparent motivation for arguing as he does. Evidently, he wants to assure the critics of the existing economic system that the conditions arousing their indignation are "normal" and "necessary." If society represses and constrains, that ". . . is not derived from a conventional arrangement which human will had added . . . to natural reality; it issues from the innermost reality; it is the necessary product of given causes" (p. 123). There is no doubt, therefore, that even Durkheim's "scientific" Rules were designed to "create a sociology which sees in the *spirit of discipline* the essential condition of all human life . . ." (p. 124, italics added).

THE STUDY OF SUICIDE

Durkheim's use of sociocultural variables to explain variations in suicide rates must be regarded as ingenious and brilliant. Here, however, we shall not concern ourselves with the empirical aspects of his study, discussions of which are widely available in the sociological literature. Instead, we shall continue to explore the values underlying Durkheim's study.

Durkheim chose to study suicide because he had hoped that from his study would emerge ". . . some suggestions concerning the causes of the general contemporary *maladjustments* being undergone by European societies and concerning remedies which may relieve it."[24] If in his earliest works Durkheim gave attention to *both* the anomic and the forced division of labor, he now focused almost exclusively on the first. The problems of modern man were a matter of "maladjustment." The most pressing task, therefore, was to develop for modern man an appropriate morality that would give him a sense of satiety, that would help him overcome his restlessness and discontent, and that would enable him to adjust happily to modern society.

Modern man kills himself, Durkheim argues, primarily as a result of two conditions: the loss of cohesion in modern society and the absence of suitable moral norms by which to orient himself. Modern man is egoistic and anomic. Both conditions can be remedied by creating a new moral code and by resurrecting and reorganizing the occupational guild so that it may serve an integrative and regulatory function under modern conditions. The most urgent task is to bring about a high degree of social integration—moral, domestic, political, and economic—because the data tend to support the proposition that "*Suicide varies inversely with the degree of integration of . . . society*" (p. 208).

A third type of suicide Durkheim called "altruistic"; this occurred when social integration was too strong. That, however, was endemic to "lower societies," and therefore no cause for concern to higher ones. A definite cause for concern, however, was the "excessive individualism" characteristic of modern civilization. So again the remedy is cohesion, consensus, and solidarity. Noting the rise in the rate of self-destruction *after* the war of 1870, Durkheim writes,

> On the morrow of the war of 1870 a new accession of good fortune took place. Germany was unified and placed entirely under Prussian hegemony. An enormous war indemnity added to the public wealth; commerce and industry made great strides. The development of suicide was never so rapid. From 1875 to 1886 it increased 90 percent. . . . (p. 244)

The juxtaposition of suicide and war, both of which result in the destruction of human life, is revealing. Given Durkheim's values and focal concerns, suicide loomed as a bigger problem than war. A rising suicide rate indicated diminishing integration. War, on the other hand, brought with it greater solidarity. Durkheim's attitude reached its logical conclusion in the patriotic articles he wrote during the great carnage that began in 1914. The translation into practice of his doctrine that the individual must subordinate himself to Society (which in practice could only mean to the State) mortally wounded him. He lost his son in the war and, brokenhearted, died himself soon afterward. Durkheim had apparently failed to perceive the dangers inherent in a "social integration" that was the product of nationalist chauvinism and that compelled men to kill one another en masse as their patriotic duty. Furthermore, it is ironic that for all of his concern with social integration, he never anticipated the extreme disorganizing consequences of World War I—social convulsions and revolutions throughout Europe and, in the end, far-reaching structural changes.

What Durkheim called "anomic" suicide is especially interesting since it was associated with both rising prosperity and economic crises. If the suicide rate increased under both circumstances, Durkheim reasoned, that must mean that the rate has nothing to do with either prosperity or economic crises per se. Rather, it is associated with the fact that both types of events are ". . . disturbances of the collective order. Every disturbance of equilibrium, even though it achieves greater comfort and a heightening of general vitality, is an impulse to voluntary death" (p. 246). In explaining that phenomenon, Durkheim elaborates his philosophy for modern man.

The needs of all other animal creatures are strictly organic in nature; they are driven instinctively to replenish the energy exhausted in their metabolic interaction with nature; once having done so, they are satisfied and crave nothing more. Natural limits are set on their craving and striving. In contrast, "[n]othing appears in man's organic nor in his psychological constitution which sets" limits on his desires. Man has needs which transcend the strictly vital requirements of his organism; those needs are "unlimited so far as they depend on the individual alone." In the absence of an "external regulatory force, our capacity for feeling is in itself an insatiable and bottomless abyss" (p. 247). That can be only a "source of torment" to man. "Unlimited desires are insatiable by definition and insatiability," writes Durkheim, "is rightly considered a sign of morbidity" (p. 247). The infinity of man's desires and goals is what really causes him pain and suffering; the only solution, therefore, is to limit his passions. Some regulative force must be imposed upon him that will "play the same role for moral needs which the organism plays for physical needs. This means that the force can only be moral" (p. 248). Since the imposed limits will be effective only so long as men recognize them as just, they must receive the sense of what is just "from an authority which they respect, to which they yield spontaneously" (p. 249). And, of course, as we have come to expect, it is "Society" which is the ultimate authority in this regard: ". . . society alone can play this moderating role; for it is the only moral power superior to the individual, the authority of which he accepts. It alone has the power necessary to stipulate law and to set the point beyond which the passions must not go. Finally, it alone can estimate the reward to be prospectively offered to every class of human functionary, in the name of the common interest" (p. 249). "Society" can and should determine the rewards to be assigned to each "function"—to the men in each occupation. "A genuine regimen exists, therefore, . . . which fixes with relative precision the maximum degree of ease of living to which each social class may legitimately aspire" (p. 249).

Durkheim perceived that the living standards of all classes, including the workers, continued to improve; nevertheless, there was no contentment. Restlessness, social conflict, and "anarchy" prevailed despite the betterment of material conditions for all. But there still remained the "relative deprivation" of those in the lower and disadvantaged strata. Therefore, society must exert moral pressure so that "each in his sphere vaguely realizes the extreme limit set to his ambitions and aspires to nothing beyond. At least if he respects regulations and is docile to collective authority, that is, has a wholesome moral constitution, he feels that it is not well to ask more" (p. 250). The only real solution to man's malaise is to curb and bridle his aspirations; only then will he be contented with his lot and strive "moderately to improve it, and this average contentment causes the feeling of calm, active happiness, the pleasure in existing and living which characterizes health for societies as well as for individuals" (p. 250).

Durkheim understood, however, that "society's" moral authority would be accepted by men only if they regard the existing "distribution of functions" as just. "The workman is not in harmony with his social position if he is not convinced that he has his deserts" (p. 250). And now there is a definite shift of emphasis in Durkheim's argument as compared with *Professional Ethics and Civic Morals.* There he argued that at least one structural change required immediate institution: the abolition of the private inheritance of wealth. That was necessary because without it the relations among men were inherently unjust. Now, in *Suicide,* he retreats from that position or, at the very least, is highly ambivalent. It is true, he writes, that "the nearer this ideal equality were approached, the less social restraint will be necessary. *But it is only a matter of degree.* One sort of heredity will always exist, that of natural talent" (p. 251, italics added). To demand of those "naturally superior" that they function without greater rewards would require a discipline even stronger than the existing one. If earlier he argued that "natural inequalities" need not be accompanied by material inequalities, now Durkheim changed his view. Since *all* social systems regulate and repress, since man can never escape altogether from social restraint, the abolition of institutionalized economic inequalities, he now tells us, would only result in a diminution in the degree of restraint. That being the case, there is no point in agitating oneself about existing inequalities and injustices; their abolition will make only a minor difference for man's existence. The main task for Durkheim, therefore, is not to change social conditions so that constraint and repression are constantly reduced, but to bring about a collective order that is obeyed and respected. Man must be given a moral education that will teach him, above all, to be content with his condition and to improve it moderately. "All classes contend among themselves," he painfully observed, "because no established classification any longer exists" (p. 253). The task, then, was to arrive at a new "classification" that all would accept.

Durkheim was impressed with the greater immunity to suicide of the poor; but his discussion of that fact becomes a celebration of poverty:

> . . . [T]he less one has the less he is tempted to extend the range of his needs indefinitely. Lack of power, compelling moderation, accustoms men to it. . . . [Poverty] is actually the best school for teaching self-restraint. Forcing us to constant self-discipline, it prepares us to accept collective discipline with equanimity, while wealth, exalting the individual, may always arouse the spirit of rebellion which is the very source of immorality. (p. 254)

Regulation, moderation, discipline, duty—those are the highest virtues. Durkheim wanted a "highly socialized" man, "for if one were highly socialized one would not rebel at every social restraint" (p. 288).

It was only the egoistic and anomic types of suicide that Durkheim regarded as morbid. The former, for example, "results from the fact that society is not sufficiently integrated at all points to keep all its members under its control. . . . Thus the only remedy for the ill," writes Durkheim, "is to restore enough consistency to social groups for them to obtain a firmer grip on the individual, and for him to feel himself bound to them" (p. 373). Durkheim therefore calls once again for the restoration of occupational groups. The individual would be firmly integrated in his group, and the groups subordinated to the State, thus yielding an "organic" solidarity. The conflictive character of the previous system would thus be eliminated.

Durkheim, of course, understood that a higher form of social solidarity presupposed the elimination of basic social inequalities. But in the context of his intellectual work as a whole, the concern with justice, so effectively articulated in his *The Division of Labor in Society* and *Professional Ethics and Civic Morals,* figures far less prominently than his concern for anomie. Anomie could only be reduced and done away with by raising "Society" to the status of the divine.

Durkheim felt the need to hypostatize and deify "Society" because he feared the moral vacuum that might result from the decline of traditional religion. In an earlier era, God was the supreme guarantor of the moral order; in giving God his due, people were in effect assuring that their relations would rest on a firm moral basis. But in his own day, Durkheim, like several other social thinkers, believed that God was dead in the moral sense. The gods are growing old or are already dead, he believed, and "others are not yet born."[25] Religion had declined as a consequence of both the dissolution of traditional society and the growth of industry and science. If religion has become a moribund institution, reasoned Durkheim, and no longer fulfills its central moral function, then present-day society is faced with a great danger: the denial of morality altogether. If no secular substitute is found for religion, then public morality will be threatened at its roots. To forestall that condition and thus to overcome anomie, it was necessary to find new gods suited to the new conditions. To discover what the nature of the new gods (that is, the new moral norms and values) must be was the task of social science. Durkheim's positivist conception of social science led him to conclude that "Society" was the appropriate new god, for it "is the highest form of the psychic life," "the consciousness of the consciousnesses." Society "sees from above" and "sees farther."[26] When one reads such descriptions by Durkheim of Society as the "Supreme God," one also understands why duty, devotion, discipline, and abnegation were his most cherished values.

NOTES

1. See Marcel Mauss's introduction to the first edition of Durkheim's *Socialism and Saint-Simon*, ed. and with an Introduction by Alvin W. Gouldner (London: Routledge and Kegan Paul, 1959).
2. Ibid., p. 2. (Hereafter all page references to this work will be indicated in parentheses immediately following the quoted passage.)
3. Émile Durkheim, *The Division of Labor in Society* (New York: The Free Press, 1965), p. 204. (Hereafter all page references to this work will be indicated in parentheses immediately following the quoted passages.)
4. Émile Durkheim, *Professional Ethics and Civic Morals* (London: Routledge and Kegan Paul, 1957), p. 12. (Hereafter all page references to this work will be indicated in parentheses immediately following the quoted passage.)
5. Émile Durkheim, *The Rules of the Sociological Method*, trans. Sarah A. Solovay and John H. Mueller, ed. George E. G. Catlin (New York: The Free Press, 1964), p. 55.
6. Ibid., p. 66.
7. Ibid., p. 69.
8. Ibid., pp. 71–72.
9. Durkheim, *Division of Labor,* p. 81.
10. Ibid., p. 102.
11. Ibid., p. 108.
12. For details about Lombroso and other key figures in the history of criminology, see Bernaldo de Quiros, *Modern Theories of Criminality* (Boston: Little, Brown, 1911), and Hermann Mannheim, ed., *Pioneers of Criminology* (Chicago: Quadrangle/The New York Times Book Co., 1960).
13. For a detailed critique of the methods employed in such studies, see George B. Vold, *Theoretical Criminology* (New York: Oxford University Press, 1958).
14. E. B. Tylor, *Religion in Primitive Culture* (New York: Harper Torchbooks, 1958), p. 8. (First published in 1871.)
15. Émile Durkheim, *The Elementary Forms of Religious Life,* trans. and ed. J. W. Swain (London: George Allen and Unwin, 1964), p. 47. (Hereafter all page references to this work will be indicated in parentheses immediately following the quoted passage.)
16. Tylor, *Religion,* pp. 12–13.
17. Bronislaw Malinowski, *Magic, Science and Religion* (Garden City, N.Y.: Doubleday/Anchor Books, 1954), p. 58.
18. Ibid., p. 58.
19. Ibid., p. 69.
20. William James, *The Varieties of Religious Experience* (New York: Collier Books, 1976), p. 42. (Originally published in 1902.)
21. Émile Durkheim, *Education and Sociology* (Glencoe, Ill.: The Free Press, 1956), p. 71. (Hereafter all page references to this work will be indicated in parentheses immediately following the quoted passage.)
22. Émile Durkheim, *Moral Education* (Glencoe, Ill.: The Free Press, 1961), p. 38. (Hereafter all page references to this work will be indicated in parentheses immediately following the quoted passage.)

23. Émile Durkheim, *The Rules of the Sociological Method* (New York: The Free Press, 1964), p. 55. (Hereafter all page references to this work will be indicated in parentheses immediately following the quoted passage.)
24. Émile Durkheim, *Suicide*, trans. John A. Spaulding and George Simpson (London: Routledge and Kegan Paul, 1963), p. 37. (Hereafter all page references to this work will be indicated in parentheses immediately following the quoted passage.)
25. Émile Durkheim, *The Elementary Forms of Religious Life* (London: George Allen and Unwin, 1964), p. 427.
26. Ibid., p. 444.

22

Karl Mannheim
(1893–1947)

Like Max Weber before him, and in a sense following his example, Mannheim accepted the suggestion that the value of Marx's method lay in the "hint that there is a correlation between the economic structure of a society and its legal and political organization, *and that even the world of our thought is affected by these relationships.*"[1] Most conspicuously in his sociology of knowledge, Mannheim considered political, legal, philosophical, religious, and other ideas in their relationship with economic and social changes. That the ideas people hold vary with changing economic circumstances and that they are "somehow connected with the social context in which they live," remained a central and guiding principle throughout his work.

Mannheim's life's work may be divided into two distinct but interrelated phases and projects. The first, for which he is more famous, is his contribution to the sociology of knowledge. It began with his doctoral dissertation entitled "The Structural Analysis of Epistemology" and culminated in his classic work *Ideology and Utopia* and in his later essays published in one volume under the title *Essays on the Sociology of Culture.* The second phase, the fruit of his reflections on the crisis of his time and on life in England during World War II, included such works as *Man and Society in an Age of Reconstruction; Diagnosis of Our Time;* and *Freedom, Power, and Democratic Planning.* It was in the latter phase that one sees most clearly the ethical commitment underlying all of Mannheim's work—namely, that sociological studies must be regarded "as a response to the challenging present." Bramsted and Gerth have observed that for Mannheim, "sociology was a specifically modern way of thought which contributes to the rational self-orientation of man in industrial society. By raising us to a new level of self-awareness, the intellectual tools that the sociologist forges open up for us an insight into the dangerous processes of the modern world with its drift toward social upheavals and world wars."[2] There was, then, a first, or German, phase in which Mannheim directed his main efforts toward a sociological analysis of knowledge and a second, or English, phase in which he attempted to use his sociology to sketch the guidelines for a rational and democratic reconstruction of society.

MANNHEIM AND GERMAN SOCIOLOGY

There were three main intellectual currents in Germany that imparted to German sociology its specific form: (1) German classical philosophy, particularly the Hegelian school; (2) nonacademic sociological thought, notably Marxism; and (3) the *Geisteswissenschaften* (a school insisting that distinctive methods were required by the cultural-historical sciences), whose outstanding representatives among Mannheim's older contemporaries were Wilhelm Dilthey and Georg Simmel. Those three currents were also most evident in Mannheim's early work. From Hegel (and Marx) he derived the conception of history as a structured and dynamic process. Seeing facts and events not as isolated phenomena and occurrences but in relation to the dominant social forces and trends "and to the whole social situation existing at any given moment derives from Hegel."[3] Since Marx, however, had already incorporated those insights into his own conception of historical change, Mannheim was indebted primarily to him for his basic approach: The changing class structure of a society resulted from changes in productive techniques and the division of labor. The ideologies of a given society in a given period bore some determinate relationship to the existing classes and to the objective conflict of interests among them.

Originally, Marxism was an "opposition theory" and was therefore outside the German academy. Eventually, however, the issues raised by Marxism not only penetrated the universities but also generated so much interest and debate that the work of outstanding thinkers such as Max Weber, Troeltsch, Simmel, Sombart, Scheler, and Mannheim himself may be viewed as the fruitful results of a critical encounter with Marxism. In Mannheim's words, what began as "a mere dispute over principles was turned into an advancement of knowledge" (p. 215). Marxism, then, together with aspects of Hegel's philosophy, were two main currents which profoundly influenced Mannheim's thinking.

The third influence, most notable in Mannheim's early essays on "styles of thought" and *Weltanschauungen*—that is, world-views—was that of German humanistic studies. In common with Weber, he accepted Dilthey's assumption that there was a fundamental difference between the physical and cultural sciences, and that the latter required a specific method. If the physical sciences were concerned exclusively with calculable external phenomena, then the cultural sciences were (and must be) concerned with the motives and values of men and the meanings of their acts. In the physical sciences, explanation (*Erklärung*)—the correlation of external facts—was quite sufficient; not so in the human sciences where "explanation" alone is most superficial. What one should strive for in studying human conduct is not mere explanation but *understanding (Verstehen)*; for that, "sympathetic intuition" is required. Of course, explanation and interpretive understanding were not mutually exclusive; but the main point for Dilthey, Simmel, Weber, and Mannheim was that, whereas explanation is sufficient in the study of physical phenomena, an *adequate understanding* of human acts always requires an involvement with the purposes, motives, and values of the actors concerned; understanding, in short, requires a concern with the mind.

In those terms, Mannheim was interested in *meaning*, because in his view the most important interrelationships and interactions of men were meaningful and communicative acts. Interpretive understanding had to be applied not only to works of art, literature, and music, but to everyday speech and acts as well. In that, Mannheim followed Max Weber, whose work he knew very well. Mannheim admired Weber's elaboration and refinement of Marx's method and in fact emulated in his own work both of those extraordinary thinkers. He saw clearly that Weber had adopted Marx's general view that changes in the minds of men could not be understood adequately without relating them to the changes in their concrete existential conditions. "The greater art of the sociologist," writes Mannheim, "consists in his attempt always to relate changes in mental attitudes to changes in social situations. The human mind does not operate in vacuo; the most delicate change in the human spirit corresponds to similarly delicate changes in the situation in which an individual or a group finds itself, and, conversely, the minutest change in situations indicates that men, too, have undergone some change" (p. 219). That remained the leading idea of Mannheim's sociology of knowledge. In his earliest essays, however, it is not yet the Marxian approach that is most evident but the ideas of Hegel, of the German historical school, and of Dilthey, Windelband, Rickert, and others. An examination of the early essays will be followed by a consideration of those in which he employed a more consistently Marxian approach.

In his doctoral dissertation Mannheim worked with some of the fundamental assumptions of Hegel and of the *Geisteswissenschaften*: A cultural element is always to be regarded as a part of a greater logico-meaningful whole. Understanding, therefore, consists in systematically placing an element in its larger logico-meaningful context. The larger *Gestalt* ("whole," "structure," "context," or "form") is what imparts meaning to its component elements. Every intellectual and cultural field has a structure of its own, asserts Mannheim, and adds in Hegelian terms: "The simpler forms can be understood, in our opinion, only in terms of this 'highest,' 'all-embracing' form" (p. 16). "System," "context," "complementariness," "correlatedness," and so on, are already implied in every concept; there is no such thing as an isolated concept, which can be demonstrated by the fact that one has a "sense" of where a given concept properly belongs "and that it will show at once if it is 'transferred' into an alien sphere, where it can only be applied 'metaphorically'" (p. 23). Even the process of "thinking" is a matter of placing a concept in its proper total framework; "a thing is taken to be explained, comprehended, insofar as we have discovered its place in the currently accepted orders, series, levels" (p. 22).

The postulate of "system" holds for the exact physical sciences as well as for philosophy, art, and literature. In the physical sciences, however, an older system is superseded by a newer one because the latter is now considered true and the former, false. The Ptolemaic and Copernican systems, for example, cannot be regarded as equally true. Art forms, on the other hand, can exist side by side without contradicting one another even while expressing different truths. Clearly, different criteria of truth and validity are involved in the arts as compared with the sciences. Once a work of art has achieved aesthetic validity it acquires something of a "timeless glory"; and although the criteria for philosophical truth are closer to those of science than to those of art, certain of its "abandoned" solutions or insights may nevertheless have a timeless quality. Each cultural endeavor has its own criteria for validity; yet all such endeavors are parts of a meaningful whole which lends them a mutual affinity and a common "spirit."

ON THE INTERPRETATION OF WELTANSCHAUUNG

It seemed self-evident to Mannheim that the manifold cultural creations of humanity constituted a unity. This truth had been increasingly obscured by the splitting up of the whole culture into apparently separate and isolated domains. Mannheim believed that the fragmentation of the concept of culture into religion, art, literature, philosophy, and so on, was a product of the various theoretical standpoints from which culture was analyzed. He should have added that the division of labor, in which there emerged professional practitioners of religion, art, literature, and so on, had something to do with the subsequent theoretical treatment of those activities as separate and autonomous domains. As a result of the division of labor and of theoretical abstraction, the concrete cultural-experiential wholes had been neglected. The "whole," of course, can refer to an individual work of art, to the pattern which emerges from the total *oeuvre* of the artist, or, finally, to "the still more comprehensive 'whole' of the culture and *Weltanschauung* of an epoch."[4]

Interpretation, then, requires that one refer to the cultural unity underlying and tying together the various creations of a given society (or societies) in a given epoch. To understand, for example, art styles and art motifs, one "must make reference to even more fundamental factors such as *Zeitgeist*, 'global outlook,' and the like. Bringing these various strata of cultural life in relation to each other," Mannheim continues, "penetrating to the most fundamental totality in terms of which the inter-connectedness of the various branches of cultural studies can be understood—this is precisely the essence of the procedure of interpretation which has no counterpart in the natural sciences—the latter only 'explain' things" (p. 36). *Weltanschauung* is thus conceived as an atheoretical entity; it is an idealistic concept, or construct, referring to the highest, all-embracing "spirit" that permeates all cultural creations ranging from the arts through customs and including even "the tempo of living, expressive gestures and demeanor . . ." (p. 38).

Mannheim suggests that every cultural product and/or social event will reveal, if one probes deeply enough, three levels of meaning: (1) the objective, (2) the expressive, and (3) the documentary. His own illustration is as follows: He is walking down a street with a friend. A beggar beckons to them, they stop momentarily, and the friend gives the beggar alms. That simple state of affairs—a "meaningful" situation—can first be interpreted from the "outside," as it were. "Beggar," "assistance," "giver," and "charity" are sufficient to reveal the meaning of the social interaction taking place; the "objective social configuration" without a knowledge of either the beggar's or the friend's consciousness gives us what Mannheim calls the *objective* meaning of the situation, the most superficial level of understanding.[5] To proceed beyond that superficial level, it would be necessary to grasp the individual intent of the alms giver. In giving the alms, the objective meaning and result of which was "assistance," the friend may have intended to convey that he was engaging in a personal act of "mercy, kindness, and compassion." To determine that, one must know the alms giver intimately; only then can one grasp the act authentically—that is, as he intended it. That is the *expressive meaning* of the act. But, knowing the alms giver intimately means that we know him in a variety of contexts; in that light, his so-called "act of charity" may reveal itself as an act of hypocrisy. The act of giving may have been not at all in keeping with his general character so that the *documentary* or *evidential* meaning of his act is really inauthentic and hypocritical. Of course, these are merely analytical levels, not clearly distinguishable from one another in real situations. In this early phase of his thinking, Mannheim believed that such analytical devices provided one with greater insight into works of art and into everyday social interaction.

Can that approach be regarded as scientific? Yes, Mannheim replies, but in the special sense of the *Geisteswissenschaften*. Surely anyone who has had, for example, considerable listening experience can perceive significant differences in the music of Mozart, Tchaikowsky, and Debussy. When it is said that those composers represent the Classical, Romantic, and Impressionistic movements, respectively, that is not a subjective judgment. Experienced listeners tend to agree that the mood conveyed in the works of each of those composers and musical movements is representative of a certain cultural period. Furthermore, art connoisseurs, students of philosophy, *and* experts in musical styles may agree that their respective cultural areas share in a given period a common theme or spirit—or, as Mannheim would say, they express a common *Weltanschauung*. Can that be *demonstrated* in any positive, empirical sense? Mannheim was not so foolish as to suggest it could. But if positivistic standards cannot be applied, does that mean that studies of cultural creations can have no rigor? One can apply relatively rigorous scientific standards, Mannheim argued, to problems of *objective* and *expressive* meaning; given sufficient background, one can describe with precision the "visible" aspects of a work of art and the relevant aspects of an artist's biography which may have affected his style, choice of subject, materials, themes, and so on. However, the third level, the *documentary*, presents special problems and difficulties. Here, Mannheim raises an issue to which he will often return in his later works: the influence of spatiotemporal location upon the interpreter:

> Unlike the two other types of interpretation [writes Mannheim], documentary interpretation has the peculiarity that it must be performed anew in each period, and that any single interpretation is profoundly influenced by the location within the historical stream from which the interpreter attempts to reconstruct the spirit of a past epoch. It is well known that the Hellenic or Shakespearian spirit presented itself under different aspects to different generations. This, however, does not mean that knowledge of this kind is relative and hence worthless. What it does mean is that the type of knowledge conveyed by natural science differs fundamentally from historical knowledge—we should try to grasp the meaning and structure of historical understanding in its specificity, rather than reject it merely because it is not in conformity with the positivist truth-criteria sanctioned by natural science. (p. 61)

To impose upon the interpretive sciences the standards of the physical sciences is to forfeit the possibility of knowledge in many areas of life. Each area of study imposes certain requirements and limits and in a sense dictates the appropriate methodological approach. Standards of precision and verification cannot be mechanically transferred from the physical to the cultural sciences without exacting a price; that price, more often than not, is that a mechanical transfer of method yields the most superficial understanding in the cultural realm.

HISTORICISM

"Historicism" is an aspect of a *Weltanschauung* that emerged in a certain period in response to definite historical conditions. After all, it was no accident, as Mannheim was fond of saying, that such concepts as "movement," "process," and "flux," conceived *organically* and applied to sociocultural phenomena and institutions, first appeared in a definite historical period. The emergence of metaphors, concepts, and theories based on the "organism" as opposed to the "mechanism" had some determinate relationship to the social conditions prevailing in Europe after the French Revolution.[6] "Historicism," then, refers to the writing of history under the influence of that *Weltanschauung*, or in Mannheim's words: "We have historicism only when history itself is written from the historistic *Weltanschauung*" (p. 85).

Under that *Weltanschauung*, historians view all aspects of human life—institutions, customs, art, for example—either developmentally or organically. Thus the structure of history, its ordering principle, may be studied from two directions: (1) the vertical or historical and (2) the horizontal or cross sectional. One can take any social institution or cultural phenomenon and trace "it back into the past, trying to show how each later form develops continuously, organically from the earlier. If one gradually extends this method to all the spheres in cultural life, then one will obtain, so to speak, a bundle of isolated evolutionary lines" (p. 86). With that, the historian has completed only half the task, for even though one now sees development in each of the lines or spheres, they are isolated and disconnected, without any recognizable relationship among them. The remainder of the task, therefore, is "to show how, at one temporal stage, the *motifs*, which have just been observed in isolation, are also *organically bound up with one another*" (p. 87). "Organically bound up" in the "logico-meaningful" and not necessarily in the causal sense.

Mannheim realized very well that the method he advocated was in some sense "metaphysical," but he insisted that it is a necessary and valuable method in the study of culture (p. 135). The Hegelian notion of Spirit or Idea as the real subject of history was a fruitful heuristic device in the study of cultural *motifs*. In rather straight Hegelian terms, Mannheim writes, "The separate *motifs* are, rather, mutually conditioning at the successive stages of evolution and are components and functions of an ultimate basic process which is the real 'subject' undergoing the change" (p. 87). Throughout this essay Mannheim employs a Hegelian mode of expression and speaks, for instance, of the historical process as permeated by "reason" and "form-giving categories"; he retains the notion of a higher, all-embracing totality that imparts meaning and unity to the apparently separate events. Hegelian influence is also evident in the historicist view of truth: Present-day systems and conclusions of philosophy are based on a reality not yet known to earlier systems. The earlier systems, therefore, are not false but incomplete. Thus one must eschew an out-and-out rejection of previous systems, by attempting to incorporate them in the newer systems.

More important, however, is Mannheim's related historicist conception of the greater truth and validity embodied in the thought of a later as opposed to an earlier historical stage. The philosophy of the Enlightenment, for example, held to an ahistorical conception of *Reason*. Those who held to that doctrine in the nineteenth century tended, therefore, to reject the later historical, organic, developmental conception of "reason." For Mannheim, they were fundamentally wrong, for the nineteenth-century exponents of the Enlightenment view failed to see the greater validity of the historical conception—namely, "that the most general definitions and categories of Reason vary and undergo a process of alteration of meaning—along with every other concept—in the course of intellectual history" (p. 91). By rejecting the historical conception, the philosophers of static reason closed themselves off from the insights derived from a dynamic organic model based on living and growing organisms. There can be no doubt, Mannheim believed, of the superior validity of the dynamic-historical conception of sociocultural reality. The newer conception must be viewed as the theoretical counterpart of the general transformation taking place in the social structure. The changed sociohistorical situation is "the basis for the emergence of a new theoretical superstructure" (p. 96). Historicism, or the historical approach, rejects the rigid alternatives of true and false and seeks instead the "truth in history itself" (p. 100). Getting at that truth, however, is not a simple matter.

Mannheim explores some of the problems involved by developing further the distinction between the *Naturwissenschaften* and the *Geisteswissenschaften*, or the physical and sociocultural sciences, respectively. In the exact physical sciences, the historical and social position (*Standort*) of the knowing subject and that person's corresponding value orientations do not penetrate the scientific content. Mannheim sees a qualitative difference in the impact of one's *Standort* in the physical as compared with the cultural-historical sciences. In the latter it is incontrovertible that, depending on whether one is a Positivist, a Hegelian, or a Marxist, the principles of selection, the direction of the study, and the categories of meaning will differ. One cannot posit an abstract, impartial knowing subject in the study of history. That is true because "historical knowledge is only possible from an ascertainable intellectual location . . . [and] it presupposes a subject harboring definite aspirations regarding the future and actively striving to achieve them. Only out of the interest which the subject at present acting has in the pattern of the future, does the observation of the past become possible" (p. 102). That is why the "historical picture of the past changes with every epoch" (p. 103).

Does that imply the relativity of all historical knowledge? Mannheim insists that *"historicism veers away from relativism"* (p. 104). The "solution" he suggests at this stage and elaborates in his later writings is that social and historical knowledge is not relative but *perspectivistic* and *relational.* That was the view held by Max Weber in his historical studies. The so-called "materialistic conception" and his own thesis on ascetic Protestantism, far from being mutually contradictory, were in fact complementary. It was not, and never could be, a question of which view was right and which wrong. Both views were simply different perspectives of a given reality and our knowledge of that reality became more adequate and was enriched as a result of the additional perspective provided by Weber. Mannheim notes that even our conception of physical objects depends on the "location of the observing, interpreting subject." The "different historical pictures," Mannheim continues, "do not contradict each other in their interpretations, but encircle the same . . . historical content from different standpoints and at different depths of penetration" (p. 105). The dialectical interaction of the theories of successive periods results in the progress of knowledge.

Thus Mannheim strives, now as later, to impart the status and dignity of science to his perspectivistic, "dialectic-dynamic type of knowledge" (p. 115). The efforts he made to distinguish the two "kinds" of science and to harmonize perspectivistic knowledge with nonrelativistic criteria of truth are noteworthy. He firmly believed that perspectivism did not imply relativism. Rather it led "to a widening of our concept of truth which alone can save us from being barred from the exploration of these fields in which both the nature of the object to be known and that of the knowing subject makes [sic] only perspectivistic knowledge possible" (p. 120). That brings to a close our consideration of what may be termed the early phase of Mannheim's sociology of knowledge. The dominant influences here were Hegel, the historical school, Husserl, and the methodology of the *Geisteswissenschaften*. In his second phase those influences, though not abandoned, are subordinated to a more consistently Marxian approach.

CONSERVATIVE THOUGHT

If in the essays thus far considered Mannheim concerned himself with thought forms or *Weltanschauungen* and their connection with other aspects of social life, that was mainly in a general and philosophical manner. Though he pointed here and there to the underlying sociohistorical conditions of a given world outlook, he did not as yet explore that relationship in any systematic manner. In his essay "Conservative Thought," on the other hand, one sees a transition to a sociology of knowledge which was to be more characteristic of his later phase: Now he concerns himself not only with styles of thought, their relationship to one another, and their place in the larger cultural context, but more explicitly and systematically with the social basis of a given movement of thought. His main efforts are now directed toward demonstrating that "the key to the understanding of changes in ideas is to be found in the changing social background, mainly in the fate of the social groups or classes which are the 'carriers' of these styles of thought."[7] That approach, clearly Marxian, may be taken as paradigmatic, for it exemplifies the method he employed throughout his later essays in the sociology of knowledge. To be sure, he retains and utilizes elements derived from the other "schools" described earlier, but the dominant influence now becomes Marxian.

To support his thesis that there is a determinate relationship between forms of thought and the existence and fate of social groups, Mannheim selects for study the conservative movement, its class basis and its historical context. Although he examines the bases of conservatism in general, he focuses eventually on one group and one country during a specific period: German conservatism after the French Revolution. In this study his "styles" and movements of thought are predominantly political, approximating what he later calls ideologies. The study of conservative thought, he shows, implies that one must study liberal thought and even socialist thought—that is, thought which in each case developed along class and party lines. How much this method owed to Marx may be gathered from a brief description of the paradigm Mannheim employed in his analysis.

To understand conservative thought one must begin with rationalism, or the philosophy of the Enlightenment. What accounted for the growth of modern rationalism was the rising capitalist bourgeoisie. Quantitative rationalism, as it appeared in mathematics, philosophy, and the natural sciences, had its parallel in the growth of the capitalist economic system: Commodity production replaced the subsistence economy, exchange value replaced use value, and the formerly qualitative attitude toward things and men became increasingly quantitative. As Marx had observed, using Carlyle's phrase, it was now the callous "cash nexus" which related man to man. This abstract attitude, Mannheim agreed, gradually came "to include all forms of human experience. In the end even the 'other man' is experienced abstractly" (p. 86). The situation Marx had described as alienation stood in sharp contrast to the *Gemeinschaft* of the Middle Ages in which—and here Mannheim quotes Marx—"The social relationships of persons engaged in production appear, . . . as their own personal relationships, and not disguised as social relations of things, of products of labor" (p. 87n). Conservatism, then, was the political and intellectual reaction against the continuing process which was destroying the older world; it called for a restoration of that world, for a return to the *status quo ante.*

The social "carriers" of the ideological reaction were mainly "those social and intellectual strata that remained outside the capitalistic process of rationalization or at least played a passive role in its development" (p. 87). They included the peasant strata, the small bourgeoisie, and the landed aristocracy. It was primarily in those strata that the older, precapitalist relationships prevailed, and consequently, where the older traditions were kept alive. Those strata and particularly their intellectual representatives resolutely opposed the philosophy of the Enlightenment—that is, the intellectual tendencies that accompanied bourgeois capitalism. The Romantic-Conservative movement thus sought to salvage the older way of life and its values: "'Community' is set up against 'society' . . . family against contract, intuitive certainty against reason, spiritual against material experience. All those partially hidden factors at the very basis of everyday life are suddenly laid bare by reflection and fought for" (p. 89). Hence, it was not the socialists but the conservatives who historically were the first opponents and critics of capitalism.

Conservatism, then, like socialism, is a new or modern phenomenon which arose as a *conscious* and *reflective* reaction against the advance of capitalism. In those terms it is fundamentally different from mere "traditionalism," from simply clinging instinctively to the old ways of life. Conservatism is the intellectual, political-ideological expression of class interests and values in a dynamic historical situation; it is a style and movement of thought that developed as an antithesis to the conditions and ideology of the capitalistic world. In Mannheim's words, "traditionalism can only become conservatism in a society in which change occurs through the medium of class conflict—in a *class society*. This is the sociological background of modern conservatism" (p. 101). The "carriers" of the conservative experience and thought express their basic *Weltanschauung* by positively emphasizing all those aspects of life and thought which are antagonistic to the life and thought of bourgeois society. With conservative ideology, the qualitative and concrete are opposed to the quantitative and abstract; landed property, not the individual, is the basis of history; organic groups not "classes" are regarded as the real units of society and history. Conservatism looks to the past, liberalism to the present, and socialism to the future.

The conservative movement, then, arose in conscious opposition to capitalist conditions and to bourgeois society; the conservative *Weltanschauung* may therefore be viewed, schematically, as a point-for-point repudiation of natural law philosophy, the mode of thought most characteristic of the bourgeois-revolutionary epoch. Natural-law philosophy included the following doctrines: the "state of nature," "social contract," "popular sovereignty," the inalienable "Rights of Man (life, liberty, property, the right to resist tyranny, and so on" (p. 117). The main methodological principles of this philosophy were

1. Rationalism as a method of solving problems.
2. Deductive procedure from one general principle to the particular cases.
3. A claim of universal validity for every individual.
4. A claim to universal applicability of all laws to all historical and social units.
5. Atomism and mechanism: collective units (the state, the law, etc.), are constructed out of isolated individuals or factors.
6. Static thinking (right reason conceived as a self-sufficient, autonomous sphere unaffected by history). (p. 117)

The conservatives attacked each and every one of those articles of faith and proposed their own to replace them. In opposition to Reason and the deductive method, they stressed "History, Life, the Nation," and the essential "irrationality of reality." They repudiated the claim of universal validity and posited instead the historically unique character of each society. For the *mechanical* conception of political and social institutions, they substituted the organic conception: Political institutions, for instance, could not be mechanically transposed from one nation to another. As opposed to the liberal, atomistic notion of a society—that is, a sum of individuals who form a contract with one another—the conservatives insisted that society was an organic unified whole. Finally, the conservatives attacked the doctrine of static reason: The norms of reason are in a process of continual historical development. German conservatism, however, developed in a peculiar way because social conditions in Germany differed in a number of fundamental respects from those in England or France, for example.

The key to an understanding of German conservative thought, Mannheim believed, was to be found in Marx's observation that "Germany experienced the French Revolution on the philosophical plane" (p. 80). In France, the conservative movement was engendered by the reaction to the actual revolutionary events. What was being fought out in the social reality was accompanied by a political and ideological conflict. In Germany, in contrast, the counterrevolution was of a purely intellectual character. Conservatism in Germany was pushed to a logical extreme; this can be attributed to the absence of a large and strong middle class which, if it had existed as in England and France, would have developed a liberal party and ideology and would have mediated between the existing political extremes. Reminiscent of Marx's critique of the Left-Hegelians for not inquiring into the relationship between German social reality and German philosophy, Mannheim writes: "From our point of view, all philosophy is nothing but a deeper elaboration of a kind of action. To understand a philosophy, one has to understand the nature of the action which lies at the bottom of it. This 'action' which we have in mind is a special way, peculiar to each group, of penetrating social reality, and it takes on its most tangible form in politics. The political struggle gives expression to the aims and purposes which are unconsciously but coherently at work in all the conscious and half-conscious interpretations of the world characteristic of the group" (p. 84).

This, then, is Mannheim's general approach. Basing himself on Marx's *Critique of Hegel's Philosophy of Law* and on Engels's *Germany: Revolution and Counterrevolution*, he attempts to explain the specific form of German conservatism on the basis of German economic "backwardness." Capitalist developments in Germany and especially Prussia lagged many decades behind the other Western countries. "Marx's view is probably correct," writes Mannheim, "and he held that the social condition of Germany in 1843 corresponded roughly to that of France in 1789" (p. 121). At the time of the French

Revolution, Germany was lacking in any real bourgeoisie or proletariat; that condition was still evident after 1848 when Engels suggested that the dismal failure of the revolutions in Germany could be attributed to its economic backwardness. The middle class was characterized by so wide a diversity of interests that it was incapable of carrying out concerted political action; its response to the French Revolution was therefore purely ideological. The only strata capable of politically effective action were the nobility and the bureaucracy. If in France, the bourgeoisie mobilized the third and fourth estates against the Church, the monarchy, and the nobility, in Germany it was the nobility "from below" that struggled against the monarchy, allied with the bureaucracy, "from above." The absence of any real popular pressure weakened the ties of the nobility to the bureaucracy so that, when the latter initiated certain state reforms in the interest of capitalist development, the reforms evoked a romantic-feudal ideological reaction. The economic, and hence class, structure of German society at the time led to the curious situation in which the bureaucracy employed the rational ideas of the French Revolution as an ideological weapon against the nobility, while that class, in turn, sought to preserve and revive its feudal privileges, and the "organic" and "corporative structure of medieval society" (p. 122). The result was a peculiarly German way of thinking, which may be termed Romantic and historicist. It became so pervasive an intellectual climate that even its opponents, Mannheim observes, "could never quite free [themselves] from its habits of thought. Heine was a Romantic despite his opposition to the Romantic school; Marx a historicist despite his opposition to the historical school; etc." (p. 123 n.)

THE PROBLEM OF GENERATIONS

In his approach to the phenomenon of "generations," Mannheim generalized Marx's conception of *class* and in that way formulated a *sociological* conception of the problem. A "generation" is not a group but a category. A "group cannot exist without its members having concrete knowledge of each other, and [it] ceases to exist as a mental and spiritual unit as soon as physical proximity is destroyed." "Generation" is a social category and what is meant by that term may best be understood by considering another category, which shares

> a certain structural resemblance to it—namely, the class position (Klassenlage) of an individual in society.
>
> In its wider sense class position can be defined as the common "location" . . certain individuals hold in the economic and power structure of a given society as their "lot."[8]

A class is not a concrete group like a small territorial community, for example. "Class position is an objective fact," writes Mannheim in straight

Marxian terms, "whether the individual in question knows his class position or not, and whether he acknowledges it or not" (p. 289). What Marx called "class consciousness" does not necessarily accompany a class position, although in certain social conditions the latter can give rise to the former, lending it certain features, and resulting in the formation of a 'conscious class' (pp. 289–90). Generations, Mannheim notes, have something in common with Marx's conception of objective class position—that is, the "similar location of a number of individuals in a social structure . . ." (p. 290).

There is no denying that the similar "location" is based on the biological rhythm of the human organism: People born in the same year share a common temporal location in the social process. Social generations are ultimately based on that fact. Mannheim is quick to add, however, that "to be *based* on a factor does not necessarily mean to be deducible from it, or to be implied in it" (pp. 290–91). The biological factor has sociological relevance and that is where the sociological problem of generations must begin.

"Social location," as the common characteristic of class and generation, refers in the first place to the limitations imposed by that spatio-temporal location: Individuals are exposed to a specific range of potential and actual experiences and excluded from others. In those terms, just as the "experiential, intellectual, and emotional data" differ for each class, they also differ for each generation. Of course, one must not ignore the stratification and varying locations of members of a single generation. "Even a mental climate as rigorously uniform as that of the Catholic Middle Ages presented itself differently according to whether one were a theologizing cleric, a knight, or a monk" (p. 291). The category of generation is important, however, because it alerts one to the following characteristics of social life:

a. new participants in the cultural process are emerging whilst
b. former participants in that process are continually disappearing;
c. members of any one generation can participate only in a temporally limited section of the historical process, and
d. it is therefore necessary continually to transmit the accumulated cultural heritage;
e. the transition from generation to generation is a continuous process. (p. 292)

Marx had distinguished the objective and subjective aspects of class, and Mannheim employs a similar distinction with respect to the category of generation. When one says that the members of a single generation share a sociohistorical location, that means that the "location as such only contains potentialities which may materialize, or be suppressed . . ." (p. 303). Whether young peasants scattered in the countryside and urban youth are an *actual* generation will depend on whether they participate *"in the common destiny"* of some sociohistorical unit.

> We shall therefore speak of a *generation as an actuality* only when a concrete bond is created between members of a generation by their being exposed to the social and intellectual symptoms of a process of dynamic destabilization. Thus, the young peasants . . . only share the same generation location, without, however, being members of the same generation as an actuality, with the youth of the town. They are similarly located, insofar as they are *potentially* capable of being sucked into the vortex of social change. . . ." (p. 303)

That is reminiscent of Marx's discussion of whether the peasants are a class.[9]

Further refining the category of generation, Mannheim notes that even within the same *actual* generation, one must distinguish the separate units which emerge in response "to an historical stimulus experienced by all in common. Romantic-Conservative youth and [the] liberal-rationalist group, belong to the same actual generation but form separate 'generation units' within it. The *generation unit* represents a much more concrete bond than the actual generation as such."[10] The *generation unit* is not necessarily a group, since its members may never come into personal contact with one another. Nevertheless, they respond similarly to the situations in which they participate; they share a certain affinity for certain principles and ways of viewing their common world of experiences. "Thus within any generation there can exist a number of differentiated, [and even] antagonistic generation units."[11] Thus Mannheim provides the means of exploring the mutual relationship of class position, ideology, and generation.

IDEOLOGY AND UTOPIA

Although the principles enunciated in these essays can apply to the general problem of "how men actually think" and to the relationship of thinking to other aspects of human action, in practice Mannheim confines his attention to the narrower question of how thinking functions in the public and political spheres of social life. Now, as earlier, his major working hypothesis is derived from Marx's celebrated idea that it is the conditions of men's social existence which tend to determine their social consciousness. Mannheim adopts that principle in its full conflictive and dialectical sense: Men "act with and against one another in diversely organized groups, and while doing so they think with and against one another."[12]

Depending on the position men occupy in the social structure and their consciousness of that position, they join together in groups and strive collectively either to change or to preserve the conditions of their existence. Like Marx, Mannheim protests the separation of thought from action. The unity of theory and action must be recognized and restored in practice so that men may gain a fuller consciousness of the consequences of their acts. For Marx, the function of theory was to guide men in changing the world; for Mannheim, similarly, the raison d'être of his sociological theory of knowledge was to provide scientific guidance for action directed toward social change—for what he eventually called *planning for freedom.*

At the very outset he points quite clearly to both the advantages and limitations of his sociology of knowledge; ". . . the ultimate criterion of truth or falsity is to be found in the investigation of the object, and the sociology of knowledge is no substitute for this" (p. 4). Relating men's ideas to the particular location they occupy in the social structure is a process quite different from assessing their truth and validity. The sociological theory of knowledge can tell us how those ideas emerged but not whether they are true or false.

For Mannheim, the sociological theory of knowledge is a peculiarly modern instrument of analysis and reflection. It accompanied the greater tempo of social change of the capitalist-industrial era, including vertical and horizontal mobility, and the more intense and overt class conflicts of that era. Such a theory never could have arisen in medieval Europe, for example, which was a relatively static society characterized by closed castes or ranks. Nobles, clerics, peasants, artisans, and merchants had their own respective views of the world which merely coexisted as isolated *Weltanschauungen*—a reflection of the relative social isolation of those strata from one another. Only with the great social mobility and communication of the capitalist era did a decisive change take place. That becomes evident "when the forms of thought and experience, which had hitherto developed independently, enter into one and the same consciousness impelling the mind to discover the irreconcilability of the conflicting conceptions of the world" (p. 7). In addition, the greater mobility, communication, and conflict which accompanied capitalist-industrial developments brought in their wake greater democratization. That gave the thinking of the lower strata a greater public significance; one example in philosophy of the attempt to formalize such thinking is pragmatism. Social changes have resulted in a social system fundamentally different from the *Gemeinschaft* of the Middle Ages and are reflected in the thought of the "free intelligentsia"—also a characteristically modern product. They are "recruited from constantly varying social strata and life situations and [their] mode of thought is no longer subject [as it was in the Middle Ages] to regulation by a caste-like organization" (p. 10).

The greater understanding which the sociological approach to knowledge facilitates becomes evident by comparing it with others. Historically, one may distinguish at least three distinct approaches to problems of knowledge: (1) the *epistemological*, (2) the *psychological*, and (3) the *sociological*. An example of the first may be seen in the various philosophical controversies between the idealists and materialists, the realists and the nominalists, the empiricists and the rationalists, and so on. To take the last dispute, there can be no doubt that the participants raised an important question. Is knowledge a result of immediate sensory experience as Locke, for example, had held? Or is it the outcome of experience mediated by a priori categories as Kant had postulated? Mannheim sided with the latter school—but with the important qualification that the categories are not a priori. The mind and all its logical categories are a social product, and without that insight the epistemological question could never be adequately resolved. Though epistemology has enriched our understanding by posing certain problems, it needs sociology to solve them.

The psychological approach has also yielded greater understanding of the form and content of certain thoughts. Biographical data, for instance, are often very illuminating since they suggest why a given thinker thought the way he did. Yet, that approach, too, has definite limitations. Studying the life of Jesus or the Apostles, for example, can never adequately convey the full meaning of the biblical saying: "The last shall be the first." A full and adequate understanding of that utterance, Mannheim strives to show, could only be gained by going beyond the strictly psychological approach to consider not only biography but social structure and history as well. Combining ideas of Marx, Nietzsche, and Scheler, Mannheim suggests that the phrase, "The last shall be the first," can only be understood if one becomes aware of "the significance of resentment in the formation of moral judgments" (p. 22). An analysis of the sociohistorical context in which the sentence was first uttered suggests "that it has a real appeal only for those who, like the [early] Christians, are in some manner oppressed and who, at the same time, under the impulse of resentment, wish to free themselves from prevailing injustices" (p. 23). The merit of the sociological approach, then, is that it sets "alongside the individual genesis of meaning the genesis from the context of group life" (p. 25).

The conditions of existence and conflict of interests between oppressors and oppressed engender antithetical movements of thought. Mannheim employs what he calls "two slogan-like concepts 'ideology and utopia'" to describe these antithetical thought forms. Early Christian thought, for instance, was "utopian" in that it expressed the resentment of the oppressed. Their weakness led them to deprecate power and to glorify passivity—for example, "turn the other cheek." The early Christians constituted a "stratum which had as yet no real aspirations to rule," thus the saying, "Render unto Caesar the things that are Caesar's." Their resentment was therefore sublimated into a mere psychic rebellion: "The last shall be the first." All the values of the Roman oppressors ("ideology") were repudiated in the counter-values ("Utopia") of the oppressed Christians. Both ideological thought and utopian thought are thus "situationally determined," not only in the sense that each reflects the different conditions of existence of rulers and ruled, oppressors and oppressed, or upper and lower strata, but also in the sense that each reflects the interests of its "carriers."

Two distinct meanings may be discerned in the development of the concept ideology, and Mannheim calls them the *particular* and *total* conceptions. The first refers to the "more or less conscious disguises of the real nature of the situation, the true recognition of which would not be in accord with [one's] interests. These distortions range all the way from conscious lies to half-conscious and unwitting disguises; from calculated attempts to dupe others to self-deception" (p. 49). The *total* conception of ideology, on the other hand, refers, for example, to the *Weltanschauung* of a class or epoch, or to the ideas and categories of thought which are bound up with the existential conditions of that class or epoch. In the *particular*, or psychological, conception one deals with an individual and attempts to "unmask" him by discovering the true personal interests he deceitfully hides or denies; in that case one designates "only a part of the opponent's assertions" as ideology while continuing to share with him a common universe of discourse and common standards of validity. The total conception, in contrast, "calls into question the opponent's entire *Weltanschauung* (including his conceptual apparatus) and attempts to understand these concepts as an outgrowth of the collective life of which he partakes" (p. 50). Examples of the *total* conception might be "conservative thought," "bourgeois-liberal" ideology, and so on. When men express such ideas it is not a matter of deceit or even "interests" in any narrow sense but rather an expression of the outlook of a whole social group or stratum whose existential circumstances they share. Marxism fused both conceptions into one and thus became a formidable ideological weapon in the hands of the proletariat and its spokesmen. "It was this theory which first gave due emphasis to the role of class position and class interests in thought" (p. 66). Soon afterward, however, the opponents of Marxism learned to use the weapon of ideological analysis and to turn it against Marxism itself. It was that process that made possible the "transition from the theory of ideology to the sociology of knowledge" (p. 67).

For Mannheim, then, the *total* conception of ideology requires *sociological* analysis, and here two formulations may be distinguished: the *special* and the *general*. At first a group discovers the *Seinsverbundenheit* or "situational determination" of its opponents' ideas while remaining unaware that its own thought is also influenced by the social situation in which it finds itself. When that is the case, Mannheim calls it the special formulation of the total conception of ideology. The *general* formulation, on the other hand, is employed when one "has the courage to subject not just the adversary's point of view but all points of view, including his own, to the ideological analysis" (p. 69). If the *general form of the total conception* is used in an investigation in a nonevaluative manner—that is, judgments are temporarily suspended as to the truth or falsity of the ideas in question—then one has a *sociology of knowledge*.

Does not the sociology of knowledge imply that truth is "relative"—that is, "dependent upon the subjective standpoint and the social situation of the knower"? To that Mannheim replies in the negative, for while the study of history from the standpoint of the sociology of knowledge does not reveal any absolute truths, that implies not "relativism" but "relationism." The probability is great that the perspective of an observer or knower will vary with his social standpoint, but the question "[W]hich social standpoint offers the best chance for reaching an optimum of truth?" still remains (p. 71). For Mannheim, then, the social basis of an idea and its validity are two separate questions.[13]

The student of a given social or historical question, even one who has a truly objective intention, is made aware by the sociology of knowledge that all points of view, including his own, are partial and one-sided. His objective posture leads him to consider carefully the many contending viewpoints, which he relates to their respective social situations. "Through this effort the one-sidedness of our own point of view is counteracted, and conflicting intellectual positions may actually come to supplement one another."[14] Our knowledge and ability to get at the truth are presumably enhanced by the very fact that one can employ a variety of perspectives through which to study a given phenomenon, and are enhanced, too, by discovering the social bases of the various perspectives.

This may be illustrated by recalling Max Weber's view. There can be no doubt that he regarded Marx's perspective as strategically important for an understanding of historical change, and his own perspective as supplementary to that of Marx. For Weber, it was not a matter of one perspective being true and the other false. Rather, by adding his own to Marx's, a richer and more adequate understanding of the origins of capitalism was made possible. One partial truth supplemented and enriched another. That was also Mannheim's attitude toward historical questions. Under no circumstances were the postulates of the sociology of knowledge to be regarded as a substitute for empirical research. "We, too, appeal to 'facts' for our proof, but the question of the nature of facts is in itself a considerable problem."[15] In the end, Mannheim believed that, however objective an analysis, there was "an irreducible residue of evaluation inherent in the structure of all thought," but that there was perhaps one stratum in society which was more capable than any other of becoming conscious of its evaluations. That was the intelligentsia.

THE INTELLIGENTSIA

It is not quite accurate to say that Mannheim found "a structural warranty of the validity of social thought in the 'classless position' of the 'socially unattached intellectuals' [*sozialfreischwebende Intelligenz*]."[16] If the impression of such a "warranty" could occasionally be inferred from Mannheim's remarks in *Ideology and Utopia* and other early essays, he makes quite clear in a later essay, devoted entirely to the subject of intellectuals, that such an impression is not the one he had intended to convey and, in fact, that it is a misinterpretation of his thesis. Mannheim's point about the intelligentsia was that they are not a class; they have no common interests, they cannot form a separate party, and, finally, they are incapable of common and concerted action. They are, in fact, *ideologues* of this or that class but never speak for "themselves."

For Mannheim, the intelligentsia was essentially a "classless aggregation," or an "interstitial stratum" which willy-nilly became "a satellite of one or another of the existing classes and parties."[17] It was "between, but not above, the classes." He is quite explicit on this score: The intellectuals are not a "superior" stratum, nor does their peculiar social position assure any greater validity for their perspectives. Their position does, however, enable them to do something which members of other strata are less able to do. It is true that most intellectuals do in fact share the orientations of one or another of the existing classes and parties. "But," writes Mannheim,

> over and above these affiliations he [an intellectual] is motivated by the fact that his training has equipped him to face the problems of the day in several perspectives and not only in one, as most participants in the controversies of their time do. We said he is equipped to envisage the problems of his time in more than a single perspective, although from case to case he may act as a partisan and align himself with a class. (p. 105)

The emphasis here is on the *potential* ability of the educated individual to adopt a variety of perspectives toward any given social issue or phenomenon. Intellectuals are *not*, Mannheim reemphasizes, "an exalted stratum above the classes and are in no way better endowed with a capacity to overcome their own class attachments than other groups" (p. 105). In his earlier essays, he explains, the term "relatively" in the phrase "relatively unattached intelligentsia" which he borrowed from Alfred Weber, "was no empty word. The expression simply alluded to the well-established fact that intellectuals do not react to given issues as cohesively as for example . . . workers do" (p. 106). Being a member of the so-called intelligentsia, then, provides no structural warranty of validity nor does it make one "privy to revelations." Apparently all that Mannheim wanted to convey in his thesis about the intelligentsia "was merely that certain types of intellectuals have a maximum opportunity to test and employ the socially available vistas and to experience their inconsistencies" (p. 106). Right or wrong, that is a considerably more modest thesis than his critics have attributed to him.

One of the main points Mannheim wanted to make with the phrase "relatively unattached" was that after the Middle Ages the intellectuals to an increasing degree were emancipated from the upper classes and unaligned as yet with the lower. The institutions in which the intellectuals could first be discerned as relatively free and detached were the *salons* and the coffeehouses. While the salons enabled individuals of different social backgrounds, views, stations, and allegiances to mingle, entry to the salon required social acceptability and was in that sense restricted. The coffeehouses, on the other hand, were open to all and thus "became the first centers of opinion in a partially democratized society" (p. 138). Membership and participation were now determined not by rank and family ties but by intellectual interests and shared opinions; the latter being especially true when the houses became political clubs. "Not the common style of living and not common friends, but like opinion constituted now the basis of amalgamation" (p. 139).

In the modern era, *some* intellectuals at least were able to escape a relationship of dependence on local habitat, institution, class, and party. To be sure, they "may have their political preferences, but they are not committed to any party or denomination. This detachment, however, is not absolute" (p. 157). *Some* journalists, *some* writers, *some* scholars, and *some* scientists "enjoy" a relatively uncommitted position which, however, has for Mannheim negative as well as positive consequences; for although it is true that the "free" intellectual has a potentially wider view, and is potentially less blinded by particular interests and commitments, he lacks at the same time the restraints of real life. He is more inclined to generate ideas without testing them in practice—that is, in the actions and consequences of everyday life. He may lose touch with reality and forget that a main purpose of thought is the orientation of action. Such observations helped illuminate the changing historical role of the intellectual.

More important for Mannheim, however, was the fate of the relatively free intellectuals in the face of the tendency so well described by Max Weber: the growing bureaucratization of all aspects of social life including scholarship and science. Increasingly, Weber had pointed out, not only the workers but the scientists and scholars were being "separated" from the means of "production" (research). That, together with specialization, which narrows the compass of thought and activity, discourages the "will to dissent and innovate" (p. 168). More and more, research, thinking, and scholarship were now carried out in the context of large organizations, private and governmental, and the increasing dependence of the mental laborer led to an increasing "intellectual dessication" (p. 168). There were now few professions that were "free" in the sense that they could be practiced independently, outside a bureaucratic context.

No matter how small the intellectual stratum may be, still it retains an important role at once diagnostic, constructive, and critical. There is nothing automatic about those functions—they do not follow "naturally" from a social position. In effect, it is only by a conscious and deliberate commitment that the intellectual can prevent his affiliation with parties and organizations from resulting in self-abnegation. His conscious posture must at all times be critical—of himself as well as of others. Mannheim recognized that the intellectuals were powerless, but he believed, nevertheless, that they could play an influential role in the preservation of freedom and in the reconstruction of society.

MAN AND SOCIETY IN AN AGE OF RECONSTRUCTION

Writing these essays as the Nazis were coming to power [18] and almost two decades after the Russian Revolution, Mannheim perceived that in Germany and Russia, as well as in those countries which remained politically democratic, the growing bureaucratization of the crucial sectors of society seemed to be a virtually inexorable process. Bureaucratization undermined democracy because it separated the people from the means of power and brought about, in Mannheim's words, "the dominance of small minorities under capitalism as well as communism."[19] In the eighteenth and early nineteenth centuries, democracy was based in no small degree on the military power of the people: "[O]ne man meant one gun, the resistance of one thousand individuals one thousand guns." Ultimately the people could use that power to safeguard democracy. In the twentieth century, the growing scale and concentration of the instruments of military power had brought about a basic change; large numbers of people could now be intimidated, terrorized, and killed by efficient, large-scale means of destruction under the control of dominant minorities. The military significance of small arms and barricades had radically diminished and the power of the people had declined accordingly.

Moreover, bureaucratic organization strives for maximum *functional rationality*—that is, it suppresses all forms of substantial rationality. Functional and substantial rationality are opposed in principle: The first requires the subordination of one's mind and self to a thing or mechanical process, while the second presupposes that men strive to master a situation and adapt it to their conscious ends. The master trend of modern industrial society—bureaucratization, or increasing formal rationalization—far from raising the capacity of Everyman for independent judgment, is in fact paralyzing and destroying it. The average individual has little or no understanding of his condition and, in effect, he has turned over to small dominant minorities "the responsibility for making decisions." Mannheim viewed that trend as the basis of "the growing distance between the élite and the masses, and [of] the 'appeal to the leader' which has recently become so widespread" (p. 59).

Left with a reduced capacity for independent thinking, and accustomed to following blindly, the average individual is also thereby reduced to a state of "terrified helplessness" and impotence when the functionally rationalized system collapses. Under those circumstances, is it any wonder that economic crises and other disruptions of the social system are accompanied by widespread eruptions of irrational behavior? "Irrationality" from that standpoint is a type of behavior generated under specific social circumstances. Man is inherently neither rational nor irrational and which type of conduct will prevail depends on the situational context. "Uncontrolled outbursts and psychic regressions," for example, were more likely to occur, Mannheim argues, in the mass industrialized society than in small groups. He observes that the functional rationalization of human behavior in industrial society brings with it "a whole series of repressions and renunciations of impulsive satisfactions," which remain repressed so long as the system works smoothly. With its breakdown, however, the repressed impulses assert themselves as wild and powerful irrational outbursts, which avail the people nothing but which are successfully harnessed by "the leaders." Irrationality, its sources and its consequences, are thus explained *sociologically.*

With that analysis, Mannheim prepared for a presentation of what appeared to him as the only solution. It was high time, he argued, that the liberal advocates of laissez faire recognized that their classic doctrine had outlived its usefulness. It is the "planlessness" of contemporary society that is the cause of economic crises and of the breakdown of "social order." Economic planning is absolutely essential if social stability is to be preserved. Not planning in the formal or functional sense, which tends toward totalitarianism, but "democratic" planning. The liberals must be made to understand, once and for all, that planning need not take the totalitarian form. With democratic, rational planning, the irrational can be transformed into a positive force, a "pure *élan*" which "heightens the joy of living without breaking up the social order" (p. 63). Against the various groups of Marxists, on the other hand, Mannheim argued that class conflict, revolution, and working-class power are not the precondition for a new society in which the substantive needs and wants of all are planned for. How does Mannheim conceive of democratic planning? He recounts that during a discussion of the possibilities of planning, someone remarked: "We have progressed so far as to be able to plan society and even to plan man himself. Who plans those who are to do the planning?" Mannheim confesses: "The longer I reflect on this question, the more it haunts me" (p. 74). Although he is not entirely happy to do so, he places his faith in "responsible élites." Let them plan for the whole society and bear responsibility for it. It is true that they are small minorities, but "the masses always take the form which the creative minorities controlling societies choose to give them" (p. 75). This élitist conception of "democracy" is characteristic of all of Mannheim's work on planning, but especially the essays in *Man and Society.*

Mannheim's reasoning seems to have been the following: The high degree of bureaucratization of the crucial sectors of social life is here to stay; the concentration of power is an irreversible process, though decentralization here and there may be possible. Periodic economic crises and now the most dramatic breakdown of all have weakened the liberal political order. The working class and its leaders are divided among themselves and seem incapable of stopping fascism; the unemployed restless masses have come under the sway of dictators who threaten to envelop the whole world in a devastating war. The only choice, therefore, is to learn what one can from the totalitarian states—namely, planning and other social techniques—and to apply them as democratically as possible toward the maintenance of order. "How it would simplify our common life," writes Mannheim, "if this power of planned persuasion were used, not for stirring up strife, but for encouraging behavior on which all our hopes of peace, cooperation, and understanding depend" (p. 261). It was not without some apprehension that Mannheim advocated the use of such "techniques"; he saw the great dangers in giving some men, a small minority, so much power over all the others. But in the end, he saw no alternative.

Since the intellectuals have no power, the only option open to those who refuse to become mere ideological spokesmen for one or another of the parties is to advise the élites. It is here that we have a concrete example of the so-called "relatively unattached intellectual," which Mannheim, no doubt, considered himself in this instance to be. The role of the intellectual was to impart scientific-sociological knowledge to the various élites so that they might govern wisely and benevolently. In some cases, the intellectuals would become an integral part of the planning authority. Here one sees an approach to social change, reminiscent of Saint-Simon's, which is at once positivistic, technocratic, and paternalistic. "The planning authority," Mannheim proposes, "should be able to decide on empirical grounds what sort of influence to use in a given situation, basing its judgments on the scientific study of society, coupled if possible with sociological experiments" (p. 266).

Apart from the sinister implication of this proposal—giving scientific knowledge to élites by which they can control the "masses"—it is naively technocratic: Planning is simply a matter of applying scientific knowledge; social change requires little more than intelligent social engineering. Somehow, science and the goodwill of the élites would be sufficient to bring about a higher "organic" solidarity, and Mannheim in fact relies on Durkheim's thesis for theoretical support. A new consensus must emerge planned by the scientific and power élites and the sole raison d'être of "social techniques" "is to influence human behavior as society thinks fit" (p. 271). "Society" in this instance quite clearly refers to the élites. Nowhere in these essays, despite his insistence on "democratic" planning, does Mannheim make provision for a genuinely democratic decision-making process by which the members of society may determine their own fate.

During World War II Mannheim retained the same general view but felt that the wartime experiences presented new possibilities to the democracies for peaceful, planned reform.

DIAGNOSIS OF OUR TIME

As a sociologist interested in social change, Mannheim, maintained that "Just as the revolutionary waits for his hour, the reformer whose concern it is to remold society by peaceful means must seize his passing chance."[20] Thus

Mannheim suggests "that Britain has the chance and the mission to develop a new pattern of society. . . ." Developing further his earlier description of the basic structural trends of modern industrial society, he calls attention, once again, to the implications of those trends. The concentration of power and the growing scale of organization were an undeniable tendency. That was true not only of the economic, political, and military spheres but of the media of mass communication as well. Clearly, those changes in what Mannheim called "social techniques" (his term for means of social control) had brought about a new situation in which large masses could now be controlled and manipulated by small groups in key positions of power. A few men, strategically placed, could make decisions affecting the lives and fate of the vast majority. That meant that "social techniques" had acquired a fundamental importance—perhaps "even more fundamental to society than the economic structure or the social stratification of a given order. By their aid one can hamper or remold the working of the economic system, destroy social classes and set others in their place" (p. 2).

One could not go back to the decentralized, small-scale social organization of the past. Although it is true that the concentration of power accompanying modern developments often fostered oligarchy and even dictatorship, they were not necessary outcomes of those developments. That the scale of social life in modern mass society requires planning has become evident in the periodic breakdowns of the economic system and in the social upheavals accompanying them. The partial "planning" that is already in effect in the "functional" rationalization of many areas of social life is clearly not what is required. Planning must be democratic and guided by substantial rationality. Mannheim was thus trying to persuade a specific English public that laissez-faire was now a useless and even dangerous doctrine, and that planning need not be totalitarian. There is a "third way" that is compatible with democracy and freedom as those concepts are understood, say, in England.

Mannheim's "third way" is a mixture of Keynesian and social-democratic measures. Now as earlier, he advances his proposals with the hope that the existing élites will recognize their wisdom and act upon them. It had become clearer than ever before that when "left alone" the economic system generated greater inequalities in wealth and income—or in "life chances" generally. Not only was that unjust, it led to social tension, conflict, revolutionary upheavals, and dictatorship. Social justice as well as class cooperation and social peace, therefore, could only be achieved by a conscious and deliberate diminution of differences in wealth and opportunity. The wealthy and advantaged will have to be enlightened enough to make some sacrifices; if they do, they may be able to hold on to a reasonable amount of their wealth. If not, they may lose all. In that way, Mannheim hopes to appeal simultaneously to the sense of justice and the long-term interests of the advantaged.

"The move toward greater justice," he writes, "has the advantage that it can be achieved by the existing means of reform—through taxation, control of investment, through public works, and radical extension of social services; it does not call for revolutionary interference, which would lead at once to dictatorship" (p. 6). With such means, moreover, the active cooperation of the liberal and conservative intelligentsia, and the Church, could be enlisted. The realization of this plan would also require the militant and systematic inculcation of the basic values of Western civilization—for example, social justice, freedom, brotherly love, mutual help, decency, respect for the individual.

Although Mannheim was appealing primarily to the élites, he was aware that the implementation of his proposals required more than their assent, even if they could be persuaded to give it. It also required the support of the working class and its leaders. These were wartime essays, one must remember, and he shared the illusions of many at the time that the wartime class cooperation would survive the war. The democracies, notably England, had demonstrated, under the Nazi attack, their courage, viability, and efficiency. Much of that could be attributed to the voluntary cooperation among the classes of English society. The experience of the Depression and the war and the fear of totalitarianism would encourage, Mannheim hoped, an even more cooperative and reformist attitude among the workers than already prevailed.

For Mannheim, the most important lesson to be learned from recent history was that revolutionary upheavals are more likely to result in dictatorships than in a good society. Socialist critics of the existing order, therefore, "will be readier to advocate reformist measures, as it is becoming obvious that recent revolutions tend to result in fascism and that the chances of a revolution will be very slight as soon as a united party has coordinated all the key positions and is capable of preventing any organized resistance" (p. 10).

Of course, increasing social justice by means of democratic social planning required international peace. Mannheim looked forward to the transformation of the wartime coalition—which included partners with different socioeconomic systems—into a lasting peacetime alliance. What William James had called a moral substitute for war could be found. Thus in an optative mood that was indeed shared by many others at the time, Mannheim wrote: "I think there is a reasonable chance at least that after the horrors of this war the tasks of reconstruction will be so urgent that they will be felt by many to be a unifying issue at least as strong as the war itself" (p. 30).

Mannheim's proposal for peaceful social change required, therefore, general goodwill, class cooperation, and the rational mobilization of resources guided by the knowledge of the social sciences. Such knowledge is an "aid to those who govern," but it can also aid the governed. Education in general but especially in the "science of society" can help the governed check the arbitrariness of the leaders. The élites must be made to understand that "the uneducated and uninformed masses today are a greater danger to the maintenance of any order than classes with a conscious orientation and reasonable expectation" (p. 43). Education for democratic planning is essential at all age levels but particularly for the young. Here something can be learned from the totalitarian states. The point, of course, is not to imitate them but to grasp the fact that the great *élan* of youth can be guided toward constructive goals. Presumably, a nationwide youth movement could be organized with a common *Weltanschauung* that would cut across class lines. Mannheim was calling for a new type of awareness, not the *partial* class awareness that furthers class conflict, but a "total" awareness in which one considers general interests not less than one's special interests. Nevertheless, the new consensus would not preclude class conflict; rather it would lend it a democratic and peaceful form. "Democracy is essentially a method of social change, the institutionalization of the belief that adjustment to changing reality and the reconciliation of diverse interests can be brought about by conciliatory means, with the help of discussion, bargaining, and integral consensus" (p. 69). Under those conditions, class struggle even preserves democracy. What is needed to make democracy safe is not the exclusion of the social struggle, but that it should be fought out by methods of reform" (p. 70).The workers, especially, should have learned by now that a "society without a governing class" is an unrealizable fantasy. The realistic aim should be "the improvement of the economic, social, political, and educational opportunities for the people to train themselves for leadership, and improvement of the method of the selection of the best in the various fields of social life" (p. 72).

There were for Mannheim at least three criteria by which one could judge whether a society was succeeding in the implementation of his proposal: (1) social control, discipline, and repression are steadily reduced to an absolute minimum; (2) controls and prohibitions are democratically decided upon and are above all "humane"; and, finally, (3) institutions are designed to help the individual make his way but also to "come to the rescue of those who have failed . . . " (p. 82).

Many of the same ideas and some new ones are developed in his essays collected under the title *Freedom, Power, and Democratic Planning*. Mannheim's "third way" may be viewed as an attempt to mediate between extremes: between those who insist on maintaining the same old routine and those who demand fundamental social changes. Speaking to both extremes, then, Mannheim is saying first to the defenders of the status quo, planning is essential to counteract the dangers of a mass society. He appeals to their sense of justice and attempts to enlighten them as to their long-term interests. To the Marxists, on the other hand, Mannheim concedes that their revolutionary theory may have been appropriate to the conditions of early capitalism—a world of scarcity, ruthless exploitation, and "life-and-death struggle between rich and poor in which the poor had nothing to lose but their chains." Today, however, the situation is different and "there are too many people who could lose by revolution."[21]

Moreover, there is another condition which all, but especially the workers, should reflect upon seriously. The "withering away" of the state after a socialist revolution was originally not an altogether silly and quixotic vision. When Marx advanced that idea he was justified in projecting into the future a historical tendency in which absolutist regimes were giving way to increasingly democratic ones. The ghastly experiences of the twentieth century, however, have demonstrated that revolutionary upheavals are followed by a strengthening of the state and that far from "withering" it becomes increasingly totalitarian. The "social techniques," the means of social control in the hands of the dominant minorities, are so efficient and powerful as to render revolution "against any totalitarian power once entrenched . . . nearly hopeless. No established totalitarian regime, whatever its political creed, can be broken from within; it takes an external war to unseat it."[22] In short, the almost certain results of any future revolution make it expedient for everyone to opt for the "third way."

This appeared as a particularly viable alternative for England and for other societies with similar conditions. In England, the main social base of planning would be the large middle class, the broad center. That base, together with highly developed democratic institutions and traditions, makes it more likely that planning would be acceptable to the majority "excluding both the reactionaries who do not want to move at any price, and radicals who think the millennium is just around the corner."[23]

Since the third way is unthinkable under conditions of international tension and war, every effort must be made to preserve peace. The beginnings of the Cold War were already visible when Mannheim wrote these essays and he understood that a third world war could be fatal for all humanity. He placed his faith in the balance of power between the United States and the Soviet Union. The danger in that, he recognized, was that the small powers could become pawns in the Great Power struggle and the main hope of preventing such a result "rests in a *tenacious insistence on fair play* on the part of political forces spread all over the world, who are truly interested in and stand for the transformation of present-day imperialism into a peaceful order."[24] Ultimately, however, it is the superpowers that have a special responsibility in this regard: "Just as the Roman Empire established its *Pax Romana* among formerly bellicose peoples, so the rule of the great powers may spare us the guerrilla wars of small brigand states."[25]

In several important respects, Mannheim's new society was quite Saint-Simonian: hierarchic, "organic," and guided by scientific-industrial élites. Because even the best planners and the most "substantial" rationality cannot avoid a situation in which "economic decisions affect some groups and classes favorably and others unfavorably," organic unity requires something more. Just as Saint-Simon had called for a New Christianity, Mannheim now proposed a New Social Philosophy based upon Christian values. There was no getting around that basic requirement of the new planned society: Basic ethical principles, enjoining altruism and self-sacrifice, had to be established. "There will, therefore, in every planned society be a body somehow similar to the priests, whose task it will be to watch that certain basic standards are established and maintained."[26] In the end, Mannheim's longing for a different world led him to believe that there was "a reasonable chance that after the war the struggle between antagonistic dogmatic systems will have burnt out and there will be a desire to develop potentialities which at present can only be diagnosed as latent tendencies of a Third Way."[27]

NOTES

1. Karl Mannheim, *Systematic Sociology* (New York: Grove Press, 1957), p. 137, italics added. For a brief discussion of Marxian and other theoretical influences on Mannheim, see Robert K. Merton's essay "Karl Mannheim and the Sociology of Knowledge," in *Social Theory and Social Structure* (Glencoe, Ill.: The Free Press, 1968), p. 544.
2. See "A Note on the Work of Karl Mannheim," by Ernest K. Bramsted and Hans Gerth in Karl Mannheim, *Freedom, Power, and Democratic Planning* (London: Routledge and Kegan Paul, 1950), pp. vii–xv.
3. Karl Mannheim, *Essays on Sociology and Social Psychology* (London: Routledge and Kegan Paul, 1953), p. 214. (Hereafter all page references to this work will be indicated in parentheses immediately following the quoted passage.)
4. Karl Mannheim, *Essays on the Sociology of Knowledge* (London: Routledge and Kegan Paul, 1952), p. 36. (Hereafter all page references to this work will be indicated in parentheses immediately following the quoted passage.)
5. In art, this level of meaning would be revealed by the purely visual content; in music, by melody, rhythm, harmony, and so on.
6. In this book "historicist" theories were, of course, considered in the chapters on the Romantic-Conservative Reaction to the Enlightenment and the French Revolution.
7. Mannheim, *Essays on Sociology*, p. 74. (Hereafter all page references to this work will be indicated in parentheses immediately following the quoted passage.)
8. Mannheim, *Essays on the Sociology of Knowledge*, p. 289. (Hereafter all page references to this work will be indicated in parentheses immediately following the quoted passage.)
9. See Marx's essay, "The Class Struggles in France," in Karl Marx and Frederick Engels, *Selected Works*, Vol. I (Moscow: Foreign Languages Publishing House, 1950).
10. Ibid., p. 304.
11. Ibid., p. 306.
12. Karl Mannheim, *Ideology and Utopia* (London: Routledge and Kegan Paul, 1960), p. 3. (Hereafter all page references to this work will be indicated in parentheses immediately following the quoted passage.)
13. An excellent critical discussion of this and other problems may be found in Merton, "Karl Mannheim and the Sociology of Knowledge" (see note 1, this chapter), pp. 543–62.
14. Mannheim, *Ideology and Utopia*, p. 76.
15. Ibid., p. 91.

16. Merton, "Karl Mannheim and the Sociology of Knowledge" (see note 1, this chapter), p. 561.
17. Karl Mannheim, *Essays on the Sociology of Culture* (London: Routledge and Kegan Paul, 1956), p. 104. (Hereafter all page references to this work will be indicated in parentheses immediately following the quoted passage.)
18. The essays were first published in German in 1935; in 1940, they were translated into English, revised, and expanded.
19. Karl Mannheim, *Man and Society in an Age of Reconstruction* (New York: Harcourt Brace Jovanovich, 1948), p. 46. (Hereafter all page references to this work will be indicated in parentheses immediately following the quoted passage.)
20. Karl Mannheim, *Diagnosis of Our Time* (London: Routledge and Kegan Paul, 1943), p. ix. (Hereafter all page references to this work will be indicated in parentheses immediately following the quoted passage.)
21. Mannheim, *Freedom, Power*, p. 27.
22. Ibid., pp. 27–28.
23. Ibid., p. 36.
24. Ibid., p. 71, (italics added).
25. Ibid., p. 75.
26. Mannheim, *Diagnosis of Our Time*, p. 119.
27. Ibid., p. 164.

Epilogue

We began this review of classical sociological theory with the Enlightenment thinkers because they, more than any of there predecessors, approached the study of society informed by the newly emerging scientific principles. Much of what they had to say appears to be vital still today. Much but not all, since some of their propositions were one-sided, as we have learned from the Romantic-Conservative Reaction.

However, the encounter between the Enlightenment and its critics has also alerted us to the one-sidedness of the Reaction. We recognize, therefore, that a fusion of Enlightenment and Romantic-Conservative elements would be necessary in any truly adequate theory and method. That is the valuable insight we gain from the "debate" between those two intellectual movements.

If the Enlightenment and the Conservative Reaction represent Parts I and II of this book's organizational framework, then the "Marxian Watershed" and the "debate with Marx's Ghost" represent Parts III and IV, respectively. I call the work of Marx and his followers a "watershed" because it was in fact an extraordinarily influential political and intellectual movement in the history of twentieth-century social thought. I have tried in the chapters on Marx and Engels to discuss their ideas objectively, with the aim of drawing out scientifically fruitful insights. Hence, just as we learn from the encounter between the Enlightenment and the Reaction, we learn a great deal from Weber, Pareto, Mosca, Michels, Durkheim, and Mannheim as they engage in a critical dialogue with the Marxian legacy.

Finally, we should observe that in studying the human condition, the classical tradition of sociological thinking had failed to place the subjection of women at the center of our concerns and that it required the special efforts of women to do so. In this book those special efforts were represented by the theoretical contributions of Mary Wollstonecraft, Harriet Martineau, and Harriet Taylor Mill.

Index

G

H

I

J

K

L

M

R

S

T